CHRISTIAN MYSTICISM:
TRANSCENDING TECHNIQUES

MARILYN MAY MALLORY

CHRISTIAN MYSTICISM: TRANSCENDING TECHNIQUES

A Theological Reflection on the Empirical Testing
of the Teaching of St. John of the Cross

VAN GORCUM ASSEN/AMSTERDAM THE NETHERLANDS 1977

The publication of this book was made possible through a grant from The Netherlands Organization for the Advancement of Pure Research (Z.W.O.)

ISBN 90 232 1535 4

248
M297

79051530

Printed in The Netherlands by Van Gorcum, Assen

Acknowledgments

Special gratitude must be extended to the fifty-four members of the Discalced Carmelite Order for their generous participation in the empirical study. Without their cooperation this study would have been impossible. The seventeen subjects who also volunteered for the physiological registrations deserve special mention. Furthermore, the author wishes to extend thanks to those members of the Discalced Carmelite Order who did not participate, but who nevertheless encouraged others to volunteer. Acknowledgment of the contributions of the various specialist (psychologists, neurologians, technicians, etc.) will be given in the sections of this study where their help is directly discussed.

The publication of this book was made possible by a grant from The Netherlands Organization for the Advancement of Pure Research (Z.W.O.) of the Dutch government.

Foreword

It is all too common today that the westerner knows more about oriental meditation than about the contemplative traditions of his own, western culture. Furthermore, what little the westerner might know is often nothing more than the accumulated pre-conceptions or stereotypes about western mysticism, with little or no basis in empirically tested fact. This study aims at shedding some light on one of the most systematized of these traditions, the so-called "Spanish Mysticism". This will be done via a depth study of the teachings of one of its main representatives, St. John of the Cross (1542-1591). These teachings are then tested empirically in an inventory of religious experience among members of the Discalced Carmelite Order, which was founded by John of the Cross and Teresa of Avila. Even today it has many thousands of members still following their teachings. The approach followed here combines many disciplines in an attempt to show the theological-historical as well as the cultural-psychological and even psycho-physiological aspects of this contemplative tradition as it is experienced today.

The inspiring example for this multi-disciplinary approach is the work of the late Professor H. M. M. Fortmann (1912-1970), a pioneer in the psychology of religion and culture at the University of Nijmegen. His works have remained largely unknown outside the Benelux because they have not yet been translated from Dutch. Following the example of Fortmann in bringing disciplines together which had grown apart, this dissertation inter-weaves theology not only with the social sciences, but also with the medical sciences. This introduces an aspect of modern science into the picture which Fortmann did not consider, perhaps because he emphasized 'bodiliness' rather than the fundamental biological reality of the body. Thus this study follows Fortmann's example, but with a 'harder', more concrete empirical approach and with a deeper theological dimension.

The empirical reality of the body is the starting point for this study, since it is the author's position that the body is the starting point for any modern spirituality, western or eastern. In chapter one, on the basis of the teachings of John of the Cross, the negative attitude of western spirituality toward the body will be presented. Chapter two will show how irrelevant this negative attitude toward bodily sensuality is for mystical advancement, based upon empirical data. The psycho-physiological study in chapter two will then go on to throw some light on the actual role of the body in contemplation. Chapter three then traces why Christian spirituality has become so negative about the body. In chapter four the author will present a phenomenological analysis, based upon a previous study by Fortmann, of the role of bodily eroticism in prayer.

Hereby the scope of Fortmann's study, *Aandachtig bidden* (1945) ('concentrated prayer'), is extended. Fortmann had explicitly excluded mystical and contemplative prayer from his study and had dealt only with liturgical and other prayer forms which are not contemplative, both formal and spontaneous prayers. Perhaps the reason why he left the prayer of mystical union out of the discussion was because of the widespread feeling among Catholics of his generation that contemplation was only for a small elite among Christians. The average Christian had to content himself with the more conventional kinds of spiritual experience. In fact, to aim purposely at more than that was regarded as a sign of presumption. Nowadays, however, the modern laity and especially the youth clearly express a growing need or spiritual hunger for contemplative experience. To meet this need, this dissertation has therefore concentrated on the kinds of prayer which Fortmann did not deal with in his dissertation. In his later years, Fortmann had a growing interest in oriental spirituality, whereby he forsook his earlier interest in western spirituality. Perhaps due to his premature death, he never reflected deeply on the relationship between western and oriental spirituality. The aim of this current study is to return to Fortmann's original starting point, western prayer, and bring this into closer relation with his later interests.

In Fortmann's study, the phenomenological method was pre-empirical. It almost had to be, because so few empirical data were available at that time on prayer. In this study the phenomenological analysis of prayer is post-empirical, appearing only at the end of this thesis. In the post-empirical stage, the advantage of the phenomenological method appears. It allows the non-specialist to understand the main lines of the phenomena (i.e. Christian mysticism) without having to deal with highly technical terminology and methodology. For this reason the reader who is not familiar with the special vocabulary and methodology of psychology or psycho-physiology is advised to concentrate mainly on chapter four.

While the preceding chapters aim mainly at clearing the air of prejudices and misconceptions about what Christian mysticism 'ought to be', chapter four tries to formulate what Christian mysticism 'really is', as far as the available data and the insights of Fortmann and John of the Cross permit. In this chapter an attempt is made to introduce the theme of the imitation of Christ in a new way, so that it becomes not only a theme for spirituality, but also a dogmatic theme. This is done by establishing a broader basis for dealing with redemption than is usual, namely by introducing the concept of 'affective redemption'. Within this expanded terrain, certain themes which traditionally belonged within mystical theology have been brought into the mainstream of dogmatics. This opens, too, a new approach to both Christology and Pneumatology. The aim in this approach is to get beyond a static, intellectualized and juridic view of redemption. Hereby redemption becomes not only the redemption of man's 'thinking self' but also redemption of his 'bodily self'.

January 10, 1977

Dedicated to the inspiring
memory of the pioneer in the
psychology of religion,
Professor Dr. H. M. M. Fortmann (1912-1970)

Preface

When one glances through contemporary popular books on mysticism or even more serious studies[1] one finds that many stereotypes and presuppositions exist regarding mystics and mystical experience. Because these stereotypes of 'the mystic' are generally taken for granted one finds theologians who conduct entire discussions or even tirades against mysticism without first considering whether their idea of a mystic is based on fact or fiction. A. Vergote points to the widely held idea that mysticism is presumably non-prophetical and opposed to an attitude of faith[2]. One sees in a discussion of 'politics *or* mysticism' the stereotype of mystical experience as it has become associated with spirit/matter dualism[3]. One finds that the 'mystical consciousness' is contrasted with rationality. Thereby mysticism and irrationality are made identical, irrationality and emotionality are equated, and thus mysticism is made identical with emotionality[4]. Without considering whether these associations are merely literary fictions, with no basis in experience, the conclusion is drawn by some modern theologians that mystical experience is other-worldly or even anti-historical.

In other disciplines, especially psychology, one encounters the stereotype of the mystic as psychopathological[5]. Put into very simplified terms, psychologists tend to conceive of mystics as being introvert, emotional, hysterical, regressive, egotistical and escapist[6]. If one considers these traits a bit more closely, it becomes clear that a mystic can not be both an introvert and a hysteric, since in Eysenck's studies a hysteric is postulated as being an unstable extravert[7]. Similarly a mystic can not be both regressive and egotistical, since a regressive is by Hood's definition[8] a type in which the concept of self has not sufficiently developed.

This sort of inconsequence is perhaps best illustrated by the fairly recent attempt of a Spanish writer, A. Roldán[9], to classify three basic religious 'types', based upon several well-known sets of psychological typologies. He established three religious types: 1) the mystic, corresponding to the sensual or affective temperament, 2) the apostolic type, corresponding to the energetic, passionate type; and 3) the moralist, characterized by the sensitive, cerebral type. His whole system is marred, however, by his own final admission that no well-known mystic in western history corresponds to the 'mystic type'. On the contrary, he states, such mystics as Teresa of Avila and others resemble the apostolic type. Something must be wrong somewhere with attempts to classify the 'mystic type' when such blatant inconsequences can occur. The hypothesis that all mystical experience can be explained on the basis of psychological disturbances is nothing more than that, i.e. a hypothesis, which needs to be proven empirically on the basis of extensive research and not on the limited chance study of a few abnormal persons. It is this empirical approach which will be followed here. It would be interesting in itself to investigate all the preconceptions about mystics and mysticism, but the aim of this work is to get beyond these commonly accepted cliches or myths about mystics. For this reason, not a 'literature study' but an experimental study was undertaken. A 'literature study' would have amounted to nothing more than the accumulation of misconceptions which have been handed down and taken at face value.

This study has been purposely narrowed down to the mystical tradition of the Discalced Carmelite Order, and to the teachings of John of the Cross in particular. Thus the operational definition of mysticism in this study is that particular kind of contemplative approach taught by the co-founder of the Discalced Carmelite Order and put into actual practice by its members. The main characteristic of this tradition is its aim to attain union with a personal God via faith which transforms man into the likeness of Christ. This is accomplished within a context of two contradictory teachings: on one hand the 'via negativa' which rejects any specific technique in spirituality, and, on the other hand, a strict affective asceticism, which is a spiritual technique par excellence. The actual content of this 'super technique' will be reviewed briefly in chapter one. Its effectiveness in stimulating and aiding mystical development will be tested in chapter two. The reasons for this inconsequence, i.e. two contradictory teachings, will be explored in chapter three. Finally, a way is suggested in chapter four whereby this teaching can transcend techniques of all sorts, both western and oriental. Hereby an attempt is made to extend to the modern laity a better understanding of the context in which Christian contemplation occurs, that is, the 'via negativa', and also of the dynamism, the erotic or libidinal energy, which gives it momentum. The aim of this study is therefore to seek precisely those facets of Christian mysticism which distinguish it from oriental meditation techniques and mystical teachings. To seek a broader, more universal approach to mysticism would reduce both the Christian as well as the oriental traditions to a lowest common denominator. This would do neither tradition justice[10].

Table of Contents

xvi

The Super-Technique of Strict Affective Asceticism

1. *The Discalced Carmelite Order*

The contemplative religious Order, the Discalced Carmelites, has been selected for this study because its mystical teachings comprise perhaps the only approach to mystical development in the Catholic Church which is still followed even today by thousands of people in a somewhat systematized and standardized manner. This Order was founded in the 16th century in Spain by St. Teresa of Avila and St. John of the Cross, as a defence of the practice of inner prayer against its persecution under Felipe II[1] and as a reaction against the relaxed state of the Carmelite Order. Although the Carmelite Order had from its very beginnings in the Middle Ages aimed at the contemplative life, the reformed branch called the Discalced, or shoeless, Carmelites (because they originally wore sandals instead of shoes as a sign of poverty) emphasized the need to regain a strict ascetical observance. Consequently the Discalced Carmelite nuns even today follow one of the strictest Rules in the Catholic Church, observing strict enclosure. The Discalced Carmelite friars, although preserving some aspects of monastic existence, nevertheless also participate in such activities as pastoral work and teaching.

2. *St. John of the Cross*

The spiritual teaching of this Order is due particularly to the systematic foundations laid by the co-founder St. John of the Cross (1542-1591 A.D.) in his literary works. He has been chosen for this study instead of Teresa of Avila because of the theological forming which his works reflect.

John of the Cross, although coming from an impoverished family, nevertheless obtained an education in the humanities from the Jesuits at Medina del Campo. In 1563 he joined the Carmelites and received permission upon his profession in 1564 to follow the primitive observance of the Carmel, a very strict ascetic ideal. He was sent to the University of Salamanca where he studied philosophy from 1564 to 1567. Following the

1

custom of Carmelite students there, he also studied simultaneously at the Carmelite College of St. Andrew. Evidence shows that he was a good student. He had already acquired in his student days the reputation of being very austere and mortified. In 1567 he began his theological studies at the University of Salamanca but left his studies prematurely to assist Teresa of Avila in founding the Discalced Carmelites. The non-reformed Carmelites resisted their activities and captured and imprisoned him from 1575 to 1578. In prison he composed much of his poetry. After escaping from prison, he continued to be active in the founding of the Discalced Carmelite Order. His period of greatest literary (prose) production was from about 1578 to 1588, under the duress of the reaction against inner prayer. With the intensification of the Inquisition in Spain around 1586 and the condemnation of 'illuministic' books, John of the Cross, too, came under suspicion even though his emphasis upon the role of blind faith and his denunciation of interest in 'illuminations' from visions clearly distinguished his teaching from that of the Illuminists[2]. He was subjected to further persecution from conflicting factions within the Discalced Carmelite Order. Due to this ill-repute into which his name had fallen at the time of his death, his works were circulated with caution in the Carmel. Many of his letters were destroyed. His works were not published openly until 1618 after an inquest by the Apostolic See had examined his orthodoxy. In the subsequent centuries his name had been cleared of suspicion and in 1926 he was declared Doctor of the Church Universal by Pope Pius XI.

His literary production consists of four main books, *The Ascent of Mt. Carmel*, *The Dark Night of the Soul*, *The Spiritual Canticle*, and *The Living Flame of Love*[3], plus counsels, letters and poems. These four main works follow a similar pattern; a poem accompanied by a commentary on its verses. *The Ascent of Mt. Carmel* describes the path to perfection via the renunciation of desires for both worldly goods as well as the goods of heaven, e.g. visions, prophecies, revelations, etc. He emphasizes the role of faith in leading the Christian to divine union. *The Dark Night of the Soul* goes further into the theme of purification, showing that man's active ascetical practice is insufficient and needs to be supplemented by an intense period of passive purgation. This is the dark night of the spirit, which is the passive counterpart of the active dark night of the senses. The dark night of the senses is the first dark night and the dark night of the spirit is the second dark night. *The Spiritual Canticle* describes lyrically the progress of the soul toward the 'Beloved', using the nuptial symbolism of 'bride's mysticism'. His final work, *The Living Flame of Love*, describes the highest experience of mystical union. Here the nuptial symbolism retreats into the background and the role of the Holy Spirit comes forward, sym-

2

bolized by flame. In all his works there is a constant emphasis upon detachment and the mortification of desire as a pre-requirement for mystical progress. This absolute detachment is underlined by his insistence upon 'nada', i.e. nothing, which indicates the complete mortification of the will. The will should be attached to nothing but God. This point will be elaborated in the treatment of his ascetical teaching in chapter one. Due to the limited space, it is not possible to give a complete account of either the life or the works of John of the Cross[4] in this short introduction.

In chapter one some current commentators on John of the Cross will be examined to see how they try to make the teachings of John of the Cross more adapted to modern times. Subsequently criticism will be given inasmuch as their attempts to 'modernize' John of the Cross leave important aspects of his teaching out of the discussion. It will be shown that large parts of his teaching can not be made to fit into a modern non-dualistic view of man. Via a dogmatic-patristic study another approach is explored, namely that of tracing the source of this dualistic view in Augustine's influence upon John of the Cross. This leads to the hypothesis for chapter two. (Note to the reader: all quotations from Spanish and Dutch will be translated by the author. Where this has been done, the initials 'MM' will appear.)

I. THE 'STATUS QUAESTIONIS' REGARDING JOHN OF THE CROSS

The story is told of how the philosopher Blondel had tried to introduce Teilhard de Chardin to the works of St. John of the Cross[5]. Teilhard indeed began to read them, but soon stopped. His reason for stopping was because John of the Cross' method or experience could not be applied to the majority of men. This statement is the starting point for this study: the teachings of John of the Cross in their present form are not applicable for spiritual instruction to the majority of (lay)men today. This is particularly regretable since his teachings constitute perhaps one of the few, if not the only, standardized, systematized approaches to mystical development which is native to the western world and which is put into practice by many followers even today, in the cloisters of the Discalced Carmelite Order. But this is precisely the problem; his is a cloister spirituality, not a spirituality designed for laymen. John of the Cross himself states:

"Nor is it my principal intent to address all, but rather certain persons of our sacred Order of Mount Carmel of the primitive observance, both friars and nuns . . . who, as they are already detached from the temporal things of this world, will better understand the instruction concerning detachment of spirit."[6](Prologue, 9, *Ascent*)

One can speculate that it was at precisely this point where Teilhard de

Chardin stopped reading John of the Cross. It would indeed seem as if John of the Cross were addressing himself to only a very small elite among Christians. But later on, in his last work *The Living Flame of Love* which he wrote for a laywoman, Doña Ana de Peñalosa, he sets himself the goal of instructing all Christians to attain mystical union (cf. stanza II, *Flame*). Nevertheless, his main work as spiritual director was not with lay people but with Discalced Carmelite nuns and friars, an orientation which influences especially his ascetical teaching. The task at hand, therefore, is to re-interpret his teachings, especially his ascetical thought, for modern lay people.

A brief survey will be given here of the most prominent modern writers on John of the Cross, to show the general lines of approach and the main points of interest in re-interpreting his teachings for modern times. It is not the intention of the author to give an exhaustive review of commentators on John of the Cross, but rather to show various kinds of approaches as illustrated by several modern studies.

Writers of an earlier generation tended to over-emphasize the influence of Thomas of Aquinas upon John of the Cross, paying too much attention to the points of divergence with Thomas. These Thomists, e.g. J. Maritain, Marcelo del Niño Jesús, A. Mager and others, devoted attention to explaining such erudite matters as why John of the Cross departed from the Thomistic two-faculty scheme or why he emphasized the theological virtues to the near-exclusion of the gifts of the Holy Spirit, in contrast to Thomas' approach. Other matters of contention were terms like 'faith' and 'supernatural', which have a different meaning in John of the Cross than in Thomas. This all must have been particularly frustrating to Thomists like A. Mager who stated, "Eine Psychologie der Mystik kann keine anderen Wege gehen als die, welche Thomas in seiner *Summa* geht."[7] Continuing this same thomistic line, one finds even relatively recent writers, like H. Sansom in *L'esprit humain selon saint Jean de la Croix* (1953), who are still preoccupied with the two-faculty schema (intellect and will) vs. the three-faculty scheme (intellect, will, and memory). Even after the second Vatican Council one finds remnants of this approach in F. Ruiz' reaction against this over-emphasis upon the three faculties. However, the very fact that he still felt the need to react against this approach reveals the continuing preoccupation with the thomistic line[8]. The result of all this thomistic preoccupation can be summed up by saying that it generally centered all attention upon defining the exact structure of the soul in John of the Cross' scheme, with a disregard for the role of the affections, emotions or eroticism in his teaching.

An approach which gets closer to the one to be explored in chapter four of this study is the dissertation of J. Peters, *Geloof en mystiek* (trans: Faith and Mysticism) (1957)[9]. He attempts to throw some light upon the central role of the affections in the whole teaching of John of the Cross by showing how the structure of the soul is determined by the central role of the will, the center of man's affections or desires. The center of the soul, where God dwells by grace, resembles a medieval city, surrounded by a wall which is man's will. This wall separates man's center from the settlements outside, which is man's sensuality. The gates in the wall are man's mental faculties and the 'interior senses' (fantasy and the imagination), through which the outer senses can penetrate through to the center.

Peters describes the ideal situation as one in which man should remain in the center of his soul, and thereby remain master of his desires. Due to original sin, however, man can not return to that spiritual center unless with the help of grace and through the practice of the theological virtues, especially faith. Unfortunately Peters did not develop further on the theme of the affections or on eroticism.

The most lucid analysis of the place of the affections in John of the Cross' thought is perhaps that of E. W. Trueman, *El crisol del amor* (trans: The crucible of love) (1963). He shows that the basic differences between the 16th century theology (and psychology) and the modern view lies in the treatment of the emotions. Trueman outlines how medieval theology and psychology, such as it was, allowed no place for the emotions as such. Rather, they were dealt with as sensations or perceptions of the senses. Emotions were sensual perceptions. The dualism between spirit and 'sense' is in fact a dualism between spirit and the emotions. The passions were movements of the sensual nature of man, the 'anima sensitiva'. The affections were nothing more than the desires of the senses as perceived in the spiritual part of man, the 'anima rationalis'. Trueman also points out that this psychological scheme in the 16th century was a function of theology and should be seen in the context of the western teaching about original sin, concupiscence and man's fallen state. It was generally accepted that the desires were not to be eliminated, but put in order or governed.

Since the Second Vatican Council, attention has been paid increasingly to trying to understand the strongly negative attitude of John of the Cross toward human desires, affections, and toward the human will in general. These studies trace the influence of Augustine upon western spirituality in general, and upon John of the Cross in particular. What is central to such studies is the problem of the dualism of spirit and matter. Two of the best studies on these issues are J. Bendiek, "Gott und Welt nach Joh. vom Kreuz", *Philosophisches Jahrbuch*, (1972), 88-105; and R. Mosis, *Der Mensch und die Dinge nach Johannes vom Kreuz* (1964).

J. Bendiek attributes John of the Cross' rejection of man's material existence and human nature as such to the influence of Augustine. This 'condemnation of human nature', as he calls it, is motivated by the teaching about original sin and is linked in John of the Cross' mystical teaching to the idea that man is totally unable to attain to God because of the effects of original sin.

"San Juan hat die Natur des Menschen 'verurteilt' in dem Sinn, dass sie ihm unfähig erscheint, zur Vereinigung mit God zu führen — und darin stimmt er wohl mit der traditionellen katholischer Dogmatik überein. Freilich, da er — im Gegensatz zu der geläufigen theologischen Meinung — in der menschlichen Natur keinerlei Anknüpfungspunkte für die übernatürliche Umwandlung in Gott zu sehen vermag, hat er wohl tatsächlich 'verurteilt', welche Verurteilung man im allgemeinen nur über die in Adam gefallene Natur auszusprechen pflegt."[10]

Bendiek shows how this condemnation extends beyond man's sensual nature to his rational faculties, by pointing to passages in John of the Cross which state that both must be thoroughly mortified in order to attain divine union. The root of the perverted will is in the spirit, not the senses (cf. *Ascent* I,1,1; II,2; *Night* II,3,1). Bendiek develops the idea that it is the doctrine of original sin which conditions the way John of the Cross approaches the 'via negative'.

R. Mosis analyzes the problem of dualism in John of the Cross and concludes that there are two sets of dualities: on one hand the dualism of sense vs. spirit (which could actually be called a triad because he divides man into sense, spirit and a 'center' of the soul); and on the other hand a dualism of the will which divides the will between attachment to creation vs. attachment to God. This voluntary dualism is based upon the first dualism of spirit/sense in a very complex way. Mosis, just as Bendiek, notices that John of the Cross is concerned with a radical corruption of man's desires, in both man's sensual and spiritual nature. He underlines that the main issue in John of the Cross' anthropology is not a platonic dualism of spirit/matter, but rather a theological understanding of man's fallen nature, based upon the idea of original sin. The theme of renouncing desires for creation comes from his idea of man's fallen state and the weakened state of his will, rather than from some dualistic view as such. Mosis cites 24 texts in John of the Cross which establish the close connection between the doctrine of sin and the subsequent division of man's will between God and creatures. As a consequence, the mortification of the passions or desires extends to both man's sensual *and* spiritual nature, since the passions affect all of man's being.

Going further, Mosis shows that the purification of the passions is always the purification of the senses, especially the 'inner senses', the fantasy and imagination. Man's sensual nature is often characterized by John of the Cross by 'under' or 'lower'. Indeed many texts in his teachings are clearly dualist. The body is like a prison (*Ascent* I,3,3). Mosis comes to the conclusion that for John of the Cross, only man's higher, spiritual being has been redeemed, not the lower part. He supports this with several texts: *Ascent* II,4,2; III,26,4; *Canticle* 18,8; *Night* II,23,14. What these texts all have in common is a sharp distinction between man's higher, spiritual being which can communicate with God vs. man's lower, sensual being, which only hinders this divine communication.

To summarize this rather subtle analysis by Mosis, one might say that although the root of the perverted desire since the Fall is in the will, nevertheless its actions are governed by the senses. This same thought has been said also about Gregory the Great, as formulated by R. Gillet[11]:

"Le désordre des appétits inférieurs est causé par un désordre supérieur antécédent; mais en pratique, le désordre inférieur commande et amène à l'acte le désordre supérieur qui, au fond, est cause."

The problem now arises as to how to extricate the mystical teaching of John of the Cross, especially the 'via negativa', from this network of Augustinian concepts? The task of making this teaching more relevant to the modern laity involves much more than merely coming to understand the roots of his pessimism. It is the aim of the rest of this study, especially chapter three, to show how the 'via negativa' is something quite distinct from the dualistic Augustinian framework into which he has placed it. This reappraisal is necessary because some writers tend to denounce the entire teaching about the 'via negativa' on the basis of the presupposition that the 'via negativa' and strict asceticism are just two aspects of the same pessimistic mentality. An illustration of this attitude is found in F. Cordero, in his article "La teología espiritual de Santa Teresa de Jesús, reacción contra el dualismo neoplatónico"[12]. Cordero contrasts what he considers the non-dualistic thought of Teresa of Avila with that of John of the Cross. He interprets the instructions of John of the Cross about not praying by meditating actively on any specific intellectual content or with imagery (i.e. the 'via negativa') as implying a rejection of man's material or bodily existence. He states: "It is typically dionysian, the doctrine of recollection of Friar Francisco Osuna: to fight to free oneself from created things."[13] (trans.: MM) This means, that Cordero associates the doctrine of the 'via negativa', originating with pseudo-Dionysius, with a dualism of Creator/creation. He goes on to state that this implies a rejection of Christ's humanity. This teaching about rejecting rational activity or the use of the imagination (the inner senses) in prayer is the central aspect of the 'via negativa'. In the teaching of John of the Cross the practice of the 'via negativa' is the pre-condition or the foundation for a growth in mystical love for God. The actual content of the via negativa will be further explored in chapter three.

Cordero therefore denounces the via negativa or the mystical teaching of

7

John of the Cross because of its supposed hostile attitude to creation as such. He concludes by insisting upon a prayer form that retains imagery, particularly that of meditation upon the humanity of Christ. Cordero's argument is faulty along two lines. First it assumes a strong dualism of matter/spirit in neo-Platonism, a point which has already been called into question by G. Verbeke (1945)[14] in his study of the problem of the 'spirit' in Augustine. Verbeke shows that the radical dualism which is usually associated with neo-Platonism actually originated with Augustine, who influenced western spirituality in the way already briefly sketched in the discussion of Bendiek and Mosis. Cordero attributes the radical dualism of spirit/matter to pseudo-Dionysius, when he actually should have directed his attacks against Augustine. That is, he attributes to pseudo-Dionysius that which belongs to Augustine. Secondly Cordero has an insufficient knowledge of the actual attitude of pseudo-Dionysius to man's material, bodily existence. This point will be amply illustrated in chapter three.

Cordero overlooks one key text in John of the Cross which instructs the soul to seek God in its inmost center and to regard the world as nothing. In this text John of the Cross quotes Augustine, not pseudo-Dionysius:

"Hence Saint Augustine, speaking with God in the Soliloquies, said, 'I found Thee not, O Lord, without, because I erred in seeking Thee without that wert within.' He is, then, hidden within the soul, and there the good contemplative must seek Him, saying: 'Whither has Thou hidden Thyself?' (*Canticle* I,4)

The question will be raised later on in chapter three as to whether there might be any text whatsoever in pseudo-Dionysius' mystical writings which John of the Cross could have possibly quoted here regarding the flight from the world. Although Cordero's argument is too ill-founded to be convincing, it serves to illustrate the way the close association of mystical theology with Augustine's view of man is often taken for granted. It will be the aim of the rest of this study to show how the mystical teaching of John of the Cross can be extricated from the framework of Augustinian concepts which surround it. Despite the short-comings of a writer like Cordero he nevertheless does recognize the existence of a very difficult problem, namely that much of the teachings of John of the Cross reflects a very negative attitude toward creation and toward human nature. This recognition of the problem seems preferable to the attempts of some authors to pass over this negative aspect.

This minimalist tendency is illustrated by two authors: G. Morel, *Le sens de l'existence selon Saint Jean de la Croix* (1960) and E. Orozco, *Poesia y mística* (1959). Morel plays down much of what John of the Cross has to say about detachment from the desires for creatures:

"Mais une tradition tenace, perpétuée jusqu'à nos jours, voudrait laisser entendre le contraire: saint Jean de la Croix aurait enseigné un total mépris du corps et des sens. Sa vie prouve qu'il

8

s'agit là d'une étrange caricature. L'oeuvre n'est pas en contradiction avec la vie."[15]

What Morel is referring to is the opinion which is sometimes expressed that John of the Cross was only strict in a certain abstract sense but not in practice. That is, his actual life was not as strict as his teachings. Morel argues from this presupposition that, if he was mild in actual example, then he must have been mild also in his teaching since the two can not contradict each other. A short review of certain episodes from Crisgóno's biography of John of the Cross calls this presupposition into question, however.

As a student, Crisógono tells, John of the Cross slept on a bed without a matras and used a log for a pillow. He wore hairshirts and used disciplines which were filled with blood. He had made a special kind of hairshirt out of a tough grass sort with hard knots in it like a fishingnet[16]. At the first monastery of the Discalced Carmelite friars at Duruelo, John of the Cross established an example of extreme mortification of the body. On one cold morning he had helped the vicar, an old man, to mount a donkey. He had fastened the vicar's habit with a pin to keep it from blowing open. By accident he pierced the vicar's leg as well. The vicar complained, but John of the Cross told him to be silent since he was just that much better fastened. Later on that day in the review of faults committed, John of the Cross again accused the vicar of complaining about the pin that stuck him[17].

Many stories are told about how John of the Cross gave so much care and attention to sick friars and nuns, even to the point of coddling them. He went out to beg money to buy medicine and food for them. These stories seem to show the mild side of John of the Cross. But although he was indulgent to the sick, he was very strict with the healthy and especially with himself. Regarding food, he always left part of his ration on the plate and on certain Fridays he ate only bread and water. For weeks he ate on the floor[18]. While on a trip, he refused to sleep on a bed or a cot, but slept on the ground. Once, while he himself was very ill (possibly because of such practices) another example of his strict asceticism came to light. Another friar was assigned to rub a lotion into his back. He discovered that John of the Cross was wearing a chain around his waist, the links of which were embedded in the flesh. When he tore it off, profuse bleeding ensued[19].

These episodes show that the concrete example of John of the Cross was everything but mild. Indeed, as Morel argues, the concrete example can not contradict the theoretical teaching. Both are very strict and advocate a heroic degree of bodily mortification. Morel's statement therefore seems peculiarly slanted.

Especially in chapter one, volume two, "Le sensible", Morel attempts to put the ascetic teaching of John of the Cross into a more positive light. He continues this line of argument in an appendix, "Note sur l'idée sanjuaniste de vide":

> "La dualité irréductible que l'on prétend découvrir dans la doctrine de saint Jean de la Croix n'est qu'une illusion — vivace — de la pensée intellectualiste qui ramène la négation à l'idée de la négation."[20]

E. Orozco adopts the approach of searching for a balanced view of John of the Cross' ascetical teaching. He tries to show that some statements which seem harsh can be balanced out with others, or with the general context, to give a more humane view. The basic question is avoided, namely, why are these negative statements there in the first place?

A more straight-forward approach is that of Lucien-Marie de Saint Joseph in his article on the current relevance of John of the Cross[21]. He calls a spade a spade, presenting concisely those points which are out-dated in John of the Cross:

> "L'actualité de la doctrine sanjuaniste est contrecarrée par une manière d'aborder les problèmes spirituels qui n'est plus la nôtre, un vocabulaire souvent désuet, une présentation scolastique, surtout dans la Montée, un accent mis sur les problèmes personnels, dans l'ignorance des problèmes communautaires, et une absence relative du sens de l'histoire."[22]

Since such attempts to minimalize the out-dated elements in John of the Cross might give the impression that his teaching is not so out-dated as the above quote would suggest, the author has found it necessary to present in the following section (II) a short sketch of the ascetical and mystical teaching of John of the Cross, proceeding from his own texts. Against the objection that such texts might have a different meaning when considered within their greater context, an attempt will also be made to present the larger context or lines along which he constructs his teaching. This approach seems more productive than trying to balance out every harsh statement with some positive statement in his writings.

II. THE TEACHING OF JOHN OF THE CROSS

A. The ascetical teaching

Matias mentions how it has become commonplace to contrast Teilhard de Chardin's vision of the world and of man with the views of John of the Cross[23]. The former accents the immanent presence and working of God in the world while the latter accents God's separateness from creation. More precisely, the rivalry in the view of John of the Cross exists within man's perverted will, which is torn between the love of God and the love of creatures. The broad outlines of this dualistic scheme become apparent by considering his development of the theme of 'spiritual freedom' and its related themes.

'Spiritual freedom' is a term which occurs again and again in the works of John of the Cross. He defines it as salvation itself (*Ascent* III,5,3); in salvation the soul is freed for the incomprehensible God (*Ascent* III,26,6) in contemplation (*Ascent* III,18,8). In this redeemed state man has freedom of heart (*Ascent* III,19,5) and can experience the freedom of God's love (*Night* II,7,4). It is God's love which brings peace and spiritual freedom (*Night* II,9,1). Complete spiritual freedom is attained in divine union, which is the goal of the mystical life (*Ascent* I,4,6). Therefore, the final stage in the process of salvation is mystical union, which is at the same time the highest degree of spiritual freedom. (*Canticle* 35,2-3)

The fullest description of 'spiritual freedom' occurs where John of the Cross deals with the themes of union and glory. In the state of union, inasmuch as it can be experienced in this life, the soul has become purified enough to enjoy a high degree of spiritual freedom. This freedom consists in having the glory which belongs to God through divine union (*Ascent* I,4,6). Glory is possessing God (*Ascent* I,12,3). God is the slave of the soul and the soul is God (*Canticle* 27,1). Here the paradox becomes evident that in the state of union the soul is transformed into God and is at the same time possessed by God (*Flame* 4,4). The heart becomes captive of that which it possesses (*Night* II,13,3). In divine union the soul possesses dominion and glory (*Counsels* 2,4) but paradoxically God's glory is that the soul's will is entirely conformed to His will (*Poems* 9,5). Here is the starting point for the voluntary dualism which accounts for the rivalry between God and creation.

In the ideal state, the soul's appetites are directed to God alone and free from all that is not God (*Ascent* II,5,4). The poor in spirit, i.e. those who are mortified in their appetites, will inherit the kingdom of heaven (*Ascent* III,44,1) (*Flame* 1,31). Because the soul has hated every other kind of possession (*Cautions* 7), God will work an immense possession of glory eternally within it (*Ascent* III,26,7), rewarding it for every passing and corrupt joy which the soul has denied itself. This is the preparation which is needed for heaven since even if the soul were to be in heaven, it would not be content there if its appetites were not suited for it (*Letters* 13,1).

John of the Cross states: "Divest thyself of what is human in order to seek God"(*Sentences* 54). This underlines what has already been mentioned, namely that in the final analysis spiritual freedom is freedom from any human appetites and the complete absorption of the human will and human nature itself in the divine. In the final state of divine union, God possesses the faculties of the soul like a ruler; he moves and commands them (*Canticle* 18,1) and the Word makes its dominion felt within the soul (*Flame* 4,4).

The opposite of spiritual freedom is freedom of desire, sensual freedom, or what is also called 'temporal freedom' by John of the Cross. This is the liberty of the world, which is slavery in the eyes of God (*Ascent* I,4,6; 19,12). Everyone is actually looking for spiritual freedom, which is the only true freedom (*Night* II,23,2), but due to man's fallen state, he chooses freedom of desire, sensual freedom. Hereby man thinks to attain freedom by possessing created goods, or even moral, intellectual or spiritual goods, but paradoxically he becomes a slave to these desired goods. The heart becomes captive of that which it possesses (*Night* II,13,3). It is not these goods themselves but rather the appetites or desires for them which hold the soul captive (*Ascent* I,11,4; 15,2). To be spiritually free the soul must be empty of appetites (*Ascent* III,3,4).

Freedom of desire is closely associated with bodily sensuality. The soul is in the body like a lord in a prison (*Canticle* 18,1). This natural life impedes spiritual freedom (*Flame* 1,31). In this fallen state the soul lives as in the slavery of Egypt. Until the appetites are put to sleep by the mortification of the sensuality the soul will not go forth to enjoy the true liberty of the union with its Beloved (*Ascent* I,15,2). The more the soul withdraws itself from sensual affections and appetites, the more it will obtain freedom of spirit (*Night* I,13,11). Due to original sin, the soul is truely captive in this mortal body (*Ascent* I,15,1). The body which is corrupted weighs down the spirit (*Night* II,1,2; *Canticle* 26,5; *Flame* 2,13). (The paraphrasing of Wisdom 9,15: 'A perishable body presses down soul', is a cornerstone in the dualistic construction behind John of the Cross' ascetical teaching.) Go forth and free yourself from the body of death in order to live and enjoy the life of your God (*Canticle* 8,2). This natural life empedes spiritual freedom (*Flame* 1,31). In mystical union God will take away the appetites of the soul (*Flame* 1,28). Free from the bother of natural passions, the soul will enjoy participation in God (*Cant.* 24,5).

This polarity between love for creatures and the love of God is absolute. There is no room in the heart for both God and creatures (*Ascent* I,6,1). In the state of perfect freedom there should be no stain or remembrance or affection in the soul regarding any creature (*Ascent* II,5,7). In such a state the soul is purified from (not in!) its appetites and affections (*Ascent* III,16,3) (Original Spanish text: 'purgar la voluntad *de* sus afecciones'). This distinction between purifying the soul *from* its affections rather than *in* its affections attests to the radical ascetical attitude of John of the Cross. (It should be added here that 'afecciones' is a technical term in John of the Cross for earthly desires, not desires for God, which are described with another term, 'ansias' (or 'deseos'), yearnings or desires. This point will be expanded upon in chapter four.) In such a perfect state the soul is not tied down to any created thing (*Poems* 1). One single desire is enough to impede the experience of God's love (*Night* II,9,1). In the final mystical union the soul is not allowed to notice anything in the world (*Canticle* 26,14). John of the Cross expresses this polarity very emphatically:

"The whole world has not the worth of a man's thought, for that thought is due to God alone; and thus whatever thought of ours is not centered upon God is stolen from him." (*Sentences* 37). "All the world is not worth one thought of man, therefore God alone is worthy of it." (*Sentences* 32)

Finally in the perfect state of divine union, the theological virtues act upon man's nature in such a way as to destroy it:

"Faith voids and darkens the understanding as to all its natural intelligence . . . Hope voids and withdraws the memory from that which it is capable of possessing . . . Charity voids and annihilates the affections and desires of the will for whatever is not God" (*Night* II,21,11).

In this 'divinized' state the soul can permit itself to enjoy creation finally because it sees and experiences everything through the Creator. Everything the senses perceive brings the soul to love God all the more, since:

"To him that is pure, all things, whether high or low, are an occasion of greater good and further purity . . . But let not him that has not yet mortified his pleasure in things of sense dare to make great use of the power and operation of sense with respect to them, thinking that they will help him to become more spiritual; for the powers of the soul will increase the more without the intervention of these things of sense . . . that is, if it quench the joy and desire for them rather than indulge its pleasure in them"(*Ascent* III,26,7).

Thus the soul can finally permit itself to enjoy creation, but only when its own human nature has been so annihilated that all its operations are divine. This is an important point, since some modern attempts at interpreting John of the Cross merely point out his essentially positive evaluation of creation, without mentioning that, for John of the Cross, man's relation to creation via his will is so fundamentally corrupt (even *after* redemption) that only after man's nature has been entirely 'replaced' by the divine nature can he permit himself to enjoy creation. Put in other words, John of the Cross is not pessimistic about creation as such, but about man's relationship to creation through his perverted will. He has a fundamental pessimism about man's will.

These references to texts in John of the Cross should serve amply to convince even the most sceptical reader that the dualism between the Absolute, God, and the relative, creation, in man's will is much more than a mere 'illusion', as G. Morel attempts to prove[24]. There are too many texts which clearly show a dualistic view in the teaching of John of the Cross. Perhaps one might be able to show how one or two texts, when considered in their context, are not as extreme as they appear here (as E. Orozco tries to show), but the general tendency of all these texts can not be denied.

B. *His mystical teaching*

The treatment of dualism in John of the Cross would not be complete if his mystical teaching were left out of the discussion. As seen in the beginning of section (A), in the definition of 'spiritual freedom', John of the Cross links spiritual freedom with the freedom for contemplation. As shown repeatedly already mystical union is the final stage in this process of purification from sensual desire. This tendency is reflected in all the preceding stages in prayer through which the soul must progress, ascending from the 'sensual' stages to the 'spiritual' stages. It is significant in this respect that the most advanced contemplatives are referred to in his vocabulary as 'espirituales', spiritual persons. He divides the three stages of prayer into beginners, progressives and perfect contemplatives.

1. *Beginners*

The beginner is practically unable to detach himself from what the senses perceive, including the inner senses of the fantasy and the imagination. They pray sensually by using the imagination to picture things about God or by making mental concepts or reasonings. This sensual prayer is called active meditation. John of the Cross teaches that the beginner should drop this form of prayer and go over to contemplation when he notices that he no longer can meditate actively with the senses. At this stage the beginner should drop active prayer and should remain in quiet, practicing a 'loving attentiveness' to God without any specific content. He should rely on blind faith instead of his own intellectual or emotional activity. The main sets of instructions regarding this stage are: *Ascent* I, ch. 13; *Night* I, ch. 9; *Flame* III,30. But until this passive state has become continuous he may have to resort to active meditation occasionally (*Ascent* II,15,1). The beginning stages of contemplation are characterized by the inability to pray. The beginner experiences God's absence rather than His presence; he proceeds by 'unknowing' rather than by knowing. His intellect as well as his emotions are in darkness. It is as if a dark cloud had been placed between the beginner and God during prayer (*Night* II,8,1). This is the first dark night, called the active night of *sense*.

2. *Progressives.*

The progressive has come through the first dark night and now enjoys the first degree of illumination, receiving many insights, intuitions and even visions or prophecies about religious matters. John of the Cross warns that these phenomena are still too closely associated with sense. The progressive is to reject them and practice pure, blind faith. The dualistic reasoning behind this counsel is based upon a kind of axiom which he repeats constantly: "God, who has no image or form nor figure can not be reached by the soul that tries to know God via forms, images, etc." (*Ascent* II,12,1; 15,4; 16,7; III,2,4; 7,2; 11,1; 13,1; 24,2; *Night* II,25,3; etc.). The state of contemplation is described thusly: "The spirit which is entirely pure, alone and away from all forms, communes interiorly with delightful calm with God" (*Counsels* 1,26). Rather than knowing God through 'forms' the soul comes to know God through blind faith, which, like cristal, is clear and clean of error and natural forms (*Canticle* 12,3). The soul should not let its eye rest upon any creaturely form in order to be able to gaze upon God in faith and hope (*Ascent* III,11,2). Consequently any intuitions, insights, visions, etc. which the soul might receive during prayer are 'forms', i.e. not purely spiritual since spirit has no form, and therefore they should be disregarded because they are less than perfect contemplation (*Ascent*, all of book II).

After the progressive has finally received some experience of God in quiet, formless contemplation he makes increasing growth in the theological virtues, and especially in faith, which empties the understanding of its base mode of operation via forms. He comes to understand without effort and experiences much satisfaction and delight in God's presence.

This is the state of the progressive when he enters into the second dark night, called the passive *spiritual* night. The first book of *The Dark Night of the Soul* exposes the imperfection of the progressive which necessitates his being subjected to a more spiritual purgation. The first night had only purified his sensual nature, but the root of imperfection lies in the spiritual faculty of the will. The second dark night purifies the will and conforms it to God's will. The second book of *The Dark Night of the Soul* describes how the spirit is purified by trials coming from the world, the flesh, the devil, but mainly from God Himself. The dark fire of God's love burns away all imperfections in the spirit. The progressive would not be able to endure this ordeal if it were not for intermittent periods of spiritual refreshment, i.e. pleasurable experiences of God's presence. Gradually, toward the end of the second dark night the progressive comes to experience this dark fire of God's love as delightful and not oppressive.

3. *The perfect contemplative.*
To summarize the development up to this point and beyond, John of the Cross makes use of the symbolism of the *Canticle of Canticles* in his book *The Spiritual Canticle*. In the final stages of mystical development the soul is united to the Beloved in a '*spiritual* betrothal' and finally a '*spiritual* marriage'. In this stage of purity the human will has been conformed to the divine will. Several metaphors describe this process of assimilation: fire

eats away at a log until it finally consumes it and the wood itself becomes fire; light shines through air which has been purified of all dust and particles; a flame is caught up and becomes one with the fire. Those who have attained to mystical union are called 'espirituales' or spiritual persons because the 'old man', i.e. the sensual man, has been replaced by the 'new man', the spiritual man (*Flame* III,74).

A few words should be said here about the place and role of ecstasy. John of the Cross considers ecstasy as a phenomenon which belongs to less advanced mystical experience because it is the result of the impact of purely spiritual communications upon the senses, which are not able to receive them. With time, the contemplative becomes more accustomed to these purely spiritual communications and the bodily senses do not become so perturbed, and ecstasy ceases to occur (*Canticle*, stanzas 13-14).

C. The link between mysticism and asceticism:
The dogmatic foundation

In the discussion of the 'status quaestionis' in the preceding section some reference was made to the influence of the concept of original sin upon the teaching of St. John of the Cross. Reference was made to twenty-four texts which R. Mosis had found where the idea of original sin is connected to the rivalry between God and creation in the works of John of the Cross. In this section more will be said about this and other underlying dogmatic themes which determine both his ascetical and mystical teaching. In chapter three (III) the problem will be explored whether this dogmatic foundation comes from Augustine, from pseudo-Dionysius or from some other source.

1. *Man's state after the Fall.*
As Trueman-Dicken has already observed in *El crisol del amor*[25] the idea of original sin, which underlies so much of the thought of John of the Cross, nevertheless receives very little explicit mention in his works, simply because it is taken for granted. The most extensive reflection on the issue of original sin and its effects upon human nature (and even then it is only a few sentences) is found in *The Spiritual Canticle*:

"... even as by means of the forbidden tree of Paradise she (the human race) was ruined and corrupted in her human nature through Adam, even so upon the Tree of the Cross she was redeemed and restored, by His giving her the hand of His favour and mercy, through His death and passion, and raising the barriers that came from original sin between the soul and God"(*Canticle* 23,2).

"This betrothal that was made upon the Cross is not that whereof we are now speaking (the 'spiritual betrothal'); for that is a betrothal which is made once and for all when God gives to the soul the first grace, which comes to every soul in baptism. But this betrothal is after the way

16

of perfection, which takes place only gradually and by stages; and, although they are both one, the difference is that the one is wrought at the soul's pace, and so is gradual, while the other is according to God's pace and thus is wrought once and for all" (*Canticle* 23,6).

In addition, some reflection on the effects of original sin also occurs in *The Ascent of Mt. Carmel*:

"For, although it is true that the unruly soul, in its natural being, is as perfect as when God created it, yet, in its reasonable being, it is vile, abominable, foul, black and full of all the evils that are here being described, and many more. For, as we shall afterwards say, a single unruly desire, although there be in it no matter of mortal sin, suffices to bring a soul into such bondage, foulness and vileness that it can in no wise come to accord with God in union until the desire be purified (*Ascent* I,9,1-3).

Summarizing the main points contained in these passages, it appears that after the Fall, human nature has been ruined and corrupted, although the 'natural being' of the soul is still as perfect as when God created it. The extent of John of the Cross' pessimism about human nature is found in his treatment of the desires. In the quote above he says that an *unruly* desire can make the soul vile. But in another passage dealing with various categories of desires, he makes no allowance for any desire which is not unruly, at least as far as voluntary desires go:

"That which I say, and that which is to the point for my purpose, is that any desire, although it be for but the smallest imperfection, stains and defiles the soul" (*Ascent* I,9,7).

In other words, there is no desire which does not cause some kind of sin, thereby impeding divine union:

"But all the other voluntary desires (in contrast to involuntary desires), whether they be of mortal sin, which are the gravest, or of venial sin, which are less grave, or whether they be only of imperfections, which are the least grave of all, must be driven away every one, and the soul must be free from them all, howsoever slight they be, if it is to come to this complete union . . . for the soul to come to unite itself perfectly with God through love and will, it must first be free from all desire of the will, howsoever slight."

"These habitual imperfections are, for example a common custom of much speaking, or some slight attachment which we never quite wish to conquer – such as that to a person, a garment, a book, a cell, a particular kind of food, tittle-tattle, fancies for tasting, knowing or hearing certain things, and suchlike . . . For as long as it has this there is no possibility that it will make progress in perfection, even though the imperfection be extremely slight"(*Ascent* I,9,2-4).

2. Redemption of the 'center' of the soul.

As the preceding quotations already indicate, the soul returns to God by getting rid of its desires, all 'desire of the will'. The problem involved here is that, for all practical purposes, man's nature, his will, remains entirely sinful even after baptism. Man only comes to God by divesting himself of all that is human, as John of the Cross explicitly states. It is not creation as such but the weakened or corrupted state of man's will which impedes this return to God. Any good thing in creation is therefore dangerous for man's weakness (*Flame* I,27).

In redemption God comes to dwell in the center of the soul by grace. In fact, God *is* the center of the soul, by grace (*Flame* 1,12). This is a presence of God which is something other than God's general sustaining presence in all of creation (*Ascent* II,5,3). It is a presence by affection which transforms the soul into its original likeness to God. This 'center' of the soul where God dwells is free of any contact with sense, the devil, or the world (*Flame* 1,9). The Spouse comes to dwell there and frees the soul from the demon and sensuality (*Canticle* 22,1). The consequence of placing the image of God in the soul's center is a mysticism of introversion:

"If one would learn how to find this Spouse . . . the Word, together with the Father and the Holy Spirit, is hidden essentially in the inmost center of the soul. Wherefore the soul that would find Him through union of love must go forth and hide itself from all created things according to the will, and enter within itself in deepest recollection, communing there with God in loving and affectionate fellowship, esteeming all that is in the world as though it were not" (*Canticle* 1,4 A).

At this point follows a quotation from Augustine: "I found Thee not, O Lord, without, because I erred in seeking Thee without that wert within." This was already pointed out in the discussion of Cordero's article on neo-platonic dualism. The background and actual location of this quote from Augustine will be given in chapter three.

Thus that part of man which was created in the image of God, i.e. the soul (*Ascent* I,9,1), and which is restored to the state of innocence by the indwelling of God there through grace, is the point of encounter in divine union. This 'center' of the soul is outside of time, a-historical. In fact, John of the Cross even goes so far as to state that the prayer of recollection in God, the prayer of union, is a prayer which occurs outside of time: ". . . because (the soul) has been united in pure intellegence, which is not in time" (*Ascent* II,14,11).

Even more typical of this a-historical view is John of the Cross' concept of what happens to the memory during divine union, since precisely in the memory is the connection with time: "The memory has been exchanged ('trocado') for eternal apprehensions of glory" (*Night* II,4,2; *Canticle* 19,4; 26,5; *Flame* 3,68). In divine union the memory, as well as all the other faculties, lose their contact with all that is temporal and thereby with all that is created.

One can conclude from this that only that part of man which John of the Cross conceives of as being redeemed is an a-historical 'center' of the soul. Neither the body, nor man's created intellectual abilities, can be the image of God. On the contrary, in divine union these faculties are assaulted ('embestido').

18

3. *Attaining the likeness of Christ.*

The fundamental dichotomy involved in the whole teaching of John of the Cross is the opposition between human nature, as historical and bodily existence, and the divine nature. The central point in his teaching is precisely the way in which man becomes transformed into the divine nature by divesting himself of all that is human, as seen in both his ascetical and mystical teaching. This radicalized polarity is based upon a certain use of the philosophical axiom which he repeats occasionally: "Two contraries, like the philosophers say, can not be contained in one subject" (*Ascent* I,4,2; 6,1; *Flame* 1,22). Nevertheless John of the Cross also states that the aim of his whole teaching is to obtain this union via Christ, who is the way to it (*Ascent* II,9,9) and man's example and light. This example which man must follow consists of the participation in the way of the cross, which John of the Cross interprets as the crucifixion of human nature.

This is evident in the following texts: Christ came to teach the contempt of all things in the world (*Ascent* II,7,8). One must renounce all and follow Christ in spiritual and interior nakedness, which is the emptiness of the desires for creatures (*Ascent* I,5,5). This divine Spouse frees the soul from the demon and from sensuality (*Canticle* 22,1). One must attain to God through suffering for Christ and in the annihilation of ones desires for everything (*Ascent* II,7,8). Evangelical perfection is the detachment and emptiness of sense and spirit from the vile and low things of the earth (*Flame* III,35; *Letters* 11,6). Man should therefore mortify his desires for creatures, since until the appetites cease, the soul can not reach God no matter how many virtues it may practice (*Ascent* I,5,6). Man owes God a debt because of redemption, which is all the love of his will (*Canticle* 1,1). The aim of all this is to restore Adam's original state when everything in creation increased his pleasure in contemplation (*Ascent* III,26,5). This state of innocence is obtained when man carries the likeness or image of Christ crucifed in himself (*Ascent* III,35,3). Crucified interiorly and exteriorly with Christ, one will live with satisfaction in ones soul (*Counsels* 2,8).

This transformation into the likeness of Christ is accomplished, not so much through man's active ascetical effort as through God's purifying action. The theological virtues are the most directly involved in this 'theandricizing' process because their role is to supplant human nature with the divine nature. Man can prepare the way for the action of the theological virtues by mortification of the desires. In fact, if the appetites for creatures are not mortified the soul will not arrive at God, no matter how many virtues it might practice (*Ascent* I,5,6). Appetites for creatures weaken the practice of the virtues (*Ascent* I,10,2). By denying the heart of natural goods, one disposes it for the love of God and the other virtues (*Ascent*

III,23,1 and *Ascent* I,13,5). On the other hand this active mortification of the senses only helps to adapt human nature to spiritual things (*Night* I,11,3). From there, the spirit has to be adapted to God, who is pure spirit. This work is done by the theological virtues, as has already been mentioned elsewhere; but for emphasis, this quote should be repeated here:

"Faith voids and darkens the understanding as to all its natural inclinations . . . Hope voids and withdraws the memory from that which it is capable of possessing . . . Charity voids and annihilates the affections and desires of the will for whatever is not God . . ." (*Night* II,21,11).

In the dark night of the spirit, which is called passive purgation, these virtues and especially faith, which is alien to all sense (*Night* I,11,4), strip the soul, both sense and spirit, of their natural powers (*Night* I,11,4; II,4,1). The human will is emptied of its affections by faith and charity (*Letters* 11,4). The action of these virtues is to drive out attachments to creation (*Ascent* III,11,2). Even attachments to pleasurable experiences in prayer are to be driven out, since these, too, are involved with sense (*Ascent* I,4,1).

The likeness with Christ is finally achieved in the 'spiritual marriage'. This does not occur, however, until the soul seduces God with the purity of its faith (*Canticle* 22,3; 31,3). This immediate association of faith, which as seen in the quotation above voids the understanding of all its natural inclinations, indicates that the mystical marriage is the culmination in this process of de-naturalizing man. This is not a marriage between human nature and the divine nature, but the complete domination of human nature by the divine. This is reflected in the frequent use of the concept of 'possession' in regard to this theme (*Canticle* 9,4,6; 12,7; 22,3; *Flame* 1,1; 3,21, etc.). Although the soul is also said to possess God in this union, what in fact remains of human nature in the 'soul' after this total annihilation is nothing. The human will has been totally conformed with the will of God. The theme of the spiritual marriage whereby the soul becomes one with the likeness of Christ is therefore a logical extension of the dualistic teaching of John of the Cross.

This brief summary of the teachings of John of the Cross presented here should make it clear why it is so difficult to adapt his dualistic views to modern man. There are so many texts which contain a fundamental dualism between God and creation, between divine nature and human nature, between spirit and sense, between desires for God and desires for creatures, etc. that it would seem nearly impossible to salvage anything in his mystical teaching which might be of value for the spiritual guidance of laymen seeking mystical union with God. Indeed his view of Christ is so fundamentally colored by this dualism between the human and the divine that one does not wonder that the Spanish Inquisition was hot on his heels[26]. Yet precisely the central reason for his being declared Doctor of the Church Universal by Pope Pius XI in 1926 was his teaching on the transformation of man into the divine in the likeness of Christ![27] This in itself would imply that much more is contained in his teaching than meets the eye.

An attempt has been made, purely on the basis of a close re-examination of the teaching of John of the Cross, by several fairly recent authors to put the thought of this Spaniard from the 16th century into a more modern framework and vocabulary. Perhaps the best of these attempts is that of Lucien-Marie, O.C.D.[28], in his book *L'expérience de Dieu* (1968), mainly because he is so aware of the fact that John of the Cross is indeed hopelessly out-dated in so many respects. This is evident in his straight-forward and highly critical summary of the short-comings of John of the Cross as quoted earlier[29]. Rather than trying to pass over these difficulties in rehabilitating John of the Cross, he faces the problems squarely, but goes on to find elements in that teaching which are still of value.

The central problem, however, remains unsolved in the work of Lucien-Marie, namely the role of the 'via negativa' in the way to mystical union. In fact, he barely devotes four pages to this theme, (in a book with 364 pages), in the section entitled 'Le Christ historique et la théologie négative'. The close association which John of the Cross makes between the 'via negativa', or man's inability to know God as He is, and blind faith is indeed underlined by Lucien-Marie. Nevertheless he remains silent on precisely the point which Cordero, in the article already reviewed, draws attention to: John of the Cross gives clear instructions to refrain from any attempts to pray with specific intellectual or emotional content. Lucien-Marie gives the impression that the 'via negativa' serves merely to warn the Christian that God will always transcend human concepts of Him, but he does not recognize the fact that the 'via negativa' is much more than a mere warning in the teaching of John of the Cross. On the contrary, it is the central point in his mystical teaching.

Rather than going into the dogmatic problem of rehabilitating John of the Cross' Christology along the lines which Lucien-Marie follows, this study will follow an entirely different route toward reaching a new understanding of the via negativa, namely an interpretation based upon an empirical study of the actual mystical development of Discalced Carmelites.

Summing up what has been illustrated so far, the teachings of John of the Cross contain two main themes: strict affective asceticism and the via negativa. Affective asceticism can be called a 'super technique' because it is a practice which extends to the follower's entire way of life, day in and day out, all day long. An oriental meditation technique which takes up only twenty to forty minutes a day during the actual meditative session is a mini-technique in comparison. The other point in his teaching, the via negativa, is a rejection of the meditative techniques of Spain in the 16th century. These consisted in imagining various scenes from the Bible or in thinking about various religious topics. One could say that John of the Cross opposed the Spiritual Exercises of Ignatius of Loyola. He undoubtedly became familiar with them during his intermediate studies in humanities at the hands of the Jesuits in Medina del Campo. However, while rejecting techniques in prayer he advocates, inconsequently, an all-encompassing technique in asceticism. The reasoning behind this inconsequence will be presented in chapter three.

Before going on to test these teachings empirically, it must be shown briefly that the potential subjects, the members of the Discaled Carmelite Order and especially the nuns, still practice this 'super-technique'. The Rule of the nuns, namely, was actually formulated, not by John of the Cross, but by Teresa of Avila. Although the commentary on the constitutions of the Discalced Carmelite nuns by Gabriel of St. Mary Magdalene[30] does state that in general the constitutions of the nuns follow the main lines of the Rule of the friars, certain differences in accent can be noted. The nuns actually live much more separated from 'the world' than the friars. The constitutions of the nuns stipulate a strict observance of the cloister. The friars, on the other hand, are allowed much more freedom of movement in connection with their pastoral duties and academic careers. Due to the nuns' stricter way of life the other aspects of the Rule are much more strictly observed, namely poverty and obedience. The practice of maintaining silence and solitude in the cell and of doing penance is much more common among the nuns than among the friars. One aspect of the nuns' constitutions which John of the Cross does not mention is the role of work in the mortification of the body. The constitutions of the nuns state, as commentated upon by Fr. Gabriel, that the nuns must get used to the fatigue which work causes. As Fr. Gabriel notes, the aim of work is mortification, and as such, it belongs also to the super-technique of strict affective asceticism:

"This mortified body we will use for work, so that through fatigue it will be even more mortified and will be made suitable to be a tool of brotherly love . . . St. Teresa in her Constitutions makes us able, in accordance with the word of the apostle, to live a life of bodily denial and incessant work, a continuous, true sacrifice of the body . . . This sacrificial offering opens wide the way to the supernatural life of the grace . . . We, who wish to be His true brides, must, just as He, generously sacrifice our bodies."[31]

Now that both the theory and the actual practice of the super technique of strict affective asceticism, i.e. the rejection of all bodily pleasure, have been sketched, the point has arrived to test its value and function in the contemplative life.

CHAPTER TWO

The Empirical Study
of Christian Mysticism

> Gregory of Nyssa (died 394 A.D.):
> "Thousands of things have been studied by them
> (physiologists, medical doctors, anatomists) of
> which none of us has any experience, because no
> instruction is given in this part of inquiry, and
> because we do not all wish to know who we are.
> For we are content with knowing heaven better
> than ourselves. Do not despise the wonder within
> you!"[1]

INTRODUCTION: SUMMARIZING THE HYPOTHESIS

The first chapter of this study sets the criteria for establishing if a subject is
a 'mystic', according to the tradition of the Discalced Carmelite Order,
based on the teachings of John of the Cross. He defines a mystic as
someone who has gone through a certain ascetical purification, involving
the suppression of all desire except the desire for God. Furthermore, this
strict ascetical purification must correspond to a certain prayer development, which consists of three stages: the beginning stage, the progressive
stage, and the perfected stage. This pattern of development is placed by
him within a framework of dualistic thought, i.e. spirit/sense dualism, the
dualism of creator/creation, and the rivalry between desire for the created
good vs. the desire for God. The first thing which the empirical study will
test will be this criterion of mystical development. This means testing to see
if mystical development corresponds to the growth in phases which he
outlines. It also means testing to see if a strict affective asceticism correlates
with this mystical development.

After establishing the validity of John of the Cross' definition of what a
mystic is, the theological and psychological stereotypes of mystics and
mysticism will be tested upon those subjects who can be classified as
mystics, according to the definition given above. The theological
hypothesis is that the dualistic framework, in which John of the Cross
places his view of what a mystic is, is not intrinsic to the mystical experience, and will not correlate when tested upon such points as the role of
asceticism, either in actual practice or merely in the attitude of the subject.

23

In conjunction with this, it is also predicted that not asceticism, but other factors such as some psychological and religious attitudes will correlate with mystical development. The psychological stereotypes enter the picture here. What is the psycho-physiological profile of the 'mystic', and of those who do not become mystics, even though they have spent most of their life in a contemplative cloister? The exploration of this psychological profile is carried out with five psychological tests and with EEG and other physiological measurements. It should be mentioned here that the EEG study to be described here is, to the author's knowledge, the first one to be done on Christian contemplatives. The EEG results will be compared with similar EEG studies on oriental meditation, to aid in exploring the specific psycho-physiological profile of the Christian mystic.

It should be made clear at the start that this empirical study is not an experiment, in the technical sense, since nothing is manipulated or changed in the experimental conditions. Rather, this is nothing more than an inventory. At the end of this chapter some suggestions will be made, however, as to possible experiments which could be set up on the basis of the data collected here.

I. THE STRUCTURE OF THE INVENTORY

A. General procedure for testing the hypothesis

It was first of all necessary to determine through some quantifiable test which prayer experiences the subjects have had recently, that is, within the last month, and in the past. By comparing these present prayer experiences with their antecedent experiences, the pattern of prayer development could be determined. To obtain this information a questionnaire or scale of prayer experiences was designed with the help of psychologists. To bring these prayer experiences into correlation with possible determining factors, the questionnaire also included items testing religious attitudes, distracting problems, and ascetical views. Furthermore five psychological 'paper and pencil' tests were given. In short, no psychoanalytic depth interviews, Rorschach tests or other non-quantifiable projective methods were used.

In order to assure a homogeneous group of subjects, only subjects were recruited within a specific cultural area, namely Holland and the Dutch-speaking part of Belgium, i.e. Flanders. All subjects were chosen from the Discalced Carmelite Order, not from the associated branch, the Calced Carmelites, or from other religious groups. The restriction to a certain cultural area and a specific spiritually-formed group assured that the interpretation of the teachings of John of the Cross would be fairly standard. The subjects had been exposed to similar spiritual publications, in the Dutch language, and to similar spiritual instruction. In fact, one friar had given spiritual conferences for years to almost all the nuns involved. Since the style and language of John of the Cross is somewhat out-dated and difficult for modern readers, the advantage of limiting the subjects to the Discalced Carmelites was that the subjects had almost all had an introduction into his thought.

B. *Subjects and methods*

The method for investigating this field therefore seemed to depend upon obtaining as large a number of Discalced Carmelite subjects as possible, ranging broadly in age, ascetical views, strictness of cloister, cultural and psychological traits. Appeals were sent out to the various Discalced Carmelite cloisters in Holland and Flanders. Of the potential ± 350 female subjects and ± 50 male subjects, only about 15% volunteerd to participate. The basis for participation was closely related to the attitude of the religious superior in each cloister to the inventory, and especially to the EEG study. This was purely a matter of individual policy and seemed to have nothing to do with how progressive (experimental) or conservative a superior was. In most cases, it was in fact just as difficult to enlist the cooperation of the experimental cloisters or groups as of the traditional groups. Altogether there were 55 subjects, one of whom had to be dropped because she did not follow instructions. There were 38 Dutch nuns, 6 Flemish nuns, and 9 friars, only two of whom are Flemish. The ages ranged from 24 to 77.

It should be noted that it was extremely difficult to obtain male subjects of any age, either in Holland or Flanders. This was unexpected since it is the male Discalced Carmelites who have the higher degree of education and whom one therefore would have expected to be the most open to scientific inquiry. However, it was the nuns who showed the most appreciation of the scientific nature of the study. The lack of prayer experiences, as later revealed in the questionnaire on spirituality, among the male subjects in general might have accounted for this negative attitude. The author suggests that either the friars resisted the empirical study because they were afraid that it would reveal their lack of prayer development, or because they thought they could contribute nothing to the study precisely because they had had so few experiences in prayer. It should be noted, furthermore, that the friars are the ones who give spiritual direction, not the nuns. Perhaps therefore the friars were concerned that their domain not be brought into question through 'outside' inquiries. The reason for the disparity in prayer development between males and females will be ex-

25

tensively discussed in chapter four.

Preliminary interviews were held with twelve subjects, coming from widely varying cloisters. On the basis of these interviews a pilot test was set up, which these twelve were asked to fill in and comment upon. On the basis of their answers and reactions the definitive version of the questionnaire on spirituality was designed. Since the items and especially the types of question differed greatly from the pilot test and the final test, the two did not generally overlap. It was decided not to ask the subjects to write essays, or to answer with a simple 'yes' or 'no', but to present them with a multiple choice type of question, which could be answered with a scale of '0' to '5'. This reduced the divergence in answers due to lack of intellectual or expressive ability, while allowing for some nuance in thought.

All the questionnaires were mailed to the subjects with the instructions to fill them in individually and spontaneously. The pilot test had already revealed that some nuns tended to fill the questionnaire in with the help of the religious superior. Since some subjects were particularly concerned about remaining anonymous, each subject was assigned a number in a private conversation. The subject was instructed to use that number and not a name when filling in the tests. Since the questionnaires were usually mailed back in a common envelope which contained all the questionnaires of the subjects in any given cloister, the subjects were interested that their fellow nuns or friars not be able to identify them.

The re-test, i.e. the second administration of the test, was given about six weeks after the first administration. In the future, the re-test of prayer experiences should be given within three weeks, to exclude the effect of long-range alternations in prayer growth. This will be explained later. The only other re-test given was the main psychological scale, the ABV, to be described presently. It was re-administered one year after the first testing.

After the data had been collected and computerized individual interviews were held with each subject in which, as a reward for their cooperation, each subject was told his/her own results in a general way. In discussing these results, the subjects often volunteerd additional information, which was either written down or recorded on tape. These interviews are reported in part in chapter four. They were important for determining the social position of the subject within the group, the prayer development of the subject, and the nature of certain intimate relationships with members of the opposite sex as well as with members of the same sex. The subjects were allowed to censor or review those parts of the interviews which are quoted in chapter four.

C. Detailed description of the tests used[2]

1. *The Questionnaire on Spirituality* (see Appendix, pp. 235-241 for the text).
Preliminary interviews with twelve of the subjects had revealed that the spiritual formation of Discalced Carmelites was fairly standard up until a few years ago, when a new form of noviciate was introduced in some communities. Since none of the subjects had been formed in this newer noviciate, they had all had a standard acquaintance with the teaching of John of the Cross. The main exception to this was a small number of nuns who had been forbidden by a former superior to read his works as well as the "Song of Songs" in the noviciate. Even these subjects had found the opportunity to read him later on. A few of the younger subjects expressed difficulty with his style and vocabulary.

a. Section one: Prayer experiences (68 items).
From the works of John of the Cross 68 quotations were selected which describe a wide variety of prayer experiences, ranging from the total inability to pray to the highest mystical experiences. However, since he refers only briefly to the beginning states, namely active rational or visual prayer, these kinds of prayer were insufficiently represented, with only 4 of the 68 items.

The instructions, which were extensive, requested the subjects to indicate with their answers the frequency with which they had experienced the things described in prayer during the last month. A high frequency of occurrence was to be indicated by circling the '5' in a scale of '0' to '5'. To indicate past prayer experiences they were to put an 'X' beside all items which they had ever had in the past. Thus, regarding present prayer experiences a gradation from '0' to '5' was possible, but unfortunately not in regard to past prayer experiences. A future, revised version of this questionnaire should take into account the desirability of providing a gradation also for past prayer experiences. This emphasis on a continuing line of development is an innovation on the usual questionnaires on mystical experience or 'peak' experiences, such as Maslow and Greeley[3] have constructed, where the orientation is restricted to separate mystical phenomena, without sufficient attention to their place within the subject's total pattern of spiritual development over a period of time.

b. Section two: Distractions in prayer (32 items).
This section included 20 items describing distractions in prayer due to disturbances from the environment and from inner conflicts. Twelve items were added, in modern language, which paraphrased various prayer ex-

periences which John of the Cross described. It was expected that these paraphrases would correlate highly with their equivalents in section one. Hereby an attempt was made to explore the possibilities of constructing a modernized version of the questionnaire, to replace the dated style and language of John of the Cross. The instructions were the same as in section one, i.e. to circle a number in a scale of '0' to '5' indicating the frequency of occurrence during the last month.

c. Section three: Ascetical views (20 items).
Twenty statements by John of the Cross on ascetical matters were selected, consisting of about ten statements which could be classified as strict views and ten statements which could be called mild views. The mild views emphasize that God's love purifies man. The strict views state that man must reject all desires except the desire for God. Included in the mild category were a few statements which state that refraining from rational or intellectual activity in prayer is necessary. The subjects were instructed to consider each item critically and carefully and to give a personal opinion. To indicate full agreement with the statement, they were to circle a '5' in a scale of '0' to '5'. Lesser degrees of agreement could be expressed by circling numbers '0' to '4'.

d. Section four: Attitudes toward John of the Cross (21 items).
These items were gathered from the preliminary interviews, where a number of subjects indicated a strong aversion to John of the Cross. The items were constructed in order to reveal the motives for this attitude. The subjects were asked if they disagreed with him on an ideological level, on the literary level (out-dated style), on the emotional level, or if they had ever read him. One special item concerned the subject's attitude toward bride's mysticism. This item was included to see if it correlated with hysteria and/or with mystical development.

At the beginning of section four were four items which paraphrased the ascetical views of John of the Cross, plus two items which described two other ascetical views which are not found in John of the Cross. It was expected that the four paraphrases of John of the Cross would correlate with the respective statements in section three.

e. Section five: The 'idea of God' test by G. Vercruysse (44 items).
This section was included to see if subjects who were advanced mystics might have a more personal idea of God than non-mystics, or vice-versa. The test by Vercruysse had been developed on a wide variety of laymen, not on members of religious communities. The subjects in this experiment, therefore, were far more homogeneous and religious than the original

28

population for which the test was designed. The instructions were to circle a number in a scale from '0' to '7', to indicate the extent of agreement with each idea about God.

f. Section six: Personal assessment (2 items).

This section was intended to see if certain subjects considered themselves to be much further advanced in contemplation than the rest of the group. Two lines, A and B, of equal length, were presented. The subject was instructed to indicate on line 'A' how advanced he thought he was. On line 'B' he was to show how advanced he thought the group was. John of the Cross states that the illusion of being very much more advanced than the others occurs at about the half-way point in contemplative development.

The Re-test.

The re-test was considerably shortened by excluding sections five and six. The subjects had given highly non-differentiating answers to section five and had shown great resistance to answering section six. The page sequence in section one was reversed to make it more difficult for the subjects to remember their original answers. Thus the re-test consisted of:

Section 1: Present and past prayer experiences
Section 2: Distractions in prayer and paraphrased prayer experiences.
Section 3: Strict and mild ascetical attitudes.
Section 4: Attitudes toward John of the Cross and paraphrased ascetical views.

The original questionnaire was in Dutch, and the translations from John of the Cross were taken from the most recent Dutch version of his works[4]. Although the place of the quotations from John of the Cross are indicated in the English version of the questionnaire presented in the appendix to this study, (see factor analysis) the text reference was ommitted in the actual version given to the subjects. The reason for this was to avoid having the subjects look up the original context of the prayer experience being described, i.e. to see if it belonged to the beginning, the middle or the advanced stage.

2. *Amsterdamse Biographische Vragenlijst (ABV) by G. J. S. Wilde.*

Sub-scales: neuroticism, psycho-somatic neuroticism, extraversion, test unreliability, social desirability. Number of items: 107. Norms adjusted for sex and age. Type of answer: choice between 'yes', '?', 'no'. Retest administered after one year.

This Dutch test was constructed by G. Wilde with items taken mainly from the 'Maudsley Personality Inventory' of H. J. Eysenck. This is the most-used Dutch personality inventory and therefore the Dutch norms are very well established. Although ideally it would have been better to have used the 'Personality Inventory' by Eysenck and Eysenck, since Eysenck's theories are so important to the psycho-physiological study to be described presently, his test could not be used at the time of this study because the Dutch norms had not yet been established. The Dutch version appeared about two years after this study[5].

3. *The Barron Ego-Strength Scale.*
One scale. Number of items: American version, 68; Dutch version by A. F. Casséé, 66; adapted version for this study, 60. Two blank answers allowed. No re-testing.

Since this scale was originally designed for a heterogeneous population, it had to be adapted to the subjects in this study, who are homogeneous in regard to religion. The six items in the original test concerning religion were dropped. This was motivated by the fact that these same six items were omitted from the Dutch version of the MMPI because they receive a different cultural value in Europe than in America. R. Hood had already observed that these six items prejudice the results on even an American religious population[6]. Therefore only 60 items were included here. Accordingly the norms had to be adjusted. Cassee's norms were lowered to 39 and 40 points, as the normal Dutch score for the average adult in this study.

4. *The Scale of Inter-Personal Values.*
Sub-scales: degree of conformity, degree of independence, altruism, leadership qualities, need for group support, need for recognition. Number of items: 30. Type of answer: choice between 'the least' or 'the most'. Separate norms for sex. Adapted to Dutch population.

This scale was particularly important precisely because the group of subjects is so homogeneous in its spiritual forming. To test for the degree of group influence, the scales on degree of conformity, need for group support, and vice-versa, the scale on the degree of independence, were especially necessary.

5. *Vragenlijst over Positief Innerlijk Welbevinden by H. J. Hermans.*
(trans.: Questionnaire on Positive Inner Well-Being) See appendix, pp. 231-234 for complete translation of the text of this scale.

Sub-scales: happy emotionality, unhappy emotionality. Number of items:

35. Type of answer: choice between "I feel like this . . .": 'very often', 'often', 'sometimes', 'once in a while', 'very rarely', 'never'. No re-administration. No Dutch norms for the adult population have yet been established. Because this scale uses two variables (happy and unhappy emotionality) it was preferred above other scales of emotionality which use only one variable (anxiety scales).

6. The 'Hysteria Scale' of the MMPI.

Only one scale. Norms adapted for sex. Number of items: 60. Type of answer: choice between 'true' or 'false'. Dutch norms established by J. Nuttin and B. Beuten. No re-administration.

The kind of hysteria tested here is conversion neurosis, as defined by Nuttin and Beuten in the manual to the Dutch version of the MMPI[7]. A factor analysis of the items in this scale indicated as being most characteristic for this form of hysteria; nausea, vomiting, retching, lack of appetite. Despite the large amount of over-lapping with items from the Barron Ego-strength Scale and the ABV, there was not much inter-correlation between these scales because the way these items are scored changes from scale to scale. That is, what is scored positively in one scale is scored negatively in another, in some cases.

7. The Lacuna.

If the number of tests had not been so great, it would have been most useful to have given a concentration test as well, since distractions in prayer might be tied in with a general inability to concentrate well. However, since the subjects were already complaining about having to fill in so many tests, even to the point where one or two refused to complete the re-tests, it would have been unfeasible to have added more tests. In the future, this could be avoided by shortening the Questionnaire on Spirituality.

8. Other personal data collected.

Every subject was questioned about his/her age, educational background, medical history and recent illnesses, record of administrative positions in the cloister or in the order, intimate relationships, amount of duties or responsibilities, number of years in the cloister, acquaintance with the writings and teachings of John of the Cross. Other possible psychological variables such as depressiveness and paranoia could have been tested with sub-scales of the MMPI, but this would have meant administering the complete MMPI. Since this is a very lengthy test, about two hours would have been needed for the subjects to full it in. Since they were already complaining about having to spend so much time on the questionnaires, this was not used.

The analyses were conducted in two phases: 1) the test reliability of the Questionnaire on Spirituality and 2) the correlations between the scores on the Questionnaire on Spirituality and the five psychological tests, plus the other personal data. The first phase was also intended to throw some light on the various kinds of prayer types, their mutual relationships, their development over the course of time, and their relationship to the expectations based on the teachings of John of the Cross, i.e. correlations with ascetical views and religious attitudes.

A. The Questionnaire on Spirituality - test reliability, sections I - IV

1. *Internal consistency* (appendix, pp. 242-244 for contents of clusters). The test of reliability based upon internal consistency of the items was conducted by using the iterative cluster analysis method of A. H. Boon van Ostade, whereby all data are reduced to digits of '0' and '1'. When the reliability is high, i.e. above 0.500, the internal consistency of the items is great, that is, they all center around a common point. This also indicates that a sufficient diversity of experience exists among the subjects to allow good differentiation. The test of reliability was conducted separately on each of the first four sections. It could not be done on the fifth section because the answers did not differentiate enough, as already mentioned.

Reliabilities:		First Test Administration	Second Test Administration
Section I:	present prayer experiences		
	Cluster A: happy experiences	0.9537	0.9587
	Cluster B: unhappy experiences	0.8124	0.8871
Section II:	distracted behavior and paraphrases		
	Cluster C: distracted behavior	0.8467	0.9032
Section III:	strict and mild ascetical views		
	Cluster D: all ascetical views combined	0.9285	0.9241
Section IV:	rejection or acceptance of John of the Cross		
	Cluster E: all attitudes combined	0.8526	0.8544

Conclusion: All the cluster reliabilities are very high, indicating that in sections one through four all the questions had a common point of orientation and that the diversity of prayer experience and attitudes among the subjects was sufficiently great. The fact that the differentiation between mild and strict ascetical views in section three did not appear in the cluster 'D' is due to the influence of conformity, as is shows in the appendix, p. 243. This means that the subjects gave non-differentiating answers on items which correlate well with conformity. In section four, although conformity also influences the answers here (see p. 244 in the appendix) in cluster 'E', a clear differentiation exists between acceptance of John of the Cross and rejection of him, as evident in the plus/minus signs by each item.

2. *Test/re-test reliabilities*

Some gauge of the group scoring pattern between the first and the second administration of the test can be obtained by comparing the clusters which resulted from each section. When the content of the clusters is similar in both administrations, the answering pattern of the group can be called consistent. Individual reliability is not tested hereby, but rather with the sub-scale for test unreliability in the ABV test. A much more refined analysis of test/re-test reliability will be presented shortly in the discussion of factor reliabilities.

Cluster A: happy prayer experiences.
The contents of this cluster in both tests were very similar. Both contained items describing mystical union and contemplation.

Cluster B: unhappy prayer experiences.
Although the items in this cluster remained pretty much the same in both tests, some shifts could be seen in the rank or sequence of some items. Those items which described the absence of God or the inability to pray correlated higher with the sumscore of the cluster in the second test than in the first test. Other items, describing active rational and visual meditation, became less important in the cluster of the second test. This indicates some unreliability, which is further confirmed in the factor unreliabilities of factors 2 and 3.

Cluster C: distracted behavior.
In both the first and second administrations of the test, cluster C lumps seemingly contradictory kinds of behavior together: tenseness, drowsiness, restlessness, yawning, etc. These items do not correlate with conformity, but rather with unhappy prayer experiences, cluster B, which correlated at 0.47 in the first test and 0.50 in the second test, with cluster C. This indicates that all these kinds of distracted behavior form a complex which accompanies prayer when the pleasurable experiences are absent. The reasons for this will be explored in the discussion of the EEG study later.

Cluster D: strict and mild ascetical views combined.
This cluster remains more or less the same in both the first and second

administration of the test, with the exception that the stricter items come to predominate in the re-test. The reason for this is that the influence of conformity is very great, especially in regard to the strict items. The fact that the stricter items prevail in the re-test indicates that the answering pattern of the group becomes even more conformistic in the re-test.

Cluster E: attitudes toward John of the Cross.
The same items appear in this cluster in both the first and the second administration of the test. In the first test the 'acceptance' items were grouped together and correlated positively with the sumscore of the cluster, while the 'rejection' items correlated negatively with it. In the second test the same grouping of the items is evident, although the plus/minus signs are reversed. Due to the influence of conformity, cluster E correlates very well (0.70) with cluster D in both test administrations.

Conclusion: the general answering pattern of the group remains nearly the same in both administrations of the test for all sections except for cluster B, unhappy prayer experiences. The increasing influence of conformity in the second test administration, especially regarding section III: cluster D, makes the first administration of the test the more reliable one, since the answers reflect a greater spontaneity. For this reason the factor sumscores of only the *first* test administration will be used in correlations with other variables.

B. *Section I: Prayer Experiences*

1. Factor analysis (see pp. 246-251, appendix for contents of factors).
The factor analysis and not the cluster analysis will be the yardstick for measuring the degree and kinds of emotionality present in prayer development. Whereas the cluster analysis is based upon a fairly rough calculation which does not deal with the raw data but with digits, the factor analysis, on the other hand, is based upon the actual answers of the subjects. The advantage of this is that fine nuances in prayer experience can come to light in the factor analysis, which would be ignored by the cluster analysis.

a. Naming the factors.
In naming the factors the assistance was asked of two neutral judges, two women who did research in the neuro-psychiatric clinic of the University of Nijmegen. Neither one had ever read the works of John of the Cross nor had any acquaintance with his teaching. The names which the neutral judges assigned to the fifteen factors are presented below. Factors 9 and 12 are omitted because they contained too few items and also because they did not correlate well with the other factors. Their content and role therefore

34

seem unimportant.

The names of the most important factors:
1. Emotionally pleasurable mystical experience.
2. The inability to pray.
3. Active, visual prayer.
4. Intellectual visions or 'thinking contemplation'.
5. Sensational mystical phenomena.
6. Active, rational prayer.
7. Emotionally neutral contemplation.
8. Emotional contemplation.
10. Distracted, troubled prayer.
11. Mixed pleasurable/unpleasurable mystical experience.
13. Unpleasurable mystical experience.
14. Very unpleasurable mystical experience.
15. Passive, restful contemplation.

*Detailed description of the content of each factor and motivation for nomen-
clature:*
Factor 1: "Emotionally pleasurable mystical experience"
All the quotations taken from *The Living Flame of Love* which describe the
highest and most intense kinds of mystical union occur in factor one,
together with ten quotations from the *Spiritual Canticle*, which describe the
prayer of union. In the quotations with the highest loadings (above 0.700)
one finds the traditional symbols which have been used for centuries to
describe mystical prayer (wine of love, fire, flame, the divine 'touch', the
wedding feast, the wounds of love, etc.). The two neutral judges emphasized the highly emotional nature of these items.

Factor 2: "The inability to pray"
The content of many of these items are words or symbols associated with
the so-called 'via negativa', i.e. the cloud, darkness, the inability to feel or
reason about God. This is not the same as a disinterest in prayer, but rather
a spiritual dryness which makes prayer impossible. John of the Cross warns
that this spiritual lethargy may be due to melancholy and not to true
spiritual development, as will be discussed further in chapter four. Both
judges noticed that this factor is much less depressive than factors 13 and
14.

Factor 3: "Active, visual prayer"
This describes meditating with the visual imagination. Both judges pointed
out the active nature of this prayer form and its emotional 'coolness', or

35

lack of emotion.

Factor 4: "Intellectual visions"
All the items here come from the passages in the *Ascent* which describe spiritual intuitions or insights. The judges noticed here, too, the lack of emotionality. The latent emotional content of this kind of illumination is discussed extensively in chapter four in the section on the Divine Wisdom. Both judges agreed that this is not the same kind of intellectual insight as the intellectual activity in factor six. One judge called it 'thinking contemplation'.

Factor 5: "Sensational mystical phenomena"
Both the judges pointed out that the visions as well as the ecstasies involved here concern things which are perceived with the senses. At the same time, these things cause sensations or spectacles. One of the judges had the impression that the bodily senses were not yet adapted to spiritual things at this stage. She thought this was a less-experienced stage. Neither judge mentioned any emotional coloring involved here.

Factor 6: "Active, rational prayer"
This involves meditating by dwelling on texts or themes or objects. Both judges thought that this prayer form is a technique for getting concentrated. Neither one made any reference to any kind of emotionality present here.

Factor 7: "Emotionally neutral contemplation"
One judge called this 'self-forgetfulness' or recollection. Neither judge saw any particular emotional 'color' in this prayer form.

Factor 8: "Emotional contemplation"
In this factor both the experience of love, union, and intellectual illumination or enlightenment are present. As in factor four, there is a latent emotionality present, as will be discussed in chapter four. The judges thought that rest and receptivity dominate here together with some emotionality (pleasurable), but to a much less degree than in factor one.

Factor 10: "Distracted, troubled prayer"
This factor describes the attempt to pray rather than a prayer experience. It involves inner conflicts and distraction. It is therefore not the same thing as the inability to pray (factor 2), but rather a period of inner torment.

Factor 11: "Mixed pleasurable and unpleasurable mystical experience"

The judges thought that the alternation of happy and unhappy experiences in this factor might indicate a rapid oscillation from one state to another. In both states the emotional tone is intense.

Factor 13: "Unpleasurable mystical experience"
The judges noticed a difference between both the intensity of the suffering and the kind of suffering in this factor, as compared with factor 11. In factor 11 the suffering is interspersed with pleasurable experiences, while in factor 13, the suffering is constant and unalleviated. Not the experience of pain dominates, as in factor 11, but rather emptiness or absence of pleasure.

Factor 14: "Very unpleasurable mystical experience"
The judges found this factor clearly more depressive than factors 2, 11, 13 and 10. They noticed certain parallels with depressive or even masochistic states in psychiatric patients. One judge considered the possibility that this might be merely a temporary state in a growth process.

Factor 15: "Passive, restful contemplation"
The judges were unsure about whether this factor describes happy or unhappy prayer experiences, although they agreed that the emphasis here is upon rest and receptivity. It could therefore be called neutral contemplation although it has some emotional coloring which is more than factor 7 has. The precise kind of emotionality could not be determined, however.

b. Determining the degrees of emotionality.
Now that the types of emotionality in certain prayer experiences have been discussed, it is possible to determine the way these kinds of emotionality are inter-correlated. The correlation matrix of these factors (see appendix, p. 252) indicates two main groups, corresponding roughly to happy mystical experiences (Cluster A) and unhappy mystical experiences (Cluster B), with the difference that the active neutral prayer forms (*active* rational and visual meditation) are left out. This shows the advantage of the factor analysis over the cluster analysis, which did not sufficiently recognize the existence of emotionally neutral experiences. These two groups are therefore:

Happy mystical experiences:
Factor 1:   Emotionally pleasurable mystical experience
Factor 4:   Intellectual visions
Factor 7:   Emotionally neutral contemplation

Factor 8: Emotional contemplation
Factor 15: Passive, restful contemplation

Unhappy mystical experiences:
Factor 2: The inability to pray
Factor 11: Mixed pleasurable/unpleasurable mystical experience
Factor 13: Unpleasurable mystical experience
Factor 14: Very unpleasurable mystical experience.

What meets the eye here is that the *passive* neutral prayer forms, i.e. factors 2, 4, 7, and 15, are included in the groups of emotionally colored factors. This suggests that the passive neutral factors nevertheless have somewhat more emotional coloring than the active neutral prayer forms. This is especially true of the passive neutral factors in the 'happy' group, whose latent emotional content will be discussed in the EEG study.

c. Factor reliabilities and emotionality.
A factor analysis was conducted on the first section, present prayer experiences only. How reliable are the answering patterns of the subjects in regard to these factors in the second administration of the test (re-test)? How well do these factor sumscores correlate with the re-test? The factor reliabilities were obtained by adding up the sumscores of the subjects on the factors in section one, for the first administration of the test only. Using the same factors, the sumscores on the second administration of the test (re-test) were also added up. This was done for present and past experiences, with the exception of factors 7 and 15, which were excluded as being less germaine. The complete list of factor reliabilities is given on p. 245 in the appendix. Reliability correlates above about 0.6750 are considered reliable. The most reliable and the most unreliable factors are shown here:

Reliability Correlates		Present prayer experiences	Past prayer experiences
Pleasurable mystical experience	(factor 1)	0.8852	0.8985
Active rational meditation	(factor 6)	0.8088	0.4534
Emotional contemplation	(factor 8)	0.7884	0.8683
Active visual meditation	(factor 3)	0.5177	0.1764
The inability to pray	(factor 2)	0.6706	0.6552

As the cluster analysis had already shown, cluster B contains some unreliable factors. Generally speaking, the emotionally positive, or happy, factors are the most reliable. They become even more reliable in regard to the long-term memory of past experiences. The emotionally neutral factors are generally the most unreliable factors. The long-term memory of these factors becomes even more unreliable. Factors 6 and 10, although reliable in the present or short-term memory, become unreliable in the long-range memory of past experiences. As the psychological scores on p. 267, appendix, when compared with the test/re-test scores (p. 270, appendix), show, the greatest discrepancies between test/re-test scores on these unreliable factors occurs among subjects with low scores on the Barron Ego-Strength Scale. These 'weak' subjects tend to give widely discrepant answers on the emotionally neutral factors in regard to both present and past prayer experiences. Such 'weak' subjects also tend to show a higher sum-score on the happy prayer experiences in the second test administration than in the first testing, although here the discrepancy is not so great that the reliability of the factor is affected.

Conclusion: Emotionally neutral experiences are more unreliable than the emotionally unhappy experiences or the happy prayer experiences. Generally the long-range memory of these neutral experiences is more unreliable than the short-range memory of them. The most reliable prayer experiences are mystical, emotional contemplative, and intellectual visionary experiences. Why are the happy experiences so reliable? The suggestion is made and supported by the author in chapter four that these happy prayer experiences involve a certain erotic, bodily experience as well as a spiritual experience. The impression which the bodily pleasurable feeling makes is the touchstone whereby the subject can easily remember the happy prayer experience. The unreliability of factor two, the inability to pray, might be due to the lack of any bodily feeling, happy or unhappy. The subject has no physical touchstone to attach the memory to. Consequently, the current mood of the subject, especially the 'weak' or unstable subject, can color both his memory of recent emotionally neutral experiences as well as his long-term memory of such things. The same explanation might apply to the two kinds of active meditation, rational and visual prayer, which involve the imagination and the intellect, but not necessarily the sensuality of the body. Very unhappy prayer experiences, on the other hand, (factors 13 and 14) are somewhat more reliable. This might be because the absence of bodily pleasure is so great that the pain this causes is also more deeply etched in the memory. In short, the reliability of the factor seems tied in with the degree of pleasure and pain it describes, with the pleasurable experiences dominating. The role of bodily sensuality will be further discussed in regard to this 'pleasure principle' in chapter four.

d. The sequence of factors in prayer development (see p. 252, appendix). The correlations between factors can be explained according to the theories of John of the Cross, who teaches that these states follow one another in a certain pattern. The fact that the high negative correlation was found between emotional contemplation (factor 8) and active rational prayer (factor 6) (-0.43) supports his teaching that passive prayer and active prayer are mutually exclusive to some extent. The high negative correlation between emotional contemplation (factor 8) and distracted, troubled prayer (factor 10) (-0.51) suggests that contemplation can only occur when inner conflict is resolved. Factor 8 also shows a fairly significant negative correlation with the unhappy prayer experiences in factors 2 (-.38) and 14, (-.35), which suggests that emotional contemplation and these forms of unhappy prayer experiences are mutually exclusive to some degree. The fact, however, that the other happy prayer factors did not correlate well, either negatively or positively, with the unhappy prayer factors implies that a subject can experience both kinds of prayer within the same month. They are not per se mutually exclusive.

The high positive correlation between very emotional pleasurable mystical experience (factor 1) and the emotionally 'cooler' forms of contemplation, factors 7,8,4,15, suggests that these are all aspects of the same basic kind of experience, namely the prayer of union.

The key to determining the sequence of these factors lies in the various degrees of unhappy prayer experience. According to John of the Cross the sequence of dark nights, i.e. unhappy experiences, should lead from the inability to pray (factor 2), which corresponds with the first dark night, to the second dark night, which is considerably more unpleasurable. Is factor 13 or factor 14 the second dark night? The fact that factor 2 correlates much better with factor 14 than with factor 13 suggests that the phase which immediately follows the first dark night is factor 14, very unpleasurable prayer experiences. At about this time, factor 10, distracted and troubled prayer also plays a role. Factor 10 correlates well with only factor 14 (0.42). This corresponds to what John of the Cross says about the inner torment which accompanies the second dark night.

After this second night comes a third night, which seems comprised of periods of relief or alternation with happy experiences. This corresponds to factors 13 and 11, which are mutually connected (0.72). The fact that factor 11 correlates more highly with factor 13 than with factor 14 suggests that factor 11 is a stage beyond factor 13. This corresponds to what John of the Cross says about the final phase of the dark night consisting of the break of dawn, i.e. a mixing of unhappy and happy experiences. Thus, in review, the sequence of unhappy factors seems to correspond to the correlation matrix. Factor 2 comes first, is followed by factor 14, which in turn is succeeded by factor 13, and finally by factor 11. This corresponds to a progression from the first dark night (the inability to pray), to the second dark night (very depressive prayer experience), to the third dark night (less unhappy), and finally to the break of dawn (mixed happy/unhappy experiences).

Pleasurable mystical experience (factor 1) can occur together with these unhappy experiences, especially with the final phase, factor 11, since it correlates the highest with factor 11 (0.32). Factor 8 (emotional contemplation) does not correlate positively with any unhappy prayer experience to any noteworthy degree. Factor 8, however, does correlate negatively with the first two phases, factors 2 and 14, as already mentioned. In fact, factor 8 is the only happy prayer experience which correlates negatively to any noteworthy degree with the unhappy experiences. This is very important, since it suggests that factor 8 is the only kind of prayer experience which continues to develop in the last phases of unitive prayer, after and beyond the dark nights. The succession of happy prayer experiences therefore seems to be traceable in the correlation matrix, too. Starting with factor 15, which is the only 'happy group' factor which correlates positively with the first and second dark nights, the prayer of neutral contemplation seems to come first in the sequence. Factors 4 and 7 then start to play a role, and continue to do so until the last phase, where they correlate positively with factor 11. Factor 1, very pleasurable experience, starts prevailing thereafter, although in connection with factors 7 and 4 and 8. Finally, factor 8 predominates, even after the last phase of the dark nights. *This all implies that factor 8 is the yardstick of advancement.*

The sequence of prayer experiences, both happy and unhappy, is shown in the sumscores of the subjects on each of the factors. The sumscores were ranked according to the total number of points which each subject had on factor 8. Using the same items as in factor 8, the total number of points in past prayer experiences of emotional contemplation were also added up. Likewise, the sumscores were calculated on each of the other factors, for both present and past prayer experiences. The sumscores are presented in the tables on pp. 253-257 in the appendix. On the left side of the table are the present prayer experiences and on the right side are the past prayer experiences, up to and including the present. The sumscores of past experiences in factors 7 and 15 are not included because they are of minor importance in the general survey of past prayer experiences. The factors are arranged in the tables in this order: factor 8 (the key factor), factors 6, 10, 3 (the factors with the highest negative correlation to factor 8), factors 1, 4, 15, 7 (the factors with the highest positive correlation to factor 8 and factors 2, 11, 13, 14 (the factors describing the dark nights). Factor 5 (sensational mystical phenomena) was excluded because so few subjects had ever had such experiences. At the bottom of the table note is made of

41

those subjects who state that they have ever experienced ecstasy (item 34, factor 5).

In addition an 'X' is placed to the far left of each subject's number to indicate which subjects thought that their prayer life was more advanced than that of the others in the group, corresponding to their answers to section six.

The sumscores are added up again, using the factors from the first test administration, but with data from the second administration of the test. This allows comparison between the sumscores of the test and the re-test. The author is aware that this detailed attention to the individual scores of subjects is not customary, but this is practically the only way to determine the sequence of phases in prayer development. A Guttman scale could not be used, although this was attempted, because it is not adapted to take oscillations or recurring phases into account. The model of prayer development is not a scale, but a zig-zag in which overlapping phases are repeated, at ever-intensified levels, and at an ever-increasing speed.

To facilitate the study of the tables of sumscores the subjects have been divided up into five groups on the basis of percentage of points on factor 8. Group I, the most advanced group, has from 80-100% of the points on factor 8. Group II, has from 60-80% of the points. Group III, the middle group, has from 40-60%. Group IV has from 20-40%. Group V, the least advanced, has from 00-20% of the points possible on factor 8. A discussion of the psychological profiles of the groups will be given in section (2.c). Here only a brief review of the groups will be given to show the general pattern of prayer development.

e. *Review of the prayer development of the five groups:*
Group I: Here one finds subjects who have the highest number of points on past prayer experiences, including both the happy and unhappy mystical factors. They have all had the experience of the 'second dark night', i.e. factor 14, and almost all have had the experience of the 'first dark night'. The re-test sumscores on factor 2, the 'first dark night', show that almost all the subjects remember having had this experience. Furthermore, most of the subjects report having had all the experiences of the 'third dark night', i.e. factors 11 and 13. Looking at their current experiences of the dark nights, the highest sumscores are generally found in the 'third dark night'. The experience of the first dark night is almost, if not completely, over. The number of points on the emotionally 'neutral' passive factors in the 'happy' group increases in proportion with the increase in points on factor 8. Thus emotionally neutral and highly emotional prayer experiences increase together. This suggests that the unhappy prayer experiences do indeed succeed each other and finally all pass away. Whereas, the happy prayer

experiences do not phase out, but build up in intensity together. What is left after the unhappy experiences go away is a combination of various kinds of mystical and contemplative experiences, both emotional and non-emotional. Practically the only subjects who report having experienced ecstasy are also in this group. The same thing applies to the other items in factor 5, i.e. sensational visions. Practically the only high sumscores on factor 4, visions and prophecies of an intellectual nature, are found here, although not all the advanced subjects here have such experiences.

Group II: The subjects here have high sumscores on factor 8, but have only about half the percent points possible in factor 1, pleasurable mystical experience, and factors 11 and 13, the third dark night. Their reports of past prayer experiences show that the development in the final phase of the third dark night, factor 11, is far behind that of group I. This group does report having had many of the experiences of the first, second and some of the third dark nights. Generally speaking the level of happy prayer experiences is proportionate to the level of unhappy experiences. The two balance each other out. Only two males placed in the first two groups, both of Flemish origin.

Group III: The present prayer experiences of this group place most of the subjects here in the half-way station of development. The past prayer reports show that many of the subjects are still in the first dark night, however. Very few have had any experience with the final phase of the third dark night, factor 11, or with intellectual visions, factor 4. Of the seven subjects who think they are more advanced than the group, six are in this middle group.

Group IV: Unlike most of the other groups, this group is characterized by a large number of subjects who report having had many prayer experiences in the past, both happy and unhappy, but who currently have very few such experiences. This group could be called the 'backsliders'. Their current prayer life consists of active rational prayer instead of contemplation. Intellectual visions, factor 4, practically do not occur nor have they in the past either. The unhappy experiences outnumber the happy ones, both at present and in the past. The reason for this lack of development seems related to a weak ego-strength, as will be discussed later. The past experiences do not form a mounting line of development, but rather are merely scattered 'peak' experiences.

Group V: The past prayer experiences of this group show that many subjects are acquainted with active rational prayer, (factor 6), the first dark night (factor 2) and troubled prayer (factor 10). Experience with intellectual visions (factor 4) and the third dark night is minimal. The first dark night dominates the picture here. Happy experiences are far outnumbered by unhappy ones. This, too, seems related to certain psychological traits, religious attitudes, and especially to the social attitude of the subject, as will be discussed shortly.

f. *Conclusion:*

Summing up the results of this section, the statistical analyses show that an oscillation or pendulum swing occurs between the happy and unhappy prayer experiences. The emotionally neutral *passive* prayer forms tend to accompany the happy experiences, while the emotionally neutral *active* prayer forms tend to accompany the unhappy experiences. The subjects tend to have greater difficulty remembering the emotionally neutral prayer experiences in the past, and to some degree, also the unhappy experiences. The subjects remember the happy experiences the most consistently. Within the same month, this oscillation can occur, since the happy and unhappy prayer experiences are not mutually exclusive, with the exception of factor 8, which is the yardstick of mystical advancement. This could be called the short-range oscillation in prayer development.

A long-range dynamic also exists. The emotionally neutral experiences develop in two directions: The passive neutral experiences increase in importance while the active neutral experiences decrease, in general. Once the active, emotionally neutral experiences begin to decrease, the oscillation between the happy and unhappy experiences begins to take place. Both happy and unhappy experiences gain in importance together, increasing proportionately. Thus two sets of opposites develop in different ways: emotionally neutral vs. highly emotional experiences. This is related to the underlying neural or psycho-physiological basis, as will be explained in the EEG study. It shows that the first phase, or basis, is the emotionally neutral, restful and passive experience of contemplation. This is both the foundation for later developments, as well as the structure or scaffolding within which the emotional experiences can occur. That is, the increase in emotionality corresponds to an increase in rest, which is the context for contemplative development.

As for the nature of the emotional development, both emotional poles gain in intensity until a 'breaking point' occurs almost at the end of this zig-zag development, somewhere between the second and the third dark night. After this point the unhappy experiences recede and the happy experiences increase. In the final phase, this becomes an ever-accelerating alternation. The final state is not a synthesis between the two poles, but a fixation at the happy pole, within a context of great rest, or emotionally neutral contemplation. Factor 8, which combines both aspects of prayer, emotionality and rest, is therefore the synthesis of the two levels or sets in prayer. For this reason, factor 8 is the key factor to prayer advancement. The question can be raised, whether those subjects in the most advanced group are at the end of the process of growth, or if they are merely in a period of temporary alleviation? Only a long-range study of the subjects could determine this.

One special group of subjects does not develop at all, but rather slides back down to the emotionally neutral, active, prayer forms. Their emotional experiences are sporadic, with the unhappy experiences prevailing. These subjects tend to have low scores on the Barron Ego-Strength Scale, as will be discussed later. On the re-test, subjects with a 'weak' ego-strength tend to show the greatest discrepancies in their answers, especially in regard to the emotionally neutral prayer forms. This does not correlate with test unreliability, as measured by the ABV, of the individual subject. Rather, it seems to reflect the actual erratic or disordered pattern of prayer experience which corresponds with this 'weak' type of subject. Such 'weak' subjects, however, do tend to show higher scores on mystical/contemplative experiences in the re-test. This suggests that they answered the first test with some caution, which they overcame in the re-test. This was not a sufficiently great difference, however, to affect the reliability of the happy factors. (This contrasts to the answering pattern of the other subjects, who tended to become more cautious and conformistic in the re-test.)

Due to the fact that conformity plays a greater role in the re-test, at least with most of the subjects, the first administration of the test gives the most reliable and spontaneous data. The further discussion of the remaining sections of the Questionnaire on Spirituality, sections two, three and four, will be based exclusively on the first test. Before going on to discuss these other sections of the Questionnaire on Spirituality, however, it is necessary at this point to bring the psychological and cultural variables into the picture. This is because these variables help to explain the results of the Questionnaire on Spirituality and throw more light on the reliability of this test.

2. *The influence of psychological/cultural variables upon test reliability*
The statistical analyses determined first of all the correlations between the separate prayer experiences in section one and the variables in the five psychological tests, plus certain personal data such as degree of education, position as religious superior, sex, age, strictness of cloister and medical history. As the table on pp. 258-264 in the appendix shows, the correlations are not very high in most cases. Happy emotionality and independence are

the two main variables involved, in association with the degree of education, the degree of experimentation in the cloister, and sensitivity to what is socially desirable.

Although the correlations between separate items involving prayer experiences and psychological/cultural variables are not very high, these correlations do become higher when grouped together in multiple and canonical correlations. The results of these computations are shown extensively on p. 276, 267 in the appendix. A brief review is given here. The sumscores on factor 8 (emotional contemplation) and factor 1 (pleasurable mystical experience) were correlated with the following psychological and cultural variables:

Canonical Correlation Analysis:		Corr. with factors 1 and 8, sumscores:
Extraversion	0.23	(emotional contemplation and
Happy emotionality	0.41	pleasurable mystical experience)
Social desirability	0.35	
Conformity	0.33	
Independence	−0.53	
Higher education	−0.48	
Administrative position	−0.30	

The probability level of this canonical correlation analysis was 0.0043, which is significant at the .01 level. The canonical correlation included four other items which involved ascetical and religious views. The canonical correlation was 0.74.

Canonical Correlation Analysis:		Corr. with factors 3, 6, 10, sumscores:
Neuroticism	0.43	(active rational and visual
Psycho-somatic neuroticism	0.32	meditation and troubled or
Introversion	0.43	distracted prayer)
Unhappy emotions	0.45	

Canonical correlation = 0.56. Probability level = 0.033, which is significant at the .05 level.

Conclusion: The tendencies which the correlations show between psychological/cultural variables, on one hand, and single prayer experiences, on the other hand, are even more clearly manifested in the canonical correlation analyses. The only psychological variables relevant to mystical/contemplative prayer are happy emotionality, social desirability, and, to some extent, extraversion. The most important cultural variables are (negatively) independence and higher education, and administrative positition as a religious superior, to some extent.

In regard to active rational and visual prayer and distracted prayer, a significant correlation is found between these 'active' prayer forms and neuroticism, introversion, unhappy emotionality and psycho-somatic neuroticism.

a. Test reliability of the individual subjects.

The variable 'test unreliability' from the ABV test correlated negligibly with only two prayer experiences, out of the 68 items. Thus the individual degree of unreliability does not affect the results of the Questionnaire on Spirituality. Rather, this 'lie scale' reflects only the test attitude of the subject toward the personality inventory. Due to item overlapping, the correlation between test unreliability and 'social desirability' is high (0.64). This means that some subjects with high scores on 'social desirability' will also have high scores on 'test unreliability', but this in no way reflects on their answers to the Questionnaire on Spirituality, at least as far as test reliability goes. There was, however, a moderate correlation between 'social desirability' and high sumscores on mystical and contemplative prayer experiences (0.35). This indicates that advanced contemplatives in the Discalced Carmelite Order are sensitive to what the group considers socially desirable. In a contemplative cloister, contemplation is socially desirable. Because they are sensitive to the ideals of the group and identify with the group, these contemplative subjects are receptive to the prayer culture of the cloister. Perhaps precisely because of this group relationship, these subjects were able to develop a contemplative prayer life. Later on, it will be shown how important to prayer development this group involvement is, in the discussion of 'independent' subjects.

Sensitivity to what is socially desirable is not the same thing as conformity. There is no correlation whatsoever between the two. Conformity measures the degree of obedience to the group pressure. Conformity correlated moderately (0.33) with mystical/contemplative prayer, and slightly with test unreliability (0.25). Conformity correlated with only 9 out of the 32 items in factor 1, mystical experiences. Since the group of subjects as a whole is much more conformistic than the general population, the question arises, why was this correlation not even higher than it is? The reason conformity plays a smaller role than might have been expected is because conformistic subjects are found at all levels of prayer development. Furthermore, in section one, the subject is asked to *recall* experiences, not to state an opinion. A memory is less open to the influence of conformity than an opinion. Where opinions are asked, conformity plays a larger role, as in sections three and four:

b. Test reliability of cultural groups.

As the chart on p. 265 in the appendix shows, there is not much correlation between the psychological variables and the cultural variables. The cultural variables were measured with the Scale of Inter-Personal Values. These also include such personal data as degree of education and degree of experimentation in the group. Since the correlations between prayer experiences and the cultural variables 'independence', 'experimental group' and 'higher education' are so similar, an inspection of the answering pattern of these groups is required. Especially 'higher education' and 'independence' show the same negative set of answers to items in factor one and factor eight, describing happy mystical experience and emotional contemplation. About 20 out of the 32 items in factor one are 'rejected'. In contrast to the fairly low correlations which the other cultural and psychological variables showed with prayer data, these negative correlations are much higher, averaging around 0.50.

That there is some connection between 'higher education' and 'experimental group' is evident in the fact that they show a good correlation (0.43). That independence plays a role here is also evident, since independence correlates at 0.37 with 'experimental group' and at 0.31 with higher education. Perhaps this connection can be explained by the fact that of the twelve subjects with a higher theological education (mostly males), five are also 'independent' subjects. Vice-versa, of the eleven highly independent subjects, almost the half are highly educated. These independent subjects are generally not much more independent than the average population, but the meaning of this variable in a cloister group takes on a different tone. The group is highly conformistic, much more so than the average population. Any degree of independence, therefore, varies proportionately much more from the group's norm than in the average population. In such a group, independence, however slight, means the rejection of the conformism of the group. The correlation between independence and conformity is high (−0.57). The question arises, why should rejection of the group's conformity include rejection of happy mystical experiences? The independent subjects reject what is socially desirable (−0.40), and contemplation is socially desirable in a cloister. The author suggests that independence in this cloistered group means the rejection, not only of the ascetical views of the group, but an indiscriminant rejection of the entire 'prayer culture' of the group. The mystical experiences would therefore automatically be rejected. It is conceivable that the variable 'independence' in a population of laymen might function in precisely the opposite way. Because the society is non-contemplative, the independent layman might cultivate an interest in mystical and contemplative experience, as a rejection of the activism and rationalism of the current culture, or what is 'socially desirable' in society.

Of the eleven independent subjects, seven are in experimental groups. An experimental group is a small group of about ten friars or nuns who have secular jobs, who do not wear a habit, and who generally only pray about 15 to 20 minutes every two days, if at all. The prayer culture of these groups has been reduced to a minimum. Since these cultural variables do

48

not correlate with the psychological variables, the motivation for leaving the group and setting up an experimental group can not be found in any psychological factor. The average age of these members of experimental groups is about 35, which is about 20 years younger than the average age of the cloistered members. The motivation for rejecting the prayer culture of the group might be the following: about ten to fifteen years ago, when the culture was not yet interested in contemplative experience, some Catholics entered the comtemplative life, possibly under the influence of some family member, some admired priest, or nun. The out-dated cloistered community had not yet adapted the noviciate to this post-war generation. With the Second Vatican Council, came a new critical attitude toward these out-dated practices. In rejecting them, these new members 'threw the baby out with the bath water', and also rejected the contemplative tradition as such. At this time, in intellectual circles, the 'God is dead' theology and secularization theology came into vogue, which increased their critical attitude toward spirituality. Such 'independent' types then set up experimental communities, oriented entirely to active, secular jobs. This explains the reluctance of such groups to participate in this empirical study of prayer. (It should be noted, however, that four subjects had entirely left the order, but had not rejected the prayer culture. They score high on factors 1 and 8.)

Despite the cultural developments of the 70's, which tend to promote a more positive attitude to spirituality in general, these 'independent' subjects persist in the mentality of the 60's. The experimental groups involved are subject to a cultural lag, which determines their negative answering pattern. Young subjects who have entered within the last five years, on the contrary, are much more appreciative of the contemplative tradition of the cloister, despite or perhaps because of their high level of education. Some of these young subjects are now among the second-most advanced group, namely group two, which has a few subjects aged between 25 and 35. For this reason, not age, but attitude is the key factor here. The 'generation of the 60's' is a group with an attitude which has not been revised in the light of the cultural developments of the 70's. This group is not unreliable, but rather non-differentiating. It gives a set of negative answers indiscriminately, regardless of the actual content of the question.

A secondary group with a set answering pattern is composed mainly of subjects who are now, or have been in the past, in an administrative position. There were 14 religious superiors among the subjects, about half of them female. They tend to reject contemplative and mystical prayer, as is evident in the negative correlation (-0.30) in the canonical correlation with the sumscores on factors 1 and 8, as already mentioned. Such subjects tend to practice active meditation and to be distracted by inner conflict.

They reject the theological virtues (−0.30), conformity (−0.21), social desirability (−0.20). Rather they are independent (0.22). They stress that purification is a matter of doing ones duty and acting justly, as will be discussed in sections three and four. The passive or receptive element is rejected in both mysticism and asceticism. Both social dependency and religious dependency tend to be rejected. One could call this an active set or a 'do-it-yourself' spirituality, based upon both a religious as well as a social attitude of independence. In some ways the answering pattern of the superiors corresponds to that of the 'independent' group already mentioned above. Both groups could be classified as socially and religiously independent types. Neither group is characterized by any specific psychological traits, except the rejection of what is socially desirable. Therefore both are cultural groups.

c. The role of the psychological variables in prayer development.

As has already been mentioned briefly, prayer development can not be explained with a scale model because it proceeds in an accelerating zig-zag of experiences, which mount in intensity. The dynamism or movement involved is a pendulum swing between a happy pole and an unhappy pole. As the intensity of the happy and unhappy experiences increases, the emotionally neutral *active* experiences decrease in importance. This spiral movement is made more complicated, however, by the distorting influence of a non-parallel set of happy/unhappy variables, namely the general psychological 'mood' of the subject. Subjects with high scores on emotional prayer score high only on happy emotionality, which can accelerate or favor this contemplative development. Unhappy emotionality can hinder it, fixing the subject at the level of the emotionally neutral, active prayer forms. Furthermore the ability to support this constant tension between pleasurable and unpleasurable prayer experiences requires a normal 'ego strength'. Subjects with a weak ego strength seem to have great difficulty bearing this tension or even the tension which comes from everyday life. They can not follow the upward, spiral pattern of development, but show merely sporadic 'peak' experiences. An inspection of the scores of these 'weak' subjects on the Scale of Inner Well-Being, pp. 267-269 in the appendix, shows that these subjects tend to have low scores on any kind of emotionality, either happy or unhappy. High scores on unhappy emotionality correlate very well with neuroticism (0.84) and to a limited degree, in comparison, with low ego strength (0.46). Neuroticism also correlates well with low ego strength (0.59). The data in the chart on p. 265 in the appendix suggests that there are two kinds of 'weak' subjects. One kind is basically unhappy and neurotic; the other kind is libidinally weak or impoverished, with low scores on both kinds of emotionality. This somewhat non-emotional 'weak' type correlates with psycho-somatic neuroticism more than with neuroticism. Psycho-somatic neuroticism correlates poorly with unhappy emotionality (0.25) and well with low ego strength (0.59).

What these data suggest is that a certain libidinal strength is needed before a subject can support the mounting tension involved in prayer development. Active, emotionally neutral, meditation is an 'escape' for these 'weak' types.

When the general emotional level of the subject is high, at least as far as happy emotionality is concerned, the subject has a much better chance at becoming a contemplative. The reason for this is possibly because the highly pleasurable mystical experiences presuppose a pre-existing emotional basis within the subject. A subject whose emotional system has not learned to handle intense emotions in everyday life will not be equipped to support the libidinal impact of intense prayer experiences, as single phenomena (peak experiences) or as a mounting spiral of experiences. The relationship with extraversion and stability which the variable 'happy emotionality' shows, correlating at 0.57 and 0.74, respectively, brings Eysenck's concept of the 'strong nervous system' to mind. Eysenck's theories about the strength and weakness of the nervous system will be explored in depth, proceeding from a psycho-physiological study which will be discussed presently.

Cultural variables can complicate this libidinal basis, however, as has already been shown. Some subjects have a high score on happy emotionality but low scores on the emotionally pleasurable mystical experiences. One can say that their general emotional level does not correspond to the emotional level of their prayer life. When this happens, some attitude is inhibiting the usual libidinal development in prayer. Two possible hindrances have already been mentioned; a 'negative set' due to certain intellectual and theological views and an 'active set' due to a 'do-it-yourself' mentality. The first kind of hindrance to the libidinal action of prayer results in the inability to pray described in factor two. As long as this mentality persists the subject will stagnate at this emotionally neutral, passive level. This is the prayer form characteristic of the least advanced group, group five. Not surprisingly, most of the subjects in this group are characterized by a very high degree of education and an experimental group. This is also the most introvert group and the incidence of neuroticism and psycho-somatic neuroticism is high. The group with proportionately the most religious superiors is the middle group. These subjects tend to think they are more advanced in prayer than the group. Out of the seven subjects who thought this, four are superiors.

What is the prayer form characteristic of the 'do-it-yourself' type, so typical of the administrative superior? As the canonical correlation analysis has already shown, such subjects tend to be impeded from reaching full prayer development in contemplation. They get to the half-way station, group three, and tend to stay there. The average age of group three is the highest of all the prayer groups. These active subjects tend to combine prayer forms, sometimes practicing contemplation, sometimes meditating actively.

The average age of the two most advanced groups is not high. The most advanced group, group one, averages about 55. The second most-advanced group, group two, averages about 45. In this group two are a few young subjects who have not been in the cloister for more than about six years. The psychological scores of most of the subjects in both top groups are extremely favorable. They are more stable than 80 to 90% of the population and very extravert. They have a normal 'ego strength', neither exceptionally high nor low. The few exceptions to this picture are unstable, weak subjects whose re-test scores show a considerable drop back down to a lower level. Males are impeded from advancing. This all implies that when the psychological conditions are good and when the right attitude is present, the development of a mystical and contemplative prayer life can happen rather quickly, at least for females.

Did John of the Cross realize the influence of these psychological factors upon prayer? He does observe that 'weak' types can not develop in prayer:

"But those who are weak are kept for a long time in this night, and He purges them very gently and with slight temptations. Habitually, too, He gives them refreshments of sense so that they may not fall away, and only after a long time do they attain to purity of perfection in this life, some of them never attaining to it at all."(Night I,14,5)

The only passage which the author can find where John of the Cross admits the necessity of a strong libidinal basis in the subject is:

"It is not necessary that the will should be so completely purged with respect to the passions, since these very passions help it to feel impassioned love (in prayer)." (Night II,13,3)

Finally, about only 35% of the total number of subjects have progressed beyond the half-way station, i.e. group three. John of the Cross states that not even the half will go on to experience the second dark night and mystical union (Night I,9,9). He does seem to recognize the influence which what he calls 'lukewarmness' and 'weakness' and 'melancholy' can have upon the experience of the first dark night, i.e. factor two. He says that this inability to pray may be merely the result of the abovementioned traits (Night I,9,3). In fact he recognizes that this prayer experience, i.e. factor two, is highly unreliable because he then pays a great deal of attention to instructing spiritual directors in how to discern the real first dark night from this resemblance of it. If one translates 'lukewarmness' with a lack of emotionality, 'weakness' with a low ego strength, and 'melancholy' with unhappy emotionality, the results of the psychological tests verify what he says.

Was John of the Cross aware of the pleasure principle in prayer and the oscillations between pleasurable and unpleasurable experiences? He states:

"Speaking now in a natural way, the soul that desires to consider it will be able to see how on this road ... it has to suffer many ups and downs, and how the prosperity which it enjoys is followed immediately by certain storms and trials; so much so, that it appears to have been given that period of calm in order that it might be forewarned and strengthened against the poverty which has followed; just as after misery and torment there come abundance and calm. It seems to the soul as if, before celebrating that festival, it has first been made to keep that vigil. This is the ordinary course and proceeding of the state of contemplation until the soul arrives at the state of quietness; it never remains in the same state for long together, but is ascending and descending continually." (*Night* II,18,3)

d. The role of prayer in psychological development

Finally, the question arises whether the advanced subjects are so stable as a result of having reached mystical union? To really answer this a long-range study should be made of the subjects in groups three and two, to see if their psychological scores improve as they advance in prayer. The only change which was evident between the first and second administration of the ABV test was, at least as far as a quick survey can discern, an increase in test unreliability. Furthermore the scores of the most advanced subjects improved generally on 'neuroticism' and 'extraversion', but this might be linked to test unreliability. The data at the moment are insufficient to answer the question.

C. Section II: Distractions in prayer

In connection with what has already been discussed about the relationship between neuroticism, psycho-somatic neuroticism, introversion and un-happy emotionality, on one hand, and active rational and visual meditation and distracted, troubled prayer on the other hand, the results of section two can now be adequately interpreted. The cluster analysis had grouped some kinds of distracted behavior together: drowsiness and tenseness. The other kinds of distracted behavior in section two were left out of the cluster. A factor analysis was made, whereby the distinctions between various kinds of distractions became clearer.

1. Discussion of the factor analysis.

The results of this section are not as important as those of the first section and therefore the factor analysis of section two will only briefly be discussed. The factor analysis on p. 271 in the appendix shows that the 'tense' items are separated from the 'drowsy' items and the 'restless' items. The fact that the cluster analysis grouped them together corresponds to their high inter-correlatedness. The same subject can do all these things within one prayer session. What the factor analysis also brought to light was another factor, "Attempted relaxation and concentration". This factor consists of attempts to raise the libidinal level of prayer by concentrating ('stilling the thoughts'), trying to awaken certain feelings and trying to remember God's presence. This is perhaps the most important factor in section two because it describes not the distracted behavior itself, but the attempt to become concentrated once the subject has become aware of the distraction. Only one psychological variable, 'neuroticism' correlated with only one item (stilling the thoughts) in this factor (0.45). In fact this was practically the only noteworthy correlation between 'distraction' items and any psychological variable. This means that distracted behavior is not necessarily related to the psychological type of the subject, but to something which belongs to the complex of prayer itself. The various kinds of distracted behavior correlated as a group with cluster B, unhappy prayer experiences (± 0.50), and not with unhappy emotionality. The four items in the factor "Attempted relaxation and concentration" also correlated well with the cluster of unhappy prayer experiences (0.47, 0.52, 0.29, 0.53). It should be pointed out that in the 'unhappy cluster', the unhappy prayer items constituted about 50% of the cluster and the neutral prayer items the other 50%. Distraction correlates usually with these neutral items, averaging 0.35, see pp. 272-274, appendix. The data show that distractions occur periencing something without being able to express it'). Item 8 correlated emotionally neutral prayer forms, both active and passive, dominate; that is, active rational and visual meditation, and the inability to pray (the first dark night), factors 2,3,6,10.

This means that active meditation on texts, themes and visual imaginings goes together with states of great distraction. Active meditation is not a form of prayer in which the subject is concentrated, but is rather a symptom of the distraction of the subject. The same thing can be said for passive, emotionally neutral prayer experiences, i.e. factor 2, and for factor 10, distracted, troubled prayer. What this indicates is that the subject is only concentrated when he is engaged in some kind of emotionally colored prayer, especially when it is emotionally pleasurable. The activation of the libido is necessary to awaken and maintain concentration in the subject. This is precisely what the factor "Attempted relaxation and concentration" describes. The subject tries to awaken the libido by remembering the point of orientation of the affections (God), he tries to stimulate the emotions for God, he restrains rational activity in favor of the libido, and calls up certain

54

other associations.

Conclusions: The fact has been brought to light that concentration in prayer occurs only when the libido is activated, especially in emotionally pleasurable prayer. When the emotional level is low in prayer distractions occur. For this reason so many distractions occur during active meditation on texts, themes and images. In short, concentration in prayer increases in proportion to the degree of libidinal involvement. This is important for the interpretation of the data from the EEG study which will be presented presently and for the whole discussion in chapter four on concentration in contemplation.

2. *Paraphrases of texts from John of the Cross*

Attempts to paraphrase the difficult and out-dated texts from John of the Cross did not produce the expected results, but did reveal some interesting connections. To paraphrase his descriptions of emotional mystical and contemplative prayer, item 8 was composed ('receiving something, experiencing something without being able to express it'.). Item 8 correlated well, ranging from 0.30 to 0.50, with only three contemplative texts and with only six mystical texts, out of the ± 35 possible in section one. The reason for this might be that the paraphrase excludes any reference to emotionality, but merely describes passivity and ineffability in mystical experience. In another attempt to paraphrase contemplation item 12 was composed ('being made restful during or as a result of prayer'). This item did not correlate at all with any contemplative or mystical text from John of the Cross. Furthermore, also contrary to expectations, the paraphrase of emotional experience in mystical union, item 20 ('being caught up in certain emotions') did not correlate with contemplative and mystical texts, but with descriptions of 'intellectual visions', in positive correlations ranging from 0.38 to 0.51. This confirms what has already been said about the latent emotional content in factor four of section one, i.e. "Intellectual visions".

In regard to active meditation, the results also went against expectations. Item 2 ('thinking about not more than two texts') did not correlate with any description of active meditation by John of the Cross. Rather, his texts describing active meditation correlated with the paraphrase 'making an effort to call up certain feelings about God'. This supports the teaching of John of the Cross, that active rational meditations should function to activate the libido, not to stimulate the intellect.

Conclusion: These findings show how difficult it is to make a good paraphrase of texts from John of the Cross. The element of emotionality needs to be expressed in precise formulations, which also include the elements of passivity and ineffability, to adequately describe contemplation. A good paraphrase presupposes a good understanding of the role of emotionality in prayer.

D. Section three: Ascetical views

Review of the data.
Page 274 in the appendix lists the six ascetical views which correlated with prayer development. These are not the strict views, but the mild views. They describe the act of trusting in God, and the purifying action of God's love, i.e. a passive receptiveness to love. The active will to love God, however, did not correlate with prayer (item 6). Included in those items which did correlate with mystical prayer are items 5 and 13, which describe the via negativa, i.e. praying by 'unknowing' or rejecting rational activity. When these items were correlated in a canonical correlation analysis with the sumscores on pleasurable mystical experience (factor 1) and emotional contemplation (factor 8), the result was a canonical correlation of 0.68. The probability level was 0.20, which is not significant (see p. 275 in the appendix). As the data here show, only three items in section three correlate very well with mystical prayer, namely the items describing the via negativa (5, 13) and the item describing trust in God (item 19). A paraphrase of item 19 in section four (item 6) also correlates well.

Turning to the strict ascetical views, a canonical correlation between them and the sumscores on pleasurable mystical experience and emotional contemplation produced a canonical correlation of only 0.22. The probability level is 0.99, which is in no way significant. This means that strict ascetical views have practically nothing to do with prayer. The very slight positive correlation which was found might be due to the distorting influence of conformity. As the chart on p. 275 in the appendix shows, conformity is closely related to strict ascetical views.

The psychological variables correlate only moderately and with only a few of the mild items. Only neuroticism and unhappy emotions correlate negatively with a few mild items. The cultural variables show more correlation. The cultural group characterized by independence, experimental group and higher education exhibits here the same non-differentiating response patterns as in section one, prayer experiences. This group rejects both the strict and the mild ascetical views.

At this point it is possible to show the relative importance of the mild ascetical views in comparison with the other variables which play a role in prayer development. In a canonical correlation analysis already briefly mentioned in the discussion of the psychological variables and the first section of the Questionnaire on Spirituality, a highly significant result was found. The mild ascetical items included in this canonical correlation analysis were two items (5, 13) which describe the via negativa and two items which describe the purifying action of God's love (19, and item 6, section four). These two 'love' items were closely correlated (0.80) and in fact express the same thought. The complete results of this analysis are on p. 276 in the appendix.

In an attempt to see if a clearer view could be obtained about the actual process of purification involved in mystical development, the same canonical correlation analysis was carried out, but the second 'love' item was dropped. It was replaced by item 4 in section four: "The process of purification consists mainly in getting rid of all excessive self-love." The results showed that this item correlated negativety with prayer development. That is, the most advanced subjects did not agree with this statement, while subjects who were not at all advanced in prayer did agree with it. The results were even more significant than the preceding analysis. The canonical correlation was 0.77 and the probability level was 0.0011 (see p. 277 in the appendix).

This merely confirms what the results of section three had already shown. The kind of purification involved is not a negative action, either getting rid of desires for anything except God or getting rid of self-love. Rather, what is involved is a positive and open attitude toward the 'in-truding' and purifying agent, God's love. This goes hand-in-hand with the practice of the via negativa. As the correlations of the individual mild items with the canonical variate of the criteria on p. 276 in the appendix show, the two items describing the via negativa actually correlate better than the two 'love' items. This means that the via negativa is even more important to prayer development than the theological virtues. The way John of the Cross inter-weaves the theological virtues and the via negativa will be explained in chapters three and four.

The variable 'altruism' correlates only with the mild views. The variable 'age' correlates only with a few of the mild views and with none of the strict views. Thus, the older nuns tend to favor the mild approach and not the conformistic, strict ascetical view. The variable 'female' correlates at 0.54 with item 19 (a 'love' item) and at 0.40 and 0.35 with items 5 and 13, which describe the via negativa. This will be touched upon later, in the discussion of the variable 'female' in the fourth chapter.

What did not correlate with prayer development were the items: 'Direct the will with love to God', and 'The soul can not purify itself in an active manner so that it might be even minimally suited for the divine union in the perfection of love'. These two statements contradict each other. One instructs man to direct his love to God with the force of his will power. The other states that man can not prepare himself for the union of love at all. The fact that neither statement correlated with prayer development suggests that neither the active not the purely passive attitude is correct. In chapter four a theological reflection will be given upon an intermediate way, the way of faith, which is to be called the active side of the passive purification. What is also important is that although the theological virtues do correlate with prayer, they do not function in the way John of the Cross taught. The item 'Faith empties the understanding of all its natural intelligence; hope makes the memory detach itself from the possession of the recollections of creatures; love purifies the will of its desires and affections for all that is not God' does not correlate with prayer development at all. This corresponds to his ascetical view that natural human desires impede God's action in prayer. As such, this item is closely related to the strict ascetical views.

Conclusion: The hypothesis of this study has been confirmed by these data. Strict ascetical views have nothing to do with prayer development, but are related only to conformity to a cloister ideal. The theological virtues and the via negativa, on the other hand, do indeed correlate with mystical prayer, but not in the way John of the Cross intended. The further theological reflection on these data will be given in chapters three and four.

E. Section four: Attitudes to John of the Cross

This section consisted of three classes of items: paraphrases of the ascetical views of John of the Cross plus a few other ascetical views, attitudes for or against John of the Cross, and attitudes about the 'spiritual marriage'.

1. *Paraphrases.*
In this section items 2,3,4,6 were intended to paraphrase both the strict ascetical views as well as the mild views of John the Cross. This succeeded fairly well, with correlations with the original texts ranging from 0.4 to 0.8. The strict views correlated just as highly with conformity as did their counterparts in section three. This means that the content of the item is nearly the same. It also means that the subject pays attention to the content, not the way it is stated nor to whether the view carries the explicit authority of John of the Cross or not. The subjects were able to distinguish between these views and the ascetical views which did not belong to his teaching, especially 'Purification consists mainly of acting justly and doing ones duty.' This item correlated rather poorly with conformity (0.25). Of the eleven subjects who indicated complete agreement with this ascetical view, six were religious superiors, out of the 14 superiors in this study. Altoge-

ther, of these 14 subjects, 10 indicated either complete agreement or nearly complete agreement by circling a '5' or a '4'. None of the advanced contemplatives agreed with this view. This supports what was already said in section one about the tendency of religious superiors to give an 'active set' of answers. This ascetical view correlated only with active rational prayer.

These first items all concerned the ascetical opinions of the subjects. Concerning actual ascetical practice, one might have expected different results. For this reason item 34 was composed: 'I have actually been able to put the counsels of John of the Cross about asceticism into practice, and I do so, day in and day out.' Only 15 of the 54 subjects indicated nearly complete or complete agreement. This item correlates well (0.50) with the cluster of ascetical views in section three and also with conformity (0.38). It did not correlate well with prayer development in factors 1 and 8 (0.20). Thus both ascetical views and ascetical practice correlate with conformity and not with prayer.

2. Bride's mysticism.

To test the subject's views on the spiritual marriage, or bride's mysticism, item 11 was composed: 'The theme of the spiritual marriage which occurs so often in the works of John of the Cross appeals to me personally." This item did not correlate with conformity at all, but did correlate negatively with 'experimental group' (−0.41), which belongs to the non-differentiating response pattern of that cultural group. This item correlated, not with prayer, but with strict ascetical views. This association with strict asceticism has nothing to do with a conformistic attitude, but seems inherently bound to a compensation mechanism. The more the subject strictly rejects all desires for pleasure, the more he or she will seek a compensation in 'bride's mysticism'. This has nothing to do with whether one really attains the spiritual marriage or not, since the correlation with the cluster of happy mystical experiences is low (0.26). When one inspects the relationship between this item and the sort of prayer experiences with which it does correlate separately, one finds a correlation averaging about 0.35 with only seven items describing pleasurable mystical experience, out of the ± 32 possible. Furthermore, this item does not correlate with the theological virtues nor with the via negativa items in section three. On the other hand this item correlated very well with the strict ascetical views (0.49).

This all suggests that the theme of bride's mysticism as it functions among this group of cloistered nuns is a compensation for the usual libidinal outlets in human sexual relationships. It did not correlate with any of the psychological variables, not even hysteria. This is very important to note, since it implies that attraction to this theme is not a psychological

59

motive but a motive inherent in the cloister life itself, i.e. the celibate life. The most advanced subjects were interviewed upon this subject. They all stated that the theme of the spiritual marriage was very important to them at the beginning of their prayer life. It stimulated their emotional orientation to Jesus, who was the main object of their prayer life then. As their prayer life has developed the object of affection has changed to the Holy Spirit. At the same time, their attraction to bride's mysticism decreased.

It should be mentioned here that this interest in the Holy Spirit coincides with an active support of the Catholic Pentecostal movement in Holland. The only subjects who are actively involved in pentecostalism are among the two most advanced groups. This recent interest in the Holy Spirit, within the last three years, has changed the libidinal orientation of their prayer life, and correspondingly their attitude toward the spiritual marriage. No conclusions about the role of this theme can be drawn for the spirituality of non-celibate laymen and laywomen, however, because the data are insufficient. More will be said about this matter in chapter four.

3. *Attitudes toward John of the Cross.*

It should be mentioned first of all that the layman, unacquainted with the 'hero worship' of John of the Cross in the Discalced Carmelite Order, at least in the past, approaches his teachings differently from a Discalced Carmelite nun or friar. One finds three attitudes among the subjects toward John of the Cross: complete rejection, conformistic acceptance of some things, rejection of passivity. The usual negative, non-differentiated set of answers which the 'generation of the 60's' showed in the other sections of the questionnaire is evident here, too. The variables 'experimental group' and 'independence' follow almost the same pattern of response — a rejection of his views on prayer (-0.38), the inability to find support in his mystical teachings (-0.32), the inability to put his ascetical teaching into practice (-0.41), and the tendency not to have ever read his works (-0.32). Thus, some subjects in this 'negative set' reject all of the teaching of John of the Cross without having ever read him! This negative answering pattern is a sign of a rejection of the 'hero worship' of John of the Cross, within the order.

The acceptance of John of the Cross has some relationship with conformity, although this is not a strong bond. Conformism correlates with only some items. Conformistic subjects tend to state that they read often in his works (0.36), that they can put his ascetical views into practice (0.38), and that he is their favorite spiritual writer (0.30). His prayer teachings do not correlate with conformity. The ability to find support in his teachings on prayer correlates poorly with conformism (0.20). Instead, it correlates well (around 0.45) with most of the items describing mystical and contemplative prayer experiences in section one. Thus subjects who report having found support in his teachings on prayer are not conformistic, but are themselves experienced in prayer.

Finally, a third answering pattern can be discerned. At first glance it might seem that what is involved is a rejection of the highly emotional tone or color of the sort of prayer experiences John of the Cross describes. Three items dealt with this issue:

Item 8: "I disagree with the theories on prayer of John of the Cross."

Item 9: "I have never had much profit from the prayer descriptions of John of the Cross because I prefer a more sober spirituality."

Item 17: "My own prayer experiences are much more sober than those of John of the Cross."

Contrary to expectations, however, these three items did not correlate with the emotional prayer experiences in section one. Rather they correlated negatively with passive prayer experiences, in which the emotional color was very subdued. Thus item 8 (above) correlates negatively with the following descriptions of passive prayer in section one:

"One understands without effort; rather one receives that which is given." (−0.56)

"The soul becomes recollected without knowing how or without doing anything of its own." (−0.41)

Item 9 (above) correlates this way with items in section one:

"The communications from God occur intimately and hiddenly in the soul; they make the active play of the inner and outer senses stop, grow still." (−0.38)

"During this spiritual slumber the soul possesses and enjoys a calmness, a relaxation and rest." (−0.35)

Finally item 17 (above) correlated positively with only one prayer type, (0.35) active rational prayer. It correlated negatively, not with the highly emotional experiences, happy and unhappy, in section one, but with the passive items already listed above, in correlations averaging around −0.35. This indicates that a certain group of subjects ostensibly say they do not like the emotional style of John of the Cross, but in fact do not like his emphasis upon passivity or receptivity. This corresponds to the 'active set' of the religious superiors, who in general insist upon a 'sober' spirituality.

Only one other variable correlated with this rejection of the highly emotional or libidinal style of John of the Cross. The variable 'hysteria' correlated with item 9 (0.28). That is, subjects with high scores on hysteria will tend to state that they prefer a spirituality which is more sober than that of John of the Cross.

61

Conclusion: First of all, the attempts to paraphrase the ascetical views of John of the Cross succeeded much better than the attempts in section two to paraphrase his descriptions of prayer. The attempts to put his highly emotional descriptions of prayer experiences into more sober, modern language were motivated by the awareness that some people reject John of the Cross because of his emphasis upon emotionality. The data from section four, however, suggest that the real 'stumbling block' for some people is not the emotionality of mystical experiences he describes, but the element of receptivity or passivity. The objection to emotional prayer experience is a sham objection.

Similarly, the enthusiasm of some subjects for the theme of the spiritual marriage ostensively indicates an enthusiasm for the prayer of union. In actual fact, however, it has nothing to do with prayer. Rather, it is a compensation for the strict affective asceticism of the subject. The theme of bride's mysticism in a group of celibate nuns might function differently from the same theme in a group of laymen or laywomen. For this reason no conclusions can be drawn until research had been done on this topic among non-celibates.

Acceptance of the teachings of John of the Cross can be a result of a certain conformistic attitude among the subjects. However, those subjects who state that they have found support in his descriptions of prayer are not doing this because they are conformistic, but because they actually have experience in mystical and contemplative prayer. Rejection of John of the Cross seems to be tied in with a general negative attitude of the 'generation of the 60's' mentality. Such a mentality rejects both the ascetical and the mystical teaching of John of the Cross, although the actual content of this teaching may be unknown to the subject, who in some cases has never even read his works. When a subject with this negative set rejects bride's mysticism, this rejection is likewise not necessarily based upon a consideration of the theme itself, but is merely a non-differentiating negative response.

III. DISCUSSION OF THE RESULTS:
THE CO—DETERMINANTS TO CONCENTRATION IN PRAYER

The model which has been established for describing prayer development is an accelerating movement which zig-zags increasingly. The dynamism involved is an erotic or libidinal energy which alternates between two poles, happy and unhappy emotional experiences. In between these two poles is a neutral area which includes both passive and active prayer forms which are emotionally subdued. The beginner starts with active, emotionally neutral prayer and goes on to passive, emotionally neutral or restful contemplation, which increases as emotionality increases. Gradually the pendulum swing between the two emotional poles starts a certain libidinal movement in prayer. This gains in momentum in an accelerating alternation between the two poles. The libidinal energy becomes increasingly intense. Finally the breaking point is reached and the unhappy 'pole' decreases in importance, while the happy 'pole' gains. The final state is a fixation at the happy pole, within a context of great rest.

The results show that some psychological, cultural and religious factors can influence the rate of this libidinal build up of energy; some factors accelerating it, others slowing it down or even bringing it to a standstill. The inter-relatedness of these three sets of variables is somewhat complicated. The psychological variables are not related to the cultural variables. Rather, both are inter-connected via a bridge, which are the religious variables. The exception to this is 'social desirability', which correlates with the psychological and the cultural variables (independence, −0.40). Due to reasons which will be explained extensively in chapter four, the 'sex' variable will be classified here as a cultural variable, since what is involved is the way western culture has influenced the way men experience God differently than women do. The cultural variables will be classified under one lable 'social dependency'. This means that the two cultural groups which reject contemplation are both characterized by 'social independency'. The negative mentality of the 60's emphasizes the rejection of the 'ties that bind' to a tradition and a group, and to an idea of God. It favors self-determination and independence, and the rejection of what is socially desirable and conformistic.

The other cultural group, the 'active set', typical of persons in an administrative position, is characterized by a do-it-yourself mentality. The variable 'administrative position' also correlates positively with independence and negatively with conformity, sensitivity to what is socially desirable, and the theological virtues. These religious superiors are independent, both in their attitude as well as in their actual freedom of independent action. The group is dependent upon them. Perhaps the reason why these correlations were not even higher than they were is because the group currently tends to elect non-leaders to such positions. These weak leaders are relatively more dependent on the group and more sensitive to what the group considers socially desirable than the strong leaders among the religious superiors. (The consequences for cloister politics will be touched upon again briefly in the conclusion.) What has been said here about the 'do-it-yourself' mentality applies to the strong administrative figure, not the weak leader. In general, neither the strong nor the weak religious superior has an advanced prayer development.

Both the socially independent groups show a tendency toward what could be called 'religious independence'. Religious dependency means a reliance upon the three theological virtues. As the data from section three show, the virtue of love means, in this context, not the active determination to love God, but rather the receptivity to God's love. That is, love functions in a receptive manner in a relationship of inter-dependency between man and God. Religious dependency also means receptivity to other kinds of gifts than just favors in prayer. It includes the ability to accept 'gifts' from within a tradition and a group organization, a common practice, an identity dependent upon the group.

The psychological variables function in two ways: they influence the openness to 'gifts', and they determine the rate of libidinal build-up in prayer as well as the kind of libidinal involvement (happy vs. unhappy). Neuroticism hinders religious dependency, especially the development of an inter-dependent love relationship with God. Likewise it hinders the intensification of emotionality in prayer by fixing the subject at the level of emotionally neutral prayer. This goes together with introversion and unhappy emotionality. All three tend to hinder any libidinal momentum in prayer. Especially unhappy emotionality blocks this development. On the other hand, happy emotionality stimulates or makes possible the development of both kinds of emotionality, happy and unhappy, in prayer. Thus the set of happy/unhappy psychological variables does not run parallel to the happy/unhappy set of prayer variables. The most advanced subjects are not the most emotional subjects, but only the most happy subjects. Subjects who are libidinally weak, i.e. with low scores on both happy/unhappy emotionality and low scores on ego-strength, can not support this build up of libidinal or emotional energy. When the emotional tension becomes too great, either in prayer or in daily life, or both at the same time, they slide back to the emotionally neutral prayer forms. Thus a normal ego strength and high scores on happy emotionality are the two main factors which favor the development of a contemplative prayer life.

Summing this up, one can say that concentration in prayer depends on the degree of libidinal involvement rather than on the degree of intellectual alertness. The tension involved in this highly-charged libidinal prayer form requires a strong psychological structure in the subject, capable of supporting the intensity of the emotionality and the tension generated from the rapid alternation between happy and unhappy states. When the psychological, or perhaps psycho-physiological, structure is weak, this network of prayer experiences will collapse again and again. In such a case, no development is possible. Furthermore the momentum can not build up if the dependency upon the final point of orientation is not well-established. The dynamic movement in prayer is the result of the ever-shortening distance between the contemplative and the goal, Christ. The forward or upward movement in prayer is caused by the attraction or pull of the object of union, Christ. This will be further worked out in chapter four. The model of prayer development can be illustrated with the movement of a pendulum. The pendulum swings harder and harder, alternating between increasingly intense emotional (happy and unhappy) experiences. Understandably this puts great demands upon the mechanism of the clock. After a certain 'break point', the intensity does not increase, but the speed of alternation does. It is as if the pendulum were being shortened, causing the pendulum to swing more and more quickly. Finally the pendulum stops, not in the middle, but on the 'happy pole'.

Perhaps the inter-relations between the co-determinants in prayer can be illustrated in this diagram:

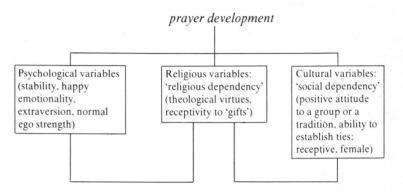

prayer development

| Psychological variables (stability, happy emotionality, extraversion, normal ego strength) | Religious variables: 'religious dependency' (theological virtues, receptivity to 'gifts') | Cultural variables: 'social dependency' (positive attitude to a group or a tradition, ability to establish ties; receptive, female) |

In the future, research should be carried out to see if these same co-determinants function in the prayer development of the laity. Furthermore, the number of male subjects should be brought into better proportion with the number of female subjects, the psychological tests should include a test of concentration, and longitudinal studies should be carried out to see if prayer development coincides with an improvement in the psychological profile of the subject. Especially the cultural variables should be well-established, since the content of these social values could vary from a cloister population to a lay population. The questionnaire should be revised as a scale of intensity of emotional experience, with three dimensions: happy, unhappy and neutral, plus a scale of frequency of occurrence. The neutral experiences should be better represented than was done here. Perhaps the appropriate model would have to be invented. Neither the Guttman scale nor the Coombs scale is appropriate for establishing prayer development over a period of time, because there are two levels being measured, intensity and frequency, with various dimensions, i.e. prayer is too complicated for a simple scale model. A factor analysis is also inadequate because it does not show the sequence of experiences.

In the preface to this study two types of presuppositions or stereotypes in regard to mystics and mysticism were briefly sketched: the theological and the psychological stereotypes. Furthermore, several predictions were made in regard to the hypothesis. The results of the empirical study will be reviewed here to test the correctness of these stereotypes and expectations.

A. Theological stereotypes

Is there such a thing as 'introvert' mysticism?
This question will be extensively answered in chapter four, where the inherently extraverted attitude of any unitive mysticism is shown. It suffices here merely to point out that extraverts, not introverts, are basically better equipped through their out-going attitude to attain mystical union. Even the phase of concentration and recollection are basically 'extraverted' activities, as the following EEG study will attempt to show through Eysenck's theories on extraversion and introversion.

Is mysticism opposed to the attitude of faith?
No. On the contrary, those items describing the attitude of faith or trust in God were among the variables which correlated the most highly with mystical advancement.

Is mysticism opposed to politics?
Not inherently. What restricts the subjects' political activity in society is not mysticism but the cloister. Concerning cloister politics, however, the role of mystics is indirect but nevertheless quite powerful. Not any of the advanced subjects here had ever been elected to any administrative office, with only two exceptions. Even these two, however, were never re-elected. Considering that elections take place every three years, this means that the group consistently and repeatedly refrains from electing mystics to office. Being excluded from elected office is not the same thing as being excluded from politics, however. The current situation in cloisters today favors the influence of mystics in politics.

The current religious superiors in the various cloisters involved in this study generally score very low on leadership ability. They are non-decisive types whom the group, which is splintered by opposing factions, has elected because no single faction could gain the majority. These are compromise figures. These non-leaders do have to make decisions, nevertheless. In many of these cloisters, the nominal leader has a right-hand man or woman to turn to in making decisions. The non-leader seeks certainty from another. In most cases, as the interviews have revealed, the superior had chosen a trusted person who has a high score on leadership. Such a strong leader would never have been able to gain the majority in an election under the current circumstances. In several cloisters, this power behind the throne was one of the advanced mystics.

Such a strong figure can only maintain such an influential position if two conditions are met: the trusted man or woman can never seek personal recognition at the cost of the nominal leader, and the actual power of such a person must remain hidden or disguised from the group, so as not to lose the confidence of the group. This requires a high degree of altruism from the trusted person. Why does the non-decisive leader turn to the mystic? The fact that altruism correlated well with contemplative experience and with the theological virtues suggests that this power behind the throne, this mystic, is more altruistic than the others in the group. Perhaps because this mystic's altruistic attitude helps him or her to maintain a broad perspective of the basic aims of the group, thereby surpassing factional differences, the mystic is able to offer the nominal leader a cadre within which he or she can make decisions. This all suggests that, in politics in general, the reason why mystics have been considered as being a-political might be because such figures have to remain hidden in order to maintain their powerful political position. The seemingly a-political pose is a front to cover up their real involvement.

Is the mystical experience purely an emotional = irrational one?
No. The degree of intellectual enlightenment increases in proportion to the increase in emotional experiences. This is seen in the proportional gain in importance of factor four (intellectual visions, or thinking contemplation) along with the gain in the emotional mystical and contemplative factors.

B. The psychological stereotypes

Is the mystic pathological?
Of the unfavorable psychological traits tested for here, none correlated positively with mystical experience. On the contrary unstable subjects tend to be unable to sustain the tension of mystical development. Advanced mystics are more stable than 80 to 90% of the Dutch population, generally speaking.

Is the mystic an introvert?
Extraversion correlates positively with mystical development, not in-

troversion. Of the 22 subjects who classify as advanced mystics, 40% are extremely extravert and only about 20% are extreme introverts. Of those who practice active rational meditation instead of contemplation, 40% are introverts and only 10% are extraverts. Thus introverts have far less chance of becoming contemplatives.

Is the mystic a hysteric?
Contrary to Hood's findings[8], hysteria did not correlate with mystical or contemplative prayer experience. Furthermore, some caution should be taken in regard to this variable since the physical manifestations of conversion neurosis included in the scale on hysteria in the MMPI can coincide with actual illness (see note p. 268, appendix).

Is the mystic unstable?
Stability, not neuroticism, correlates positively with mystical development. Unstable subjects can have erratic mystical experiences, but it is very rare when they manage to develop beyond a few scattered peak experiences.

Is the mystic characterized by a low 'ego-strength'?
The advanced mystics in this study have normal scores on ego-strength. Subjects with low scores on ego-strength have great difficulty in maintaining a high developmental level of contemplation. They usually manage to have only scattered peak experiences, and then fall back to active, rational meditation.

Is the mystic egotistical?
The variable 'altruism' correlates positively only with contemplative experience and with the theological virtues. Furthermore, contemplation correlates positively with sensitivity to what is socially desirable.

Is the mystic highly emotional?
The answer is yes and no. There are two variables involved, happy and unhappy emotionality. The advanced mystics tend to be highly emotional in the happy sense and very unemotional in the unhappy sense, i.e. regarding anxiety. The fact that happy emotionality correlated negatively with neuroticism (-0.74) should remove the pejorative connotation which being highly emotional has. The subject who is highly emotional as far as unhappy emotions go, or anxiety, is very rarely an advanced mystic. A great deal more will be said about this in the following EEG study. The ability to support the strain of intense mystical experience seems to presuppose, among other things, a strong nervous system capable of intense happy emotionality. Subjects who are low on ego-strength and who might

68

be classified as subjects with a weak nervous system tend to be rather unemotional in both directions, happy and unhappy. Precisely because their libidinal level is too low, they can not attain to lasting mystical union.

C. Is the hypothesis confirmed?

Yes. Strict affective asceticism relates in no way to prayer development. The co-determinants to development in prayer are psychological, religious and social variables. The traditional rejection of bodily sensuality in favor of 'spirit' is irrelevant to mystical development. The implications for the rennovation of the spiritual tradition of the Discalced Carmelite Order are great. There is no inherent relationship between the strict cloistered life, based upon the cultivation of the 'spirit' at cost to the body, and prayer. Theoretically therefore the contemplative tradition of the Discalced Carmelite Order could just as well be taught to the laity, stripped of the teaching of the 'super technique' of strict affective asceticism. The data clearly show that the core of the Carmelite tradition which is authentic is the emphasis upon the 'via negativa' and the theological virtues. So far the data have merely shown what the 'via negativa' is not. The following psycho-physiological study aims at uncovering more about the actual psychological and even psycho-physiological mechanism behind the 'via negativa'.

V. THE PSYCHO-PHYSIOLOGICAL STUDY
OF CONCENTRATION IN PRAYER

Introduction

As the discussion of the results of the psychological study in the preceding sections has already shown, concentration in prayer is a result of the degree of libidinal involvement. The libido is activated in contemplative prayer. Distractions occur when this libidinal level is low. The distracted subject tries to combat distractions by calling up associations through active meditations on themes or texts, which awaken the emotions. When this does not succeed, a combination of seemingly contradictory behavior patterns occurs: drowsiness, tenseness, restlessness, irritation, sleepiness. The question arises, why can some subjects become libidinally involved in prayer with more ease and more rapidly than other subjects? What do the psychological variables 'happy emotionality', 'extraversion', 'ego strength' and 'stability' have in common? How can they influence this build-up of libidinal concentration in contemplation? This psycho-physiological study aims at throwing some light on these matters by applying Eysenck's theories on the 'strong nervous system' to concentration in contemplation. Before stating the hypothesis of this study, some background information must be given about Eysenck's theories and about other physiological studies of (oriental) contemplation. After this has been done, an EEG experiment will be presented which the author and the EEG department of the University of Nijmegen conducted[9], in which concentration in contemplation is brought into relationship with Eysenck's theories. As far as the author knows, this is the first attempt anyone has made to connect the two. The results of this study will form the basis of the phenomenological analysis of concentration in prayer, in chapter four.

Since this study is in many ways a modern testing of the insights and intuitions of H. Fortmann's dissertation on concentration in prayer (1945)[10], his ideas will be brought into the discussion of the results of this psycho-physiological study, as a preliminary to the more extensive discussion of his ideas in chapter four. Especially his views on the role of the body in prayer are relevant here. The body is the starting point for the study of concentration in general, and for the study of concentration in prayer in particular.

A. Eysenck's theories on the 'strong nervous system'

Although much criticism has been given of Eysenck's theories, they still manage to inspire research because they suggest a way to explore the neurological basis of personality. Eysenck's theories are relevant here because the data already presented show that the libidinal basis of concentration in prayer might be a 'strong nervous system' and also because the EEG data and response characteristics which Eysenck predicts one will find for the strong nervous system correspond to the data gathered from (oriental) meditation.

Eysenck's theories involve two variables, extraversion and stability. The strong nervous sytem is based upon these two traits. Although Eysenck builds upon Jung's personality theories, his views on extraversion/introversion differ on one main point. Jung defined an extravert as someone whose libido is attracted positively toward the environment. An introvert is someone whose libido in negatively related to the environment, and positively attracted to his inner, subjective world[11]. Thus, extraversion/introversion are concepts inherently linked with the libido, i.e. with happy or unhappy emotionality. Eysenck, however, separates the libido from extraversion/introversion by postulating two circuits: the cortico-reticular circuit which determines extraversion/introversion, and the limbic circuit, which determines the libidinal activity. Although he suggests that the two circuits are linked, he does not work out either the way they are linked or the degree to which they are connected. The data from this study suggest that Eysenck is right. Extraversion correlated at 0.57 with happy emotionality and at −0.46 with unhappy emotionality. Thus, there is some connection. However, another variable, 'neuroticism', correlated much better with emotionality. Neuroticism correlated at −0.74 with happy emotionality and at 0.84 with unhappy emotionality. There are thus two dimensions or circuits involved here, which inter-act. The variable 'ego-strength' might possibly be the measure of the strength of the nervous system, because it correlates well here with both circuits. Ego strength correlates at 0.50 with happy emotionality and −0.46 with unhappy emotionality. On the other hand, it correlates at −0.59 with neuroticism. The strong 'ego' is based upon both extraversion and stability.

What is the nature of these two circuits? The background of Eysenck's theories is formed by, among others, Pavlov's concept of cortical inhibition. The Russion school of neurophysiology based upon Pavlov has developed a whole system of distinctions between different kinds of neurological inhibition, only one of which is being considered here[12]. Eysenck's theory of cortical inhibition begins with Pavlov's theory that a strong nervous system possesses a state of equilibrium in dynamism. That means that it maintains a balance which prevents it from over-reacting to stimuli. A weak nervous system lacks this steady control and is too-easily and too-readily stimulated.

In his book, *The Biological Basis of Personality* (1967)[13], Eysenck presents what he calls a 'weak theory' to explain the underlying neurological basis of these two pivotal dimensions or circuits, extraversion/introversion and stability/instability. To account for extraversion/introversion he sketches a cortico-reticular loop. Neural messages are relayed along ascending pathways to the cortex and also are sent to the reticular formation, which in turn sends 'arousal' messages to the cortex. Depending on the sort of message, the cortex instructs the reticular formation to keep on sending arousal messages or to switch to 'inhibition', i.e. the blocking off of such messages. Both arousal and inhibition must be considered as active processes. When 'inhibition' messages predominate the nervous system is guarded against over-reacting to stimuli. This corresponds to the orientation of the extravert. When arousal messages predominate, the system is sensitized or aroused to the environment. In this case, this corresponds to the introvert orientation. The paradox in this theory is that an introvert tends to be negatively oriented toward his surroundings precisely because he is overly sensitive to it. That is, his threshold of reaction to stimuli is low. He is too easily and too rapidly aroused to stimuli, and therefore he withdraws.

To explain the basis of stability/instability (neuroticism), Eysenck proposes another loop involving the visceral brain and the reticular formation. The 'visceral brain' includes the hippocampus, amygdala, cingulum, septum, and hypothalamus. It could be called the seat of the emotions. The theory of Eysenck postulates that a 'weak nervous system' will react emotionally to even mild stimuli. Stability becomes equated with unemotionality, or equanimity. The stable nervous system reacts slowly and only moderately to emotional stimuli. The strong nervous system, in Eysenck's view, can withstand all emotionally activating stimuli. Hyperexcitability is characteristic, therefore, of the weak nervous system, i.e. of the neurotic.

At this point, criticism begins to enter the picture. As J. F. Orlebeke[14] has pointed out. Eysenck bases his proof of this view of neuroticism upon several experiments which worked with scales of anxiety, not neuroticism as such. Such experiments show that stable subjects have low scores on anxiety, or unhappy emotionality. But since such scales work with only one variable, the other aspect of emotionality, i.e. happy emotionality, is left out. Eysenck then concludes prematurely that stable subjects are therefore not easily aroused emotionally. The data from this study show that only one kind of emotionality, i.e. unhappy emotionality, correlates with neuroticism positively (0.84). Happy emotionality, which is not the same thing as equanimity but rather also involves excitability, correlates negatively with neuroticism (−0.74). Thus Eysenck's theory is wrong here. Instability is not identical with the degree of emotionality, but rather with the kind of emotionality. On the contrary, subjects in this study with low scores on both kinds of emotionality tend to have low scores on ego-strength, and high scores on psycho-somatic neuroticism. Thus the strong nervous system is characterized by high thresholds to stimuli in the cortico-reticular loop (extraversion) and low thresholds to happy emotional stimuli (and high thresholds to unhappy emotional stimuli, i.e. anxiety) in the limbic circuit. Stability is the absence of anxiety, not the absence of emotions. In this case, Jung's distinction between positive and negative libidinal attraction is more useful than Eysenck's distinction between strong and weak libidinal excitation. The problem in Eysenck's theories is his attempt to introduce the concepts of arousal and activation into the two loops. The whole discussion would be simplified if he were to set these two concepts temporarily aside and would work with types of neurological function rather than with levels of functioning. Now that his theories on emotionality have been explored, his theories on extraversion need some further explanation.

Eysenck's theories on extraversion/introversion have met with more success than his theories on emotionality. His publications are extensive collections of experiments conducted by himself and others to test his theories. These are reviewed here briefly in regard to stimulus thresholds of extraverts and introverts[15]. In a test for pain tolerance with heat stimulation, eight of the ten extraverts withstood the radiation for twenty seconds; none of the introverts did. Extraversion correlated with pain tolerance at 0.69. In another experiment, four drops of lemon juice were placed on the tongues of extraverts and introverts for twenty seconds. Extraverts showed almost no increase in salivation. Introversion correlated with salivation increase at 0.71 on 100 subjects. In a test of reaction to auditory stimuli, introverts had significant lower thresholds to noise than extraverts. In research on conditioning which measured the rate of eyeblink as a reaction to puffs of air, introversion correlated at 0.40 on 144 subjects with conditioning. After thirty trials, extraverts still showed no conditioning, while 46% of the introverts did. These and many other such experiments on thresholds to stimuli show generally positive results. They indicate that extraverts will not react as readily to stimuli as will introverts, and they will condition more slowly. A more thorough, critical review of such experiments is found in J. Orlebeke[16].

The same problem arises here, too; the concept of levels of functioning. According to his theories, extraverts are not as aroused as introverts. Introverts react faster because they are more aroused, i.e. more alert. Orlebeke's study on the GSR of extraverts, however, leads him to conclude that introverts have a low arousability in comparison with extraverts at the initiation of a task. On the other hand, stimulation leads to faster inhibition of the arousal in extraverts, which occurs to a lesser degree in introverts[17], at least if the stimulus is monotonous. Orlebeke notices that anxiety (neuroticism) disrupts or interferes with the function of the cortico-reticular loop. Unstable introverts then become over-aroused. The problems with Eysenck's theories which have been mentioned here reoccur when he formulates predictions about the relationship between EEG data and extraversion.

Eysenck derive two minor premises from his main premise that extraversion is caused by inhibition. He deduces that 1) inhibition can be measured by testing the speed and degree of reaction to stimuli, and 2) inhibition is equal to low arousal, which should be evident in abundant slow (alpha) waves in the EEG. Introverts, on the other hand, should have fast (beta) waves, because they are more aroused. Eysenck's views had to be revised when an experiment by R. Savage[18] indicated that clear results are obtained only when the variable 'neuroticism' is included. Stable extraverts produce abundant alpha waves; unstable introverts produce predominantly fast beta waves. Eysenck then concluded that unstable extraverts would have predominantly very slow theta and delta waves, corresponding to his theory of extraversion and low arousal[19].

In a number of experiments designed to test these theories about extraversion, stability and EEG data, much less success was achieved than in the experiments designed to test his first minor premise about thresholds to stimuli. A. Gale presents a review[20] of many of these experiments. The findings are rather contradictory. Some experiments find abundant alpha in introverts and not in extraverts, while others find the opposite. Gale concludes that under experimental conditions in which the subjects are moderately aroused, the extraverts will produce abundant alpha, but he leaves the influence of neuroticism unnoticed. Gale points out that such experiments contain many possible sources of error:

"We have now come to the end of this serial comedy of errors. We have witnessed a strange phenomenon: a dozen or more studies which apparently were designed to ask the same question yet which yielded very different answers. The question, 'Is there a relationship between extraversion and the EEG?'appears to be quite simple and straightforward. However, a little 'unpacking' of the question reveals a horde of difficulties. The problem areas are: selection of subjects, choice and use of inventory, techniques of EEG measurement, implicit set within the subject, bias within the experiment, experimental instruction, experimental paradigm, statistical tests, and finally, the rationale for the whole procedure."[21]

In Gale's own experimenting in this area, the factor of neuroticism accounted for the unexpected results in the subjects. In an experiment which bears directly upon meditation, Gale et al.[22] investigated the relationship between personality types, imagery capacity and alpha waves. The theory of Eysenck, and also of Jung, had supposed that the introvert would have a richer inner world of experience and of imagery than extraverts. Research in this area, however, had shown that extraverts can report richer imagery than introverts. Eysenck adjusted his theory by adding the idea that the extravert is stimulus-hungry, unlike the introvert who withdraws from stimuli. The extravert seeks inner stimulation by imagining things. The introvert, who already is overstimulated would reject inner stimulation and imagery. Gale suggests that neuroticism modifies this theory. Neurotic introverts have a high imaging ability, he finds. He concludes that neuroticism must somehow impair the introvert's usual inhibition on imagery. High anxiety states go hand-in-hand with inner imaginations, fantasies. Gale's findings are confirmed by this study, which produced data showing that introversion, neuroticism, unhappy emotionality (anxiety) and psycho-somatic neuroticism all form a complex which correlates well with active visual and rational prayer, and with inner distraction due to inner conflict[23]. Furthermore, the item describing the attempt to 'still the thoughts' correlated well with neuroticism (0.45)[24], not with introversion or extraversion.

This all suggests that 1) the concept of arousal and/or activation only confuses the matter and does not explain anything, and 2) although two circuits are involved, they must be considered together, since they interreact. The strong nervous system is characterized by both extraversion and low anxiety (and high scores on happy emotionality). Before Eysenck's views on emotionality can be revised, however, research on emotionality should reject the current great diversity of methods for determining emotionality[25], in favor of a single scale of emotionality, using two variables (happy vs. unhappy states). There is evidence that slow alpha waves do correspond to the strong nervous system, which includes both extraversion and stability. In the light of these theories, the data from EEG experiments on oriental meditation can now be reviewed. These data suggest that cortical inhibition is the neural mechanism involved in forms of meditation which reject imaginings and intellectual activity, in favor of a more libidinally-oriented consciousness.

B. Survey of the background literature on oriental meditation

R. L. Woolfolk[26] gives a very complete general survey of all published research up until about 1975 on the physiological correlates of oriental contemplation. Comparing nineteen experiments on various kinds of Yoga, Zen, and transcendental meditation, he finds a general tendency of the electroencephalographic (EEG) activity to slow down, producing increased abundance of alpha waves with slower frequencies and higher amplitudes. Evoked responses to auditory stimuli vary somewhat. Zen practictioners respond briefly to clicks but show no alpha augmenting response and do not habituate. Yoga practictioners show this same response pattern *before* practicing Yoga, but do not respond at all during yogic practice. The data on response patterns in transcendental meditation are contradictory. Some reports do show habituation while other reports show no habituation. Woolfolk treats the data on metabolic reduction in transcendental meditation (TM) cautiously, concluding that the data were obtained under highly delicate conditions and need to be subjected to more rigorous control. TM claims, namely, that the TM technique brings the body into a state of metabolic inactivity which is unlike sleep. This is the basis of the TM movement's claim that meditation is a special state of consciousness, entirely unlike all the usual states of consciousness. The purpose of this section is to bring this claim into question, by showing that both the EEG data and the response characteristics correspond precisely to what Eysenck predicts one will find in stable extraverts, i.e. in the strong nervous system.

Since Woolfolk's purpose was to give a broad, general survey of these experiments, he did not pay much attention to the possible reasons for the

SUMMARY OF DATA FROM ORIENTAL MEDITATION
(adapted from Woolfolk's article)

Technique	Physiological Data	Rating
kriya Yoga (Das & Gastaut, 1955) (highly experienced subjects)	Faster EEG, increase in heart rate. No response to stimuli.	Poor, measurements taken in field under highly variable conditions
râja Yoga (Anand et al, 1961) (highly experienced)	Slower EEG (alpha) No response to stimuli.	Excellent, laboratory conditions
hatha Yoga (Wenger & Bagchi, 1961) (moderately experienced)	Decrease in SR level, decrease in respiration rate, increase in heart rate, increase in blood pressure	Poor, initial readings not comparable before meditation and relaxation periods
Soto Zen (Kasamatsu et al, 1957) (highly experienced)	Slower EEG (alpha, theta)	Adequate, lab. study. Meditation period too short
Soto Zen (Hirai, 1960) (highly experienced)	Slower EEG, decrease in respiration rate	Adequate, lab. conditions
Soto Zen (Kasamatsu & Hirai, 1969) (moderately and highly experienced)	Slower EEG (alpha, slow alpha, fast theta). Startle response to stimuli, but no habituation or blocking.	Excellent lab. conditions
TM (Wallace, 1970) (moderately experienced)	Slower EEG, increase in SR level, decrease in O_2 consumption, decrease in heart rate	Excellent lab. conditions, statistic comparisons made
TM (Wallace et al., 1971) (moderately experienced)	Slower EEG, increase in Sr level, decrease in O_2 consumption, decrease in blood pressure	Excellent, lab. study, statistical analysis
TM (Schwarts, 1973) (moderately experienced)	Slower EEG, increase in SR level, (not significant from controls)	Excellent, appropriate control group
TM (Banquet, 1973) (moderately experienced)	Slower EEG, but in some stages faster EEG observed.	Excellent, lab. study, statistical analysis
TM (Orme-Johnson, 1973) (moderately experienced)	Galvanic skin response more stable	Excellent, statistical analysis
TM (Pagano et al., 1976) (moderately experienced)	39% of time spent in wakefulness; 42% of time in sleep stages I & II; 17% of time in sleep stages III, IV (no REM periods)	Not reviewed by Woolfolk since published after 1975.

76

varying physiological results between Yoga, Zen, and TM. He maintains that research in this area should not concentrate on proving the special merits of any particular type of meditative technique, but rather should attempt to discover the basic underlying physiological mechanism involved in all meditation techniques. This reduction of various meditative traditions to their lowest common denominator is not supported by the empirical results, however. Woolfolk all too easily overlooks the differences in data collected from the various oriental techniques in an effort to establish the claim to a distinct 'meditative consciousness'. Therefore it is necessary to devote some attention to the differences in the various oriental techniques in an effort to understand why different traditions produce different data. These differences in data are clearly visible in the adapted chart (p. 76) which Woolfolk gives of these experiments.

1. *Yoga techniques*
Woolfolk notes that one of the first physiological studies of Yoga by N. Das and H. Gastaut (1955)[27] produced exactly the opposite results of later yogic experiments. Instead of slowing down, the EEG activity accelerated, producing faster alpha frequencies and very fast beta with unusually high amplitudes. The technique involved was that of kriyâ Yoga, which is not the same as other forms of Yoga, such as râja Yoga or jnana Yoga, or tantric or kundalini Yoga, to mention only a few of the various yogic techniques. In kriyâ Yoga, the attention is concentrated upon a light which one imagines to appear between the eyebrows in the middle of the forehead. Das & Gastaut call this a less-evolved, more primitive technique. The practitioner experiences that this light gets more intense and becomes a multitude of stars in which one can discern the aspect of the divinity. Upon reaching this climax, the practitioner becomes very pale and does not react to the environment, apparently losing consciousness. This is a technique which one practices for many hours at a time. Accordingly the EEG and other physiological registrations were made for many hours in one session. This is one main point of difference with all the other EEG experiments, in which the meditation period was about 20 to 30 minutes.

Of the seven subjects tested, Das & Gastaut claim that ónly one reached samadhi, or ecstasy. This conclusion seems to have been based exclusively on the EEG data, with no other parameters or even the subjective experience of the subject being reported. In all seven subjects, and especially in this one, the alpha production decreased greatly and fast beta activity increased. During the supposed state of ecstasy in this one subject, the beta rhythm accelerated up to 40 Hz, with the unusual phenomenon of amplitude increase, op to 50 microvolts. Since such results resemble muscle artefacts, Das & Gastaut pay particular attention to pointing out various differences between these data and muscle artefacts. In a footnote at the end of this article, the authors mention having heard that other kinds of Yoga produced abundant alpha activity. They conclude that either those subjects were less advanced or that different techniques produce different data. They themselves offer the suggestion that not only cortical inhibition might be involved, but also hormonal activity, i.e. emotional or libidinal activity. In kriyâ Yoga, namely, no cortical inhibition is generated, since the yogi is taught to work with imaginings and fantasies, in contrast to other kinds of Yoga. What is involved here seems instead to be a highly emotional state. How else could the practitioners meditate for hours at a time without falling asleep? The conclusion seems to be, provisionally, that meditation techniques which do not involve cortical inhibition (i.e. the suppression of ideational and imaging activity), but which do involve libidinal activity, will produce fast beta activity, faster heart rate, and possibly other signs of high emotionality. The lack of response to stimuli might be due to this emotional absorption, the limbic circuit interferring with the cortico-reticular circuit which relays sense perception messages.

An entirely different kind of technique is that of hatha Yoga, which consists mainly of voluntary control over visceral functions such as bodily temperature, perspiration, water retention, pulse rate, breath retention, etc. The older yogis produced faster heart rate, lower finger temperature, greater palmar conductance, high blood pressure in a study by M. Wenger & B. Bagchi[28]. In this study no EEG recordings were made, so no direct comparison with that of Das and Gastaut is possible. The physiological data do suggest that here, too, some increase in emotionality is present. Another study on hatha Yoga by Bagchi and Wenger[29] produced abundant alpha activity in the EEG with good amplitude modulation.

Another kind of technique, râja Yoga was studied by B. Anand et al.[30]. This technique consists of taking a certain sitting position, doing breathing exercises and fixing the attention on some object. It should be mentioned that these practices formed also the preliminaries to the other technique, kriyâ Yoga. However, instead of going on and imagining some object of concentration with the fantasy, the practictioner of râja Yoga suppresses his imagination by fixing his attention on a concrete object in front of him. Both conceive of ecstasy or samadhi as an experience or encounter with the divinity which one 'feels' mounting upwards in the body, toward the forehead. Both also have the ideal of complete insensitivity to the environment during ecstasy. The EEG data on râja Yoga show prominent alpha activity which could not be blocked by stimuli. The alpha production did not desynchronize although some humping occurred. Anand observes that those subjects who had a well-marked alpha activity during resting periods showed greater aptitude for maintaining the practice of Yoga, and also showed more zeal to continue it. Unfortunately, no other physiological data were registered. Therefore, no comparison can be made with hatha Yoga.

Râja Yoga seems to encourage cortical inhibition because it clearly does not teach the practitioner to imagine or fantasy anything. The emotional level may or may not be high. The data are insufficient to allow conclusions. The fact that at least one of the subjects had trouble with sleepiness (hump activity in the EEG) suggests that the emotional level might be low. The fact that in both kriyâ and râja Yoga inhibition of stimuli response occurred suggests that the cortico-reticular loop is involved somehow. The fact that practitioners of râja Yoga who had great alpha abundance normally were better able to meditate suggests that this meditation is not necessarily a unique kind of consciousness, but is merely the enhancement of the cortical inhibition already present in the subject, through a combination of techniques. One might call such a state an artificial or cultivated extraversion.

2. Zen techniques.

All the EEG studies on Zen involve the Soto Zen sect, not the Rinzai sect. Rinzai Zen centers around the practice of a mental puzzle, or koan. Soto Zen consists of several things: a certain sitting position, called Zazen, which is a lotus position; an ascetical training under the guidance of a Zen master, or Roshi; and a meditation whereby the attention is concentrated or fixed upon the object of union. In many ways Soto Zen resembles the technique of râja Yoga, except that Zen does not strive toward complete insensitivity to the environment, but rather emotional distance. In other words, not the cortico-reticular loop is the main area of concern, but the limbic circuit. Zen tries to dissociate the two loops, so that the Zen practitioner can maintain sense perception but without its usual emotional accompaniment. This state of mind is described by T. Hirai[31]:

"In Zen of the Soto sect there is no theme or topic or objective. No point of interest. No problem solving. No koans. No conscious efforts or rational thoughts. They don't seek to enter the state of oblivion or ecstasy, but on the contrary, to see or clearly perceive what they see or hear. Minds become 'transparent'. This is a positive effort, not passive. The mind isn't affected by those outside things. Ecstasy or oblivion is a positive experience, too. Ecstasy, however, is strictly prohibited. One is always aware of the surroundings."

Hirai's description might seem to suggest that there is no emotional or libidinal involvement in Soto Zen. A Zen monk whom Hirai interviewed, however, states that Soto Zen is directed to an object of identification, Buddha. The final aim is not just equanimity, but union with this object:

"Even though religious services are indispensable to the training of the monks in Soto Zen particular importance is placed on Zazen. Zazen is practiced not merely to enter the spiritual state of enlightenment, but in the Soto sect its great significance is ascribed to the religious truth that Gautema became enlightened though the practice of Zazen under the badhi tree. The image of Gautema sitting quietly with an enlightened spirit after having gone through all kinds of suffering and difficulties is, according to them, the way Zazen should be. Therefore, the main object of Zazen is said to be to get closer to that image of Buddha meditating quietly and experiencing in person the same process of 'enlightenment' as Buddha. This sitting quietly is called in the Soto sect 'Shikan-daza', meaning just to sit. Through maintaining this effort for a certain period, one would reach the spiritual state of the so-called 'mu-ga' or 'zammai', which means no-self or pure consciousness. Zazen is the spiritual training which includes the process briefly described as follows: instead of developing other thoughts, one sits first quietly and maintains the effort to concentrate ones attention internally. Then gradually and naturally one reaches the spiritual state of 'mu-ga'.

At first, one is somewhat disturbed by sounds, heat, cold, etc. but gradually these ideas pass away. The emotions (desire, anger, hatred, etc.) stop along with the halting of the thinking activity, which is accompanied by emotions. The association of some memory or idea disturbs the effort to concentrate on one point or symbol. Finally these ideas go out of the mind like calm water and the mind is very quiet and calm. This is usually thought to be the climax of the Zen meditation but it is not really true. The final stage is the central point on which the attention was focused and a unity with it."[32]

This orientation toward the object of identification is also present in the actual design of a Zen hall where the monks meditate. Each monk has his assigned seat, called 'Tan' (unit). He assumes a certain sitting position, either a half or a full lotus position. The book on Zen teachings, *Zazen-gi*, gives very explicit details about just how one should sit. When the disciple slumps and does not keep his back straight, the monitoring monk taps him with a stick. A bell signals the beginning of the meditation session. The monks meditate with their eyes open, keeping their gaze fixed on some point. The image of the Buddha is placed in the front of the Zen hall. The fixed seats are on platforms, presumably lined up so that the monk can get a full view of the Buddha image. In short, the whole design of the Zen hall is meant to awaken sense associations, tied in with sounds, bodily posture, and fixed sitting arrangements directed toward the object of identification and concentration, the image of Buddha. This all implies indirectly that some emotional involvement is latently present in Zen Buddhistic meditation, although very subdued. The meditation is directed, not at forgetfulness alone, but at absorption in Buddha. This is latently more emotionally loaded than the dissolving or unity with the innate object of râja Yoga, which could just as well be a vase as a statue. The Zen meditation seems to suppress some emotions, i.e. only those which distract from the orientation toward the Buddha image. Râja Yoga seems to suppress all emotions.

Is anything of this possible latent emotionality evident in the EEG data? The problem involved here is that the EEG is not specifically oriented toward any particular emotional state. It can only give a very general idea of the state of agitation or arousal of the subject. Physiological measurements should have been taken of heart rate, blood pressure, GSR, etc. as in Yoga. Unfortunately these were not done in the studies by Kasamatsu and Hirai. The only indirect way, therefore, to deduce any emotional activity is to see if the subject falls into sleep during meditation. Presumably, if he were emotionally concentrated, he would not become drowsy. A. Kasamatsu and T. Hirai[33] showed that during Zen sessions conducted in the laboratory, the alpha activity became more abundant and slowed down, producing higher amplitudes. This pattern did not develop into a de-synchronized pattern or sleep spindles. Drowsiness, called 'konchin' is suppressed in the Zen training. Auditive stimuli produced a startle reaction but no alpha blocking which lasted more than a second. Neither did habituation occur. Only one subject became drowsy, as far as the experimentors could tell, and a click stimulation produced the normal alpha arousal reaction with prolonged blocking of alpha. The more experienced monks produced an increase in theta waves, which were unusual in two respects. They did not de-synchronize and develop into the stage which usually follows, i.e. drowsiness with sleep spindles. Also, they had a very high amplitude, which is unusual. These theta trains appeared only after the subject had been meditating for about 15 to 20 minutes. The control subjects did not produce this slowing of the alpha nor the theta trains. They responded to click stimulation with the alpha augmenting response and with habituation. Thus Zen meditation does seem to contain some element, presumably an emotional involvement, which keeps the subject from falling asleep. One Zen master, however, clearly warns that this wakefulness has to be cultivated, since the beginner in Zen tends to become drowsy and distracted:

"Während man noch ein Anfänger ist, . . . kommen beim Zazen verschiedene störende Gedanken in einem auf. Wenn man sich so einigermassen ans Sitzen gewöhnt hat, so dass einen die Beine nicht mehr schmerzen, und man immer mehr Fassung gewinnt, wird man leicht schläfrig. Selbst solche, die ziemlich lange zu schlafen pflegen, geraten, auch wenn sie nicht geradezu schläfrig werden, leicht in den Zustand einer Art Abwesenheit bzw. Zerstreutheit. Wenn dabei dann mit einer gewissen Hartnäckigkeit störende Gedanken aufkommen, so reden wir von der Krankheit der Verwirrung (sanran). Wenn man in Schlafsucht oder Zerstreutheit gerät, so reden wir von der Krankheit des Versinkens. Beim Zazen soll das Bewusstsein nicht verschwinden, sondern in eine rechte, ordentliche Verfassung kommen, die diese beiden Zustände ausschliesst."[34]

The fact that Zen aims at a state free of visual and imaginative content as well as free from ideational content suggests that Zen cultivates inhibition in a way similar to râja Yoga. The theta waves might be just another aspect of the slowing down of the EEG already apparent in the slow alpha waves. Both might be tied in with cortical inhibition, since the reaction to sense stimulation is minimal. What is being inhibited here is the reaction to both the 'outer' directed senses (hearing, seeing, etc.) as well as the 'inner' directed senses, i.e. the imagination and the fantasy. The problem is that inhibition, if carried too far, leads to drowsiness and then to sleep. The technique in Zen, then, is not only the special sitting position, but especially the orientation toward the object of identification, the Buddha. Since intellectual activity is suppressed, this orientation must be on the emotional level. The reason beginners in Zen do have trouble with drowsiness might be because they as yet have no network of emotional associations with the Buddha which would activate them. Zen, therefore, is a technique for cultivating inhibition, or extraversion. It develops a dissociation between the emotions and the reactions to sense stimuli in a way similar to that of the Discaled Carmelite tradition, namely through affective asceticism and by orientation toward an object of union and identification. The two steps in meditation which the Zen monk described in the quote on p. 81 coincide with two kinds of Christian contemplation, namely the non-emotional stage of self-forgetfulness and the emotional contemplation of divine union, factors 7 and 15 vs. factors 1 and 8, as already described in the preceding sections of this chapter. In a way, this brings to mind the scholastic distinction between acquired contemplation and 'infused' contemplation, except that the state of divine union is not so much a matter of something being 'infused' as of the subject being attracted out of himself toward the object of identification. This applies to both Zen and Christian mysticism.

The similarities between the Zen experience of ecstasy and the Christian experience of ecstasy also seem to exist. In Zen, even in ecstasy, the subject remains aware of his surroundings, despite being absorbed in the object of union. The eight subjects in this study who reported having ever experienced ecstasy all stated that they had never been unaware of their surroundings. They were aware of conversations, sounds, movements, etc., but could not respond to them because of the absorption in divine union. These subjects reported also that this extreme stage of absorption passed away as they became more experienced and more used to it. Later on, they were able to respond if necessary to the surroundings during ecstatic experiences. The two most advanced subjects in this study stated furthermore that the ecstatic absorption had developed into a more or less continual state, which was not as intense as in the beginning.

Woolfolk's ratings of these experiments seems to proceed from the view that an experiment conducted under laboratory conditions is per se better than an experiment done in the field. In the case of meditation techniques which depend in part upon a network of emotional associations linked to a place, a special time, a special reference point or object of identification, special sounds, etc., the results obtained in the usual place where the associations have been built up might be better than results obtained in a laboratory where all these sensory stimuli are absent. The subject has to awaken the usual emotional associations in a strange environment which in no way stimulates these associations. Woolfolk overlooks the fact that Kasamatsu and Hirai took their registrations first of all in the Zen hall, during a period of 8 days while the monks were in spiritual retreat. Only afterwards did they select the most experienced monks and bring them to the laboratory for controlled experiments. Woolfolk seems to overlook hereby the latent emotional basis of the oriental meditation techniques already reviewed. His yardstick is transcendental meditation, which can be investigated in a laboratory because the emotional coloring or basis is somewhat different.

3. *Transcendental Meditation*
The third oriental meditation technique or tradition which has been subjected to extensive EEG studies is transcendental meditation, as taught by the Maharishi Mahesh Yogi. The technique consists of repeating a special meaningless sound, the mantra, and making no special efforts at ideational, emotional or imaginative activity. The exercise with the mantra is repeated for two sessions of twenty minutes daily. A specially trained teacher assigns the appropriate mantra to each individual subject, based upon a consideration of that person's own type. The subject is required to keep his particular mantra secret, and to undergo a special initiation ceremony. At the initiation the new member presents his 'offerings', sweet fruits, etc.. The teacher recites in Sanskrit a long list of the line of descent, i.e. the sequence of TM teachers who have passed on the secret of the mantra, a phenomenon which resembles what Catholics call 'apostolic succession'. Once the follower has been initiated he belongs to a group with a fairly well-knit organization. He thereby assumes certain obligations, such as paying a certain sum for admission and keeping in touch with 'checkers'. The checkers control to see if the follower is applying the technique correctly. Thus there is a network of 'gifts' or traditions, customs, structures, etc. which the follower receives upon joining. These form the framework in which the associations which aid concentration can be built up. The object of identification is the Maharishi himself, whose pictures appear on posters and book covers and advertisements. His presence is made especially nearby through the practice of showing video tapes in which the Maharishi teaches his followers. The advantage of this living and moving representation of the object of identification above that of a static image is that it all the more easily awakens emotional associations. In short, the technique itself, i.e. the mantra, is but a part of a larger network of 'techniques' which act to stimulate associations whereby meditation is made more accessible. The advantage of this highly secularized movement

is that it provides non-religious persons, who nevertheless seek a form of meditation, with a great many of the structures and techniques for meditation which religions offer, but without the usual religious connotations.

The question is, can this secularized meditation, based on a mantra with no emotional or ideational content, awaken the emotional associations necessary to maintain concentration in meditation? Does the TM follower fall asleep? How does the TM follower make the connection between the mantra technique, on one hand, and the object of identification, the Maharishi, on the other? This is perhaps the main difference between TM and the other meditation traditions already discussed. The Yogi can either imagine the aspect of the deity or can concentrate on an object. Both actions are part and parcel of the meditation itself. In Soto Zen, the image of the Buddha is present both literally and figuratively before the Zen monk. The very sitting position of Zazen imitates the Buddha's sitting position. Here, too, the act of concentrating on the object of identification is all part of the meditation exercise itself. In Christian prayer, the image of the object of identification can be a crucifix, statue, a picture of Christ, or possibly one of the saints. But at the same time, the inner identification with Christ accompanies this act of concentration. Thus the Christian contemplative orients his attention while praying toward either the representation of Christ placed before him and/or the representation of Christ within him. This will be further worked out in chapter four.

With this in mind, the problems which the TM practitioner encounters become evident. He can practice the technique without any point of orientation. He is explicitly taught to refrain from imagining anything, such as the face of the Maharishi. Also, he may not reflect during the practice of the technique, for instance upon the Maharishi's teachings. The content of the mantra itself in no way points to the Maharishi, but rather points to the meditator himself. It is his own private, secret mantra which somehow is custom-made for his own particular 'type'. Unlike the Christian contemplative or the Zen monk, the TM follower is not taught to strive to attain the inner likeness to the object of identification, i.e. a personal object which can be personally assimilated. Rather he is taught to assimilate abstract qualities like 'cosmic consciousness'. Although the Maharishi himself states that TM aims at a union of love with a personal God, the actual content of the TM teaching centers around secular virtues or abstractions like 'deep rest', 'relaxation', 'creative intelligence'. In short, there is nothing in the mantra technique itself which would bring the TM meditator beyond the first stage of rest and into the second stage of ecstasy, simply because there is no attracting agent outside the self.

Is there any evidence of emotional involvement in TM, on one hand, or of drowsiness and sleep, on the other hand? Most of the EEG studies on TM show a slowing of the EEG, i.e. more abundant alpha with slower frequencies. The recent study by R. Pagano et al.[35] shows that transcendental meditators can spend as much as 60% of the meditating time in some stage of sleep. Another recent article by H. Benson[36] maintains that any simple, repetitive mechanical relaxation technique, such as repeating the word 'one', will produce the same physiological data as transcendental meditation. R. Wallace et al.[37] found that in TM the heart rate decreased, as did also breathing rate and metabolic activity. It is most unfortunate that the experiment by Pagano did not replicate these physiological measurements. The possibility exists that the metabolic reduction might be the result of drowsiness and sleep. Wallace maintains that the slowing of metabolic activity was so extreme that an entirely different state than sleep is involved. Later experiments, however, have had trouble replicating Wallace's findings. Why did not Banquet[38], Schwarts and Orme-Johnson[39] subject such findings to repeated testing?

With such studies as those of Pagano and Benson the original attempt of researchers like Wallace to prove that transcendental meditation is an entirely unique state of consciousness has been subjected to substantial criticism. What do the TM data indicate? Unlike the data on Yoga, which indicated a degree of physiological activation, TM shows a slowing down of all bodily functions. Unlike Zen, where the alpha developed into very unusual theta trains and where no drowsiness occurred, TM seems to show an alpha pattern which can become very regular or synchronized, but which can just as often develop into various sleep stages, i.e. de-synchronization, flattening of the alpha and theta waves, delta waves and sleep spindles. This suggests that the TM practitioner can indeed achieve a certain inner rest through the technique, but that the problem of becoming drowsy and sleepy is greater than in the other oriental techniques. One could postulate that the reason for this is that the mantra evokes far too little emotional associations in itself and the teaching of the TM ideals is far too abstract. The movement does not connect the attraction of the object of identification, the Maharishi, with these ideals in a sufficiently direct way. Perhaps this is because the Maharishi does not aspire to becoming a minor deity and also because the TM movement does not intend to become a religion. Rather it refers to itself as a science of creative intelligence or the art of living. Here the element of emotional involvement is minimized. The problems involved in trying to concentrate on a set of abstract ideals, rather than on a person who embodies these ideals, will be further dealt with in chapter four. For the moment, it seems sufficient to speculate that the EEG and other physiological data on TM show that TM works at the level of the cortico-reticular circuit, helping the subject cultivate a higher level of inhibition. The absence of emotional stimulation, however, makes it difficult for the TM subject to maintain a steady state of wakefulness. If the effects of the TM technique extend beyond the meditation sessions into the daily life of the subject, as the TM movement maintains is the case, then one would expect these subjects to have trouble staying awake during the rest of the day, too.

These attempts to subject to criticism the TM claim that meditation produces a unique state of consciousness have been given additional support by other writers. V. Emerson[40] compares the differences in response characteristics and EEG data of Yoga and Zen, and concludes that belief systems can influence neuro-physiology. There is no one specific meditative consciousness, but various kinds of meditative consciousness, shaped by various traditions. An even more critical article is that of N. Doxey[41] (1972). He also underlines the differences between Yoga, Zen, TM, and the so-called 'high alpha state'. He concludes that the data from Zen are consistent with the aims of Zen, i.e. to exist in the here-and-now, in the immediacy of the phenomenal world. For this reason, the inhibition of stimuli was not complete. Yoga, with its strong world-denying quality, with its belief that the phenomenal world is all illusion, logically produces complete inhibition of response to stimuli. He calls into doubt whether the EEG is even able to prove that a distinct state of consciousness exists, pointing to a large amount of evidence that similar EEG patterns need not necessarily be accompanied by similar changes in other physiological variables[42].

Doxey observes that while TM and the conditioned 'high alpha state' both produce great alpha abundance, the other physiological data are entirely different. The 'high alpha state' can be induced without any physiological change. On the other hand, the same visceral changes can occur in entirely different states of consciousness. He concludes, citing L. Johnson[43]:

"On the strength of a wealth of evidence of this nature, Johnson (1970) concludes that EEG and autonomic activity cannot be used to define states of consciousness. The state of consciousness of the subject must first be known before the physiological significance and possible behavioral meaning of the EEG and autonomic responses can be inferred . . . I would suggest instead that we look upon the evidence from multiple levels of analysis to provide converging indicators of these hypothetical processes."[44]

This all goes to emphasize the importance of the subjective reports of the subjects, their spiritual forming in a specific mystical tradition, their degree of development in that tradition, their individual personality traits, etc. The kind of multi-level empirical study which has been conducted and described in the preceding sections in this chapter was lacking in all the physiological studies reviewed here. In such an inter-disciplinary study, the physiological registrations then do not function to 'prove' any unique state of consciousness in meditation, but serve rather to help both the meditator and the non-meditator to understand more about the bodily effects of a particular meditative tradition. The role of physiological data would be comparable to their role in the study of the emotions. One does not need physiological data to 'prove' that emotions exist. Indeed, physiological measurements are not specific enough to distinguish between various kinds of emotions. However, such data do help one understand more about what such emotions can do to the bodily processes. In both cases, one must first know the subject's state of consciousness before the physiological data can be interpreted.

This indicates one point which all the experiments on meditation discussed until now have overlooked, namely, the need to establish the connection between the subject's normal state and the meditating state. The studies on Zen merely registered for a few minutes before the meditation session to obtain the baseline. The experiment on râja Yoga by Anand et al. only mentions in passing something about the EEG data in the resting period of the subjects. In most of the studies the control is a group of subjects who do not practice the meditation technique, rather than the meditative subjects themselves. If the meditators had been used as their own controls, more data could have been gathered to show the variance between the subject's baseline and the subject's meditation session. However, in these studies reported here, one finds a minimum of time spent in establishing the baseline. The baseline, if established at all, was determined by recording for a few minutes immediately before the meditation session. The problem here is that the subjects are so conditioned to meditate, that the usual meditative associations are awakened merely by assuming the usual meditative position. Hirai especially mentions how the baseline recordings were contaminated by this conditioned effect.

This oversight seems inherent in the general approach of such studies. The researcher's interest is concentrated almost exclusively upon a certain technique. In TM, it is the secret mantra, in Zen it is the particular sitting position called Zazen, in kriyâ Yoga it is pin-pointing consciousness upon a place in the middle of the forehead, in râja Yoga it is a combination of sitting, breathing and concentration exercises. The technique is isolated from the subject's way of life. Whether a technique's effects extend beyond the time of meditation to affect the rest of the subject's day is left out of the discussion. What is especially important, and unfortunately entirely left out of the inquiry in such studies, is whether a certain way of reacting in general might affect the subject's success in practicing any meditative technique. It is therefore regretable that none of the EEG studies reported here include any data on such personality traits as emotionality, extraversion/introversion, neuroticism, ego-strength. How does the subject's usual threshold to stimuli relate to his response characteristics during meditation? Especially in TM, the response characteristics are overlooked. Thus nowhere does one find mention of recordings being made on different days before the meditation sessions, to determine the baseline, or mention of scores on personality inventories. The degree of advancement in a particular meditative tradition is also rather neglected. The experimentors seem to equate the time the subject has practiced the technique with the subject's state of advancement. The only exception to this is the study by Kasamatsu and Hirai, where a Zen master, or Roshi, was asked to rate the degree of advancement of the subjects. Although the Zen master's ratings did not always agree with the EEG findings and although no statistical comparisons were made, still some correspondence was reported in a chart. In short, an important set of parameters is absent in these experiments, simply because too much attention is focused on the particular technique and too little attention is paid to the subject practicing the technique.

C. Relating meditation to personality theories

Practically the only attempt, to the author's knowledge, to consider the psychological function of the meditative technique without treating the technique as a sort of magical cure-all, is the study by B. Glueck and C. Stroebel[45], "Biofeedback and Meditation in the Treatment of Psychiatric Illnesses" (1975). In their study of 77 psychotic patients, they achieved very little success in treating such patients with biofeedback or autogenic training. TM, however, enabled them to achieve results in combination with psychotherapy within a short time. This study is practically the only one on meditation which shows how relative the value of the particular technique is. They suggest that the effective agent is not the technique as such, but rather the way it opens up repressed libidinal material in the subject. The effect on the limbic system, or the libido, of the subject is central. Biofeedback and autogenic training failed because the subjects became bored with them. TM, however, held their attention for longer periods of time, although even here one-third of the patients stopped meditating very shortly. Glueck and Stroebel speculate that TM supplies a powerful input stimulus to the limbic system.

The theory of Glueck and Stroebel can be criticized on various points, even though their basic insight seems to correspond to what has already been suggested in the review of the neural mechanism behind meditation techniques. Their theory assumes, as did Eysenck, that unstable subjects are over-activated in the limbic system, i.e. they are too emotional. One could perhaps rectify this by stating that unstables are over-anxious. The criticism already given of Eysenck's views on emotionality applies here, too. Their theory states that the rest which TM produces, even in highly tense or anxious neurotics and psychotics, sedates cortical or ideational activity. Once these areas, especially those associated with speech, are inhibited, repressed libidinal material can surface. A parallel might be the use of hypnosis in psychotherapy, which allows unwanted or repressed memories to surface. Thus, cortical inhibition of rational activity, especially of speech, allows the libido to predominate. In the case of psychotics, the high anxiety state is reduced or sedated by the steady repetition of the mantra so other libidinal material which is usually repressed can come to light. At this point psychotherapists can apply psychoanalytic techniques with success. Indeed they must guide the patient at this stage.

The problem with the theory of Glueck and Stroebel is that its neural basis is rather faulty. They seem to assume that the left side of the brain is the seat of the intellect, and the right side of the brain is the seat of the emotions. They speculate that when the subject applies the TM technique, the activity of the left side of the brain is suppressed and the activity of the right side predominates. These ideas are rather imaginative speculations about the split in brain functions which R. W. Sperry discovered[46]. Sperry discovered that he could relieve certain kinds of epilepsy by cutting the connecting tissues between the left and the right side of the brain. Experiments showed that the right side, which is mute, does indeed have or can develop its own memory, will and perception. In Sperry's work, however, this split in functions was induced by surgery. In meditation no such severation occurs. Furthermore Sperry could find no specific function of the right side except perhaps manual dexterity. Therefore, Eysenck's theory of the limbic circuit, which involves the 'visceral brain' seems more suited to explaining the split in function, i.e. intellect vs. emotions, than the hypothesis about the right side of the brain. Put into Eysenck's terminology, their theory might then be re-stated as such: in meditation cortical inhibition is increased just to the point where the subject becomes drowsy. The intellectual activity of the imagination is sedated and thereby anxiety is reduced. If the subject does not fall asleep at this point, the repressive mechanisms of the libido become weakened, and unwanted feelings can surface. Indeed, Glueck and Stroebel report that covert psychotic tendencies became overt in the behavior of some of the patients. To keep this liberation of libidinal material from having a destructive effect upon the unstable subject, the psychotherapist must begin with psychoanalytic techniques at this point. This suggests that the reason why one-third of the patients discontinued TM might be because they were unable to handle the unwanted libidinal material, and reverted to their usual repressive mechanisms. Although Glueck and Stroebel seem to criticize the TM movement because it does not provide its followers with the necessary psychotherapeutic guidance, the function of the TM checkers might inadvertently provide this counseling. The TM follower is obliged to go to a checker once a month, every month for the first year in TM. The checker could refer the unstable subject to a psychologist if he reported having emotional disturbances during meditation.

Does only TM relax the repressive mechanisms, or do also other meditative traditions function in this way? Each meditative tradition has an institution of the spiritual leader, who guides the follower. In Yoga, it is a swami. In Zen, it is the Roshi. In Christian meditation, it is the spiritual director. In Zen, the Roshi studies the character of the follower, assigns him special tasks to improve his view of life, and guides him when he encounters problems with hallucinations or the 'demon' (makyo). The Zen master already quoted warns against various sicknesses of the mind which the beginner can encounter in Zen. He refers to persistent thoughts which keep arising during meditation, which he calls the sickness of distraction. This same Zen master then explains how to combat this sickness and come to terms with the enemy. The enemy is the uncontrolled thoughts, hallucinations, impulses, etc. which arise in Zen. He calls it a serious battle in which one either kills or gets killed. But it is a battle which has to be fought. Falling asleep is enough to make one lose the battle. The 'enemy' might be Glueck and Stroebel's repressed sexual frustrations, hostilities, etc. The battle might be the attempt to attain psychotherapeutical integration of the unwanted libidinal material into the rest of the subject's personality.

A parallel can be found in John of the Cross' instructions to spiritual directors. He, too, warns the contemplative against the 'enemy', which he describes as 'the demon, the world, and the self'. He, too, describes a state of complete spiritual vertigo and confusion which arises during and because of prayer. John of the Cross instructs the contemplative to tell all his/her experiences in prayer to the spiritual director. He observes that the contemplative seems to realize himself what he has actually experienced only upon telling it to the spiritual director. It is the role of the spiritual director to root out the experiences which come from the 'demon' and to guide the contemplative away from them completely. These instructions to spiritual directors take up a great deal of space in his works: *Ascent* II, ch. 18; *Night* II,7,3; *Flame* III,30-63. It is quite possible that the greater the emotional content of the particular meditative tradition, the more other, unwanted libidinal material will also be activated during meditation, since the same limbic circuit is being aroused. In Christian mysticism, where the emotional level is quite high, as the preceding sections have already shown, the problem of the unrepressed 'demon' or the 'enemy' becomes more acute than in meditative traditions where all emotionality is subdued. The problems, then, become all the greater the more the contemplative advances in mystical union. This might explain why factor 10, distracted, troubled prayer, coincided with the more advanced stages in prayer, rather than with only the beginning stages. Much more will be said about this in chapter four.

Whereas Eysenck seems to consider the traits of extraversion/introversion and anxiety to be hereditary, these results suggest that both traits can be enhanced or decreased through meditation. Oriental meditation seems to help the subject cultivate extraversion, or inhibition of both external stimuli and internal stimuli. With the inhibition of internal stimuli such as the fantasy and the intellect, the limbic circuit seems to gain a more predominant role than is usually the case. Jung suggested that oriental meditation might establish a balance between thought and emotion, and between extraversion and introversion[47]. The data, however, suggest that oriental meditation accentuates extraversion and happy emotionality. Hereby it strengthens the nervous system.

D. The empirical study of Christian prayer[48]

The time has now come to present the psycho-physiological study of Christian contemplation and Christian meditation. Before going any further, these terms have to be clarified. What oriental spirituality calls 'meditation' is what western spirituality calls 'contemplation', i.e. a receptive state in which all active rational effort is rejected in favor of restful attentiveness to the object of identification. What oriental spirituality calls a 'concentration exercise' is called meditation in Christian spirituality. It consists of an active effort to concentrate by reasoning on themes, texts or imaginings. Christian spirituality contains both the active and the passive prayer forms. The point of inquiry or the hypothesis is that Christian contemplation will produce the same EEG results as an oriental contemplative tradition which is very similar to it, for instance Soto Zen. This is because the same neural basis is assumed to underlie both traditions of contemplation. The hypothesis can be stated formally in this way:

1. The hypothesis.
In the reasoning which leads up to the hypothesis there are three steps: a first main premise (with a minor premise), a second main premise (with a minor premise) and a conclusion. This is illustrated in the diagram on p. 92.
1) The first main premise (1-a): extraversion is due to cortical inhibition;

stability is due to the absence of negative emotionality (anxiety) and the presence of positive emotionality.

The first minor premise (1-b): Since experiments suggest that both factors together, extraversion and stability, produce abundant alpha activity in the EEG, one would expect stable extraverts to have more alpha abundance than unstable introverts.

2) The second main premise (2-a): The data in the study already described show that Christian contemplation correlates well with stability and ex-traversion. Active meditation and distraction correlates with neuroticism and introversion.

The second minor premise (2-b): Stable extraverts have an advantage in Christian contemplation because they have a greater ability to inhibit stimuli. The final deduction (3): Therefore concentration in Christian contemplation is a function of cortical inhibition and stability, which should be evident in abundant alpha activity in the EEG when the subjects practice it. Active meditation, on the other hand, is a function of excitation rather than inhibition. Therefore, this should be evident in decreased alpha abundance during the practice of it and increased beta abundance.

The hypothesis: two things are predicted

3-a: During contemplation, abundant alpha activity and slowing of the alpha frequencies should appear, greater than the baseline.

3-b: During active meditation, alpha abundance should decrease and beta activity should increase, differing from the baseline.

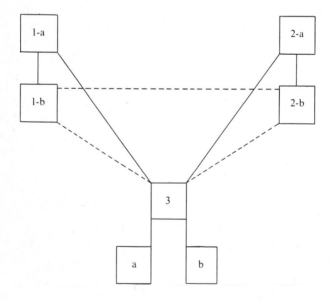

It would be difficult to predict the other physiological data since the contemplative prayer form consists of both restful and highly emotional states, which seem to occur in some kind of inter-action. Due to this emotional basis, however, one would not expect the subjects who are contemplating to become drowsy.

2. *Subjects.*

From the 54 subjects used in the broader psychological study already discussed 17 subjects volunteered to participate in the physiological study. As in the case of the 54 subjects, the motivation for participation was closely linked with the attitude of the religious superior in the group. Since there was considerably more resistance to the physiological study due to the fact that the subjects would have to travel away from the cloister to the clinic, only a few subjects could be recruited. Of the 17 subjects who did volunteer three had to be dropped because medication interfered with the EEG data. The total number of subjects was therefore 14. Of these about half were introverts and half were extraverts. Roughly speaking, about half could be classified as 'poor contemplatives', based on the fact that they had sumscores below the 50% level on contemplative prayer (factor 8) and mystical experience (factor 1), already discussed in this chapter. About half of the subjects were males. Of the ten highly advanced contemplatives in Group I, already discussed, five volunteerd for these EEG registrations. The ages ranged from about 28 to 65 years. Six were from moderately traditional cloisters, two were from moderately experimental groups, and six were from very experimental groups. Subjects were interviewed to establish their medical history and to determine the presence of factors which might distort the data. The only resulting distortion found was the prolonged use of certain medications which could not be discontinued, as already mentioned.

3. *Methods*[49].

The recording sessions were highly exploratory because no previous EEG studies on Christian contemplation had as yet been done to the author's knowledge. A variety of attempts were made to discover the conditions under which the nuns and friars could pray the best. Due to individual differences, it was decided to use each subject as his/her own control throughout the experiment. (Technically speaking, this study was not an experiment, however, but merely an inventory.) The recording conditions were not optimal due to the fact that the initial registrations had to be made in quarters not originally designed for research where the subject had to sit next to the EEG machine and had to endure a noisy environment. Furthermore the magnetic tape recorder for recording the EEG data for computerization was not available until later on in the experiment. Later registrations were made for the most part in new premises not yet fully equipped for research. Due to these handicaps the empirical study presented here must be considered merely as a pilot study in preparation for a more extensive study under better research conditions.

a. Preliminary recordings.

Since the nuns are accustomed to praying together in a chapel for about two hours a day in a kneeling or semi-sitting position, various attempts were made to find out if they could pray in a laboratory in a controlled situation. About one-half of the subjects were used for these first attempts. The recording conditions were highly variable; various positions (sitting, reclining), instructions, and ways of fixing the electrodes (glueing vs. a salt paste, held in place with a rubber cap, a quicker method).

The reason for trying to find a quicker method for applying the electrodes (glueing them on takes about 30 to 45 minutes) was because the subjects became drowsy while sitting for so long. The quicker method was abandoned, i.e. the rubber cap method, because it irritated the subject during prayer after the first ten minutes. The practice of engaging the subject in conversation during the application of the electrodes counteracted the drowsiness. (Coffee could not be given the subject because it distorted the EEG data so clearly.)

Although some subjects had originally insisted upon praying in private behind a curtain, these objections were dropped once they became accustomed to the clinic. After the recording sessions the subjects were interviewed to find out if they had been able to pray as they normally did, if the sitting or lying position was good, if certain sounds or movements were distracting, if they had become drowsy, etc. Some of the subjects remarked later that this first session, made in a reclining position, was their best 'prayer session' in the whole experiment. The reclining position was abandoned, however, because it favored artifacts from eye movements. The sitting position was chosen for the rest of the registrations. One subject had prayed with his eyes open, just as the Zen monks. He was instructed to pray with his eyes closed in order to insure a standardized recording. Since the subjects were generally rather nervous the first time in the clinic, care was taken to explain something about their EEG results to them individually so that they would not think the researchers could 'read their thoughts'. No equipment was available at the start of this experiment for making magnetic tape recordings. Only visual assessments were made.

b. Routine EEG Recordings.

To determine the baseline, routine or standard EEG recordings were made on a different day from the 'prayer session', in order to avoid the contamination of the conditioned response of praying upon sitting quietly (in the preliminary registrations some subjects showed the same phenomenon as the Zen monks, i.e. they began getting into the mood for contemplating merely by taking a certain sitting position). The instructions were the same as those given to patients in the clinic; alternating periods of 'eyes open' and 'eyes closed', plus periods of photic stimulation and hyperventilation. The subject sat in a chair next to the EEG machine in a sound proof room. The electrodes were mounted according to the 10-20 system of Jasper and were held in place with a rubber cap. These sessions lasted not more than about 20 minutes. In retrospect certain faults in this procedure can be found: the instructions should have been as nearly like those given in the 'prayer' sessions, to make a nearer comparison possible. That is, the subjects should have been instructed to keep their eyes closed during the whole time. The photic stimulation and the hyper-ventilation should have been replaced with auditory stimulation. These evoked responses should have been elicited during both this standard recording as well as during the 'prayer' session. Only visual assessments were made, in a report that was written up véry soon after the recording session, as well as a quantified report that was worked out about two years after these registrations were made.

c. 'Alpha' recordings.

Since the main emphasis in oriental EEG studies on meditation was on the slowing down of the alpha rhythm and the increase in alpha abundance, these registrations were designed to concentrate on those regions of the head where the most alpha usually occurs, namely the occipital and parietal regions at the back of the head. Twelve electrodes were mounted according to a non-standard pattern. ECG, eye movements, respiration and neck muscle tension were registered. All recordings were bipolar. Registration sessions lasted about 20 minutes each, beginning roughly about 10:00 a.m. As in the standard sessions, the subject sat in a chair next to the EEG machine. Two sessions were planned. The first session was a 'routine' one in which the subject was instructed to relax and not to pray. The problems in this procedure have already been discussed, i.e. the subject begins to get in the mood to pray just by sitting quietly. To counter-act this tendency the subjects were not told that a prayer session would follow immediately. After this first routine session, a short pause followed in which the subject was told that in the second session he/she would be instructed to pray. The prayer session followed and lasted about 20 minutes. Both sessions were recorded on the magnetic tape recorder. After the prayer session each subject was asked to indicate his/her level of concentration during the 20 minutes by plotting it on a graph. Short interviews were held and recorded on tape in which the subject described what he/she had done during prayer. Although this procedure did counter-act the conditioned tendency of the subjects to pray during the standard or routine session, another problem turned up; namely by the time the subjects had gone through the routine session and the pause, they were becoming drowsy and/or irritated. The unexpected instruction to pray for another 20 minutes was an unwelcome surprise. Thérefore the best procedure seems to be to make the baseline recording on a different day than the prayer recording. Let the subject know when he/she will be expected to pray so that they can be getting into the mood ahead of time. These 'alpha' recordings had the effect of accustoming the subjects to praying under laboratory conditions and as such were preparatory to the subsequent prayer sessions.

d. 'Push button' recordings.
Since the results of the 'alpha' recordings showed no appreciable difference between the routine and the prayer registrations, attention was then concentrated upon distinguishing levels of concentration during prayer and upon theta waves as well as alpha waves. The subjects were instructed to indicate periods of lowered concentration in prayer by pushing in on a device held in the hand. Twelve electrodes were mounted according to the 10-20 system of Jasper (see diagram, below) plus recordings were made of the ECG, eye movements, neck muscle tension, respiration. Although this had the advantage of including electrodes in the temporal areas, the exclusion of the occipital area (01, 02) was perhaps an error.

BIPOLAR MONTAGE (model 891)   MONOPOLAR MONTAGE (1-8) (model 891)

Subjects sat in a private room, connected via a cable to the EEG machine, which was in another room. This represented optimal laboratory conditions; the only recording thus made under these conditions was the 'push button' registration. Subjects were observed via a one-way window and notes were made with an indication of time when subjects changed posture, opened their eyes or in some way produced artifacts. These were subsequently removed from the magnetic tape recording. Time: $\pm$ 10:00 a.m. The instructions were the same for both 15-minute sessions: to pray with the eyes closed and to indicate moments of distraction, i.e. lowered concentration, by pushing the button in. After the first 15-minute session, in which bipolar recordings were made, a short pause followed. Subsequently for another 15-minute session monopolar recordings were made. After these sessions, the subjects were once again asked to indicate the course of their prayer session or level of concentration by plotting it on a graph. This was especially necessary in the case of a few of the most advanced subjects who had not indicated any period of distraction by pushing the button. They generally indicated no great difference in level of concentration during the sessions. The policy was adopted of selecting a period of about 10 seconds at the beginning of the session to represent the period of lowest concentration. Both sessions were subjected to a visual assessment of the results. As in the case of the routine or baseline registrations, two visual assessments were made: one immediately after the recordings and another one quite some time afterwards.

4. *Results.*
a. Visual assessment: baseline vs. 'push button' prayer session.
The baseline was established on the basis of the visual assessments of the standard recording described under 3-b. Since there was a discrepancy between the first visual assessment and the second one in about 13% of the cases the first visual assessment was taken as the yardstick in cases of disagreement. The motivation for this choice was the fact that the first assessment generally agreed the most with the computer results in the 'push button' registrations. A statistical comparison was made between the visual assessment of this standard recording (both alpha and theta data) and the visual assessment of the bipolar 'prayer' recording in the 'push button' session described under 3-d. The visual assessments were made with a double blind. Neither the operant nor the directing neurologist, Dr. Notermans, were told either the psychological scores of the subjects nor their scores on the questionnaire on spirituality. The features extracted in this visual assessment were:
i.　level of arousal: drowsy, relaxed, irritated, tense, combination[50].
ii.　form of the alpha waves: waxing and waning, desynchronization,

synchronization, hyper-synchronization.
iii. localization of the alpha waves: no spreading, spreading to temporo-basal, spreading to temporo-frontal.
iv. localization of theta waves: no spreading, some spreading to parietal-occipital, considerable spreading to parietal-occipital.
v. alpha abundance: very little (6-10%), little (10-30%), normal (50-75%), very much (90%).
vi. theta abundance: very little, little, normal, very much.

In all six cases (i-vi) a test of significance was done for the difference between the two means: 1) the baseline EEG recording (baseline) and 2) the 'push button' bipolare prayer recording (prayer). The results of the t-test for dependent samples are shown below:

Table A: t-test.

Variables	Means Baseline	Prayer	Corr.	t (dependent)	Probability
1. arousal level	3.07	3.07	0.474	-1.64 (-12)	1.00
2. synchronization, alpha	2.79	2.50	0.735	1.470	.165
3. alpha spreading	1.50	1.57	0.313	-0.322	.752
4. theta spreading	1.64	1.57	0.202	0.366	.721
5. alpha abundance	3.07	2.79	0.812	2.28	*.041*
6. theta abundance	2.71	2.64	-0.090	0.29	.776

(number of degrees of freedom = 13)

In table A the probability that the value of t will be exceeded is shown in the far right column. Only in the case of variable (5), alpha abundance, was the difference between the two means, baseline vs. prayer, significant (0.04) at a 0.05 level of significance. This means that there is a significant *reduction* in alpha abundance during the prayer session, as becomes evident when one compares the two means. No significant difference was found for all the other variables. As Table VI, p. 282 in the appendix shows, those subjects whose alpha abundance decreased during the prayer session were subjects who have a non-contemplative prayer life. They have low sumscores on the factors 1,8, and 15 (mystical experience, emotional contemplation and non-emotional contemplation, respectively). (The way the sumscores were obtained is explained on p. 38, chapter two.) Contrary to expectations, however, they are not always practicing active, rational meditation nor do they have distracted, troubled prayer. In most cases, they exhibit those signs of distracted behavior already signalled in section two of the Questionnaire on Spirituality, that is, a combination of drowsiness, tenseness, irritation and restlessness.

As the rest of the data in Table VI show, subjects who are not good at contemplating tend to have a decrease in alpha synchronization during the prayer session. Subjects who are good at contemplating, i.e. who have high sumscores on factors 1,8, and 15, do not show any noteworthy changes between the baseline recording and the prayer recording. No further statistical comparisons were made for the differences between the two means. A t-test for independent samples on the differences between baseline and prayer recordings of contemplatives vs. non-contemplatives could not be made because of 1) the small number of observations in each group and 2) the small variation in the difference scores.

A correlation matrix was made using the same variables as those above, plus the relevant psychological variables, neuroticism (N) and extraversion (E). The relevant factors from the prayer experiences in the first sections of the Questionnaire on Spirituality were included: factor 6 (active, rational meditation), factor 10 (distracted, troubled prayer), factor 8 (emotional contemplation) and factor 15 (non-emotional contemplation). The complete correlation matrix is presented on p. 280 in the appendix. A summary is given here:

Table B: Correlations.

	Baseline: alpha abundance	Prayer: alpha abund.	Baseline: synchronization	Prayer: synchron.
Factor 6 (active meditation)	-0.60	-0.49	-0.09	-0.15
Factor 10 (distracted prayer)	-0.49	-0.36	-0.17	-0.37
Factor 8 (emotional contemplation)	0.03	0.38	0.50	0.76
Factor 15 (non-emotional contemplation)	0.13	0.43	0.53	0.75
Neuroticism	-0.27	-0.50	-0.60	-0.78
Extraversion	0.15	0.33	0.70	0.42

Although no appreciable changes occurred during the prayer sessions in comparison with the baseline scores, a certain pattern emerges here which does tend to meet expectations somewhat. In accordance with expectations, active meditation and distracted, troubled prayer (factors 6 and 10) correlated negatively with alpha abundance. Also according to expectations, contemplation (both emotional and non-emotional) correlated positively with alpha abundance. This means that the general level of alpha abundance of active rational meditators and distracted, troubled subjects is

99

lower than the general level of alpha abundance of contemplative subjects.

Also according to expectations, neuroticism correlates negatively with alpha abundance while extraversion correlates positively with alpha abundance.

Synchronization of alpha activity is also important here. A reduction in alpha synchronization, i.e. regular, symmetrical waves, occurs when a subject can not contemplate during the prayer session. However, such subjects are not necessarily practicing active rational meditation nor distracted, troubled prayer. For this reason alpha synchronization does not correlate well with factors 6 and 10 either during the baseline recording nor during the prayer recording. The very high positive correlations between alpha synchronization and contemplation, both for the baseline and the prayer recordings, shows that the general level or degree of alpha synchronization of contemplatives is great all the time. The same can be said of the high negative correlations between alpha synchronization and neuroticism both during the baseline and prayer recordings. Unstable subjects tend to have very little alpha synchronization at any time. Extraversion correlates much better (and positively) with alpha synchronization during the baseline recording than during prayer. This means that extraverts who can not contemplate tend to show a decrease in alpha synchronization during prayer. Very little more can be said about the changes between the baseline and the prayer recordings for the various types of subjects (unstables, extraverts, good and poor contemplatives, etc.) because the correlational method is not well adapted or adequate for explaining such phenomena.

Summing up what has been found until now, subjects who are good at contemplating will tend to produce the same high degree of alpha abundance and the same regular or synchronized alpha waves which experienced Zen and Yoga practitioners produced. However, in the case of Christian contemplation, this EEG pattern does not appear suddenly during the prayer session, but seems to be the general or normal EEG pattern of the subject in the wakeful state. Subjects who already have this expected EEG pattern are therefore also better able to contemplate.

Although the correlation matrix gives some insight into the interrelationships between the various variables, a factor analysis shows the pattern of inter-relationships more clearly. Table C, pages 102-103, the oblique factor analysis, shows three main groups or factors: 'emotionality', 'contemplation', and 'active, rational meditation'. The correlations between these three factors show that the first two, emotionality and contemplation, are closely related, correlating at 0.60. The third factor, active meditation, correlates almost equally well, but negatively, with both of the first two factors. What is the difference between the factor 'emotionality' and the factor 'contemplation'? In the factor, 'emotionality', the psychological variables which correspond to the limbic circuit predominate, while extraversion (i.e. the cortico-reticular loop) plays only a secundary role. In this factor, the EEG variables associated with the 'strong nervous system' also have high loadings. The contents of this first factor can be interpreted this way: subjects who are experienced in non-emotional contemplation (and only secundarily in the more emotional forms of contemplation) tend to be relaxed both normally and also during prayer. The degree of alpha synchronization is high, both normally and during prayer. Thus non-emotional contemplation is linked, paradoxically, with high happy emotionality and low anxiety in the subjects. Or, happy, stable subjects (not necessarily extraverts) can achieve a non-emotional contemplative prayer level, but will not necessarily become advanced mystics.

The second factor, 'contemplation', combines all three kinds of contemplation. Contemplation is associated here with alpha synchronization, relaxation and alpha abundance during prayer. Extraversion is predominant, and stability is only secundary. This suggests that stable subjects who do go on to develop the deeper forms of contemplation, i.e. the experience of ecstasy and union, will tend to be extraverts. Thus, extraversion and thereby cortical inhibition in the cortico-reticular loop plays a dominant role in the more emotional, deeper kinds of contemplation. The limbic circuit plays only a secundary role, also paradoxically. The inclusion of the cultural variable 'independence' in the second factor suggests that those stable extraverts who do become advanced contemplatives are more dependent than the subjects who merely attain to non-emotional contemplation, i.e. inner rest. The importance and meaning of the variable 'independence' has already been dealt with in the preceding sections.

Finally, the third factor, 'active, rational meditation', suggests the following profile of the non-contemplative subject. Such subjects have reduced alpha abundance and are more tense during the baseline recording than during prayer. The exception to this are unstable subjects. During prayer, this abates somewhat because the subject becomes more relaxed. Nevertheless the reduced alpha activity is still evident. The subject who practices active, rational meditation is not necessarily unstable, but does tend to be introvert and independent. Inner distractions due to imaginings and conflicts (factor 10) tend to accompany active meditation. All these data suggest that active meditation is a function of excitation in the cortico-reticular loop. The role of the emotions, i.e. the limbic circuit, is negligible. Active meditation is an emotionally neutral prayer form. This confirms the hypothesis to some extent: active meditation consists of activation of the inner stimuli (fantasy, imagination), an activity which takes place in the cortico-reticular loop. The prediction that during active meditation, alpha abundance would decrease significantly was not confirmed. No decrease occurs during meditation. Rather subjects who generally tend to have little alpha abundance in their usual wakeful state will tend to pray using active rational meditation. Hereby they seem to extend their general high imaging ability to the practice of prayer.

The other prediction, namely that alpha abundance would increase during contemplation, was also not confirmed. No significant changes occurred when advanced contemplatives began praying. However, subjects who are not good at contemplating do have reduced alpha abundance. In general, advanced contemplatives tend to have a high degree of alpha abundance all the time. Such 'high alpha state' subjects seem to extend their usual inhibition of imaging to the practice of prayer. These subjects, who tend to be very stable and low on anxiety, and extravert, produce the same EEG patterns as the Zen and Yoga practitioners produce. However, instead of producing this EEG pattern only during prayer they produce it all the time.

Table C: Oblique Factor Analysis

Factor 1: "Emotionality"

Item	Loading
Happy emotionality	0.9576
Unhappy emotionality	−0.9560
Level of arousal, prayer EEG	−0.9513
Neuroticism	−0.8981
Alpha synchronization, prayer EEG	0.8805
Alpha synchronization, routine EEG	0.7808
Non-emotional contemplation (factor 15, section 1)	0.6752
Level of arousal, routine EEG	−0.6308
Emotional contemplation (factor 8, section 1)	0.5498
Extraversion	0.4778
Mystical experience (factor 1, section 1)	0.4451
Alpha abundance, prayer EEG	0.4277

Factor 2: "Contemplation"

Emotional contemplation	0.9988
Mystical experience	0.9223
Non-emotional contemplation	0.9096
Alpha synchronization, prayer EEG	0.7840
Independence	−0.7196
Level of arousal, prayer EEG	−0.6224
Alpha synchronization, routine EEG	0.5689
Extraversion	0.5145
Alpha abundance, prayer EEG	0.4749

Happy emotionality	0.4734
Unhappy emotionality	−0.4705
Neuroticism	−0.4477

Factor 3: "Active, rational meditation"

Active, rational meditation (factor 6, sec. 1)	0.8671
Alpha abundance, routine EEG	−0.6863
Distracted prayer (factor 10, section 1)	0.6488
Level of arousal, routine EEG	0.5697
Non-emotional contemplation	−0.5620
Alpha abundance, prayer EEG	−0.5469
Extraversion	−0.4883
Theta spreading, routine EEG	−0.4624
Mystical experience	−0.4616
Theta spreading, prayer EEG	−0.4430
Independence	0.4420
Alpha spreading, routine EEG	−0.4417
Alpha synchronization, prayer EEG	−0.4374
Emotional contemplation	−0.4095

(cut-off line is 0.4000)

Correlations among factors:

	1	2
1	1.0000	
2	0.5961	1.0000
3	-0.4523	-0.5278

Factors one and two clearly show that synchronization of the alpha waves is an EEG variable which is more characteristic of contemplation than alpha abundance. Furthermore, alpha synchronization correlates well with the traits of the 'strong nervous system' and negatively with the traits of the 'weak nervous system'. This suggests that in the future this variable should be subjected to automatized analysis, rather than alpha frequencies, amplitude, and total power in the alpha band. This might possibly be done through the plotting of coherence, as described and adapted to the study of meditation in an article by A. S. Gevins, et al.[51].

b. Power density spectral analysis.
The results of the computerized data were taken from the 'push button' prayer recording only. They measured periods of good concentration during prayer vs. periods of poor concentration during prayer. A detailed report of this multi-variate analysis of variance of repeated measurements is presented on pages 277-283 in the appendix. No analyses were made on

the physiological data because a visual inspection revealed no noteworthy changes. The technical difficulties involved in the 'push button' recording have already been mentioned. Good contemplatives often indicated no periods of poor concentration. Poor contemplatives, however, sometimes were so restless that it was almost impossible to obtain a representative period without artifacts. One subject was so restless that he had to be dropped from this analysis. The total number of subjects in this analysis was therefore only thirteen.

Only two aspects of the power density analysis were further analyzed in this statistical analysis. One was 'total power', which is the amplitude squared. This is expressed in the formula, MMV2, or microvolts, squared. This was calculated in the various bands, i.e. delta waves (1-3 Hz, or cycles per second), theta (4-7 Hz), alpha (8-12 Hz) and beta (13 + Hz). The other variable analyzed was 'average frequency', that is, the average number of cycles per second (Hz) in each band. The other variables (peak power, peak frequency, and relative power) could not be used because they were so highly dependent with 'total power' and 'average frequency'.

The computation of the combined means showed that extraverts have more total power than introverts in the alpha band during both periods, that is, during the good and the bad periods of concentration. The analysis of variance, however, produced no significant difference at the usual 0.05 level of significance. At the 0.10 level, the use of which is highly uncommon, a significant difference was found between the total power production of extraverts versus introverts in the alpha band. In regard to 'average frequency', extraverts tend to have slower frequencies in the alpha band than introverts. No significant difference was found in the statistical analysis, however (see Table IV, p. 281 in the appendix).

Extraverts tend to have spreading of the alpha activity to the temporal areas. Alpha activity is more restricted to the temporal areas in introverts (see Table V, p. 281 in the appendix). Alpha and theta spreading occurred just as much during periods of good concentration as during periods of poor concentration in prayer. This supports the results of the visual assessment.

When extraversion and introversion are left out of the picture and when one considers only the general differences between the data on periods of concentrated prayer vs. periods of poor concentration, no significant difference is found at the usual 0.05 level of significance. At the 0.10 level (the use of which is not standard practice), a difference is found in the total power in the alpha band. The mean scores (page 279, appendix) clearly indicate that the total power in the alpha band *decreases* during periods of good concentration in prayer and *increases* in periods of poor concentration. This supports the results of the t-test which was made with data from the visual assessment. There, too, a reduction in alpha activity was found during periods of prayer. However, if this reduction in alpha activity were due to distractions, as has already been suggested, then the periods of *poor* concentration should have shown a decrease in alpha activity. It was assumed that periods of poor concentration would correspond to periods of distraction. The kind of distraction involved would *not* be distractions coming from the environment because these recordings were made under optimal conditions in a sound-proof room. What is involved is inner distraction.

5. *Discussion: The neural basis of concentration and distraction in prayer.*
Fortmann suggests that there are two kinds of distraction: distraction due to a lowered degree of attention and distraction which is a quantitatively different kind of attention than that of attention in concentrated prayer[52]. The results of the t-test of dependent samples and of Table IV suggest that the reduction in alpha abundance occurs in the first case. Due to a lowered degree of attention, the subject becomes drowsy, restless and also tense and irritated. Why is this type of subject inattentive during prayer? The low scores on any emotionally colored prayer form suggest that the libidinal involvement of this subject in prayer is quite low. This type of subject is tense during the prayer session, in the so-called periods of good concentration, and is busy trying to arouse certain feelings toward God. This reduces the amount of alpha production. When this does not succeed, this subject then stops praying and relaxes. In these so-called periods of poor concentration, the alpha production therefore increases. As this repeats itself during the prayer recording, the subject becomes more and more tense and irritated during prayer, and at the same time, less and less attentive. Alpha production continues to decrease. The subject is highly aroused, but not attentive, during prayer.

The quantitatively different kind of distraction is that described by factor 10, distracted, troubled prayer. Due to inner conflicts which surface during prayer, the subject becomes distracted. He combats this by meditating actively and rationally or visually on some topic or text. Such subjects tend to have reduced alpha production at all times, which might be due in part to their introvert, unstable psychological profile. This type of subject is highly aroused and attentive, but nevertheless distracted from the actual object of his prayer, libidinal or emotional involvement with the object of identification. The libidinal level of this prayer type is also very low. Thus in both cases, distraction is the result of a low libidinal level during prayer. In the first case the reason for this could be any of the cultural and religious factors already mentioned in chapter two. In the second case, especially the psychological variables seem to play a role (see

Table VIII, p. 283).

It is important at this point to consider distracted behavior. The periods of poor concentration and distraction seem to be periods of relaxation. The subjects changes position, opens his eyes, moves his hands or feet, yawns, looks at the watch, etc. This understandably produces many artifacts. Indeed, there were so many artifacts during such periods that it was very difficult to obtain a representative ten seconds for the automated analysis. This suggests that these periods of movement *are* representative. What should have been quantified was therefore this behavior, i.e. the amount and kind of artifacts produced in periods of poor concentration. Fortmann reports that it has been found that animals can not maintain a state of attention if they are not allowed to move their bodies[53]. He applies the same principle to man. The subject tries to bolster his level of attention (not arousal) by movement. If Fortmann is correct then these periods of muscular movement are actually aids to concentration, rather than hindrances to it. Fortmann suggests that the alternation of various positions in liturgical prayer (sitting, kneeling, standing, etc.) has a function in maintaining the level of attention through bodily movement. Subjects who are libidinally involved in deep prayer often indicated no periods of poor concentration nor did they change position.

The role of muscle movement can perhaps best be illustrated by comparing the mean scores on 'total power' in the alpha band of subjects 02 and 13 with the mean scores of the other subjects (see Table I, p. 279, appendix). Both unstable subjects, one an extravert and the other an introvert, used muscle techniques. Hereby, they extended their hands, palm upwards, in front of them. When they felt they had achieved inner rest and relaxation, they turned the palms downward. When they felt the tension rising again during active meditation, which both practice to a great degree, they turned the palms upward. The continuous exertion of muscle contraction involved in keeping the hands in this position seems to help them relax a little bit. Other subjects generally produced more alpha activity during the periods of 'poor concentration', while they produced less alpha during periods of 'good concentration', i.e. they became more tense during concentrated prayer. These two subjects, however, produce a small increase in alpha activity during concentrated prayer. Both subjects practiced this muscle technique spontaneously in exactly the same way, and without any knowledge of each other. The fact that neither subject produced the abundant alpha waves which oriental meditation techniques produce means either that this technique is not sufficient to reduce anxiety, or that the EEG experiments on oriental meditation have not yet been done on such extremely unstable subjects as the two described here. The continuous muscle contraction and the discomfort this causes might be the principle behind the effectiveness of the special sitting position, the lotus position, of Zen and Yoga.

Reviewing what has been observed up until now, one can postulate that concentration in contemplation involves two phases, which are based upon two corresponding neural circuits as outlined by Eysenck. In the first phase, the subject achieves inner rest and recollection. He does this by lowering the anxiety level and relying upon his own natural ability to suppress imaginings or inner stimuli. Subjects who are high anxiety types are assaulted at this point by inner conflicts and inner distractions. They then take a detour into active meditation. This is also what Gale's findings suggest. The first phase of inner rest can be achieved only if the subject can inhibit inner stimuli in the limbic circuit as well as in the cortico-reticular loop. This corresponds to non-emotional contemplation and to the 'via negativa', which is the suppression of all rational or visual imaginings. This stage is represented in the factors 2, 7, and 15 in section one, in the Questionnaire on Spirituality.

Why can some subjects attain this first phase while others stay at the level of active meditation and inner distraction? The data suggest that in Christian contemplation insufficient aid is given to subjects who are not equipped from birth with a strong nervous system. During contemplation the degree of alpha abundance and alpha synchronization does not increase, as in oriental meditation. Rather during Christian contemplation the pre-existing strong nervous system, with its associated EEG characteristics (alpha abundance, etc.), is only maintained, but not enhanced or increased. What is missing in Christian spirituality, therefore, is a technique which strengthens the nervous system by lowering anxiety and increasing inhibition. For this reason, unstable subjects especially will have trouble inhibiting the imaginings and inner distractions which arise when the usual repressive mechanisms are relaxed, as the article by Glueck and Stroebel has already shown. They stay therefore at the level of active meditation and inner distraction, corresponding to excitation, not inhibition, in the cortico-reticular loop.

The second, more emotional, phase is made possible by the fact that the first phase makes the libido more accessible. By inhibiting cortical activity, especially ideation and speech, the emotions can come to predominate. *This is therefore the mechanism behind the so-called 'via negativa'.* Those stable subjects who do go on to this second phase will tend to be extraverts. This suggests that the deepening emotional involvement is made possible by the continuing inhibition of inner stimuli in the cortico-reticular loop. This explains the close association between factor one ('emotionality') and two ('contemplation'). The first phase, factor one, is the foundation for later developments and the kind of non-emotional contemplation (factor

15) involved here is also a framework within which the later developments can be built up. For this reason, as the factor sumscores show, emotionally neutral, passive contemplation (factor 15) continues to gain in importance until the final state of mystical union. The inhibition of inner stimuli is not a phase which fades out as emotional involvement deepens. Rather, precisely this inhibition of stimuli, which stable extraverts are better equipped to do, makes this emotional growth possible.

Returning now to the specific meditative techniques, only kriyâ Yoga seems to leave this first stage out. It stimulates emotional involvement, presumably, without first establishing a basis in inner rest and relaxation. The question arises whether this might lead to emotional imbalance in the subject. In the Christian spiritual tradition, especially in the prayer methods of the Jesuits, inspired by Ignatius of Loyola's Spiritual Exercises, this first phase is reduced to a minimum. Only outer stimuli, distractions from the environment, are reduced. Inner stimuli, i.e. the imagination and the fantasy, are excited. The emotional involvement and also the intellectual reflection which comprise the second phase have not been given a basis in inner rest. Also, the libido has not yet been made accessible. The subject can thereby attain to 'intellectual contemplation' perhaps, but not to the prayer of union.

By contrast, TM seems to over-emphasize the first phase to the neglect of the second phase. TM does not offer the subject an object of identification toward which the emotional involvement can be directed. Consequently, the meditator tends to become drowsy, since there is insufficient limbic activation to offset the increase in inhibition in the cortico-reticular loop. The TM follower is left to find the object of identification in his 'true self'. Both the mantra technique and the ego-directed goals, the 'virtues' of TM, make the TM follower turn inward. This search for connaturality with the divine within the 'true self' precludes the possibility of ecstasy. There is no agent apart from the meditator to draw the subject out of himself. Consequently the libidinal, erotic level in TM is either very subdued, or entirely absent. The problems which arise when the 'true self' of the subject comes to the surface, due to the relaxation of the repressive mechanisms, are illustrated by Glueck and Stroebel. The 'true self' is not as ideal as it should be. To get beyond this emotionally disturbing stage, the TM follower would have to find another model of his 'true self' which counteracts his imperfect self, a model which is separate and distinct from the subject himself, but which can be assimilated. Because this object of identification is missing, the TM follower has difficulty in reaching the second phase in contemplation.

6. *Conclusion.*

One could conclude that the reason why some subjects can achieve this libidinal build-up of emotional involvement in prayer better and more quickly than other subjects is because they were born with strong nervous systems. Christian spirituality does not offer subjects with weak nervous systems enough aids to lower anxiety and increase inhibition of inner and outer stimuli. Oriental meditation techniques could perhaps be assimilated into Christian contemplative traditions to supplement this lack. On the other hand, western spirituality might be able to supplement these oriental techniques with a deeper-reaching approach to the object of identification though its emphasis upon the erotic, libidinal encounter with the object of ecstasy. The way this is achieved in the contemplative tradition of the Discalced Carmelites will be explained in chapter four. Especially a technique such as TM would thereby receive an erotic dimension, whereby more of the world of human experience, i.e. the libido, would be integrated into the experience of inner peace and relaxation.

7. *Evaluation and suggestions for future research.*

An experiment such as this is in fact merely an inventory since nothing is manipulated or changed. The ways such an inventory could be improved have already been touched upon. The baseline should be established with particular care by making recordings on different days than the contemplative sessions. The instructions in the routine session should be as parallel as possible with the instructions for the contemplative session to make comparisons possible. Behavior should be recorded and quantified. The subjective experience of the subject should be given more attention. Each subject should be interviewed after the contemplative session to establish exactly what he was doing at that time.

A true experiment, in the technical sense of the word, might be set up whereby nuns and friars or monks who are not able to concentrate during prayer could be taught an oriental meditation technique such as TM. One could then check over a period of time to see if alpha abundance and coherence increased. Or TM followers who are Christians could be instructed in the way to attain deeper emotional involvement in meditation. One could see if the parameters of emotionality (heart rate, GSR, etc.) show increased activity.

CHAPTER THREE

The Roots of the 'Via Negativa' in John of the Cross

"To come to that which you do not know,
you have to go a way you do not know;
To come to that which you can not feel,
you have to go a way you can not feel;
To come to that which you do not possess;
you have to go a way you do not possess;
To come to that which you are not,
you have to go via that which you are not."

St. John of the Cross, *Ascent*, I,1,14.

INTRODUCTION

The Zen master of Karlfried Dürckheim tells the tale of a wondrous cat who was able to capture a ferocious rat simply by doing nothing. The other cats were quite astounded and asked him the secret of his success. The wondrous cat called a meeting and one by one he asked each cat what his special technique was for catching rats. After each cat had described his special technique the wise cat pointed out that each technique has its limitations; one technique emphasizes only physical skill, another stresses mental acumen only, while another relies on tricks and illusion. The wise cat concluded that techniques fall short because they make one rely on ones own skill; to really succeed one has to transcend self-reliance. Finally the wondrous cat told of an even more wondrous cat who did nothing but sleep the whole day, but the rats were so afraid of him that they all stayed out of his neighborhood[1].

The frustrating aspect of this tale is that the wondrous cat never really tells the other cats the content of his wondrous art. What distinguishes the passivity of this cat from a charlatan who really does nothing? The story implies that there are all kinds of passivity and that a cat that seems to be doing nothing may in fact be doing a great deal.

The preceding chapter has described several meditative techniques and has found certain points of comparison between them and Christian mysticism. Nevertheless, the element of reliance on any special technique is absent in Christian mysticism. What then is the content of the special art of the Christian contemplative? What distinguishes the contemplating Christian from a sleeping Christian? The preceding chapter indicates that the key factor in Christian mysticism is the so-called 'via negativa' rather than strict asceticism, i.e. the denial of any pleasure in anything except God. The empirical results show that many subjects think that the technique for succeeding in mysticism is strict asceticism; an opinion related to conformity to the cloister ideal of the Discalced Carmelite Order. This chapter will try to answer two questions: 1) what is the content of the art of the Christian contemplative, the 'via negativa', and 2) how could this 'via negativa' have become so mistakenly associated with strict asceticism, considering that this is a logical contradiction: the 'via negativa' is an anti-technique, and strict asceticism is a kind of super technique? In this chapter, proceeding from a detailed consideration of the spiritual and intellectual formation of John of the Cross, the route will be traced whereby he came to associate the 'via negativa' with strict asceticism. The starting point is therefore: how could he be so right about mysticism and so wrong about asceticism?

The status quaestionis regarding the 'via negativa':

A few explanatory comments must be made at the very beginning concerning the 'via negativa'. This term, as well as the term 'mystical theology', owes its origin and development to an unknown Syrian monk of the 6th century, A.D., who called himself 'Dionysius the Areopagite', alluding to the biblical story in Acts, ch. 17, 15-34 which tells of a certain Dionysius the Areopagite who became a follower of Paul. Since it was commonly believed that the writer of the works *Mystical Theology, Celestial Hierarchy, Ecclesiastical Hierarchy, The Divine Names,* etc. was really the Dionysius referred to in the Bible, his writings carried a great deal of authority until this century, when it became commonly accepted that the actual writer was from the 6th century. As this view became accepted a kind of rejection of the pseudo-Areopagite set in, perhaps from disillusionment. This rejection was also motivated by the discovery of strong neo-Platonic elements in his teaching. Considering that the original Dionysius the Areopagite described in Acts had been portrayed as a Greek who rejected the 'wisdom' of Greek philosophy to follow the 'foolishness' of a crucified and resurrected Christ, the discovery of Greek philosophical patterns of thought in these writings was a double disillusionment.

In the article by Lucien-Marie already referred to in chapter one[2], he calls the influence of the 'via negativa' in the teaching of John of the Cross a result of a certain lack of assimilation of the thought of pseudo-Dionysius. In another book, the same author goes even further in denouncing pseudo-Dionysius:

"Nous sommes alors amenés à demander si une docilité – non fondée, puisqu'elle reposait sur une donnée fausse: la quasi-inspiration de l'aréopagite, supposé disciple de saint Paul – à une certaine tradition mystique d'inspiration néoplatonicienne, n'a pas abouti parfois, chez saint Jean de la Croix, à une présentation de l'expérience mystique qui ne concorde pas avec celle qu'il en a faite quand il s'est tenu aux textes de l'Écriture ou à sa propre expérience, enrichie de celle de tant d'êtres qu'il avait acheminés à l'union à Dieu."[3]

This opinion, shared by many writers, considers the 'via negativa' as being antagonistic to the Christian emphasis upon Christ's humanity. This rejection of the 'via negativa' goes so far that writers like Lucien-Marie even say it is not founded in mystical experience at all, but only in philosophy. The empirical results of this study, however, clearly show that the 'via negativa' as developed by John of the Cross, is a central aspect of Christian mystical experience.

The theological problem, therefore, is how to appreciate the teachings of the pseudo-Areopagite in an unbiased manner, so that his psychological insights and true theological depth can once again be recognized, not because of some supposed connection with the Areopagite of Acts 17, but purely on the basis of their own merit. It will be shown that the theological short-comings which his views on mysticism do contain have largely been remedied by John of the Cross. Vice versa, some themes in pseudo-Dionysius remedy short-comings in this Spaniard[4].

I. DISTORTING INFLUENCES UPON THE 'VIA NEGATIVA' IN JOHN OF THE CROSS

This section will attempt to show that the sort of denunciation of the 'via negativa' which one finds, for example, in the writings of Cordero and Lucien-Marie already quoted presupposes that mystical theology is inherently bound to the dualism of spirit/sense. In order to show that mystical theology in its original formulation with pseudo-Dionysius did not necessarily contain this kind of dualism this chapter will begin with a detailed consideration of the actual texts of pseudo-Dionysius. The contrast with the mystical theology of John of the Cross will be underlined. The rest of this first section will trace the way the teaching of pseudo-Dionysius became distorted through the influence of later developments.

A. What is the 'via negativa'?

It should be clear at this point that the 'via negativa' in the context of John of the Cross is not so much apophatic theology as such, but rather a form of prayer deduced from it. It is a set of practical instructions about prayer characterized by the rejection of active rational/visual thought such as calling up thoughts or images about God, biblical scenes, religious themes with the aim of awakening certain feelings toward God. What is rejected therefore is not so much the use of reason but rather the active effort involved, on both the rational as well as the emotional level.

Thus John of the Cross states: "He who wants to join with God in union should not go the way of the understanding" (*Ascent* II,4,4). "The more one thinks God is like that which one understands about him, the more one loses of the supreme good and the more one is delayed in going toward it" (*Ascent* II,4,6). "Faith tells us that which one can not understand with the intellect" (*Ascent* II,6,1). "In order to arrive at Him, one should rather proceed by not knowing than by knowing" (*Ascent* II,8,5).

The concrete instructions are: ". . . contemplation is secret and hidden from the very person that experiences it . . . it gives the soul an inclination and desire to be alone and in quietness, without being able to think of any particular thing or having the desire to do so. If those souls to whom this comes to pass knew how to be quiet at this time, and troubled not about performing any kind of action, whether inward or outward, neither had any anxiety about doing anything, then they would delicately experience this inward refreshment in that ease and freedom from care" (*Night* I,9,6). "It is well for those who find themselves in this condition to take comfort, to persevere in patience and to be in no wise afflicted. Let them trust in God, Who abandons not those who seek Him with a simple and right heart, and will not fail to give them what is needful for the road, until He bring them into the clear and pure light of love . . . What they must do is merely to leave the soul free and disencumbered and at rest from all knowledge and thought, troubling not themselves in that state, about what they shall think or meditate upon, but contenting themselves with merely a peaceful and loving attentiveness toward God . . " (*Night* II,10,4).

Several comments can be made here on these instructions. What John of the Cross clearly does not teach is any kind of technique for meditation or concentration. He states that there are many people who have practiced some kind of meditative technique with great spiritual profit until they arrive at a point where they have gotten all they can out of that way of meditating and need to progress. They experience a kind of spiritual dryness and need to be instructed in what to do next. His aim is to help people who have arrived at this point to transcend the meditative technique, whatever it may be, and go on to develop a true spiritual depth (*Night* I,8,3). He does this by instructing them to substitute reliance upon ones own insights or feelings by another kind of reliance, namely the practice of blind faith in God. It should be emphasized that he never says the soul should do nothing. Rather it should learn to practice the virtue of faith, combined with hope and love. He recognizes that it takes time to develop this attitude and that from time to time more advanced souls will have to resort to some meditative technique when they are not caught up in the experience of infused contemplation (*Ascent* II,15,1). He does not reject active prayer as such but rather regards it as a preparatory exercise in concentration. He gives three signs by which the beginner can discern when he has arrived at the kind of spiritual dryness he describes (*Ascent* II,13,1-8; *Night* I,9, 1-9; *Flame* III,32-33). He says that it is necessary that all three signs occur because just one or two of the signs might indicate merely a state of melancholy. It is relevant here to mention that this stage of spiritual dryness, the first dark night, factor two, did indeed correlate with unhappy emotionality. Factor two was so unreliable because of the influence of psychological variables (see discussion on pp. 38-39, chapter 2).

What one notices in such instructions therefore is their psychological approach. John of the Cross has developed from the 'via negativa' a practical guide to advancement in prayer, based upon his observations of the prayer development of the many nuns and friars who confided in him. The fact that so many subjects were able to find their own mystical/contemplative experiences expressed in his teachings in quotations which did not correlate with the variable 'conformity', shows that the prayer development he traces is true to life in many respects. John of the Cross himself admits that some exceptions can occur:

"And after this manner God continues to lead the soul step by step until it reaches that which is the most interior of all; not that it is always necessary for Him to observe this order, and to cause the soul to advance in exactly this way, from the first step to the last; sometimes He allows the soul to attain one stage and not another, or leads it from the more interior to the less, or effects two stages of progress together. This happens when God sees it to be meet for the soul, or when He desires to grant it His favours in this way; nevertheless His ordinary method is as has been said" (*Ascent* II,17,4).

What the empirical results signify is that his teachings on prayer development do correspond highly with the actual experience of the subjects. The question which then arises, however, is how can John of the Cross be so right about prayer and so wrong about asceticism? What leads him to connect the 'via negativa' to strict asceticism? Why is there practically no correlation between mystical/contemplative prayer and strict ascetical views or strict ascetical practice?

Oddly enough, John of the Cross himself admits that strict asceticism and mystical experience do not necessarily go together:

"God grants these favours to whom He wills and for what reason He will. For it may come to pass that a person will have performed many good works, yet that He will not give him these touches of His favour; and another will have done far fewer good works, yet He will give him them to a most sublime degree and in great abundance" (*Ascent* II,32,2).

114

The fact that this inconsistency with his own teachings did not lead him to re-examine thoroughly his views suggests that not observation of authentic experience but rather logical deductions from a whole body of theological-philosophical-monastic concepts and ideals formed that basis for his ascetical rigorism. The aim of this study, therefore, is to show how the course of his intellectual and spiritual formation influenced the way he came to read the 'via negativa' in the works of pseudo-Dionysius. It is important to go into this historical aspect deeply since it traces in a nutshell the course of development of western mysticism and asceticism. In John of the Cross' spiritual formation all the elements are incorporated which came to distort the original mystical theology of pseudo-Dionysius.

> B. *How dualistic is the original 'via negativa'*
> *of pseudo-Dionysius?*

In this section a close examination of three translations of the *Mystical Theology* and the *Divine Names* of pseudo-Dionysius will show how the personal views of the translator affect the degree to which pseudo-Dionysius is guilty of spirit/sense dualism. In fact, this short exposé will show that pseudo-Dionysius is only as dualistic as his translator. After that, attention will be turned to the exact nature of the 'via negativa' in his writings. For this reason a study of pseudo-Dionysius demands a critical review of the translations. Although the three translations presented here are not the only ones in existence, they serve well to illustrate the issues involved.

Beginning with the key texts which present the basic ideas of the 'via negativa' certain interesting discrepancies between the translations come to light. The three translations presented here are the well-known one of E. von Ivanka, *Von den Namen zum Unnennbaren*; the lesser-known work of W. Tritsch, *Dionysios Areopagita: Mystische Theologie und andere Schriften*; and the relatively well-known one by M. de Gandillac, *Oeuvres Complètes du Pseudo-Denys L'Aréopagite*[5].

Translations of *Mystical Theology*, ch. 4 (Migne, *PG*, 3, 1040 D):

Ivanka: "Wir sagen also, dass die Allursache, die über allem ist, weder seinslos ist, noch leblos, *noch vernunftlos, noch geistlos, noch ein Körper* ist . . ."

Tritsch: "So sagen wir es dann: der Urgrund des Alls, über alles hinaus, was Schöpfung heisst, kann *nicht Stoff* sein, *nicht Geist, nicht Wesen,* nicht Leben, *nicht Bewusstsein; nicht Körper* . . ."

Gandillac: "Nous disons donc la Cause universelle, située au delà de l'univers entier, n'est *ni matière exempte d'essence,* de vie, *de raison ou d'intelligence, ni corps;*"

Confronted with such contradictory and different translations, the author,

115

who is in no way a philologist or classicist, nevertheless is thrown back upon the original Greek text: "οὔτε ἀνούσιος ἐστιν, οὔτε ἄζωος, οὔτε ἄλογος, οὔτε ἄνους, οὐδὲ σῶμα ἐστιν". Translated literally; "not without essence, not without life, without reason, without spirit, not a body." The translation of Ivanka appears therefore to be the most accurate. One wonders how Tritsch pulled the denial 'nicht Stoff' out of thin air. Of the three translators Tritsch clearly allows himself the most liberty in translating. He thereby completely turns the meaning of the denials around; instead of saying that the universal Cause is not *without* spirit (nous), Tritsch says that he is *not* spirit. Gandillac adopts an interesting tactic. Where the Greek text says 'nous', he says 'intelligence', instead of 'spirit'. Ivanka uses 'spirit' to translate 'nous' in this text; 'reason' or intelligence he uses to translate 'logos'. Later it will be shown that the way one translates 'nous' is the key point to be watched. The original intention of pseudo-Dionysius is more subtle than Tritsch would have it. The text does not state that the universal Cause is neither spirit nor body, but rather that it is not without spirit (which nevertheless does not say that it *is* spirit) and is not a body. Here pseudo-Dionysius does not clearly state that God is above spirit/body dualism. In the following text, however, he does: *Mystical Theology*, ch. 5(1045).

Ivanka: "Noch weiter emporsteigend sagen wir, dass er weder Seele ist, noch *Denkkraft*, noch Vorstellung, Meinen, Sagen oder Denken hat ..."

Tritsch: "Noch höher steigend sprechen wir jetzt aus, dass dieser Urgrund nicht Seele ist und auch nicht *Geist*. dass ihm weder Einbildungskraft zu eigen sein kann noch Meinung, noch Vernunft, noch Erkenntnis ..."

Gandillac: "Nous élevant plus haut, nous disons maintenant que cette Cause n'est ni âme, ni *intelligence*; qu'elle ne possède ni imagination, ni opinion, ni raison, ni intelligence ..."

The Greek text is: "... ὡς οὔτε ψυχή ἐστιν, οὔτε νοῦς· οὔτε φαντασίαν, ἢ δόξαν, ἢ λόγον, ἢ νόησιν ἔχει· οὐδὲ λόγος ἐστιν, οὔτε νόησις· οὐδὲ λέγεται, οὔτε νοεῖται·"

The important word here is 'nous'. Interestingly enough, Ivanka changes his tactic here. In the first text presented (1040 D) he translated 'nous' with 'spirit'. Why does he not do that now? Gandillac follows his earlier tactic, translating 'nous' with 'intelligence'. Only Tritsch clearly lets pseudo-Dionysius say that this Cause is not spirit. The points of view of the three translators begin to come to light. Tritsch is trying to emphasize the view that God is above spirit/body dualism. Ivanka on the other hand tries to avoid the issue by translating 'nous' with 'intelligence', similar to the way Gandillac does. Only when pseudo-Dionysius states that the Cause is not *without* spirit (nous) does Ivanka translate 'nous' with 'spirit'. This is even more evident if one reads Ivanka's introduction to his translation, where he briefly outlines the neo-Platonic hierarchical schema present in pseudo-Dionysius: "Gott, Geist, Seele, Stoff." Here, Ivanka translates 'nous' with 'spirit'[6]. This all suggests that Ivanka can only understand the 'via negativa' in a spirit/body dualism and that he structures his translation accordingly. Thus in texts like the one above, 'nous' has to be translated with 'reason', 'intelligence', etc. One sees the same tactic in Gandillac. This is even more obviously affected here, where Gandillac is thereby forced to repeat the word 'intelligence' in the same phrase, since he is using 'intelligence' to translate two Greek words, 'nous' and 'noèsin'. Since in a translation, just as in any good prose, one usually tries to avoid using the same word repeatedly by looking for a synonym, the fact that Gandillac did not resort to the word 'spirit' for translating 'nous', but in fact preferred to repeat the word 'intelligence', clearly shows his bias.

The final text in pseudo-Dionysius where the position is so clear that no one can get around it, is *Mystical Theology*, ch. 5 (1048):

Ivanka: "Nicht Eines, nicht Einheit, nicht Gottheit, nicht Güte, nicht *Geist* – so wie wir dies kennen."

Tritsch: ". . . nicht die Eins oder die Einheit oder Göttlichkeit oder Güte oder Schönheit oder *Geist* in dem Sinne, in welchem wir Menschen es begreifen könnten."

Gandillac: ". . . ni un, ni unité, ni déité, ni bien, ni *esprit* au sens où nous pouvons l'entendre."

The Greek text: ". . . οὐδὲ ἕν, οὐδὲ ἑνότης, οὐδὲ θεότης, ἢ ἀγαθότης, οὐδὲ πνεῦμα ἐστιν ὡς ἡμᾶς εἰδέναι . . ."

The reason all three translators could agree here is because pseudo-Dionysius used the word 'pneuma' instead of 'nous'.

The clearest case of the way in which the translators influence the way pseudo-Dionysius comes to be understood is one very difficult passage which discribes the three movements of the soul to God. It is precisely this passage which writers like Stiglmayr and others pick out to show the supposed spirit/body dualism or the introversion of pseudo-Dionysius: *Divine Names*, ch. 4,9 (705 B).

Ivanka: Interestingly enough, Ivanka does not even attempt to translate this complex passage. Rather he summarizes it. It is this summary which is revealing for his bias: 'Bei den Seelen ist die kreisende Bewegung das Sich-Sammeln der Seele vom Äussern und das Sich-zurückwenden . . . zum Geistigen, das um-sich-selbst-Rotieren das Erleuchtet werden durch die geistige Erkenntnis, wenn auch nicht auf geistige und 'einsseiende' Weise, sondern auf verstandesmässige und diskursieve Weise, die geradlinige Bewegung das Emporsteigen vom Sinnbildlich-Äussern zum *Geistigen, Innerlichen*, Einigen."

Tritsch: "Die geradlinige Bewegung der Seele endlich ist jene, in welcher sie weder in sich selbst sich vertieft . . . noch auch dialektisch aufnimmt und lernt . . . sondern lehrend und wirkend in ihre Umgebung hinaustritt – aber auch da lässt sie sich von den Aussendungen anregen, doch alle mannigfachen und vervielfältigenden Symbole führen sie dann wieder zu den einfachen und geeinten Begriffen des Guten und Schönen empor."

Gandillac: "Son mouvement enfin est longitudinal lorsque, plutôt que de rentrer en soi et de tendre à l'union intelligible . . . elle se tourne vers les réalités qui l'entourent et prend appui sur le monde extérieur comme sur un ensemble complexe de multiples symboles pour s'élever à des contemplations simples et unifiées."

Ivanka states in his paraphrase of this text that the straight movement of the soul to God is a movement from all that is sensual and exterior to an inner, spiritual place. The translations of Tritsch and Gandillac both clearly show that the text actually says exactly the opposite. In the straight movement, the soul turns to the *outward* world and transcends *via symbols*, not via purely spiritual means. There is no reference to an inner, spiritual movement here at all. Instead, the movement is extravert, not introvert. Furthermore the whole issue of spirit/body dualism is simply absent. It is precisely here that Ivanka's presuppositions come to the surface, i.e. when he starts paraphrasing pseudo-Dionysius. The disparity between that paraphrase and the actual text is so clear that Ivanka's other tactics in translating pseudo-Dionysius become transparent.

The Greek text (705 B) to the passage treated above is: ". . . οὐκ εἰς ἑαυτὴν εἰσιοῦσα . . . ἀλλὰ . . . ἀπὸ τῶν ἔξωθεν . . ." ("Not entering within itself . . . but . . . turning to outward things.")

Indeed, considered even superficially, a logical contradiction seems evident between the ecstatic mysticism so characteristic of pseudo-Dionysius and the mysticism of introversion which Ivanka advocates. 'Ecstasy' itself means 'standing outside oneself', and *not* entering into ones innermost 'spiritual center'. The necessity of this extraverted attitude is emphasized by pseudo-Dionysius himself at the very beginning of *The Mystical Theology*, ch. 1 (997 B-1000 A):

Ivanka: "Denn durch das von allem Gehaltenwerden freie und rein von allem gelöste Heraustreten ('Ekstase') aus Dir selbst wirst Du, alles von Dir abtuend und von allem gelöst, zum überwesentlichen Strahl des göttlichen Dunkels emporgehoben werden."

Tritsch: "Denn erst wenn du dich von allem ganz entäussert hast, vornehmlich aber von dir selbst, unaufhaltsam und absolut, und ohne jeden Rest leer bist, erst dann wirst du dich in reinster Ekstase bis zu jenen dunkelsten Strahl erheben können . . ."

Gandillac: "Car c'est en sortant de tout et de toi-meme, de façon irrésistible et parfaite que tu t'éleveras dans une pure extase jusqu'au rayon ténébreux de la divine Suressence . . ."

The Greek text: ". . . ὑπὲρ πᾶσαν οὐσίαν καὶ γνῶσιν· τῇ γὰρ ἑαυτοῦ καὶ πάντων ἀσχέτῳ καὶ ἀπολύτῳ καθαρῶς ἐκστάσει πρὸς τὴν ὑπερούσιον του θείου . . ."

In Ivanka's version, the reference to renouncing oneself is left out. The text is made to read, 'Once you have renounced everything you will go out of yourself . . .'. Tritsch in this case gives the more accurate translation.

118

Although he turns the sequence around and says that you first have to drive out everything from you, *then* you have to become empty of yourself, he corrects this inverse order by adding the words 'vornehmlich aber von dir selbst', thereby putting the self-emptying ahead of every other kind of renunciation. Gandillac gives an even less accurate translation of this phrase, and then glosses over the rest of the passage to produce a smooth, but inaccurate translation. In both the translations of Tritsch and Gandillac, the self has to go out from everything, including its very self. In Ivanka's version, however, the reference to renouncing oneself is absent. The resulting translation connects renunciation of creation with ecstasy and excludes all reference to the extraverted movement of going out of oneself as also a kind of purification; instead going out of oneself becomes the consequence of renouncing creation. One begins to see how writers like Cordero and Lucien-Marie and others could conclude that the 'via negativa' is inherently linked with the flight from creation, depending on the translation they happened to read.

The original intention of pseudo-Dionysius seems to be an extraverted movement whereby the self passes from an intellectual attempt to grasp God to an emotional one. Ivanka himself notes this[7], but is so clearly predisposed to see spirit/sense dualism in pseudo-Dionysius that he can not integrate this insight into the way he translated the Greek texts. The real nature of the ecstatic movement becomes clearer when the theme of 'eros' is introduced and is placed in a christological context, namely in *Divine Names*, ch. 4, section 13 (712 A):

Ivanka: "Die göttliche Liebe ist aber auch ekstatisch, da sie den Liebenden nicht mehr sich selbst angehören lässt, sondern dem Geliebten. Und das zeigt sich auch darin, dass die höheren Wesen durch ihre Fürsorge den niedrigeren angehören, die gleichgeordneten durch ihr Zusammenhalten (einander), die niedrigsten aber durch göttliche Rückwendung zu den ersten (den höheren angehören). Deshalb sagt auch der grosse Paulus, als ein von der göttlichen Liebe Besessener und teilhabend an ihrer ekstatische Gewalt, mit gottbegeistertem Munde: "Ich lebe, aber nicht mehr ich, sondern es lebt in mir Christus." (Gal. 2,20). So spricht er als ein wahrhaft Liebender, der, wie er selber sagt, aus sich heraus zu Gott getreten ist und nicht mehr sein eigenes Leben, sondern das des Liebenden als ein überaus geliebtes lebt."

The roles of eros is central to the dynamism of pseudo-Dionysius' mysticism. One wonders therefore why Ivanka leaves out almost all the passages on 'eros' in his translation of pseudo-Dionysius (sections 11, 12, and most of 14 in ch. 4, *Div. Names*). The difference between pseudo-Dionysius and later mysticism, such as John of the Cross, lies here. A similar idea regarding ecstasy occurs, too, in John of the Cross. But with this difference — it is connected with spirit/matter dualism. Thus, he adds, after expressing a thought similar to the one above: "The soul lives more where it loves than in the body it animates" (*Canticle* 8,3). This statement paraphrases the biblical texts of Mt. 6,21 and Lc. 12,34: "Where your treasure is, there will your heart be, too." (This phrase was a common saying in the spiritual literature contemporary with John of the Cross.) What is noteworthy here is that pseudo-Dionysius makes no reference to the soul living more where it loves than in the body. In fact, it would seem as if he were rather indifferent to the whole spirit/body issue. For that matter, so are the biblical texts cited above, too. This indifference becomes even clearer in the passage where pseudo-Dionysius raises the question whether 'eros' is spiritual or bodily: *Divine Names*, ch. 4, 15 (713 B).

Ivanka: This section as well as all the rest of ch. 4 is simply left out of Ivanka's translation. He explains that these concluding sections in ch. 4 are a long discourse on good and evil. This does not justify excluding them, however. These texts are crucial because precisely here pseudo-Dionysius states his positive attitude toward matter, the body, nature, etc.

Tritsch: "Lasst uns den Eros verstehen als sei er göttlich, als sei er ein Engel, als sei er ein Leib, als sei er ein Geist, oder als sei er eine geistleiblich sehnende Seele. Lasst uns ihn auch verstehen als die einigende Kraft der Schöpfung".

Gandillac: "Par désir amoureux, qu'on parle de celui qui appartient à Dieu, ou aux anges ou aux intelligences ou aux âmes ou aux natures, nous entendons une puissance d'unification et de connexion, qui pousse les êtres supérieurs à exercer leur providence ..."

Greek text: "Τὸν ἔρωτα, εἴτε θεῖον, εἴτε ἀγγελικὸν, εἴτε νοερὸν, εἴτε ψυχικὸν, εἴτε φυσικὸν εἴποιμεν, ἐνωτικήν τινα καὶ συγκρατικὴν ἐννοήσωμεν δύναμιν ..."

The translation by Gandillac implies the following; since 'erotès' can be both spiritual beings (angels, spirit, intelligence) as well as bodily ones (physical or natural beings), eros itself must be a force of union in all of creation. Tritsch's translation takes a little too much freedom with the text. He renders "εἴτε νοερὸν, εἴτε ψυχικὸν, εἴτε φυσικὸν" with 'geistleiblich sehnende Seele', which is more of an interpretation of the text than a translation of the text. He furthermore translates 'ton erôota' with 'eros', which is not entirely correct; pseudo-Dionysius refers here to 'erotès' in the plural, not to the abstract noun 'eros'. Tritsch's translation would make it seem as if pseudo-Dionysius were saying that eros can be understood both as body or spirit, *as well as* a force of union. Gandillac's translation says that because 'erotès' can be both spiritual and bodily beings, eros itself must surpass this distinction by being above spirit/body dualism. At this point pseudo-Dionysius introduces the concept of eros as a dynamic force of union. In the rest of chapter four he further develops on this dynamic view of eros and makes no further mention of whether eros is bodily or spiritual. Despite Tritsch's intentional option against dualism, it is Gandillac's translation which best reveals the anti-dualistic attitude of pseudo-Dionysius, simply because it is a more faithful rendition of the original text.

120

How could Ivanka leave out such a central body of texts as the second half of chapter four? The clue is still his predisposition to think of mystical union as occurring between man's spirit and God: "Die mystische Einigung vollzieht sich dadurch, dass der Geist nicht nur die Sphäre des Sichtbaren und des Vorstellbaren, sondern auch die des *Denkbaren* hinter sich lässt..."[8]. It should have read, "... sondern auch die des *Geistlichen* hinter sich lässt." This is illustrative of Ivanka's tendency to translate 'nous' with 'intelligence' or 'thought' whenever pseudo-Dionysius says that God is above the spirit, 'nous'. This seems contrary to the original intention of pseudo-Dionysius, who interchanges 'nous' with 'pneuma' with the same lack of regard for philosophical distinctions, or rather indifference to them, as his attitude toward eros shows.

The difference between John of the Cross' view of the force of love for God and the view of the Areopagite is the way John of the Cross connects this theme with the subjection of man's sensual nature and his rejection of love for anything else but God (*Ascent* III,28,6; *Night* II,11,4; *Canticle* 30,1). In order to underline the positive attitude of pseudo-Dionysius toward matter, and the body in particular, it is necessary to contrast the frequent reference which John of the Cross makes to Wisdom 9,15 ("The corrupted body weighs down the spirit.") to the complete lack of this text in pseudo-Dionysius. Rather the Areopagite states: (*Div. Names*, 4,27-28, 728)

Tritsch: "Noch weniger ist das Böse in den Körpern ... Aber nicht einmal für die Seele ist der Körper eine Ursache des Bösen (obwohl man dies häufig sagen hört).

Gandillac: "Le mal n'appartient pas non plus aux corps ... Que le corps d'autre part ne soit pas pour l'âme la source de son mal, c'est chose évidente ..."

Tritsch: "Nicht einmal das sprichwörtlich gewordenes Urteil der Menge ist wahr, das Böse beruhe in der Materie, sofern sie die Materie sei (und als solche den Geist herabziehe). Auch das Nur-Stoffliche nimmt Anteil an Ordnung, ist der Schönheit fähig, und seine Form kann Sinn ausdrücken ... Sobald man aber auch noch daran erinnert, dass die Materie für Aufbau und Vollendung des Weltganzen notwendig ist — wie kann dann irgend jemand noch behaupten, die Materie sei ein Übel?
Darauf wird gewöhnlich erwidert, die Materie schaffe zwar nicht selbst Bosheit in den Seelen, ziehe aber die Seelen zum Bösen hin. Wie kann das richtig sein? Viele Seelen richten doch Blick und Sinn nach dem Guten? Das wäre nicht möglich, wenn schon die Materie selbst unbedingt zum Bösen hinzöge ... Zuletzt der Einwand, dass die Menschen den Lockungen der Materie blind zum Bösen folgen, sobald es ihnen nicht gegeben ist, sich auf sich selbst zu besinnen, und dass die unbeständige Materie ihnen unentbehrlich sei. Sollte also das Böse notwendig sein und das Notwendige ein Übel?" (728 D - 729 B)

(Gandillac's translation, which will not be given here, agrees generally with that of Tritsch, except that what Tritsch puts between parentheses is not in the original text but rather is his own interpretation of the text.)

Tritsch: "Er werde uns nach unserem Erdenleben, unserem ganzen Wesen gemäss – unsere Seelen, sage ich ausdrücklich, samt unseren mit ihnen wesenhaft verbundenen Leibern – in ein vollkommenes Leben versetzen und in die Unsterblichkeit."

Gandillac: "... et, ce qui est plus divin encore, il (God's love) nous promet de nous transférer tout entiers (je veux dire corps et âme unis) à la vie parfaite et à l'immortalité" (*Div. Names*, ch. 6,2 (856 D).

What these texts show is pseudo-Dionysius' positive attitude toward the body and toward matter, in contrast to his contemporaries and also in contrast to John of the Cross. In the text quoted above it is God's love, eros, which gives immortal life to both man's soul and body. The Areopagite's views on eros as a dynamic force which surpasses spirit/body dualism account for his extraverted and cosmological mysticism in which all levels of creation are attracted by God's love back to Him. This is quite different from the mysticism of introversion which pits the 'outer' world against the 'inner, spiritual' world:

Tritsch: "Zu ihm strebt alles Geschaffene entsprechend der Natur jedes Einzelnen empor und vereinigt sein Streben mit allen anderen Einzel-Eroten zum höchsten umfassenden Gesamteros." (*Div. Names*, ch. 4, 16; 713 C)

In this passage pseudo-Dionysius presents his vision of a hierarchy of 'erotès' which encompasses all of creation, *Div. Names*, ch. 4, 15 (713 B):

Tritsch: "Lasst uns ihn auch verstehen als die einigende Kraft der Schöpfung, als die allverbindende, als die allvermischende Macht, als den heiligen Anreiz, der alle höheren Wesen treibt, dass sie die Fürsorge für Schwächere übernehmen, der die Gleichartigen lockt, dass sie enger zusammenwirken, in heiligem In-und Miteinander, und der die Schwächeren zur Hingabe an die Höheren verleitet und ihnen die Hinkehr zu den übergeordneten süss erscheinen lässt ..."

(Gandillac's translation, for purposes of conciseness, will not be given where Tritsch's translation more or less agrees with it.)

Thus the preceding quotations should make it clear that the 'via negativa' of pseudo-Dionysius in no way implies a rejection of matter, of the body or of creation, but rather surpasses these distinctions due to its erotic dynamism. A short review of some modern commentators on pseudo-Dynosius reveals, however, that the predisposition to denounce pseudo-Dionysius along these lines is strong.

J. Bernhart[9] traces the medieval theme of the 'seelengrund', the equivalent of the a-historical center of the soul in John of the Cross, to pseudo-Dionysius' text 'kuklike eis heauten eisodos' (*Div. Names*, ch. 4, 9; 705 A). This text, which has already been discussed, describes the inward movement of the soul, a circular movement. In the original text the connotation of a pure spirit withdrawing from the created world is absent. Rather, what pseudo-Dionysius seems to intend is a movement of concentration of the soul's forces from distractions toward unity. As the rest of that passage makes clear, the straight movement of the soul attains unity by an outward movement. In an article of Ivanka, to be discussed later, the origin of the 'seelengrund' will be traced back to Augustine and not to the Areopagite. Another author, M. Walderman[10] maintains that pseudo-Dionysius did not know the love of a personal God; rather 'eros' is directed only toward the abstract philosophical concepts of the good and the beautiful. The text already quoted from *Div. Names* ch. 4, 13, describing Paul's love for Christ, clearly contradicts this accusation. Most of the reproaches against pseudo-Dionysius concentrate on this point, namely the supposed lack of a personal God in his scheme of things. Hence R. Roques, the well-known commentator on pseudo-Dionysius, states:

"Nous chercherions en vain chez Denys une doctrine du Maître intérieur, présent au plus intime des âmes, d'une présence directe, agissante, amoureuse. Et cette absence n'est pas entièrement rachetée par le pneumatisme, pourtant très généreux, qui anime de haut en bas et de bas en haut tout l'échelle hiérarchique ... D'abord le contact unitif de l'âme avec son Dieu n'apparaît qu'au terme d'une dialectique négative extrêmement rigoureuse, dont il n'est d'ailleurs pas le fruit. C'est à dire qu'il doit être extrêmement rare et bref. Il n'est accessible qu'à une catégorie de chrétiens privilégiée et particulièrement forte."[11]

It is true that the theme of the inner Teacher is absent in pseudo-Dionysius; that is a theme more appropriate to Augustine. What is not accurate, however, is the accusation that no personal God acts directly and lovingly on the soul. On the contrary a text from the *Divine Names* clearly refutes this reproach: ch. 4, 14 (712 C)

Tritsch: "In diesem Sinne nennen ihn die Verfasser Heiliger Schriften liebenswert und zur Liebe uns anreizend, und nennen Ihn schön und gut. Aber sie nennen Ihn auch Ursprung – oder Personifizierung – der Liebesleidenschaft und der Liebesfürsorge ..."

Gandillac: "Mais enfin que veulent dire les théologiens lorsqu'ils appellent Dieu tantôt désir et charité, tantôt digne d'un amoureux désir et d'une aimante charité? De l'amour il est la cause et, en quelque façon, le producteur et l'engendreur.... C'est pourquoi on l'appelle à la fois Aimable et Désirable, parce qu'il est Beau-et-Bon, Désir et Amour parce qu'il est une puissance qui meut et qui entraine vers lui."

Greek text: "Ταύτη δὲ ἀγαπητὸν μὲν καὶ ἐραστὸν αὐτὸ καλοῦσιν, ὡς καλὸν καὶ ἀγαθόν· ἔρωτα δὲ αὖθις καὶ ἀγάπην, ὡς κινητικὴν ἅμα καὶ ὡς ἀναγωγὸν δύναμιν ὄντα ἐφ' ἑαυτὸν ..."

As usual, Tritsch adds his own interpretation to the text, i.e. 'Personifizierung', a word which does not appear in the original Greek text. Nevertheless Tritsch seems to have drawn the logical conclusion that the source of love must in some way be personal and active in attracting creation toward him.

Furthermore, what Roques says about the unitive contact with God being reserved to a small elite, and then only after a very rigorous dialectic, leaves the whole theme of eros out of the discussion. In pseudo-Dionysius the force of eros clearly attracts all of creation, even the lowest beings, to the Father of all. What Roques refers to here, rather, is pseudo-Dionysius' description of the spiral movement of the soul, which attempts to reach God through a dialectic of reasoning. But the whole context of that passage, already quoted and discussed (*Div. Nom.* ch. 4,9) makes it clear that this whole rational approach is less adapted to attaining God than the direct movement, which rejects the use of reason for the dynamism of love.

Perhaps the most negative evaluation of pseudo-Dionysius is that of J. Vanneste, who maintains that the mystical theology is purely a philosophical construction, with no basis in any experience[12]. This view echoes that of Lucien-Marie. Here Ivanka, on the contrary, sees a positive point in this objective approach of pseudo-Dionysius:

"... griechisch (ist) auch die Weise, in der diese mystische-intellektuale Gotteserkenntnis nicht auf die subjective Innerlichkeit des persönlichen Erlebnisses beschränkt wird."

"... was sich jedoch nicht in der Steigerung ihrer persönlichen subjektiven Kräfte äussert (wie es doch zweifellos etwa der Fall ist bei Chrysostomus, Gregor von Nazianz, Hieronymus und Augustinus), sondern in einer die ganze Subjektivität übersteigenden Schau, die sie zum Werkzeug einer fundamentalen und fontalen Anbetung macht."...

"... er war darin noch für die Hochscholastik − und gerade für den diskreten Objektivismus des Aquinaten − das unentbehrliche Gegengewicht zur quellenden Subjektivität Augustins."[13]

J. Stiglmayr[14] nevertheless calls attention to the fact that pseudo-Dionysius does refer to the subjective experience of the 'touches of the divine' (*Div. Names*, 7,3; 8,3 and 9,2). It is precisely these 'touches' which John of the Cross will comment upon as being the highest personal experience of the divine. It is perhaps Stiglmayr's evaluation of pseudo-Dionysius which comes the closest to grasping his thought. He makes the astute observation that there is a kind of cleavage between the works of pseudo-Dionysius on the celestial and ecclesiastical hierarchies, on one hand, and his mystical works on the other hand. He recognizes a definite christological trend in the former works more than in the later ones; Christ is the co-fighter in the battle whereby the image of God is restored in man[15]. In the mystical works this theme is absent, as Ivanka notes[16]. Stiglmayr says that the Middle Ages had so distorted this idea of restoring the image of Christ that it came to mean the unmaking of the image of creatures in man. In pseudo-Dionysius restoring the image of Christ means eliminating the dispersion of the soul's forces in multiplicity, so that God's light can unite the soul and help it to climb upward. God is not found in some purely spiritual center of the soul; on the contrary God is 'hyper noun', above the spirit (*Letter* 1)[17]. Under the influence of the divine light creation becomes transparent, a mirror of divine wisdom (*Div. Names*, ch. 1,3). What Stiglmayr leaves out of the discussion is the idea which pseudo-Dionysius develops that all levels of creation ('erotès') help each other to reach the divine eros. Thus, despite his general good grasp of the original intention of pseudo-Dionysius' christology and his mystical theology as a whole, even Stiglmayr makes one statement which the texts of pseudo-Dionysius seem to contradict:

"Die Passivität der menschlichen Seele in mystischen Erlebnissen ist übermässig betont und die bewusste Mitwirkung des Geschöpfes in den höheren Stadien so gut wie ausgeschaltet."[18]

Here Stiglmayr refers to the outpouring of the divine light as a sort of mechanistic action of God. This conception seems in contradiction with what pseudo-Dionysius says about the active participation of the 'erotès' on all levels of creation in bringing creation back to union with the 'Gesamteros', the Father of all (cf. the text already quoted from *Div. Nom.* ch. 4, 15; 713 B). In fact, what is most striking in the study by Stiglmayr is precisely the fact that there is no mention of the central role of 'eros' in mystical theology. This might possibly be due to the fact that Stiglmayr concentrates his attention mainly on the works, *The Celestial Hierarchy* and *The Ecclesiastical Hierarchy*, and not on the mystical works.

Summary: What is the 'via negativa'?

From the fore-going it is now possible to say what the 'via negativa' in pseudo-Dionysius is, or more important, what it is not. It is the way to experiencing God's transcendence by recognizing the inability of the human intelligence to grasp God, and by striving to approach this transcendent God through cooperation with the force of the divine eros which penetrates all of creation and attracts it to the source of all eros, the Father of all. Just as God is not spirit, as we might understand it, so, too, God is not eros, as the human understanding might picture it. Rather the divine 'eros' is so different from the human conception of 'eros' that what man considers eros to be is but a shadow, a defection, of the divine eros (*Div. Nom.* ch. 4, 12; 709 C). In this ecstatic experience of the 'Gesamteros', the Christian is caught up in the love of Christ and lives, not in himself, but in Christ. This movement toward union with God is not one of introversion, but rather an extraverted, ecstatic movement of the whole cosmos. Neither matter, nor the body, not the desires for material or created goods impede this ecstatic movement. The problem now arises, however, what does impede this movement toward unity with the divine? Why do so few Christians attain to mystical union? This is the lacuna in the thought of pseudo-Dionysius which must now be closely examined.

C. The root cause of the distortion of the 'via negativa'

How did the distortion which Stiglmayr mentions come about, namely that

125

the Middle Ages came to interpret the struggle to attain to the likeness of Christ as a struggle to eliminate the image of creatures in man? How could this dualistic interpretation be read into what pseudo-Dionysius says about the 'via negativa'? The argument to be developed here is that pseudo-Dionysius did not offer a sufficient explanation for the fact that so few Christians reach mystical union. His reflection on sin is too limited, too optimistic. This left a void or a lacuna, which later ages came to fill up with ideas from Augustine. Thus one encounters in pseudo-Dionysius no hamartiology which could act as an opposing force to the views of Augustine which later came to dominate the general tendency of western mysticism. J. Gross, in his monumental study of the doctrine of original sin, *Entstehungsgeschichte des Erbsündendogmas*[19], shows that in the Syrian background of pseudo-Dionysius no reflection on original sin had developed. Indeed he recounts that when the Syrians heard for the first time of Augustine's teaching on original sin, their reaction was one of shocked disagreement:

Isaac of Antioch: "Denn es gibt Auswärtige, welche lehren dass der Mensch keine Freiheit des Willens habe, dass es vielmehr Gott sei, der diejenigen rechtfertige, die ihm gefallen . . . Abtrünniger, Sohn der Hölle, so genau hast du Gott erforscht?"[20]

Gross states that the logical place for a reflection on sin in the writings of pseudo-Dionysius should have been at the end of chapter four in the *Divinis Nominibus*, where he does raise the question whether the force of the divine eros also extends to the demons; what is there in creation which impedes the attraction to union with God? Pseudo-Dionysius, in keeping with his general optimism, states that nothing in creation can impede union with God, since the soul is free to chose its course of action. The problem then arises, as to what is evil, and he concludes that evil is lack of being:

"Böse ist nur Mangel, Abwesenheit, Schwäche, Unordnung, Ungleichgewicht, Irrtum, Zielverwechslung oder Ziellosigkeit, etwas Ungekonntes, Misslungenes, Unschönes, Sinnloses, Geistloses, Lichtloses, Lebloses, Liebloses, Unfruchtbares, Unstetes, Unbestimmtes, Ungesetzliches, Unbegrenztes, Kraftloses oder Träges, das in keiner Weise aus sich selbst etwas ist — ein Nichtwesen schlechthin" (*Div. Nom.*, ch. 4, 32; 732 C-D).

"Böse ist nur die Unfähigkeit, Eigenschaften zur Vollendung zu entfalten, die naturgemäss gegeben sind und entfaltet werden sollten: dies ist für die Natur ein Übel" (*Div. Nom.* 4,26; 728 C).

In a few other texts pseudo-Dionysius does speak of such matters as purification, sin, perfection, cleansing from sin, and evil: *Celestial Hierarchy* III,3; *Ecclesiastical Hierarchy* II,1,3; 3,4-7; III,3,1 & 7. In these texts purification means bringing the soul back from the multiple to the 'one'. Man's many thoughts, desires, etc. must be brought back to a unity. It lies in man's free will to perfect his inner 'one', which was implanted in man's nature at birth[21]. As L. Bouyer[22] has pointed out, purification in this sense does not mean 'apatheia', which is based upon the idea that the soul is disordered and that these disorderly passions or desires must be put back into order. Dionysius rarely mentions desires, disorderly or not; rather he speaks of 'Unverstand', ignorance, or erroneous desire. He expressly says that the soul is free to decide its own course of action, since matter can not impede it. Purification is doing away with ignorance by a return to the 'one', in order to open the eye of the soul to divine illumination.

Gross concludes:

"Beim unserm angeblichen Paulusschüler findet sich, so können wir schliessen, kaum eine Spur jenes Sündenpessimismus . . . Ein Abgrund aber gähnt zwischen dem areopagitischen Optimismus und dem augustinischen Erbsündenpessimismus."[23]

In view of the fact that Augustine's concept of evil as a lack of being is rather similar to that of pseudo-Dionysius, due to their mutual neo-Platonic roots[24], Gross concludes that the pessimistic teaching on original sin by Augustine must come from Manichean elements and not from neo-Platonism, which considered multiplicity as the central impediment to the 'One'. Gross postulates that the optimism of pseudo-Dionysius was meant to be a reaction against Manichean pessimism regarding matter. Many very thorough studies have been made on Augustine's development and his views on original sin[25]. It is not the point of this inquiry to determine what Augustine thought on the matter, but rather to try to determine which elements in Augustine's teaching John of the Cross came into contact with and how they influenced him. Once this connection between Augustine's views and John of the Cross has been established via a historical study, to be presented in the following section, it will be possible to see how the 'via negativa' became distorted with certain dualistic concepts in the thought of John of the Cross.

D. Augustine's influence upon John of the Cross

As already mentioned in chapter one, several contemporary commentators on St. John of the Cross have pointed out that the starting point for understanding the dualism present in his writings is the doctrine of original sin, attributed to the influence of Augustine upon his theological formation:

"Finally, that pessimism which exudes in the pages of St. Augustine which makes us regard with distrust all that which is the own work of man, and that which sprang in the Doctor of Hippo from the importance given by him to grace in opposition to that which Pelagian and his satelites took away from it; this full-fledged pessimism exudes also, although extremely dissimulated, in the works of John of the Cross, and I do not doubt about its augustinian origin."[26]

For reasons which will be discussed in this section it is very difficult, however, to prove that John of the Cross ever read any of Augustine's works, except for short selections from *The City of God* and other scattered texts which had been incorporated into the breviary homilies of the Carmelite liturgical Office. No extensive study has ever been made, to the author's knowledge, of Augustine's influence upon John of the Cross. What follows in this section is therefore for the most part the author's own explorations into the issue, aided by the few existing studies on the matter. Since the author is not a historian, the method to be pursued consists mainly in a study of doctrinal and textual similarities, with a few historical notes.

1. *Peter Lombard: one indirect source.*

The Carmelite scholar, Efrén de la Madre de Dios, has devoted some attention, 'en passant', to Augustine's influence upon John of the Cross. He states:

"Perhaps his favorite Father was St. Augustine, . . . if anyone influenced St. John of the Cross besides the books of the Carmel, it was St. Augustine."[27]

Efrén attributes this influence to an indirect source, Peter Lombard's *Sentences.* Due to an ancient tradition, the *Sentences* were still being taught at the University of Salamanca at the time John of the Cross studied theology there in 1567-1568. The Statute 12 of Salamanca at that time states:

"In the chairs of theology from prime until vespers they are to read the four books of the *Sentences* of the Master, as the Constitution orders, in this way: that they read the parts of St. Thomas the first year from the first question until fifty 'de angelis'. . ."[28]

Crisógono explains this statute by stating that it was the practice to read first the subject matter prescribed by the Statutes, then subsequently the professor would give a critical exposition of the subject matter[29]. Thus Lombard was first read, then commented upon via Thomas' commentary on the *Sentences*. Since the *Sentences* dealing with 'de angelis' occurs only at the beginning of book two, of the four books, it is clear that first-year theology students only studied book one of Lombard, second-year students studied book two, and so forth.

In book one of the *Sentences,* which John of the Cross must have studied, one finds a discussion of man's three faculties (intelligence, memory and will) and their relationship to man's ability to know the Trinity. Since this element from Augustine's *De Trinitate* is indeed incorporated in the works of John of the Cross, to the dismay of the Thomists, Efrén's standpoint in this issue seems substantiated. Peter Lombard did indeed play a mediating role between Augustine and John of the Cross.

On the other hand, Augustine's doctrinal views on original sin and man's

128

fallen state are treated only in book two of the *Sentences* of Lombard, which John of the Cross never studied at Salamanca because he stopped his theological studies there at the end of the first year. This is a particularly important point, since if he had studied book two along with Thomas' commentary on Lombard, he would have been exposed to Thomas' correction of Lombard's and thereby of Augustine's views on man's fallen nature. Gross points out that Thomas considerably mellowed Lombard's views, substituting a more optimistic view under the influence of pseudo-Dionysius' writings:

"Im Gegensatz zum Lombarden lehrt Thomas nachdrücklich, dass die sittliche Wahlfreiheit, kraft welcher der Mensch Gutes oder Böses tun kann, durch die Sünde zwar verschlechtert, keineswegs aber aufgehoben wurde. (*Comm. Sent.* II, d.28, q.l., a.a. ad. 2) ... Aus eigener Kraft, ohne Gnade, vermag der Mensch viele gute Werke zu verrichten, jedoch keine verdienstlichen ... Dem bereits stark angeschlagenen Erbsündenpessimismus Augustins versetzt Thomas den Todesstoss mit der These von der wesenhaften Unveränderlichkeit der Natur, die durch die Sünde nur des ihr hinzugefügten Gutes, keinesfalls aber ihrer sittlichen Fähigkeiten beraubt wurde."[30].

This explains why John of the Cross, despite his theological training, could have been unexposed to Thomas' revision of Lombard's and Augustine's views. The biographer Bruno de Jesús María surmises that John of the Cross probably had the time and the opportunity to teach himself more theology when he was rector of the Carmelite College at Baeza (1579-1582), where he came into frequent debate with the professors of theology at the University of Baeza[31]. A close inspection of the accounts of these debates, however, suggests that not dogmatic but exegetical matters were the topic of discussion.

This lack of an exposure to Thomas' commentary on book two of the *Sentences* is further suggested by John of the Cross' own treatment of the problem of sin and man's fallen nature. In Book II, d. 31, Lombard states 'Idem non habitat peccatum in anima, sed in carne', quoting Augustine in *Contra Julianum* (ch. 4 and 9), adding a discussion of the active and passive effects of sin upon the soul. This discussion is taken up by Thomas who states, as Gross has already mentioned, that man's nature is unchangeable; being created in God's image it must necessarily retain that image even after the Fall. John of the Cross, however, as Bendiek states (cf. section 1, chapter one) condemns human nature, considering it incapable of attaining to God, even after redemption. In practically the only reflection which John of the Cross makes on human nature explicitly (*Canticle* 23,2), he states that with the Fall human nature was ruined and corrupted.

A further study of Lombard's discussion of original sin brings one interesting point to light; where Lombard speaks of sin's effects, John of the Cross substitutes the word 'desires', making all desire equivalent to sin. Indeed in the discussion of the various degrees of sin (*Ascent* I,9,1-4), John of the Cross states that the soul, in order to come to divine union, must be free from all desire of the will, howsoever slight. This signifies, for all practical purposes, that there is no desire of the will which is not some kind of sin. Man's will, even after baptism, is totally perverted. This treatment of human nature and sin suggests, at the most, an auto-didactic study of book two of *Lombard's Sentences*, and no acquaintance with Thomas' commentary on it.

But the problem of Augustine's influence upon John of the Cross is more complicated, due to the extreme asceticism which John of the Cross develops from the idea of original sin. Where did he get his inspiration for an asceticism which is more extreme than anything found in Augustine's views? How could the so-called 'augustinian pessimism' lead to John of the Cross' statement that the soul must be purified *of* all its desires and not *in* its desires? The theory to be advanced here is that this radicalization of Augustine's views came from a typical Carmelite source, namely the primitive Rule of the Carmel itself, *The Book of the Institution of the First Monks*.

2. *The Book of the Institution of the First Monks.*

In a study of the possible contact which John of the Cross might have had with this *Book*, the primitive Rule of the Carmel, O. Steggink[32] points to the obvious fact that John of the Cross must have read it during his noviciate since upon profession in 1564 he had received permission to follow the primitive observance. All his biographers and commentators are convinced that John of the Cross had read the *Book of the Institution*.

This *Book* is of central importance because in it are set down the four sorts of desires which the Carmelite monk must renounce: 1) all possessions, 2) the desire of the flesh, 3) contact with the world, especially women, and 4) love of oneself and of ones neighbour when this is not based upon love of God. In dealing with the desire of the flesh, chapter four in *The Book* reviews briefly the teaching derived from Augustine about concupiscence as original sin:[33]

"Behold, I was conceived in iniquities, and in sins did my mother conceive me (Ps. 50,7). It is from this original sin in which man is conceived that it happens that the flesh of man 'lusteth against the spirit' (Gal. 5,17) . . . Therefore, my son, if you wish to be perfect and to arrive at the goal of the eremitic monastic life and to drink of the torrent there: 'Go towards the East', namely, against the original cupidity of the flesh . . . Wherefore, 'if any man will come after Me, let him deny himself and take up the cross daily and follow Me' (Luke 9,23) 'Whosoever doth not carry his cross and come after Me, cannot be My disciple' (Luke 14,27).

If you wish, therefore, 'to come after Me', 'towards the East', that is, against the original cupidity of they flesh, listen how you must carry the cross . . . Just as anyone who is already crucified cannot move or turn his members anywhere as he should wish, but clings immovably just where the executioner has fixed them, likewise must you, to be crucified, be so fixed and deny yourself that you turn your will not to what my will has bound you; so that 'you may live the rest of your time in the flesh, not after the desires of men, but according to the will of God" (I Peter 4,2).

In chapter six the monk is instructed to aim at the highest degree of perfection by following the first two commandments. Those who become attached to any creature become as abominable as it. In a further exposition on this point chapter seven states that all fleshly desires are completely opposed to the love of God. When the monk has no other desire than God, then only is his heart free from sin. Here therefore is the source for John of the Cross' view that desires for creatures and the desire for God are completely opposed. It is this typically Carmelite source which leads him to develop his radical views on asceticism, proceeding from an extreme concept of the implications of original sin and concupiscence. This explains how he can arrive at an asceticism which is more radical than anything found in Augustine, while nevertheless under the influence of Augustine's views on sin, and their interpretation under the influence of Gregory the Great.

3. Gregory the Great.

Although the intellectual and spiritual formation of John of the Cross is beginning to become clearer, at least as far as his ascetical views are concerned, his views on the mysticism of introversion have yet to be explored. There is strong evidence that his particular formulation of the mysticism of introversion comes only indirectly from Augustine, through the influence of Gregory the Great. At about the time John of the Cross was beginning to observe the primitive Rule of the Carmel, around 1564, he was also studying at the University of Salamanca. He was enrolled as a student of philosophy from 1564 to 1567. Students finishing their philosophy course and wishing to be admitted to the school of theology had to write and defend a thesis. The earliest biographer of John of the Cross, Jesús María Quiroga in 1628, stated: "He mixed together with the scholastic material which he studied (at Salamanca) particular reading of mystical authors, especially St. Dionysius and St. Gregory."[34] Quiroga maintains that he obtained this information by consulting fellow students of John of the Cross who were still living. These fellow students testified, according to him, that John of the Cross had written a thesis on the true nature of contemplation in defense against deviations of his time, probably the illuminists. That thesis has been lost, unfortunately, but Quiroga states that his defense of it was considered excellent.

Although until recently some commentators on John of the Cross considered this story of the lost thesis to be the product of Quiroga's fantasy, a study[35] by Matias shows that candidates wishing to be admitted to the school of theology at Salamanca did indeed have to write and defend a thesis. Therefore there is no immediate reason to doubt what Quiroga states about it, and also what he says about the readings in Dionysius and Gregory.

The biographer, Crisógono, considers it more than likely that John of the Cross read Gregory the Great's primary mystical work, *Moralia in Job*:

"It is not possible to doubt that the author of the *Spiritual Canticle* had read the *Moralia*, which was passed from hand to hand then among all spiritual persons as an excellent code of perfection."[36]

He also maintains that John of the Cross' mode of doing biblical exegesis was like that of among others, St. Gregory:[37]

"That is because his exegesis is generally symbolical in the manner of Saint Augustine, St. Ambrose and St. Gregory and not as exaggerated as that of Origen and Clement of Alexandria . . . a continuation of the patristic exegesis of the best times."

Crisógono attempts to establish certain textual similarities between some passages in *The Spiritual Canticle* and the *Moralia*. What is of interest here is the correspondence which he notes between Gregory's formulation of the 'via negativa' and that expounded by John of the Cross:

Moralia 5,66: ". . . quia nimirum mens cum in contemplationis sublimitate suspenditur, quidquid perfecta conspicere praevalet, Deus non est." (PL 75,746 A)

Moralia 5,62: "Hanc nimirum substantiam cum animus cogitat assuetus rebus corporalibus, diversarum imaginum phantasmata sustinet. Quae dum ab intentionis suae oculis abigit manu discretionis, postponens ei omnia, jam hanc aliquatenus conspicit. Quam si necdum quid sit apprehendit, agnovit certe quid non sit." (PL 75, 713 C; 75, 509-76, 782)[38]

R. Gillet, in his article on Gregory the Great in the *Dictionnaire de Spiritualité* makes several observations on Gregory's mysticism which are especially germaine to the discussion. He mentions three themes which characterize Gregory's mysticism: the agnosticism of love, the agnosticism of faith and the impediment which the corruptible body forms to union with God[39]. God is perceived through faith (*Moralia* 16,54, PL 75, 1147b): "Nam et qui jam eum fide tenent, adhuc per speciem ignorant." Also *Moralia* 16,55, 1148b: "Etsi jam Deum per fidem novimus, qualiter tamen sit ejus aeternitas . . . non videmus." *Moralia* 10,13 PL 75, 927d: "Per amorem agnoscimus."

These elements of the 'via negativa' are tied in here with a dualism of spirit/matter. The participation with the divine occurs in the 'mens' the apex of the soul, a term which Gregory uses frequently[40]. The text from Wisdom 9,15 ('The corruptible body weighs down the soul'), which was so frequently employed in the dualistic scheme of John of the Cross is used here, too (cf *Moralia* 10,13; *Moralia* 8,50; 30,53); owing to the influence of Augustine.

The study which throws the most light upon the relationship between

Gregory the Great and the way the 'via negativa' became associated with the mysticism of introversion is that by B. Aubin, "Intériorité et extériorité"[41]. This study is a close inspection of the dualism of interiority/exteriority in the *Moralia in Job*. A calculation of the frequency with which Gregory uses these two terms reveals that he refers to interiority 1459 times and to exteriority 1027 times. Aubin attributes this dualism to the influence of Augustine, but adds that Gregory surpasses even Augustine in this respect. He uses the term 'interior' to describe the soul, the heart, wisdom, the divinity, Christ, the church, and the kingdom of heaven. He uses the term 'exterior' to describe evil, life, concupiscence, desire, and man. Aubin indicates at least 24 texts in the *Moralia* where the dualism of interiority/exteriority is tied in with the dualism of body/soul. Furthermore, he notes 39 texts where original sin is associated with the interior/exterior theme. In the *Moralia*, Christ is described as coming to recall man to the interiority which he lost with original sin. It is due to original sin that man's desires are turned to the exterior world.

What is striking in the vocabulary of Gregory the Great is that the symbol of 'darkness', so typical of pseudo-Dionysius' 'via negativa', has a completely different meaning in Gregory. For pseudo-Dionysius darkness ('skotos') is the abode of God; it is a divine darkness in which man experiences contemplation. For Gregory, darkness means the darkness and ignorance of sin. J. Baruzi[42] has made a study of the double usage of the term 'darkness' in John of the Cross, and has discovered that he uses it in the sense of Gregory the Great, i.e. being in sin (*Flame* III,3, etc.), as well as in the sense of pseudo-Dionysius, i.e. a ray of darkness, dark contemplation.

With Gregory the Great's influence upon John of the Cross through the *Moralia in Job* almost all the pieces of the puzzle are in place. In Gregory one sees how a dualistic view of man based upon Augustine's views on original sin is connected with themes like the agnosticism of faith and of love, although the central theme of the via negativa, i.e. the divine darkness, is not present. Only one piece in the puzzle connecting the via negativa with a mysticism of introversion is still missing, namely the final link between the vocabulary of pseudo-Dionysius and the mysticism of introversion. This link is not to be found in Gregory the Great simply because he shows no acquaintance in the *Moralia* with the terminology of pseudo-Dionysius. This missing link is to be found in another source which mediated the influence of Augustine and pseudo-Dionysius together, namely the apocryphal work attributed to Augustine, the *Soliloquia*.

4. *The pseudo-Soliloquia.*

It was the biographer Crisógono who drew the most attention to the indirect influence of Augustine upon John of the Cross through pseudo-Augustine, the unknown monk(s) or cannon(s) of the 13th century who wrote three works which are usually published together: *Meditationes, Soliloquia*, and *Manuale*[43]. The apocryphal *Soliloquia* (not te be confused with the authentic *Soliloquia* of Augustine himself, PL 40, 863-898) is a devotional work which weaves together various popular motifs from Augustine and many well-known passages from the psalms used in the liturgical Office. Among these sayings adopted from Augustine one finds quotations from the authentic *Soliloquia*, the *Confessiones, De Trinitate*, etc. The tone of the work is highly emotional and pathetic, stressing man's misery in his fallen state. This work is important because, of the five times which John of the Cross cites Augustine, two refer explicitly to the apocryphal *Soliloquia* and two mention passages which occur in this *Soliloquia* as well as the authentic works of Augustine. Only one other quotation from Augustine occurs which can not be traced back to the apocryphal *Soliloquia*. Not even Crisógono went into much detail concerning this influence of the *Soliloquia* on John of the Cross, and therefore it is necessary to take up the matter where he left off. These five explicit quotations from Augustine are very unusual in the works of John of the Cross because he almost never cites an author by name nor does he refer very often to any specific book of another author:

"... St. Augustine, talking with God in the *Soliloquies* said: 'I found Thee not, O Lord, without, because I erred in seeking Thee without that wert within.' " (*Canticle* stanza 4) (*Solil.* ch. 31) (Although a similar idea occurs in the *Confessions*, bk. X, ch. 27, nowhere does exactly this quotation occur.)

"St. Augustine, talking with God in the *Soliloquies* said: 'Miserable man that I am, when will my littleness and imperfection be able to have fellowship with Thy uprightness? ...' " (*Ascent* I,5,1) (*Solil.*, ch. 2; also in the authentic *Soliloquia*, cf. Migne PL vol XL,866).

"And it is to be observed that, as St. Augustine says, the question that the soul puts to the creatures is the meditation that she makes by their means upon their Creator." (*Cant.*, stanza 4, exposition; stanza 5, expos.) (*Solil.*, ch. 31) (also found in *Confessions*, bk. X, ch. 6).

"St. Augustine said to God: 'Let me know myself, O Lord, and I shall know Thee.' " (*Night* I,12,5) (*Solil.*, ch. 1) (Also in the authentic *Soliloquia* I, ch. 2).

The only time John of the Cross cites Augustine without using a text found in the apocryphal *Soliloquia* is a paraphrase of *Sermo. IX de Verbis Dom. in Ev. Math*, in fine:

"For, as St. Augustine says, love makes all things that are great, grevious and burdensome to be almost naught." (*Night* II, 19,4) (not in the *Soliloquia*).

Although it is difficult to determine just how John of the Cross came upon such an obscure text, the possibility exists that this text, just as all the direct quotations which John of the Cross takes from Gregory the Great, comes from the breviary homilies[44].

The fact that John of the Cross refers explicitly to other authors so rarely (four times to Gregory the Great, four times to pseudo-Dionysius, five times to Thomas, twice to Boethius, and twice to Teresa of Avila) suggests that the apocryphal *Soliloquia* played a very special role in his spiritual life. This hunch is further supported by one more piece of evidence, the testimony of his secretary and closest companion, Juan Evangelista, who maintained that a certain book of St. Augustine was continually in the cell of John of the Cross. It should be recalled here that the quotations from John of the Cross clearly show that he had no idea that the *Soliloquia* were not the work of St. Augustine; the fact that this work was apocryphal was a later discovery.

The statements of the secretary, Juan Evangelista, O.C.D., made over a period of years in letters and testimonies to the Apostolic See, show some interesting inconsistencies which suggest an attempt to conceal the exact title of this work of St. Augustine; presumably because it was suspected by the Spanish Inquisition:

"He (Juan Evangelista speaking in the third person) never saw any books in his cell save a Bible, a volume of Saint Augustine and a Flos Sanctorum." (Ms. 12,738 f⁰ 981) (According to A. Peers: "This document appears to be an incomplete draft of a deposition prepared for the Beatification process."[45])

"He was very fond of reading in Holy Scriptures, and I never once saw him read any other books than the Bible (almost all of which he knew by heart), a certain Father Augustine, *Contra Haereses*; and the Flos Sanctorum." (Ms. 12,738, f⁰ 559) (trans. MM) (Written to the Fathers Definitors of the Consulta for the Beatification process.)

". . . Saint Augustine, *Contra Gentes* . . ." (Ms. 12738, f⁰ 37, Málaga).

"I never saw him open a book, nor had he one in his cell, save a Bible and a Flos Sanctorum, for he always read the life of each saint upon his festival." (Ms. 12,738, f⁰1431; letter to Fr. Jerónimo, an early biographer, dated 1630) (Juan Evangelista was at that time 68 years old.) (trans. MM)

"Being a learned man, he (nevertheless) did not have any books in his cell except for a Bible." (Ms. 8568, f⁰115) (MM) (1630 A.D.)

These statements of Juan Evangelista are odd in several respects. First of all, considering that Augustine did not write any book whatsoever called either *Contra Gentes* or *Contra Haereses*[46], but rather *De Heresibus*, and further taking into account the fact that the subject matter of *De Heresibus* is a description of 4th century heresies, it seems most unlikely that John of the Cross would have been so enthralled by its contents that he would have continually had it by him for his spiritual inspiration, his 'livre de chevet'.

When one examines the final deposition which Juan Evangelista wrote for the Beatification process (Ms. 12738, f⁰559) one sees that in fact he did not say that St. Augustine wrote *Contra Haereses*, but rather that 'a certain Father Augustine' (text: 'un padre Augustín') wrote it. It has been the oversight of the biographers of John of the Cross that they ignored this slight nuance between f⁰559 and f⁰981 (perhaps because many of these biographers were Frenchmen with no knowledge of Spanish); they have always assumed that the author of the '*Contra Haereses*' was indeed Augustine, the Bishop of Hippo. As to the other fictitious title, *Contra Gentes*, which Juan Evangelista attributes to St. Augustine; the mere fact that this secretary, who, too, was a learned man, could so easily interchange titles suggests that something foul is afoot; he was trying to lead his inquisitioners astray. The fact that the rough draft, f⁰981, was more precise about the name of the author and less precise about the name of the book in question is also noteworthy. This suggests that f⁰981 was the least contrived version; the attempt to cover up the real title came later. This also perhaps explains why Juan Evangelista in his later years dropped all mention of both St. Augustine and the book in question altogether. The subject matter was too hot.

The remaining question is, therefore, which book of St. Augustine might have been suspected by the Spanish Inquisition of heresy? M. Bataillon mentions in his study, *Erasmo en España*[47], no book of Augustine which was suspected. He does, however, mention that the *Soliloquia* of pseudo-Augustine contained what could be called heretical views. He states that this book was of capital importance because it stressed certain themes of the Reformation: man can not do anything without grace (ch. 15). Stressing predestination, the book states that even the prayer of those who are predestined to condemnation becomes a sin (ch. 25). Chapter 31, which is particularly pathetic, could be construed as supporting the Reformation. Because it affirms predestination with force — the elect are protected by the omnipotent hand of God to such a point that all they do is turned into good, even the sins they commit (ch. 25) — it was highly questionable. The question arises, however, why did John of the Cross not hesitate to cite the *Soliloquia* so explicitly if it was under suspicion? The answer seems to lie in the fact that up until about 1588 the Inquisition had concentrated its attacks mainly on illuminists. Only in the later index of G. Quiroga in 1588 is explicit mention made of books which through either the negligence of the authors or through the malice of heretics, could be used to support the opinions of the 'enemies of the faith', meaning groups of Lutheran sympathizers discovered in Seville and Valladolid. Another motivation for placing some books on Quiroga's index was the 'unsuitable use of the vernacular language', i.e. translations into Spanish[48]. The Spanish translation of the *Soliloquia* had already gone through five editions in the first half of the sixteenth century. The last one was made by the Spanish Jesuit, Rivadeneyra, at Medina del Campo in 1553. After this translation no others appeared, suggesting that from that time on the *Soliloquia* in the Spanish version was under suspicion. The fact that John of the Cross refers to it as the '*Soliloquios*', i.e. the Spanish title, and not as the *Soliloquia*, the Latin title, shows that he was familiar with it in the Spanish version, either the one of Rivadeneyra or one of the earlier ones. It is not unlikely that either during his humanistic studies under the Jesuits at Medina del Campo from 1559-1563 or during the Carmelite noviciate from 1563-1564 at Medina del Campo, John of the Cross could have come into contact with the Spanish version and then have continued to read it later on in life.

The evidence suggests that if the *Soliloquia* was prohibited, then it must have occurred some time much later than the time during which John of the Cross was still alive and writing. The Index of G. Quiroga contains no reference to either the *Sololoquia*, or the other two works with which it was usually associated, the *Manuale* and the *Meditationes*. No book of Augustine is mentioned either, except for Erasmus' version of Augustine's *Confessions*[49]. Since the Apostolic inquiries into the sanctity of John of the Cross began early in the seventeenth century, it would seem plausible that the *Soliloquia* might have been on the Index of 1614 and that for this reason the secretary of John of the Cross took so much trouble to hide its influence on him. The author, who was unable to find a copy of the Index of 1614, leaves it to the historians to investigate this matter further.

Assuming therefore on fairly reasonable evidence that the book of Augustine which John of the Cross always had in his cell was probably the apocryphal work, the *Soliloquia*, particular attention can now be paid to its content. The testimony of Juan Evangelista says that the other two books which he kept in his cell were works which he read very often and regularly: he knew the Bible almost by heart and he consulted the Flos Sanctorum on the feast day of each saint. It seems therefore most likely that the other book in his cell, i.e. the *Soliloquia*, was also a book which he read often and regularly. This seems highly probable, too, considering its meditative or devotional content; it is the kind of book which allows a continual re-reading for devotional inspiration. M. Bataillon suggests that this was one of the favorite popular books of devotion used by the masses in Spain, as a reaction against the decline of the quality of preaching, which had become either too abstract and scholastic or too infantile[50].

The main importance of the *Soliloquia* in the spiritual and intellectual formation of John of the Cross lies in the way it combines the vocabulary of pseudo-Dionysius' 'via negativa' with several themes of Augustine's and Gregory the Great's mysticism of introversion. Here, too, one finds the frequent use of Wisdom 9,15 ('The corruptible body weighs down the

137

spirit'.) in connection with a frequent reference to concupiscence and the misery of man's fallen state, especially in chapters 12 and 21. In his fallen state man is in a prison (ch. 23). All man's hope and desire should be in God (ch. 23); God keeps watch over man's desires (ch. 14).

In several of the thirty-seven chapters in this book the theme of 'darkness' occurs, used in the sense of Gregory the Great, namely the darkness of sin, and *not* in the sense of the darkness of contemplation: chapters 3,4,6,10,11,12,13,15,16,17,26,29, and 33. All these chapters dwell on the contrast between the darkness of sin, ignorance, concupiscence, the devil and death, on the one hand, and the light of God's illumination on the other hand. In chapter 28, however, an interesting deviation occurs, where the symbol of the 'cloud', so typical for the 'via negativa' enters the discussion:

"Nam et secundum legem quam dedisti patribus nostris in igne comburenti montem, et in *nube tegente aquam tenebrosam*, quicquid tetigerit immundus, immundum erit."

This reference to Psalm 18,12 is highly significant because John of the Cross incorporates it into his description of contemplation. The difference between his use of the symbol of the cloud and that in the *Soliloquia*, is that in the *Soliloquia* God communicates with man in a cloud which covers the dark waters of man's impurity. This same thought is repeated in chapter 33:

"Sero te cognovi lumen verum, sero te cognovi. Erat autem nubes magna et tenebrosa ante oculos vanitatis meae."

In John of the Cross the cloud of darkness is precisely the abode of God's wisdom; it is dark, not so much because of man's sin but because the light of God transcends man's natural understanding:

"So immense is this spiritual light of God, and so greatly does it transcend our natural understanding, that the nearer we approach it, the more it blinds and darkens us. And this is the reason why, in Pslam xvii, David says that God made darkness His hiding place and covering; and His tabernacle around Him dark water in the clouds of the air. This dark water in the clouds of the air is dark contemplation and Divine wisdom in souls, as we are saying." (*Night* II,16,11)

It should be mentioned here that the *Moralia* of Gregory the Great did not mention the 'cloud' in this sense. The only reference to the cloud in the *Moralia* which illumined the flight from Egypt (book 2, ch. 35,57) refers to the darkness of sin, not the darkness of contemplation. The cloud in this passage, however, is connected with one very important theme in both the *Soliloquia* and in John of the Cross, a theme lacking in pseudo-Dionysius: the illumination through faith. In the *Moralia* the cloud illumines the night through faith. This same theme is worked out also in the *Soliloquia*, but in a somewhat different way; whereas for Gregory faith is the way of unknowing, a kind of blind faith, in the *Soliloquia* faith is belief in the articles of the Creed, as will be shown.

The chapter in the *Soliloquia* which John of the Cross makes the most use of is chapter thirty-one, and with good reason; here precisely is the connection made between Augustine's introverted mystical experience and the 'via negativa' and the illumination through faith. The dwelling place of God is within man, who was made in the image of God; this is the theme which is worked out in chapters 19,20,27 and 30 in the *Soliloquia*. This is further elaborated in chapter 31, where this interior image of God is contrasted with exterior things, where God is not present:

"Ego erravi sicut ovis quae perierat, quaerens te exterius, qui es interius. Et multum laboravi quaerens te extra me, et tu habitas in me, si tamen ego desiderem te. Circuivi vicos, et plateas civitatis huius mundi, quaerens te et non inveni, quia male quaerebam foris quod erat intus."

There follows a long description of how the soul searched for God through the use of its senses, seeking the Creator in the creatures. The soul then states that God illumined it whereby it could know God. At this point the soul asks how it could be possible that it knows God, since God is incomprehensible? There follows a long list of negations, which echo the negations found in the *Mystical Theology* of Dionysius:

"Tu quippe solus Deus . . . quoniam super omnem essentiam intelligibilem, et super omne nomen quod nominatur, non solum in hoc saeculo, sed etiam in futuro superessentialiter et superintelligibiliter esse dinosceris, quoniam superessentiali et occulta divinitate, super omne rationem, intellectum, et essentiam, inaccessibiliter, et imperscrutabiliter habitas in teipso ubi lux inaccessibilis, et lumen imperscrutabile et incomprehensibile et inenarrabile, . . ."

Such negations are repeated again for several lines. The soul then resolves its dilemma by stating that it knows God through the grace which came through Christ and through faith. Chapter 32 is a continuation of this thought, in a review of the content of that faith, namely the Creed, which is presented in full.Thus faith here is not the blind faith of Gregory and John of the Cross, but the adhesion to a body of doctrinal teachings. Chapter 33 then develops the theme of illumination through faith in these revealed truths.

This investigation into the indirect influence of Augustine upon John of the Cross does not pretend to be complete. Something could still be said about the augustinian tendencies in the teachings of, for example, Baconthorpe, the Carmelite theologian whose works were required reading in the carmelite College of St. Andrew at the time John of the Cross studied there[51]. Perhaps the dualism between spirit/sense and Creator/creation could also be traced back to the influence of popular spiritual writers of his time, particularly Bernardino de Laredo's *The Ascent of Mount Zion* and F. de Osuna's *Third Abecedario*[52]. However, since this study does not pretend to be a historical investigation, and since the evidence that John of the

Cross read these works is so indirect and obscure, it seems sufficient to restrict this study to the most likely sources of his theological and spiritual formation. Very little has been said of the influence of Thomas Aquinas because so much attention has been paid to this aspect in past studies, and also because precisely that point under consideration, namely the 'via negativa', plays such a small part in the body of Thomas' writings[53]. As to the possible influence of Tauler, Ruysbroeck, Eckhart and other mystical writers, the evidence that John of the Cross ever read them is more conjecture than anything else; since other studies have dealt in great detail with such matters, there is no need to touch upon them here.[54]

II. JOHN OF THE CROSS' SYNTHESIS BETWEEN PSEUDO-DIONYSIUS AND AUGUSTINE:

It is not difficult to reconstruct the intellectual and spiritual forming whereby John of the Cross came to read pseudo-Dionysius through the 'eyes' of Augustine. The fact that he was familiar with the writings of pseudo-Dionysius is attested to by the statement of Quiroga that he had read St. Dionysius during his student years at the University of Salamanca. Textual evidence, namely the four times he quotes pseudo-Dionysius also supports this alleged acquaintance with pseudo-Dionysius (*Ascent* II,8,6; *Night* II,5,3; *Canticle* 14,16; *Flame* 3,49). In addition to this, he quoted pseudo-Dionysius in conversations. Doña Ana de Peñalosa testified that he had quoted pseudo-Dionysius' statement that it is love which leads to ecstasy.[55] To Eliseo de los Mártires he quoted pseudo-Dionysius saying that to cooperate with God in the salvation of souls is the most divine work.[56] Eulogio de la Virgen del Carmen in an article in *Dictionnaire de Spiritualité*[57] comments that in the *Ascent*, chapter 9, where he discusses the 'via negativa' John of the Cross uses even the same biblical passages as those cited in the *Mystical Theology*, chapter 1, of pseudo-Dionysius. Eulogio goes into a thorough comparison of parallel teachings in the writings of John of the Cross and pseudo-Dionysius. What is lacking in his study, however, is a close examination of their divergences. Some attempt has already been made in section B of this chapter to point out the central deviations, but these and other points will be dealt with further here, in a brief review of certain key issues.

A. The starting point: the doctrine of original sin

Whereas pseudo-Dionysius seems to consider multiplicity as the central impediment to divine union, John of the Cross concentrates most of his attention on the desires as the root cause of this impediment. This is based upon a pessimistic view of man's corrupted will, which he probably formulated under the influence of Peter Lombard and *The Book of the Institution of the First Monks*. The reason why John of the Cross could read this pessimistic view on man's perverted will into the teachings of pseudo-Dionysius is because pseudo-Dionysius offered no counter view on the exact nature of sin. John of the Cross fills up this vacuum in the pseudo-Areopagite's teaching with a view of man's misery in his fallen state (the *Soliloquia*), his absolute inability to perform any good without grace (again the *Soliloquia*), and the doctrine of original sin which he obtained from Lombard and *The Book of the Institution*, plus its extension to a spirit/matter dualism (Gregory).

With this background of ideas, John of the Cross then comes to understand what pseudo-Dionysius says about God not being like anything created as implying that a rivalry must exist between desires for creation and desires for God, between sense and spirit:

"... it is clear from the very fact that the soul becomes affectioned to a thing which comes under the head of creature, that the more the desire for that thing fills the soul, the less capacity has the soul for God; inasmuch as two contraries according to the philosophers can not coexist in one person-.. affection for God and affection for creatures are contraries ... for what has the creature to do with the Creator? What has sensual to do with spiritual?" (*Ascent* I,6,1)

The fact that pseudo-Dionysius also states that God is not like spirit completely escapes the attention of John of the Cross. Furthermore, he overlooks the fact that the ideal of apatheia is absent in pseudo-Dionysius; no special mention is made in the pseudo-Areopagite's writings about directing all one's desires to God; rather the accent is upon participating in the attractive power of the divine 'eros' which penetrates all of creation. All levels of being are 'erotès', i.e. forces involved in attracting lower beings to the divine eros. The cosmological unity of movement toward God is almost completely lacking in John of the Cross; in the *Spiritual Canticle* he concedes that creatures can reflect God's handwork, but he states clearly that creatures can not lead the soul to God.

The result of this double dualism between desire for creation vs. desire for God, and the dualism of spirit/matter is that pseudo-Dionysius' instruction about not trying to reach divine union through intellectual reasonings is placed within a dualistic context: it seems to imply the rejection of all forms in prayer because they are 'sensual'. The 'via negativa' then comes to imply the striving for a purely 'spiritual' prayer. Hereby the highly positive attitude of pseudo-Dionysius toward matter and the body is completely left out of the picture. Furthermore the important role of Christ in the 'via negativa', i.e. the focus of the ecstatic experience, is overlooked. Thus, Christ seems to have no role in such a purely 'spiritual' prayer form.

In fact, John of the Cross has the same blind spots as Ivanka, i.e. he reads pseudo-Dionysius the same way Ivanka reads him.

B. The radicalization of the 'via negativa'

It has already been briefly mentioned in section A that John of the Cross maintains that neither man's reason nor his affections are able to attain to God since man can neither think nor reason about God as he really is nor can man love God as he should be loved. In contemplation man is passively enlightened in his intellect and passively infused with divine love. All man does is practice the theological virtues, but these in turn act by 'divinizing' man's faculties, supplanting their human functions with divine functions. In the radicality of this viewpoint John of the Cross introduces the element of passivity, an element lacking in the thought of pseudo-Dionysius, where man participates in the attraction of the divine eros, just as all levels of creation participate in it. A brief discussion must be made at this point of the problem of epistemology in regard to mystical experience, since the problem of passivity/activity is connected with the issue of knowledge.

Pseudo-Dionysius:
Ivanka, in reviewing the basic anthropological views of pseudo-Dionysius, observes that the idea of the soul being essentially divine is absent in his system:

"... in der Lehre vom Wesen der Seele die Idee ihrer wesenhaften Göttlichkeit, wonach sich die Erkenntnis Gottes auf die im Seinsgrunde der Seele bewahrte Identität mit Gott gründet, zugunsten einer Lehre aufgegeben hat, die nich einmal sosehr die Gottebenbildlichkeit der Seele betont, wenn sie die übervernünftige Erkenntnis Gottes in der Einigung mit ihm erklären will, als die Göttliche und vergöttlichende Kraft der Liebe, die Gott der Seele mitteilt, um ihre Erhebung zu ihm zu ermöglichen."[58]

The result of this viewpoint is that pseudo-Dionysius makes no use of any concept like the 'center' of the soul, i.e. the point of encounter between God and man. The level of the emotions is the level at which the mystical union occurs. As already shown, the problem of whether love (eros) is corporeal or spiritual is a matter of indifference to pseudo-Dionysius.

Augustine:
In contrast with pseudo-Dionysius, Ivanka points out the presence of such themes in Augustine's view of knowledge:

"Das eigentliche, geistige Wesen der Seele besteht in ihrer Zuwendung zu Gott, der Fähigkeit zur Erkenntniss Gottes . . . Diese Fähigkeit bestünde aber nicht, die Zuwendung des Willens zu Gott im Glauben, die die Seele für die Erkenntnis bereit macht, wäre nicht möglich, wenn ein Funken dieser Erkenntnis nicht unverlierbar im Wesen der Seele bewahrt bliebe (De Trinitate bk. 14, 4,6)."[59]

Ivanka shows how this view of an essential spark of knowledge of the divine in the center of the soul is connected with the whole framework of the mysticism of introversion: the basic concepts of turning inward, rejecting sense and sensual imagery (*De Trinitate* bk. X, 8,11) and turning the will to God in order to become like God (*De Trin.*, X,5,7). Thus here in Augustine one finds the origin of the epistemological system of John of the Cross. Here, too, the dualism of spirit/body is the underlying motif. Augustine says:

"Certainly, they would not labor under such difficulties in understanding this, and scarcely arrive at anything certain, unless they were enveloped in a penal darkness, and burdened with a corruptible body that presses down the soul (Wisdom 9,15)."[60]

Here, therefore, is the starting point for the spirit-body dualism which John of the Cross adopts, even using the same scriptural reference again and again, as already said.

Peter Lombard:
Just as in the problem of original sin, what is involved is not so much what Augustine thought on the matter but which aspects of his thought John of the Cross came into contact with. One important intermediary, as already discussed, between Augustine and John of the Cross was Peter Lombard. The issue of epistemology is dealt with in Book I, dist. III of his *Sentences*: 'How the creatures can know God.' This section relies exclusively on Augustine's *De Trinitate*. It teaches that there is a trace of the trinity in creation (*De Trin.* bk. X). The image of God remains in the mind, which is the best which is in man and is therefore capable of God. The mind is like the trinity in its three faculties; intellect, will and memory. The mind is incorporeal (*De Trin.* bk. XIV, 7 & 8; bk. XV, 7). The mind is like the trinity, not because of its three functions as such, but because it can apply these functions to the creator (Bk. XIV). At this point the main divergence with John of the Cross comes to light, namely here the faculties are active, whereas in John of the Cross they are passive under the action of the theological virtues.

Thomas Aquinas:
As already mentioned in section (D), first-year theology students had to study Lombard's *Sentences* together with Thomas' commentary on them. At the passage in Lombard mentioned above, Thomas makes a correction of Lombard, and also of Augustine. Drawing upon chapter one in the *Divine Names* of the pseudo-Areopagite, Thomas adds that even the incorporeal mind is not like God and can only know him through created 'fantasmata'. Since God can not be fantasied as he really is, not even the

143

incorporeal mind can know God. We know God by the influence of the divine light, which does not make use of fantasmata. This essential aspect of mystical theology was later to be incorporated into the teaching of John of the Cross, but within the augustinian anthropological framework of a 'center' of the soul and its three faculties. In resolving problems caused by combining these two traditions (Thomas and Augustine), John of the Cross came to differ with Thomas on one point. Thomas agreed with Lombard that the image of God is in the mind ('intelligibilis') and not in man's sensuality. (Since he considered the memory as being sensual, however, it could not be the image of God. Hence the reduction to a two-faculty scheme.) Thomas responds to the objection in pseudo-Dionysius (*Cel. Hier.*, ch. 6) that even the intellect does not belong to this image, by saying that human reason partakes of the divine intellect darkly. Thereby it can ascend to God via the creatures (quoting *Divine Names*, ch. 7). It was precisely at this point that John of the Cross departed from Thomas and followed another route.

In the *Spiritual Canticle* John of the Cross agrees that the soul can discern traces of God in creatures, but adds that these traces can not lead the soul to God. He quotes as his authority, not pseudo-Dionysius but (pseudo-) Augustine in the *Soliloquies*: 'I found Thee not, O Lord, without, because I erred in seeking Thee without that wert within.' The consequences of this standpoint have already been discussed. The problem remaining is why this insistence upon man's inability to know God via any action or created intermediary? In Augustine, Lombard and Thomas it is man's actively seeking intellect which can know God, although darkly and in an enigma.

Aristotle:
The main problem which John of the Cross had to resolve was how to retain the augustinian anthropological framework of his epistemological system while at the same time incorporating the aristotelian axiom, 'Nihil est in intellectu quod prius non fuerit in sensu' (quoted in the *Ascent* III,3,2). Trueman-Dicken outlines briefly the problem involved[61]. For Augustine, all intellectual activity was purely spiritual communication, whereby the intellectual activity of the incorporeal mind bypassed the senses. The idea of immediate intellectual perception came under fire when the views of Aristotle were introduced in the west. The problem such an axiom causes for the epistemology of mystical experience is, how can what is supposed to be purely spiritual communication enter the soul while bypassing the senses? Where or how could purely supernatural communications be communicated to man? Thomas of Aquinas attempted to reconcile Augustine's view with that of Aristotle by re-interpreting the

144

concept of immediate knowledge of God to mean merely reflective knowledge. Ivanka points out that Thomas hereby distorted the original intention of Augustine:

"Wenn Augustin von der unmittelbaren geistigen Selbsterkenntnis der Seele als dem Medium der Erkenntnis der geistigen Welt spricht, so meint er dabei nicht die reflexive Erkenntnis, aus der wir auf das Dasein anderer geistiger Wesen schliessen können, wie es der hl. Thomas auslegt (*Summa* I, q. 88, a.l, ad.1); wenn er von der unmittelbaren Erkenntnis Gottes in unserem Innern als der Voraussetzung jeder Erkenntnis spricht, so meint er nicht nur, dass unser Erkenntnisvermögen eine Mitteilung des göttlichen geistigen Lichtes ist, wie es Thomas erklärt (*Summa* I, q. 88, a. 3, ad. 1). Er spricht vielmehr von einer wirklichen Erkenntnis Gottes im eigenen Innern der Seele die, wenn auch nur keimhaft, so doch im Wesen dasselbe ist, wie die mystische Erkenntnis von Gott und die Anschauung Gottes."[62]

The problem must have been particularly urgent for John of the Cross when he was a student of philosophy at Salamanca. The philosophical training offered there was aristotelian, the Statutes requiring the students to read Aristotle's works in full:

"The regents of Summulas are to read the terms and short logical pieces until Christmas . . . Item, in the second year of logic, from the first of St. Luke's feast day until the end of May they are to read *Perihermenias*, and all the rest of Aristotle's logic . . . From the first of June until vespers in the vacation they are to read the *Physica* of Aristotle. Item, in the third year they are to read *De generatione et de caelo* and all the rest of philosophy."[63]

According to Crisógono, after reading these required texts the professor would then comment upon them, drawing from many sources:

"Aristotelian to the core, the majority of the professors however did not draw back from refuting doctrines of the Philosopher and of St. Thomas, opposing them with platonic elements and even with conceptions of arabic origin."[64]

Considering the wealth of opposing views being taught to him, it is therefore understandable that John of the Cross would adopt an eclectic rather than a purely thomistic viewpoint on epistemology.

Baconthorpe:
As to the content of the studies at the Carmelite college of San Andrés, which John of the Cross attended during the same time he went to Salamanca, Crisogono states that Baconthorpe, the main theologian studied there, was also aristotelian, but at the same time an advocate of Augustine's views:

"It is a teaching which is original on many points. Aristotelian at heart, like all the scholastics, Baconthorpe deduces from the principles of the Stagirite conclusions opposed to those which Scotus and St. Thomas deduce from the same principles. Thus, in the theory of knowledge, without rejecting either the terminology nor the psychological mechanism of knowing which they admit, he comes out with an idea of direct and immediate perception. He only admits mediated knowledge in the order of the senses. Intellectual knowledge, according to Baconthorpe, is immediate and direct."[65]

The influence of Baconthorpe is possibly much greater on John of the Cross than is usually supposed by his commentators. Baconthorpe, too, worked with Augustine's three faculty schema. Crisógono states that the idea of assigning a theological virtue to each faculty was the most original find of John of the Cross. He claims that not Thomas nor any other scholastic had thought of this possibility. But the revised, annotated version of Crisógono's biography edited by Matias includes a reference in the footnotes to Baconthorpe's teaching about the action of two (faith, hope) theological virtues upon the faculties. (He left out the virtue of love.)[66] Confronted with all these varying epistemologies, John of the Cross had the opportunity to work out a solution for himself. As one of the earliest biographers of John of the Cross, Fr. Jerónimo de San José, attests, he was particularly interested as a student in the problem of how God can communicate himself, being pure spirit, to man without going through the senses:

"The part of philosophy which deals with the nature and the properties of the soul, he studied with particular care, trying to understand well its offices and effects in the body; the faculties, organs and senses through which it works. The way it has of understanding in this exile (after the Fall), through dependence on forms and sensible images, which philosophy in the Schools calls phantasms. How these, being material, produce others which are more noble and of a spiritual nature. How the understanding conceives some as dark or obscure and others as clear, forming in the act of understanding a vivid image of the object and the thing understood."[67]

Although today such subjects would be more appropriate in classes on neurophysiology, John of the Cross was clearly interested in establishing a psychological basis for mystical knowledge, using the philosophical concepts of his day. He had to reconcile what he was being taught at the Carmelite college of San Andrés with what he was being taught at the University of Salamanca.

The solution of John of the Cross:
F. Ruíz takes up the problem of John of the Cross' epistemology where Trueman-Dicken leaves off. Ruíz maintains that John of the Cross' solution to the problem of divine communications was through the use of the concept of the 'center' of the soul whose object was God, but whose subjective working depended on the three faculties. The purifying action of the theological virtues must precede the infusion of grace by adapting man's nature to the supernatural. The dynamism of grace and God's presence in the soul through grace in the soul's center make this infusion, or passive experience of God possible (*Ascent* II,4,2). This infusion of grace, in turn, orients the faculties even more toward the supernatural, via the working of the theological virtues upon each respective faculty. Thus the reason behind John of the Cross' radical asceticism in which human

nature itself must be irradicated is his idea that man's intellect must be supernaturalized or divinized before it can receive 'infused' grace. He reasons that for man to experience God's grace in mystical union, man's natural way of knowing via the senses must be radically eliminated and supplanted by a divine way of knowing in which God alone is the agent and man is totally passive.

Therefore any kind of intellectual activity which does not come via the senses is by definition 'passive' or 'supernatural'. Ruíz states:

"For John of the Cross everything is passive which is accomplished without the intervention of bodily sense (*Ascent* I, ch. 9) . . . The saint applies the term 'passive' to favors and graces which no one today would consider as such."[68]

In this way the 'via negativa' became radicalized to mean the denial of man's nature and of creation in general. Here, too, the dualism of spirit/body plays a central role in connection with the doctrine of original sin since it is the idea that a corruptible body (after the Fall) impedes the spirit (Wisdom 9,15) which underlies the distinction between knowledge via the senses and immediate knowledge. The problem of the epistemology of mystical experience is very complex and will not be further discussed here. What is important for this study has already been dealt with, namely the reason why John of the Cross had to resort to such a radical position regarding man's passivity during contemplation. In some respects it is understandable that the Spanish Inquisition would attack him on precisely this point.

Returning back to the original mystical theology of pseudo-Dionysius, the question arises whether he could have avoided this radical standpoint. The fact that pseudo-Dionysius did not work with Augustine's concept of a 'center' in the soul which communicates with God, but rather placed the mystical encounter on the level of eros suggests that pseudo-Dionysius would have found the whole issue of immediate and mediate knowledge a misplaced concern. Rather he might have avoided the whole issue because of his indifference to spirit/sense dualism in the first place. The point which he might have labored upon would then be the way in which love (eros) is a means of knowing God. This approach will be worked out in the following chapter.

Not all that John of the Cross has to say about the 'via negativa' is detrimental. On several points he improved the teaching of pseudo-Dionysius on both the doctrinal level as well as the psychological level. The empirical results clearly show that the role of blind faith is just as central to mystical development as 'unknowing', and in fact seems to be inter-related.

147

In pseudo-Dionysius no mention is made of the role of faith in his mystical works[69]. This is particularly striking, since the 'model' or inspiration for pseudo-Dionysius, namely Proclus, had already come to the conclusion that man was completely unable to come to union with the divine without faith. Proclus was a pagan philosopher, who, unlike his foregoers among the neo-Platonists, was convinced of the complete fallen nature of man and man's inability to come to the divine merely through his own 'eros pronoètikos'. Perhaps as an overreaction to the pessimism of Proclus, pseudo-Dionysius went too far in his optimism about man's ability to love God without help from God's part. From Gregory the Great, John of the Cross seems to have gotten the inspiration for developing the theme of unknowing faith. This find becomes the central doctrinal focus of his teaching through which he can launch a counter-attack on the illuminists and thereby avoid having Christian mysticism degenerate into mere sensationalism of visions, ecstasies, prophecies, miracles, etc. True, he also placed the theme of faith in a dualistic context but that does not take away its positive value in improving the doctrinal content of the 'via negativa'.

In his development of the theme of the 'dark nights' John of the Cross adds another Christian note which was absent in pseudo-Dionysius, namely the salvific role which suffering can have in helping the Christian attain the likeness of Christ. The reason this was lacking in pseudo-Dionysius' mystical works is because he was not describing a salvific route, i.e. the 'via negativa' was not so much the way to redemption as such but rather what Ivanka calls "Erlebnismystik und Gnadenmystik"[70]. It is the great contribution of John of the Cross that he was able to incorporate the 'via negativa' in its essential aspects into a greater redemptive framework. The way he did this will be studied in depth in the following chapter (IV). Perhaps the basic reason why pseudo-Dionysius could not integrate the 'via negativa' into a Christian view of redemption was because of his too-optimistic view of man. He does not offer an adequate explanation for why so few Christians reach mystical union. He develops no theory of what sin is or why human history is imperfect. From Augustine John of the Cross obtains a view of man which recognizes the role of sin in explaining human imperfection and the difficulty man has in attaining to union with God.

From the concept of sin and the need of man for redemption, John of the Cross can then work out the theme of restoring the likeness of Christ, a theme which was lacking entirely in pseudo-Dionysius' mystical writings. It is this personal link between the Christian and Christ which serves as a correction to the metaphysical and objective style of pseudo-Dionysius' cosmological perspective. But unfortunately the influence of Augustine colors this personal dimension to his mysticism, reducing the focus of concern to man's innermost experience whereby the breadth of the original

148

cosmological perspective is reduced, but not entirely lost (cf. *Flame*, 2,10).
It is perhaps this augustinian atmosphere in the writings of John of the
Cross which repelled Teilhard de Chardin because it comes into such sharp
contrast with the breadth and scope of his own vision. It must be observed,
however, that in the last writings of John of the Cross, *The Living Flame of
Love*, he seems to break out of the confines of this too-personal idea of God
and regains something of the original perspective of pseudo-Dionysius, in
which the principle agent in man's divinization is the force of God's love,
rather than the Spouse or the Beloved of bride's mysticism. But here, too,
John of the Cross incorporates this theme into a Christian doctrinal
framework which was missing in pseudo-Dionysius. For the Areopagite,
this force of love (eros) was also described in Scripture in language which
personified it (*Divine Names*, ch. 4,14). But it remained for pseudo-
Dionysius in the first place a philosophical concept, i.e. the attraction
which the good and the beautiful exert upon creation. For John of the
Cross the force of love is the Holy Spirit. In his last writings he develops this
into a whole trinitarian perspective.

In conclusion, John of the Cross emerges from this fore-going sketch as a
true mystical theologian seeking to integrate the aspects of the 'via
negativa' which are supported by experience into a broader Christian
perspective. Unfortunately his main area of concern is out-dated, the
spirit/sense dualism. What remains of value today are the doctrinal points
which he integrated into mystical experience, trying to extend the concept
of redemption to man's psychological development as a whole.

III. CONCLUSION: CONNECTING THE PSYCHO-PHYSIOLOGICAL
AND THE THEOLOGICAL BASIS OF THE 'VIA NEGATIVA'

The content of the special art of the Christian contèmplative can now be
more closely defined. The 'via negativa', or the anti-technique, of Christian
mysticism is the rejection of man's reliance on his own mental or emotional
abilities to reach mystical union. Instead of self-reliance, the 'via negativa'
teaches one to rely on the divine darkness, the divine force of love, the
divine intelligence, in the practice of dark faith. This is an extraverted
attitude, an openness toward receiving something from outside oneself
from a God who is ready to communicate himself to all of creation because,
as pseudo-Dionysius states, good wants to communicate itself, i.e. all that is
good wants to share itself. The 'via negativa' is a highly optimistic view of
the goodness of God and of man's ability to open up to the communicative
God. The basis of the whole system of Christian mysticism is therefore the
idea of God's reciprocity and man's receptivity. The content of the art of

Christian mysticism is not passivity but rather receptivity, or even better, reciprocity. In the act of contemplation, man is busy reciprocating to God's initiative in love.

As the earliest biographer of John of the Cross, Jesús María Quiroga, stated in 1628, the mystical teaching of John of the Cross is directly and purposely formulated as an attack or correction aimed against the many meditative techniques propagated in his day:

> Leaving the opinions and human artifices which were new, he based himself upon apostolic doctrine where St. Dionysius and St. Thomas declare that the understanding of divine things in order to participate in them should not follow the path of similarities with things we do know; rather by the light of faith and the negation of all allegories. And in this manner he exercised in quiet of mind divine contemplation from then on and prepared himself to receive from God the highest gifts of perfection and divine wisdom, which he subsequently communicated to others."[71]

The original purpose of John of the Cross, as stated in *Night* I,8,3, is to instruct those who have used a meditative technique to advantage for some time, but who have arrived at a kind of spiritual plateau. His anti-technique is designed to help such people advance further by teaching them to let go of all techniques. This does not necessarily mean that he rejects techniques; rather he teaches a certain nonchalance in their regard. It is entirely possible that an advanced contemplative could combine the practice of the 'via negativa' with some technique that aids recollection or concentration. The point which John of the Cross seems to want to make is that the final goal is beyond any technique, and to attain such a goal one has to go a way which leaves all technique behind in the end. The technique itself should never become that goal: "In order to come to that which you do not know, you have to go via a way you do not know" (*Ascent* I,1,14).

The conclusion from the foregoing chapter (II) was that apparently two phases exist in contemplation: the via negativa and the via unitiva. This could possibly correspond to what pseudo-Dionysius tries to formulate in his description of the three movements toward God: the circular way, the spiral way, and the straight way. In the circular way, he states that the soul concentrates its attention and force inwardly. This might correspond to the via negativa as the first phase in contemplation. The subject turns his attention away from both inner and outer distractions. This is not a rejection of creation, but merely a rejection of distractions. Secondly, in the spiral way, a certain dialectic occurs between two opposites. Here, pseudo-Dionysius seems to suggest that this dialectic involves reasonings and discursive thought. The data in chapter two, however, suggest that the dialectic involves a spiral movement between two libidinal poles, happy vs. unhappy experiences in prayer. At the end of this dialectic, both the first phase of recollection or rest and the second phase bring the contemplative to a balance or rest in dynamism, to use Eysenck's terms. There can be no ecstasy (ek-stasis) without rest (stasis). The straight movement to God is an ecstatic movement toward the object of union and identification, Christ. What pseudo-Dionysius says here is very appropriate: the subject grasps hold of a symbol which triggers or catalyzes the ecstatic movement.

Although pseudo-Dionysius seems to suggest that these three ways to God are separate paths, they nevertheless seem to constitute the same movement, although in different phases. The data in chapter two show that the first phase continues to play a role in the following phases. The second phase continues until almost the very end, i.e. mystical union. The ecstatic phase, on the other hand, seems to be present, although to a lesser degree, almost from the beginning. Indeed it is the object of identification, the symbol, which sets the dialectic movement off. In simpler language, what seems to happen in contemplation is 1) the forces of the libido have to be concentrated together, 2) the libido is lauched upon a spiral journey toward the object of desire, 3) this momentum attains a certain balance in dynamism, whereby the final thrust toward ecstatic union is possible. The psycho-physiological study concentrated upon the first phase, i.e. rest. The fourth chapter will concentrate upon the second and third phases.

CHAPTER FOUR

Concentration in
Christian Contemplation

"Wie für ihn (John of the Cross) im wesentlichen
das mystische Leben gelebte Dogmatik ist, so ist
auch seine Dogmatik und vor allem seine
Gnadenlehre nichts anderes als ein Stück
theologischer Mystik."[1]

INTRODUCTION: THE METHOD EXPLAINED

1. *Is prayer experience ever 'authèntic'?*

Now that the preceding three chapters have attempted to clear away many
distortions of mystical experience, the time has come to try to formulate
what 'authentic' Christian mystical experience is. This will be done by
following the phenomenological method of H.M.M. Fortmann, to be explained shortly. Before discussing Fortmann's study of prayer, however, a
few comments must be made about his later work. After writing his dissertation in 1945 he then turned his attention to the psychological analysis
of problems which modern man has in regard to traditional religious
themes. He was an intuitive writer, whose mixture of scientific objectivity
and religious conviction might have seemed naive, had he not come to a
reflection upon the appropriateness of what he called a 'second primitivity'
or a second naivete in the psychology of religion. By this he meant the
ability to accept all the criticism of naive religiosity which modern science
has expressed, while preserving an openness to religious insights and
reports of religious experience, as possible sources of truth. This could be
called 'educated naivete'. A concrete example of Fortmann's approach will
be given on pp. 218-219, in his discussion of what lies beyond death.

Twenty years after his dissertation, Fortmann published a reflection on
his method, *Als ziende de Onzienlijke* (trans: as if seeing the Unseeable
(1964-1968)[2]. One could say that he began as a pastorally oriented writer,
dealing with specific problems in spirituality, and worked his way on to a
more general, reflective approach[3]. Fortmann was not primarily a specu-
lative or rationalistic thinker, but rather an intuitive observer of reality with
a rudimentary empirical instinct. The problem which came to occupy
Fortmann, and which dominates *Als ziende de Onzienlijke*, is the problem

152

which any intuitive thinker eventually runs into — how can one be certain if the intuition or the perception is true or false? For this reason Fortmann deals with the whole issue of erroneous perception and projection. When this issue is applied to prayer, the question then becomes — how does one know if one experiences the 'real' God or merely a 'god' of ones own making? Religious experience could arise merely from projection, which has no perceptual basis in reality, but merely interprets reality in function of ones own feelings and tendencies. Fortmann does not work out his own view or definition of projection, but rather restricts his endeavor to criticizing the theories of others (Freud, Jung, Marx) on projection. After forming a rather vague idea of what projection actually is, he then devotes his efforts to distinguishing erroneous perception from projection. Projections are systems closed to perception. Perception, even when erroneous, is dictated at least in part by the reality being perceived. Erroneous perception can be one-sided, rigid and incomplete, based upon the observation of too few data, but it can never be completely dissociated from the reality being perceived[4]. For example, one can mistake a stone for a hare, but that is only possible if the stone resembles a hare, at least at a distance. Participation with the object being perceived is the basis in reality for the perception. In projection, there is no participation with the object.

When applied to mystical experience something of this distinction is discernible. In erroneous mystical perception, the wrong interpretation is given to a real experience. An example of this might be the one given by John of the Cross (*Ascent* II,19): a holy man who has a vision. In this vision he hears the words, 'You will be delivered from the hands of your enemies.' The holy man interprets this to mean that he will escape them, but instead he is killed by them. The vision should have been interpreted to mean that he would escape them by being granted salvation — his enemies were the enemies of his soul, not his immediate persecutors.

A vision can be authentic even though the interpretation of the vision is wrong. For this reason, John of the Cross rejects all visions and prophecies. God can go unconditionally or immediately to man, but man can not receive this divine communication except through his own interpretive processes, processes which are conditioned by man's psychological, cultural and religious perspective. The source of that communication, God, is nevertheless not subject to man's interpretation and can act independently. This seems to be the lesson in the example which John of the Cross gives. God's self-communication and man's participation in it, raises man up to the level of that which made the perception possible, thereby making man surpass himself. In prayer, participation establishes perception. This is the inner logic of the 'via negativa' which makes delusion or projection impossible. As has already been mentioned in chapter three, the central

153

concept of the via negativa is the teaching that the 'light' of man's fantasies, thoughts, emotions or imaginings only obscures the light of God. For this reason John of the Cross insists so strongly that the only way to union or participation with God is on God's own terms, which surpass man's abilities. There is a basic difference between prayer to a 'fantasy god' whom one meets on ones own terms, and prayer in which one is overwhelmed by God on his terms.

In this context it is germaine to note that the most reliable kind of prayer experience in the Questionnaire on Spirituality, described in section one, was mystical union (factor one) (see p. 245 in the Appendix for the factor reliabilities). A most unreliable factor was factor two, which described the inability to pray due to the absence of a feeling of God's presence. Thus in the experiences of the subjects, the absence of the feeling of God's presence was more unreliable than the feeling of God's presence in prayer. This implies that in factor two, the inability to pray, the subject is projecting his own situation onto God. The subject feels absent from God and therefore assumes that God is also absent from him. The inner contradiction is the logical premise that if God does exist, then he must by definition be present everywhere all the time. Therefore the subject's feeling of a lack of participation in God's presence can be a projection, with no basis in reality other than the unreliable inner world of fantasies and subjective impressions. A much deeper study of this matter appears in the dissertation of S. Troelstra, *Geen enkel beeld. Mystieke weg, deprojektie en individuatie bij San Juan de la Cruz* (1977). (Trans: Not any image. Mystical way, deprojection and individuation by San Juan de la Cruz.)

2. *A review of Fortmann's analysis of concentration in prayer.*
Fortmann's dissertation was entitled (translated): *Concentrated prayer — A psychological study of the characteristics, the possibilities and the limits of concentration in prayer.* If Fortmann had stuck to this proposed schema (that is, the limits, characteristics and possibilities of concentration in prayer) his thesis would have been much more cohesive than it actually is. The schema of his dissertation is poorly organized, evidence of an early work. It begins with a short reflection on a much-too-broad subject — the history of the psychological study of concentration in general and the relationship between this kind of concentration and concentration in prayer. After this hasty review, he then narrows his study down to the phenomenology of concentration and distraction in prayer. He touches only briefly upon the basic issue, namely the kind of relationship to God which prayer presupposes. He then devotes a disproportionately large amount of space to describing concentrated prayer behavior. Unfortunately he did not pay the same amount of attention to distracted prayer

154

behavior. The EEG study already discussed in chapter two reveals how important distracted behavior is. The second half of Fortmann's book deals with the inner and exterior factors which influence prayer. He admits the problem which phenomenology has with causality. For instance, one might observe that a subject can not pray when he feels listless. To say that he can not pray *because* he is listless might be false, however. Both listlessness and the inability to pray might be due to a third factor, such as illness. Only an empirical experiment could determine the causal relationship involved here. Fortmann ends his thesis abruptly without tying the various sections together.

Due to the poor organization of Fortmann's dissertation, the author has found it more helpful to follow the hint already contained in the title of Fortmann's thesis, namely to discuss the characteristics, limits and possibilities of concentration in prayer. Since this study goes much deeper into various aspects of prayer, and in fact deals with a different kind of prayer than Fortmann did — contemplation — only some of his observations and intuitions are relevant here. These will be reviewed here because they form the background of the discussion to follow.

3. *The pre-conditions to concentration in prayer.*
The most important product of Fortmann's preliminary reflection upon concentration in general is his conclusion that concentration is not an entity in itself but rather merely the result of complete orientation toward some object, either through reflection or perception. Concentration is the by-product of orientation to something, with a disregard for other things. It is a choice among multiplicity[5]. In order for a person to achieve such complete orientation he must, according to Fortmann, do two things: 1) achieve an inner consistency of aims and values which gives him inner integration or harmony, and 2) then go on to find the adequate or appropriate approach to the object of orientation, by identifying with it. One becomes like that which one contemplates.

These two things are only the final steps toward concentration. They presuppose a few preliminary steps; namely the adoption of a positive attitude toward the object of orientation, the motivation for continuing this positive attitude, and a consequent openness or sensitivity to the general background or field in which this object is placed. When applied to the issue of concentration in prayer, the problem arises that many people are already pre-programmed to relate negatively to prayer because they identify prayer with the required behavior of a 'churchly' set of believers. Many experiences with parents, schools and society have already 'trained' some people to identify the God of prayer with the 'god' of an institutionalized form of Christanity. When these experiences are characterized by parental or ecclesiastical or social pressure the result can be that the person loses all ability to adopt a positive attitude to God based upon a personal and spontaneous choice. This was especially the problem in Fortmann's study because he dealt with forms of prayer which are more closely bound to the formal, institutionalized life of a particular church. The advantage of contemplative or mystical prayer is that its association with any specific church organization is very loose. The object of such prayer is therefore not necessarily the 'god' of an institution. In fact the essence of the 'via negativa' is the concept that God is beyond what man or any human institution might conceive him to be.

Fortmann begins the discussion of prayer by asking, 'How do we experience our relationship to God?' What form does this relationship assume? Is prayer a monologue or a dialogue? Since Fortmann was considering mainly liturgical and formalized prayers, such as the rosary, his answer was that prayer is a monologue. He justifies this by making two categorical statements: 1) Although God may 'listen' to these prayers, the person praying has no way to experience God's listening, and 2) God may answer prayers, but this, too, can not be felt by sense perception. It would have been more accurate of Fortmann to have said that empirical science has difficulty verifying whether God answers prayers, since many interpretations of events are possible, but the person doing the praying can nevertheless state that he has experienced or perceived that God did answer his prayer.

Fortmann goes on to describe prayer as building upon an 'I-Thou' relationship[6]. A contradiction appears here, however. If prayer is a monologue, then no I-Thou relationship could exist. The author suggests that prayer should be classified as something in between a monologue and a dialogue, like a letter. When a person writes a letter, he knows that the person he is writing to is not listening at that moment and he can not be absolutely certain that the person will answer. Yet some kind of inter-relationship must exist between the writer and the person being written to, since otherwise one would not have written the letter at all. In prayer, some kind of inter-relationship with an entity outside oneself is presupposed, since one would not pray at all if prayer were just talking with oneself. This would be like writing a letter to oneself — it is a lot of trouble with no purpose. The comparison with a letter is too limited, however. Prayer includes a wide spectrum of kinds of communication, including non-verbal communication. Perhaps in an I-Thou relationship, the non-verbal communication could include all the various degrees of intimacy present in a love relationship. The question as to whether the I-Thou relationship to God can exist only in a private prayer form or in a communal or group form of prayer is a false dilemma. The private and the public forms of prayer are not categorically opposed, but rather supplementary to each other. The main problem involved, whether in individual or communal prayer, is whether the object of that prayer is God and not some projection or an erroneous perception. In private prayer, the object of prayer should not become ones own 'fantasy god'. In group prayer, the object of prayer should not become the group, but should remain directed in a dialogue to an entity which confronts the group, a God not of ones own making. When the group becomes the object of prayer, then erroneous perception has taken place since the image of God which is present in man, individually and collectively, has been mistaken for God himself. This perception is incomplete, one-sided and rigid, i.e. the characteristics which Fortmann gave to erroneous perception. Fortmann recommends group prayer especially to neurotics, who have greater difficulty in putting their personal problems aside in private prayer.

Fortmann states:

"In the same train of thought one must say that a personal prayer is easier than really joining in with a community or communal prayer. This latter means that one puts ones own needs aside for the sake of the group. And now this is noteworthy, that many neurotics have trouble with exactly this point (putting aside their problems). Probably one could consider this as a real impotence, a lack of expansiveness, and thus one must be very cautious with making moral qualifications. They would willingly be otherwise, they would like to be able to loosen their grip on themselves, but they can not. Their level is too low. Perhaps for such people the more impersonal liturgical prayer is the right means to be able to come to a pure attitude to prayer."[7]

The empirical data presented in chapter two confirm this insight of Fortmann's to some extent. The variable, 'need for group support', obtained from the Scale of Inner-Personal Values, correlated negatively with another variable, 'altruism', from this same scale (-0.52), and positively with neuroticism (0.20) and unhappy emotionality (0.26). Altruism, on the other hand, correlated negatively with neuroticism (-0.30) and positively with contemplative experiences (see p. 265 in the appendix). The variable 'independence' correlated positively with 'need for group support' (0.31) and negatively with altruism (-0.50). As the discussion of this variable 'independence' has already pointed out, independence in this context means the inability to establish intimate relationships. The picture which these data sketch is the following: subjects who are highly independent and who therefore reject intimate relationships, have a need for group support, perhaps because it is more impersonal. They find more ability to lose themselves in the group and in group prayer. Such non-intimate subjects tend to be neurotic and unhappy. Private prayer, and contemplation or mystical prayer, i.e. the prayer of union, is very difficult for them. It presupposes a high degree of dependency, the ability to establish intimate, non-verbal communication, and altruism.

157

Now that the presuppositions of prayer have been dealt with, the three main areas of concern can be discussed: the characteristics of concentration in contemplation (section one), the limits to concentration (section two) and the possibilities of concentration or its goals (section three).

I. THE CHARACTERISTICS OF CONCENTRATION
IN CHRISTIAN CONTEMPLATION

A. *The motive: the pleasure principle, or affective redemption*

In his discussion of the motives for concentration, Fortmann remarks that it is not difficult to concentrate on someone you love. Attention is possible to the degree to which one is attracted to the object. What we are attent to in the loved one is not some abstract quality such as wisdom or friendliness, but his or her person as the bearer of a concrete realization of those qualities. That is made all the more possible because we are confronted in the loved one with a bodily appearance. We can see the loved one, hear and touch him or her. We experience the personal qualities of the loved one in the first place because of that person's 'intruding' presence. Through this sensual perception the abstract values become perceptible to us[8].

It is strange that Fortmann does not go on and apply this same line of reasoning to the I-Thou relationship between man and God. Rather, Fortmann says that the love of God does not exist in the emotions, but in the will to serve and honor God[9]. He defines the 'love for God' as a purely spiritual light, which can resonate or rebound in the affect. But the person praying finds no support in an object which can be perceived by the senses[10]. This line of reasoning seems illogical. How could attention to God and the resonance of God's love in the emotions be possible without any sensually perceptible love? Why should the kind of attention to God be so different from the kind of attention to a loved one? Fortmann does not consider that when the loved one is God, the sensual perception of God's intruding presence is the basis of concentration in prayer. The theological basis for considering the sensual, bodily perception of God's love as a real possibility in prayer is given by E. Schillebeeckx, who says that since the body is the only basis of perception, it is the required point of reference for human consciousness as well, including the way man knows God[11]. This explains the high reliability of the answers of the subjects on the Questionnaire on Spirituality, concerning mystical or contemplative experiences. The subject can remember the prayer experience because his touchstone is the bodily reaction it caused.

The subjects in the most advanced prayer group were asked about their experience of bodily or sensual perception in prayer. The general tendency was to experience sensual or erotic feelings intensely at the beginning of their prayer life. During the intermediate period, the second dark night especially, these erotic experiences were replaced with either feelings of spiritual desolation or, sometimes, peace and rest. In the periods toward the end of the second dark night the erotic feelings recurred, when the experience of God's love lasted for longer periods. One sister was very articulate in expressing the erotic side of prayer, in the beginning stages. Her statements are presented anonymously here:

MM (interviewer): "Some sisters claim that in prayer there is first a moment of intense spiritual contact with God and only afterwards does a bodily sensation or repercussion occur."

Subject: "No, they occur simultaneously . . . In the beginning during prayer it occurred so intensely that I had difficulty to stop praying."

MM: "Was that bodily enjoyment, the whole body?"

Subject: "Yes, you experience in your whole body a feeling of pleasure, precisely as a woman you experience your body. In the beginning I had difficulties because of this, namely that I had very strong sexual feelings. I talked first of all with Fr. X, but he didn't understand what I was talking about. Then I talked with a Father in Rome, who immediately understood what I meant. He said that that was very common, that it was just a repercussion of prayer and that I should not worry about it."

MM: "Thus he had had experience in directing other people who had this problem?"

Subject: "Yes, and I think he also has personal experience with this. He relieved me. In the first place, he said I was not to be worried about it. He told me where I could look it up in John of the Cross. Since I saw prayer as something which I did for God this pleasure was merely adventitious. Before I entered the cloister I had a confessor who made me very worried about it. He said that it was a mortal sin just to give in to such feelings . . . So try to figure out when you give in or not. Now I can laugh about it, but in the beginning I had a terrible time about it. Someone told me that as long as I didn't try to awaken such feelings there was no sin. But just try to pray so that such feelings don't come to the surface! The Father in Rome said not to worry about it. I then tried to pray as attently to God as possible, but the more attent I was the quicker such feelings occurred."

MM: "Was that a stage in a growth process? How is it now?"

Subject: "In the beginning it was very intense but now I experience God's presence in peace and rest. But not the strong bodily repercussions."

MM: "Has the intense experience of God's love also disappeared?"

Subject: "Yes, that is actually true. I no longer have the intense bodily feelings like getting warm and all that sort of thing. No longer."

In the rest of the interview the subject told about how she was currently in a period of spiritual and psychological torment, corresponding to a change from a traditional cloister to a more experimental life style. A follow-up interview about a year later, after the transition had been made, revealed that the experiences of God's love, with the bodily repercussions, had returned.

It was much more difficult to get the older, more advanced nuns to talk about erotic or bodily experiences in prayer, although they did agree that such things occurred. Since none of the male subjects had advanced as far as the top group, no males could offer their observations on this matter. One of the most advanced nuns described erotic experiences in unitive prayer:

Subject: "You can feel yourself really embraced during prayer and you receive something like a kiss, which also has a repercussion in the body — you feel it in your whole body."

MM: "Is the experience of love during prayer the most intense when the bodily repercussion is absent?"

Subject: "I think so, but that is also a growth process. The 'radiation' or repercussion in the body comes afterwards. That is, you get first of all the intense 'touch', then this bodily experience comes after that and is also less important. The first 'touch' goes more to the heart. But I find this distinction somehow artificial. Every 'touch' has a resonance in the body; you just don't notice it anymore."

MM: "How does this relate to your experience of bodily contact in relationships with good friends?"

Subject: "The human 'touch' becomes then a symbol of something holy."

MM: "Would you call this bodily or sensual enjoyment in prayer impure?"

Subject: "Only egoism can make a love relationship impure. This occurs when you try to pull the other down to your level, to take possession of God or of the friend, as the case may be. When you love someone egotistically you put him on a lower level than he really should be. I think that you can only have a truly pure love relationship with a friend, in the sense of non-egotistical, if you also have a very deep prayer life, since that is what really purifies you of egoism. After a very deep 'touch' of God you experience the liberation of God's Spirit which is in you . . . a blooming of the grace which came through baptism and confirmation. Your own spirit is made free in order to make room for the Spirit of God and you become the possession of the Holy Spirit, possessed by the Spirit. The greatest pain is that you can't take others, i.e. friends, with you to experience this. A point always comes when they can't follow me anymore."

It was very difficult to get the other more advanced subjects to talk about the erotic aspect of prayer, or to mention any bodily perception specifically. The most detailed description of the bodily aspect of deep prayer remains therefore the observations of John of the Cross:

"And in this way the soul enjoys here all the things of God. He communicates to it strength, wisdom and love, beauty, grace and kindness, etc. Since God is all these things, the soul tastes them together in one single touch of God, according to its faculties and its substance.

And from this good of the soul at times the unction of the Holy Spirit rebounds in the body and it enjoys according to its sensual part; all its members and bones and marrows — not as weakly as usual but with a feeling of great delight and glory, which you feel even in the tiniest arteries of the feet and the hands; and the body feels so much glory in that of the soul that after its manner it glorifies God, feeling him in its bones . . . And therefore since all one might say of this would be less than it is, it suffices to say, regarding both the bodily as well as the spiritual delight that it tastes of eternal life." (*Flame* II,22)

Returning to Fortmann's observations at the beginning of this section, the remark that through sensual perception of the loved one, abstract qualities become perceptible, applies to prayer, too. The sensual perception involved in prayer, as the above-mentioned quote and the interviews show, is

160

a 'touch', which the body feels and experiences erotically, not just genitally but in the whole body. This bodily and libidinal aspect of prayer is further worked out by A. Vergote in a psychological approach to the phenomenology of mysticism:

"Certainly tradition bases the so-called supernatural order on the natural desire for God. But this desire became conceived of as a metaphysical, intellectualized entity. Its orientation was conceived of intellectually, which was indeed unavoidable within a philosophy which thinks of man according to the order of the theoria.. Let us not forget that the thinking self is secondary; the first self is the bodily self, that is the libidinal self."[12]

"The nature of man is in the very first place not a metaphysical structure with an existential orientation to the transcendental. It is first of all libido, which avoids frustrations and seeks satisfaction in bodily experiences of pleasure. Further it seeks this in cultural values which transform the search for pleasure through language and symbol, without repressing it."[13]

Even Vergote, however, does not draw the logical conclusion, i.e. that bodily eroticism is not sublimated in mystical or religious experience in Christianity. Instead of stating that eroticism is part and parcel of the Christian experience of God, Vergote states:

"The purified recognition of the God-Father of Jesus Christ is, psychologically speaking, a high cultural achievement which demands a far-reaching sublimation of the libido."[14]

Perhaps the problem which both Fortmann and Vergote have with admitting eroticism in the Christian experience of God is due to the fact that both are men and the Christian idea of God is too masculine. The feminine aspect of God, the Divine Wisdom or the Sophia, which would be the correct reference point for a man's libidinal experience of God, has been neglected in western spirituality. For this reason, women rather than men can admit the erotic side of religious experience in Christianity in the west. This will be further elaborated upon on pp. 171-178, in the discussion of bride's mysticism.

Both John of the Cross and pseudo-Dionysius the Areopagite make God the source of erotic desire. The force of God's love reaches out and attracts man's heart to mystical union. This opens a new perspective for dealing with the phenomenon of eroticism in mystical experience. Instead of considering it as a sublimation of unsatisfied human sexual desire[15] the possibility is suggested that the opposite occurs, that is, man projects his unsatisfied desire for God, an erotic desire, onto other objects of desire including man-woman sexual contacts. This all points the way for a future approach to spirituality which is the particular task of the church in a society which is becoming more and more aware of the central significance of eroticism in giving a meaning to life. In his book, *Die Auferstehung des Eros* (1971), K. Ledergerber suggests that new psychological insights show the value of eroticism in healing man: "Liebe im ganzheitlichen Sinn als Quelle der Heilung und des Wachstums."[16]

Ledergerber criticizes the church for emphasizing the restrictions which it places upon eroticism. He pleads for a more positive approach:

"Nicht durch einen Drahtverhau der Abwehr von Exzessen, sondern durch Ziel- und Sinnge-bung eines elementaren, aber noch chaotischen Dranges finden wir das Mittel zu einer neuen Lebensfülle im wahrhaft befreiten Eros."[17]

Here he refers to the church's task in spirituality of freeing eroticism from its captivity in modern society, or what Jung called 'domesticated libido'[18]. He means especially the task which spirituality today has of satisfying an increasing hunger in society for erotic satisfaction, a hunger which Leder-gerber sees reflected in the widespread use of sex in advertisements. He interprets this exploitation of sex as a sign of man's current lack of erotic satisfaction rather than his being super-saturated with it. Such commercial representation of eroticism appeals to modern man and woman precisely because it seems to promise an erotic satisfaction which modern life in fact withholds[19]. In this light recent ecclesiastical pronouncements against erotic excesses have entirely misunderstood the spirit of the times. Instead of repressing erotic excesses, the church would do modern man more of a service by showing him a way to give eroticism a goal, a meaning. Leder-gerber sees it as the future project of Christian spirituality to enlarge the current perspective of psychology regarding love, eros and agape, and to integrate eroticism into the Christian concept of love. He proposes a reconciliation between the ideal of Christian existence, Christ, and erotic-ism. Unfortunately he does not work this reconciliation out.

Before such a reconciliation can occur, the problem regarding erotic satisfaction, the pleasure principle, and altruistic love has to be resolved. The neo-Freudian, N.O. Brown, states the problem:

"The aim of Eros is union with objects outside the self; and at the same time Eros is fun-damentally narcissistic, self-loving. How can a fundamentally narcissistic orientation lead to union with objects in the world? The abstract antimony of Self and Other in love can be overcome if we return to the concrete reality of pleasure and to the fundamental definition of sexuality as the pleasurable activity of the body, and think of loving as the relation of the ego to its sources of pleasure. Narcissistic love is fundamentally a desire for pleasurable activity of one's own body. Our problem then is: How does the desire for pleasurable activity of one's own body lead to other bodies?"[20]

John of the Cross does indeed reflect briefly — too briefly — on the relationship between self-love, pride, and the tendency man has to seek himself even in the pleasurable experiences in prayer. In his early work, the *Ascent*, he attempts to formulate an ascetical teaching whereby the heart becomes purified of this egotistical form of erotic desire by practicing a strict affective asceticism, i.e. rejecting all desires except the desire for God. The problem arises that the heart can also find egotistical pleasure in the experience of God's love. John of the Cross spends the last part of the

Ascent and all of the *Dark Night* in trying to work out a formulation whereby the heart can enjoy erotic pleasure in prayer without becoming egotistical. He comes to the conclusion that God's love has the paradoxical effect of producing erotic pleasure while at the same time purifying the heart of its self-love. Or as Fortmann stated, in affective prayer the libido is 'self-cleaning' because it is less directed to its self[21].

The empirical study in chapter two shows that his first formulation, affective asceticism, bears no relation to mystical advancement. This implies that rejection of erotic pleasure in objects other than God in no way combats self-love. The fact that John of the Cross' statements about the purifying action of God's love in man's heart did indeed correlate highly with mystical prayer development suggests that his second formulation is the correct one. God's love and the erotic pleasure it produces in man paradoxically purifies man of his self-love, opening the heart up to mystical union. It is regretable that John of the Cross reflected so briefly on the actual psychological and theological basis of this paradox.

K. Ledergerber, in the work already mentioned, supplements what John of the Cross has to say regarding the purifying action of erotic pleasure:

"Lust wird fälschlicherweise nur als Egoismus angesehen ... Das Erleben des menschlichen Sexualaktes beweist unmittelbar, dass Lust nicht nur ein Nehmen, sondern auch ein Geben ist ... Dieses Untergehen des Egoismus, dieses über das selbstische Nehmen hinausgehende Mehrbekommen zeigt, dass in Wirklichkeit Lust etwas Gnadenhaftes ist, real und symbolhaft, im menschlichen Erleben, und die sexuelle Umarmung ein Akt mystischer Einigung sein kann. Schmerz und Lust sind Formen der Selbstaufgabe. Vom Schmerz wissen wir es zum Genüge, von der Lust nicht."[22]

As a remedy to Ledergerber's tendency to accentuate the sexual aspect of eroticism special reference should be made here to a work by J. van Ussel, *Intimiteit* (trans: intimacy)[23]. Van Ussel prefers to emphasize the aspect of personal intimacy in eroticism, rather than the aspect of sexuality, which can be impersonal and non-intimate. So also he prefers to accentuate a broader view of eroticism in mystical experience. Here, too, he agrees with Ledergerber in assigning to eroticism a role in healing and developing man:

"There are people who give to the term eroticism yet another meaning. In this case it involves a kind of religious feeling, something that unites and binds and transcends the boundaries of time and space. Then eroticism is something like God's breath over his creation. Things which appear to be separate are experienced as being connected with each other. Man is small, powerless, temporal, mortal and can not answer the question about the meaning of his existence. But if he opens himself up, then he receives eyes that see 'more'; he feels and knows more. He becomes big, great and important, because he participates in transcendence, a metaphysical, cosmical, mystical or religious experience. The view of life and the world becomes a whole, everything is connected with everything else."[24]

In this broader view of eroticism, the connection with the metaphysical and transcendental aspirations of man, the 'desiderium Dei', is made possible. The pleasure-seeking eros is at the same time a drive toward healing, or wholeness. It aims at a kind of redemption from affective splintering or disintegration. This will be referred to in the rest of this study as affective redemption. The broader, cosmological aim of eroticism, which was so self-evident in pseudo-Dionysius, is also reflected briefly in the last writings of John of the Cross, where he describes mystical union:

"God awakens many kinds of reminiscences in the soul . . . but this reminiscence which the soul wishes to describe here, which the Son of God gave to it, is in my opinion the most sublime and produces the most good in the soul because this reminiscence is a movement which the Word makes in the substance of the soul with such greatness, dominion and glory and with such softness, that it seems to the soul as if all the balsams and fragrant spices and flowers of the world are mixed, turned and revolved in order to give their sweetness; and as if all the kingdoms and dominions of the world and all the powers and virtues of heaven are moving; and not only this, but also all the virtues and substances and perfections and graces of all created things shine and make the same movement, all at once and together. For inasmuch as St. John says (1,4): 'all things in Him are life, and in Him they live and are and move' . . . Just as, when the earth moves, all material things that are upon it move likewise, as if they were nothing, even so, when this Prince moves, He carries His court with Him, and the court carries not Him." (*Flame* 4,4)

The theological value of John of the Cross is the way he incorporates eroticism into a thoroughly Christian view of redemption. He attempts to work out a mystical teaching of redemption which avoids a static, intellectualized doctrine of salvation. The central aim of his endeavor is to relate the concept of redemption, which can become too abstract if isolated from psychological insights, to man's experience of an on-going redemption during his lifetime development. To show the true depth of John of the Cross' approach, it will be compared briefly here with a similar attempt by a near-contemporary of his, Andreas Osiander.

A. Osiander was a Protestant theologian in Prussia who died in 1552. He attempted to construct a mystical doctrine of justification based on, among other things, the teachings of Meister Eckhart. However, he differed from Eckhart, who worked with a concept of a divine presence in the ground ('grunt') of the soul[25]. Osiander did not place this point of contact with the divine in the structure of the soul as such, but rather in man's practice of the virtues of faith and love[26]. This followed the lines of Luther's thought: "The spiritual man is the man who relies upon faith."[27]

S. Ozment[28] interprets this as meaning that Luther denies any natural covenant with man whereby man could have any connaturality with the divine. Hereby Luther denies the basis of medieval spirituality. Ozment states:

"Stated as forcibly as possible, we will argue that Luther's Reformation theology originates in and develops as a highly polemical answer to the anthropology of late medieval mystical theology."[29]

164

Luther's emphasis upon faith was a reaction against an exaggeration of the powers of some part of the soul which was assumed to be connatural with the divine, to unite man with God. For Osiander the task was a matter of developing an experiential basis for redemption which worked with this Lutherian concept of the spiritual man as the man of faith, rather than with ontological terms which presupposed some divine part of the soul, such as the 'synteresis', the 'spark', or the 'ground'. He attempted to construct a mystical approach to justification by stating that man is justified in proportion to God's presence in him through faith. The more God dwells in man, the greater his degree of justification and also of divinization. Through the indwelling of the image of Christ in man through faith and love, man is cleansed from sin and united with God.

Opposing a static, juridical view of redemption, Osiander tried to develop a dynamic view of redemption as a process which grows during man's lifetime, as man grows in faith and love. Osiander's views involved him in vehement conflicts with Calvin and Lutheran theologians. Rather than go into the points of conflict, it is sufficient here to note that later generations of theologians attacked him on an entirely different point, namely because he did not accomplish what he set out to do. His teaching on justification was no less intellectual and abstract than that of his opponents. The reasons for this failure are his too-sober vocabulary and the lack of an experiential basis in the emotions. The element of pleasure was absent. For this reason Osiander could not adequately state what it would feel like to be divinized, since the indwelling of God did not produce any delight. Thus Osiander's attempts to widen the scope of Protestant theology, which concentrated on imputing justification to man, failed. He used the same vocabulary as his opponents, which was a static, juridic vocabulary. Instead of giving the virtues of faith and love an emotional basis, he made them into abstract concepts.

Perhaps it would be too much to expect of a Prussian, Protestant theologian to accomplish this goal. In comparison, the vocabulary of the fiery little Spaniard, John of the Cross, seems unusually adapted to that purpose. For this reason the first part of his teaching which this chapter will examine will be the actual vocabulary in which he formulates his teachings on affective redemption. What seem at first glance to be merely emotive expressions will be placed within a broad, functional framework whereby they come to express the idea of an on-going redemption at the level of man's libidinal existence. Using the idea of christological and pneumatological eroticism, John of the Cross develops a whole view of man's path to redemption along the lines of the affections. His main contribution is the way he extended Luther's somewhat narrow formulation of the spiritual man as the man of faith. For John of the Cross, the spiritual man is the man

165

of faith, hope and love. Unlike Osiander, he accents the emotional basis of these theological virtues and consequently works out an appropriate vocabulary for dealing with them. Eroticism, the force of love, hereby receives a much broader context than that of either Ledergerber or van Ussel. It becomes the gateway to 'shalom', the peace of reconciliation in the union of love between man and God. Theology has for centuries been dominated by a reflection on faith, and in recent years by a reflection on hope. The time has now arrived for theology to reflect extensively on love, in both its bodily and spiritual aspects. This urgent necessity is underlined by W. Schubart, who states:

"Das Religiöse und das Geschlechtliche sind die beiden stärksten Lebensmächte. Wer sie für ursprünglich Widersacher hält, lehrt die ewige Zwiespältigkeit der Seele. Wer sie zu unver-söhnlichen Feinden macht, zerreisst das menschliche Herz. Und es ist zerrissen worden! . . . Denn wenn es nicht gelingt, Religion und Erotik in eine neue, nahe, und glückliche Beziehung zu setzen und die Menschenwürde mit der Geschlechtlichkeit auszusöhnen, wird es nicht zu jener Wiedergeburt der Religion kommen, auf die heute viele hoffen und von der sie alles erwarten. Wenn es aber gelänge, es erhielte der Eros eine neue sakrale Würde, die Religion neue vitale Kraft, und der Mensch, hart' geworden in den Irrtümern von Jahrtausenden, zerrissen und seiner Einheit beraubt, fände mit der Einheit auch den verlorenen Frieden seiner Seele wieder."[30]

In a recent empirical study by A. Greeley it was discovered that Catholics have an inhibition against experiencing God in and through sexual ex-perience, in contrast to non-Catholics[31]. The aim of this study is to help formulate a modern spirituality for laymen in which this inhibition is removed, by emphasizing the libidinal action of the theological virtues in affective redemption. This attention to the libidinal field is the key which opens the deeper content in the teaching of John of the Cross.

B. The field of attention: the libido

The preceding section discussed the motive for interest in contemplation, namely the pleasure principle. An attempt was made to show how the interest in contemplation springs from a corresponding interest in eroti-cism, a term which is shown to contain both elements of bodily pleasure and a more general, cosmological or metaphysical pleasure — the pleasure of being as such. The desire for pleasure, when given meaning and an aim, can lead to what the author calls 'affective redemption'. The problem to be dealt with in this section is to find a new way of interpreting John of the Cross so that this general field of attention, the libido, comes to the fore-front. In the brief summary of the teachings of John of the Cross presented in chapter one, the orientation was negatieve, i.e. finding fault with the dualism of spirit/sense in his works. In this section, the exposition will be purposely slanted to highlight certain aspects of John of the Cross which tend to escape notice when one concentrates upon his ascetical teaching or the dualism in it. The elements presented here therefore do not represent a balanced or complete review of his teachings, but serve rather to show in a highly selective perspective that the role of eros is a central one in his teaching, forming the basis of his views on affective redemption. The intention here is to present a new lens through which certain aspects of John of the Cross can be read and interpreted. This is an innovation in the method of interpreting his works, since to the author's knowledge, no previous attempt has been made to approach his works explicitly from an erotic or libidinal orientation. (Perhaps this is because most of the commentators on John of the Cross are celibates.)

1. *The vocabulary of desire.*
The starting point for this section is J. Peters' observation:

"We are of the opinion that the line of thought of St. John of the Cross is precisely this; namely that man is redeemed along the line of the affections, whereby the benefits of salvation come to him through both the objective content of faith and in the psychological order, through subjective faith, i.e. the attitude of faith."[32]

This perspective gives the modern reader a key to understanding much of what John of the Cross has to say about the origin and effects of man's desires. Much more is involved here than a reflection upon the path of mystical development. Rather, his is a systematic study of man's ability to love, carried to the most intense degree. One would not be far from the truth to postulate that all that really interests John of the Cross is passion, and then passion in its most extreme form, namely mystical union with God.

What makes John of the Cross interesting, theologically speaking, is the way he incorporated this libidinal view of man into his view of redemption. Whereas Thomas of Aquinas reduced the concept of 'desiderium Dei' to an intellectual desire, the desire to see God[33], John of the Cross establishes a much broader context within which to deal with such a theme. 'To know God' is in the first place to experience God in a love relationship, from which knowledge, wisdom and illumination flow. It is the particular merit of John of the Cross that his view of affective redemption did not exclude the role of man's intellect. Indeed the illumination of man's reason is integrated into the whole path of mystical development, but then in close connection with the soul's growth in divine love.

The fact that John of the Cross' main interest in the affections is reflected in his vocabulary. He devotes very little attention to the usual abstract concepts in which redemption is generally expressed. Regarding the basic intellectual abstractions of traditional theological reflections on salvation, John of the Cross has a rather scanty interest. The *Concordance*[34] of his works shows that he has only a few sentences of commentary on baptism, the eucharist, the sacraments, the Fall, Adam, paradise, sinners, sins, salvation, predestination, evil, justification, redemption, mortal and venial sins. On the Trinity, he has only one page of comments, two pages on the eternal Father, four on the Son of God, four on Jesus, five on the Holy Spirit and only one-half a page on the humanity of Christ. He refers in 17 pages to God with the general term 'Dios', however. Fine trinitarian distinctions do not occupy his attention. Nor do fine psychological distinctions interest him. He has only 2½ pages on the flesh, one paragraph on incorporeality, and 1½ pages on corporeality. By contrast, he has 29 pages on the soul ('alma'). Even the usual issues in mysticism do not seem to attract his interest. He has only two pages on divinization, only one page of references to illumination, three pages on purification, only one page of comments on mysticism as such, and only one paragraph on ecstasy. On the other hand, he has 17 pages on mystical union itself. Thus the picture that is emerging from this review is that of a very poorly developed vocabulary regarding the usual areas of theological speculation: trinitarian distinctions, psychological distinctions and even mystical distinctions. His main area of interest is in God as such, the soul as such, and mystical union between the two.

Now that the lack of precision in his theological and psychological vocabulary has come to light, the contrast with his highly developed use of terms regarding the libido becomes clear. John of the Cross sets about forming the 'new man' in the likeness of Christ with a vocabulary, not of theological concepts about redemption, but with a vocabulary of man's desires. This preoccupation with the affections is evident in two things: 1) the fine precision of terms describing various degrees or nuances of desire, and 2) the exactness of terms for describing the object of desire, either God or creatures. Thus he is interested in the degree and the kind of desire in man.

This is evident in the amount of attention he pays to the will (11 pages), to the appetites (10 pages), to pleasures (8 pages), to the affections (8 pages), to sensual desires (11 pages), and to the purgation of the appetites (8 pages). His vocabulary for expressing degrees of desire is especially rich: movements of the will (movimientos de la voluntad), inclinations (inclinaciones), leanings (asimientos), likings (aficiones), fondnesses (afectos), affections (afecciones), attachment (arrimo), yearnings (ansias), tastes (sabores), appetites (apetitos), desires (deseos), delights (gozos), pleasures (gustos), passions (passiones), covetousness (codicia), avarice (avaricia), concupiscence (concupiscencia), vice (vicio); to like (querer), to desire (desear), to love (amar), to crave (apetecer), to love vehemently (adamar); to please (agradar), to be pleasing (gustar), to satisfy (contentar) (satisfacer) (hartar), to enrapture or intoxicate (embriagar).

John of the Cross has a highly developed system of technical terms for denoting the object of desire, either God or a creature. He has 14 pages on the love for God and 17 pages on the love from God, 'amor de Dios' vs. 'amor'. When referring to the erotic desire for God he uses a certain set of terms, 'ansias', or yearnings, and the symbol of the flame. 'Ansias' occurs five times in his earliest work, the *Ascent*, 16 times in the *Night*, and 15 times in the *Canticle*. In his last work, the *Flame*, this term appears only once. Its function is replaced in the *Flame* by the symbol of the flame, which he uses forty times. This seems like a final development in his work, since the symbol of the flame occurs only once in the *Night*, not at all in the *Ascent*, and only four times in the *Canticle*. Unlike the pseudo-*Soliloquia*, which used the term 'concupiscencia Dei', John of the Cross never refers to the desire for God as concupiscence, perhaps because he reserves this term to express the desire for creatures. Similarly the act of desiring creatures is expressed by the verb, to crave ('apetecer'), a verb which is never used in regard to the act of desiring God. Rather to describe the act of desiring God he uses the word, to desire ('desear'), a verb which is reserved almost exclusively for this purpose.

For designating erotic love, John of the Cross has a special term, 'force of love' (fuerza de amor). Eroticism here does not mean what it has come to mean in common language, namely sexual desire[35]. Rather, it should be defined as that form of desire which strives toward union or intimacy[36]. In the terminology of John of the Cross no real equivalent for eros or eroticism can be found simply because Spanish has no satisfactory word for translating this Greek word, eros. Latin, the ancestor of Spanish, too, has no real equivalent for 'eros'. Translators of pseudo-Dionysius into Latin usually translate 'eros' with 'amor' and use the terms 'dilectio' or 'amor beneficus' or 'caritas' to translate 'agape'. John of the Cross' equivalent for purely sensual pleasure in love is luxury ('lujuria'). His equivalent for agape is charity ('caridad'). But apart from the term 'amor', he seems at first glance to have no other way to translate eros. Thus, in quoting the text from pseudo-Dionysius which says that it is eros which leads to ecstasy, John of the Cross says to Doña Ana de Peñalosa that it is love ('amor') which leads to ecstasy[37].

The aspect of dynamism or a motor, which so characterized eros in pseudo-Dionysius[38], is also present in the special term which John of the Cross devised, namely 'force of love'. Therefore this term seems in fact to be a more accurate translation of 'eros' than 'amor'. Here, too, a certain fine precision occurs. The references in John of the Cross to the force of love can be divided into three main classifications: 1) there are about 18 references to God's force of love for man, 2) about 31 references to man's

169

force of love for God, and 3) about 12 references to man's force of love when directed to creatures[39]. In regard to the force of God's love, John of the Cross states explicitly that this is the Holy Spirit:

"And thus the soul loves God with the will and the force of the same God, united with the same force of love with which it is loved by God; the which force is the Holy Spirit."(*Cant.* 38,3)

In addition to this term, he develops a whole family of symbols for expressing desire and its effects: fire, a burning flame, a spark, a wound, an inflamation of the heart, a flaming sword, and so forth. The content and use of these symbols will be discussed in section three, the possibilities of concentration in contemplation, or its goals.

It is with this vocabulary of terms and symbols about desire that John of the Cross constructs a theology of affective redemption. The locus of salvation is precisely here, in man's ability to love and desire. The deepest center of man, the locus of mystical union, is not some part of the soul which is connatural with the divine, but the seat of man's affections, the 'center' of his soul where the theological virtues have their action. In this broad libidinal context, John of the Cross surpasses the inspiration of Osiander, who, too, tried to place mystical union in man's practice of the theological virtues rather than in God's immanence in the soul.

Returning to the exposition of John of the Cross' teachings in chapter one, it is now possible to re-interpret his views against the background of this general orientation toward the libido. As chapter one pointed out, he conceives of man as having a purely spiritual 'center'. Contrary to expectations, however, nowhere does he refer to this center as being immaterial. Neither is it ever called a spark or a part of the divine by nature, but rather by grace. This center, according to John of the Cross is the deepest part of man to which his desire, the force of his love, his virtue and even his whole being can attain (*Flame* 1,11). The soul will unite with God according to the degrees of love which the soul's center is capable of reaching. This capacity to love varies from person to person, and therefore John of the Cross repeats again and again that the soul will experience God according to its own abilities and after its own manner. The soul which comes to love God with all the force of its operation and movement of the will, will arrive at its very deepest center, which is God himself by grace (*Cant.* 21,1). When the Holy Spirit wounds the soul in its center, it wounds the soul in its substance, virtue and force, inflaming it in love (*Flame* 1,14).

At this point it appears possible to give another interpretation to the 'center' which avoids the seemingly dualistic meaning it had in chapter one. Although John of the Cross uses terms which do belong within a dualistic framework, what attracts his attention is not the problem of the immateriality or the incorporeality of the 'center' of the soul. In fact, in all

170

his writings he refers only three times to the term 'incorporeal', and then only in regard to 'incorporeal' visions. Rather, his whole field of attention is oriented around the theme of desire. The spirit, in this context, is the voracious desire for God in man's heart. This explains his rebuke of spiritual directors who 'do not know what sort of thing the spirit is' (*Flame* 3,54). He means spiritual directors who do not understand the workings of the heart and of desire. Indeed, the writings of John of the Cross, with their general orientation toward the libido, seem more like a study in eroticism than an exposition on spirituality. It is not without reason that some say that John of the Cross could give lessons to lovers. This seems entirely in keeping with his intention, since he himself defined mystical theology as the science of love (*Cant.* 27,5).

2. *John of the Cross' study in eroticism.*
a. Eros in contemplation: bride's mysticism.
The starting point for a depth study of the nature of eroticism in affective redemption is not the usual presentation of 'bride's mysticism'. Bride's mysticism is the application of the nuptial symbolism of the "Song of Songs" of the Old Testament to the experience of union with God. The usual presentation pictures God as masculine and the human soul as feminine. The argument to be advanced here is that John of the Cross develops a man's version of bride's mysticism, or what could be called 'bridegroom mysticism'.

The usual presentation of bride's mysticism has fallen into disrepute for both psychological and theological reasons. Theology has come to see the nuptial symbolism of the "Song of Songs" within a collective relationship rather than a purely individual context. This means, that theology has come to emphasize the merits of this symbolism for describing the collective bond between the people of God (Israel, or the Church) and God (Yahweh, or Christ)[40], rather than the bond of love between the individual soul and God.

Psychologically the way this theme functions today in the spirituality of celibate women is as a compensation for repressed erotic desire. The data in chapter two clearly show that bride's mysticism correlates with only one variable, namely a strict affective asceticism in which all desires are rejected except the desire for God. This theme in itself may in fact be necessary and even beneficial in the beginning of a woman's prayer life, since it helps her to establish an affective or erotic motivation to pray. But this theme in a strictly celibate life style in which all other human affections are strictly monitored becomes too literal. The Bridegroom becomes pictured as an all-too-human lover. At this point the development beyond this stage toward union with a 'faceless' God is impeded because the motivation is too narrow. God's transcendence can not be accepted; the anthropomorphic aspect of bride's mysticism comes to predominate.

The point of criticism is not the anthropomorphic elements in bride's mysticism as such, but rather their actual content, and their motivation.

Regarding the content of bride's mysticism, traditionally God is pictured as being entirely masculine. The soul is designated as feminine because the union with God was conceived of as one-sided: God gave himself and man had merely to receive passively. Since receptivity was identified with femininity, the part of man which could unite with God had to be seen as a feminine soul[41]. This basic idea is inspired indeed by the biblical presentation of God: Israel is the unfaithful wife and Yahweh is the forgiving Spouse. Yet in bride's mysticism, as it has developed in the west, this original motif is exaggerated. The feminine aspects of God which are also present in the Bible, such as the feminine character of God's wisdom, and the masculine aspect of the Christians as the adopted sons of God, is disregarded.

This tendency to picture God as exclusively masculine has led in the west to the predominance of a woman's spirituality. Contrary to what feministic theology might maintain, this over-masculinization of God is detrimental to men, not to women. Women reap the benefits of this manly God. They are the ones who can use this as a springboard to an emotionally rich prayer life. It is the men who are short-changed, at least those who are not homosexual. They have great difficulty in establishing the affective motivation which would serve as the basis for a rich, libidinal approach to God. In the past perhaps the emphasis on Mary and the female saints, pictured as young women and not as matronly figures, helped men to counteract this over-masculinization of God. Mary, St. Teresa of Avila, St. Thérèse of Lisieux, St. Bernadette and others provided men with an emotional access to God. However, in recent times together with the down-playing of devotion to the female figures, there has arisen an increasing emotional sterility in the prayer life of men and even a distrust of this libidinal approach to God. The difference in the libidinal 'color' between the spirituality of men and women has recently been investigated in an unpublished thesis by P. van Ginneken[42]. Comparing the spirituality of a large number of Benedictine nuns with many Benedictine monks, he observes that a great difference exists. The nuns emphasize the libidinal aspects of the religious experience, such as love and joy. The monks, however, reject most anthropomorphical and libidinal references to God.

This results in many cases in a spirituality in which the men tend to pre-maturely reject the 'warm' side of spirituality. Instead they often emphasize an empty, somewhat depressed attitude of ascetical distance toward bride's mysticism. Van Ginneken warns for exaggerations on both sides — against the stagnation at the anthropomorphic stage in the case of the nuns, and against a colorless and too-abstract spirituality in the case of the monks.

The solution for the problem seems not so much to be a re-instatement of marial devotion to its former glory, but rather the discovery of feminine traits in God. The eastern Orthodox spirituality has for centuries recognized a feminine character, the Sophia, who represented God's wisdom. This corresponds to the feminine character of God's wisdom in the wisdom literature in the Old Testament. In the Septuagint, for example, loving God's wisdom is described as 'falling in love' (Wisdom 8,2). Orthodox inconography represents the Sophia, furthermore, as a young woman who is not a mother. She is the erotic, not the motherly, side of God. This corresponds, too, to the lack of a fatherly image in Christ. The Sophia is a concept parallel to the Word[43], the Son of God. This close association with Christ excludes any parental identification, either motherly or fatherly, in the Sophia.

When the object of mystical union is a feminine Sophia, rather than the masculine Christ, the identity of the other partner, man, also changes. Rather than being a receptive, 'feminine' partner, man becomes the pursuing, active virile partner. He goes in search of wisdom, the Sophia, who lets herself be found. The starting point for developing an erotic approach to contemplation is therefore still nuptial symbolism, but not necessarily in the usual sense. The Bride can be both the soul as well as the Sophia, God's divine wisdom. The Bridegroom can be both Christ, as well as the soul. What has been changed is not the anthropomorphical approach, but the 'sexuality' of this approach. What must be changed is woman's exclusive dominion over this theme. Men, too, have a libidinal need for the erotic dimension in prayer which such symbolism opens up. The way John of the Cross developed a masculine version of bride's mysticism will be explored at this point, now that the motivation has become clear.

The role of the Divine Wisdom, the Sophia, or the feminine aspect in the Word is essential to the nuptial symbolism in which John of the Cross describes what could be called 'bridegroom' mysticism. He states at the very beginning of his work that what he is describing is union with the Divine Wisdom (*Ascent* I,2,4). She is the Divine Bride of the soul. This reference to the Divine Wisdom occurs repeatedly throughout all his works, usually with a capital letter to designate a personification of the divine, rather than an abstract quality of God. There is only one passage in which the Divine Wisdom is clearly masculine: in *Cant.* 24,3 the Divine Wisdom communicates with the Bride, which is the soul in this case. Usually the Divine Wisdom is associated with the Son of God (*Ascent* II,15,4; *Cant.* 2,7; 5,1; 14,4; 15,25; *Flame* 2,16), as a parallel concept but in

173

feminine terms, since the Spanish word for wisdom ('sabiduría') is itself feminine. It would be untrue to state that the object of union is for John of the Cross always a feminine aspect in God. He mixes this 'feminine' terminology with the more traditional, masculine idea of God.

The greatest use of nuptial symbolism occurs in John of the Cross' work, *The Spiritual Canticle*. Although this work was clearly under the influence of a similar commentary on the "Song of Songs" by Fray Luis de León[44], it also seems to be partially under the influence of a woman who was 27 years older than he, namely Teresa of Avila. Indeed, one edition of this work says that he wrote it for Mother Teresa, although most of the other editions state that it was written for a close friend of hers, Mother Ana de Jesús[45]. In this work John of the Cross advises his readers to consult the works of Teresa of Avila if they wish to know more about such things as raptures and ecstasies (*Cant.* 13,7). The nuptial symbolism which predominates pictures God as the Spouse and the soul as the Bride. In this respect, his view of 'bridegroom mysticism' is as yet partially still dominated by a woman's spirituality. The action of the soul, however, reveals some masculine traits. The soul goes out looking for the divine Spouse, who retreats like a coy maiden.

Only after John of the Cross had his last contact with Mother Teresa did he write his 'masculine' version of bride's mysticism, in the full sense, namely *The Living Flame of Love*. This was written four years after his last meeting with her and also five years after the death of his own mother. In this work the nuptial symbolism retreats into the background. When it is used, it is sometimes turned around; the Bridegroom becomes the soul and he experiences God as a woman who gives her breasts to the soul, so that the soul can drink in this love (*Flame* II,35). The soul exclaims, upon experiencing God, "Beauteous art thou in thy footsteps and thy shoes, oh, prince's daughter," (*Flame* III,5). In this work, an important step beyond these anthropomorphic references to God is made. John of the Cross associates the Holy Spirit with bringing man to union with the Divine Wisdom (*Flame* I,17). From that point on, the role of the Holy Spirit becomes increasingly greater and the role of nuptial symbolism decreases. God, the object of union, becomes 'faceless', neither masculine nor feminine.

b. Correcting bride's mysticism: pneumatological eroticism.
This last development in the mystical theology of John of the Cross could be seen as a final corrective to the bride's mysticism in his earlier works. This does not mean that the erotic element is surpassed. On the contrary the erotic symbolism is increased in intensity. The means to erotic union, however, has become a neutral agent, the force of love of the Holy Spirit. In contrast to his earlier works in which only 22 references to the Holy Spirit

occurred in the *Ascent*, only 4 references in the *Night*, and only 25 references in the *Canticle*, this final work contains 49 references to the Holy Spirit.

The erotic aspect of the work of the Holy Spirit as the 'vinculum unitatis' is evident in the way John of the Cross associates the Holy Spirit with his technical term for erotic desire, the 'force of love', as has already been mentioned. Although the object of union is the Christ, who possesses infinite force of love (*Flame* II,2), the active principle or dynamism which approaches man and gives him the force of love with which to go to God is the Holy Spirit.

"My will, united with divine love, no longer loves basely and with its natural force, but with the force and the purity of the Holy Spirit." (*Night* II,4,2)

Other key texts which give this meaning to the 'flame' of the Holy Spirit in igniting the force of love are: *Night* II,4,2; 11,7; 13,9; 16,9; *Canticle* 13,1; 30,11; 31,1; 38,3; 38,4; *Flame* 2,2; 2,3; 2,5; 2,10; 2,13. What this indicates is that affective redemption, and mystical union, can be developed at a certain stage without recourse to nuptial symbolism. The force of love is almost never associated with the 'Spouse'[46]. It should be noted here, too, that pseudo-Dionysius developed his mystical theology without a single reference to bride's mysticism, despite the central role of eroticism.

This pneumatological eroticism, as it might be called, is a corrective to the anthropomorphical tendencies of bride's mysticism. A corrective, but not a substitute. The object of bride's mysticism can become a super-personal 'Spouse' pictured in terms which can become all-too-human under certain conditions. In contrast, the kind of eroticism expounded in pseudo-Dionysius and in John of the Cross is the force of an erotic love which approaches man in an intimate and personal way, but which nevertheless remains faceless. It is highly significant, in this context, that the theme of the spiritual marriage did not correlate in the empirical study described in chapter two with mystical advancement in unitive prayer. This means that although the most advanced contemplatives had indeed gone through a stage of enthusiasm for bride's mysticism, they had not remained at that stage. Rather, they tended to show a growing interest in the Holy Spirit, as reflected in their enthusiasm for Pentecostal movements. What is also important to note is that these subjects are women, not men. This means that the attraction of the Holy Spirit in establishing the erotic contact with God applies in this study to women only.

However, pneumatological eroticism is suited to inspiring both a masculine as well as a feminine spirituality, at least in the West. (In the oriental Orthodox Church, the Holy Spirit is considered to be feminine.) The fact that the sexual identity of the Holy Spirit is ambiguous in the west makes it possible to use the Holy Spirit as a basis for both a masculine as well as a feminine idea of God. Its erotic significance has been underestimated, however, perhaps because it is symbolized as a dove in western art. The reasons for this are given by Fortmann:

"In such a situation the symbol has the function of resolving contradictions. When destructive and constructive elements can be brought together in one symbol they are easier to deal with. Now the dove was especially suited to this because it seems to reconcile many opposite qualities in itself. It represents sexual seduction and phallic power but also the innocent platonic love and tenderness. It suggests with its clapping wings an intrusive power but it suggests a friendly intimacy when it sits in its cage or on a stick. As a sacrificial animal it softens the feelings of guilt, but through its strutting and its feathers it is the picture of haughtiness and vanity. Even if the dove is a masculine animal, it has soft, round and therefore feminine forms. It is thus an androgynous compromise and that was appropriate, considering the eternal uncertainty of the church about the question whether one should call the Holy Spirit masculine or feminine . . . For the choice of the dove as a divine symbol the church has paid a high price. The Spirit of God itself has been made tame. This is because in the further development, with the Victorian period as the climax, the dove became increasingly the symbol of a bourgeoise and sleepy peace, a tame existence without conflict, without sex, without anxiety, in one word: without vitality . . . The church itself however should be the most powerful symbol of the divine Spirit. But in order to be that she must be dynamized herself."[47]

Just as the role of the Holy Spirit is a corrective to the kind of eroticism involved in affective redemption because it can not be reduced to a mere compensation for lack of eroticism in human contacts, so, too, the role of the Holy Spirit corrects the bodily experience of eroticism in prayer. That is, the role of the Holy Spirit corrects both the motivation of erotic experience in prayer as well as the actual way it is experienced. In the beginning of mystical prayer the beginner experiences what John of the Cross calls 'spiritual luxury'. With more experience, the true contemplative surpasses this more sensual kind of pleasure and comes to experience pleasure in the Holy Spirit. This does not mean that spiritual delight replaces sensual delight, but rather that the way it is experienced is changed. The beginner experiences this delight egotistically, within his isolated self. The advanced contemplative experiences this same delight, but in communication with the Holy Spirit, in identification and participation. John of the Cross goes into the matter in detail:

"For when the spirit and the sense are pleased, every part of a man is moved by that pleasure to delight according to its proportion and nature. For then the spirit, which is the higher part, is moved to pleasure and delight in God; and the sensual nature, which is the lower part, is moved to pleasure in the sense, because it cannot possess and lay hold upon aught else, and it therefore lays hold upon that which comes nearest to itself, which is the impure and sensual. Thus it comes to pass that the soul is in deep prayer with God according to the spirit, and, on the other hand, according to sense it is passively conscious, not without great displeasure, of rebellions and motions and acts of the senses, which often happens in Communion, for when the soul receives joy and comfort in this act of love, because this Lord bestows it . . . Now as, after all, these two parts are combined in one individual, they ordinarily both participate in that which

176

one of them receives, each after its manner; for, as the philosopher says, everything that is received is in the recipient after the manner of the same recipient. And thus, in these beginnings, and even when the soul has made some progress, its sensual part, being imperfect, oftentimes receives the Spirit of God with the same imperfection. Now when this sensual part is renewed by the purgation of the dark night which we will describe, it no longer has these weaknesses; for it is no longer this part that receives aught, but rather it is itself received into the Spirit. And thus it then has everything after the manner of the Spirit." (*Night* I,4,2)

". . . in that visitation of the Divine Spirit the spirit of the soul is enraptured with great force, to communicate with the Spirit, and destroys the body, and ceases to experience feelings and to have its action in the body, since it has them in God (*Canticle* 13,6)

These texts do not actually imply that bodily delight in prayer is replaced by spiritual delight. Indeed as the quote from *Flame* II,22 on page 160 has already shown, John of the Cross considers bodily delight as glorifying God just as much as spiritual delight, since it is a fore-taste of eternal life in which the body, too, will participate. Rather, the direction of the delight is changed. Whereas the delight is received into the beginner, the delight of the advanced contemplative is received into God, in communication with the Holy Spirit.

The contrast between John of the Cross' use of eroticism and that of the Platonic tradition is precisely at this point. Plato, in the *Republic*, describes the erotic, heterosexual relationship between the feminine sophia and man[48]. Despite the suggestiveness of such phrases as the idea of leaving wisdom, sophia, 'baren and unfulfilled', the bodily aspect of eroticism is used only metaphorically. It is the general opinion of certain scholars that the introduction of the body into the erotic love of things eternal, is due to a Christian source (Origen) and is unplatonic[49].

In John of the Cross the body participates in this erotic love literally and not metaphorically. The basic difference between the erotic love of the One in Platonism and the Christian erotic love of God is not so much the actual physical basis of the love, but rather the object of that love. In Platonism, the object of erotic love is an impersonal and unresponsive Wisdom, or the One or the Good or Form. The Christian object of love, the Sophia, is personal and responsive. The consequence is that the love of man for God, the human 'eros pronoètikos', must also be personalized. This is the main reason for the difference between the metaphorical use of 'eros' in Plato and the personal, bodily eroticism in Christian bride's mysticism. The intimacy of the human experience of God in the spiritual marriage is a parallel to the intimacy of the object of that union, the personalized God. Even the Holy Spirit, being the member of the Trinity with the least distinct personality, is still capable of approaching man in a personalized way.

Returning now to Fortmann's observation that it is not difficult to concentrate on someone you love because abstract qualities are made present in the loved ones bodily appearance, which awakens sensual perception, this exposition of the characteristics of concentration in contemplation has tried to show that a similar line of reasoning applies to prayer. The bodily or sensual experience of God's love is the basis for concentration. It supplies both the motive for concentration − the pleasure it gives − as well as the general point of orientation, the libido. Once this basis has been laid, the path to further development in contemplation is opened.

C. Degrees and kinds of concentration in contemplation

Fortmann describes the growth in concentration and interest in prayer in two phases: 1) spontaneous growth and 2) practice or controlled growth[50]. The first kind of interest in prayer occurs when a person discovers that it is adapted to his aims or desires in life. In fact this means that the person has been attracted to prayer because it rewards him with some kind of pleasure. Due to this attraction he begins to deepen his knowledge of prayer and to start practicing it. But this kind of spontaneous interest is dependent largely on the rhythm which governs his libidinal interest. This interest comes and goes under the influence of the milieu, of his bodily rhythms, and of changing interests toward other fields of life. Therefore this first kind of interest in prayer is rather short-lived.

If a person wants to establish a set rhythm in which the interest in prayer can recur regularly, he will have to regulate that interest so that it becomes independent of changes in mood and circumstances. He does this by realizing the value of the object (contemplation, in this case) and by consciously aiming at it. In other words, he will have to exercise his interest. One could search for a reason or a motive which would explain why a person might go on to practice contemplation in this conscious way. Fortmann concludes that a whole complex of motives might exist, based upon a single basic orientation of the will. In the case of contemplation this means that a person's aims in life have become oriented around the libido. In the last analysis, the strength of a person's will toward achieving a goal is the main motive. Thus one would expect a person with a strong will to adopt this determined approach, rather than a person with a weak will.

The actual exercise of concentration in prayer, or contemplation in this case, grows along certain lines. First comes the phase of hard duty, of will power without much success or reinforcement with pleasurable experience. The practice of a technique or a certain procedure during such sessions aids the will to contemplate. The value of such practices is that they establish a habit, which overcomes distractions. Hereby the person is increasingly made aware of the distinction between his usual routine and this contemplative period. Such techniques might include Yoga, Zen, Transcendental Meditation, the spiritual exercises of Ignatius of Loyola, the rosary, or the mere repetition of certain psalms or simple prayers. At this point Fortmann goes into an extensive treatment of the various kinds of formal and spontaneous prayers. He does not deal with contemplation, however. The result of these prayers is that distractions decrease, inner harmony increases and the affect comes to resonate with the will. The practice of the technique or meditation becomes enjoyable in itself. The interest in the meditative technique becomes spontaneous and habitual.

The instructions about how to progress beyond this point are found, not in Fortmann, but in John of the Cross. He assumes that a person will begin to develop his interest in contemplation along the lines of some meditative practice, which serves to train the person in concentrating his attention and affection on the object of his meditation (*Night* I,8,3). After having experienced a certain degree of spiritual growth, the beginner reaches a kind of spiritual plateau. A 'spiritual dryness' sets in and the beginner no longer finds any desire to practice the meditation he used to enjoy so much. He experiences an emptiness, both intellectually and emotionally when he tries to practice his usual meditation. This is an entirely different kind of distraction than that of the person who has no real interest in contemplation or whose interest is rather capricious. John of the Cross gives three signs which indicate when this spiritual dryness is the result of a real spiritual growth, and not just due to some temporary fluctuation in mood, corresponding to the rhythms of the libido. These three signs are presented in three blocks of texts: *Ascent* II,13,1-8; *Night* I,9,1-9; *Flame* III,32-33. They are: 1) along with a disinterest in these 'divine values', comes a disinterest in anything whatsoever, 2) the memory is burdened with guilt feelings and care, caused by the fear that one is back-sliding, and 3) no matter how hard one might try, one can not meditate or reflect or feel the effects of the meditation the way one used to. Certain beginners with a weak will will experience this spiritual dryness only occasionally (*Night* I,9,9). Those who have a strong will will come to experience this phase continuously.

John of the Cross gives various reasons why this period in prayer occurs. In his dualistic formulation, he states that God is leading the beginner from the prayer of sense to the prayer of the spirit. Sometimes he states that God is leading the beginner from an active to a passive prayer form. In one passage, however, he gives a more psychological motive for this period of transition — the beginner is penetrating deeper levels of his ability to love. He is learning to love better. A person who insists on trying to continue with the beginning practice of meditation is like someone who keeps on peeling an orange, without ever stopping to eat the fruit.

"Since, then, the conduct of these beginners upon the way of God is ignoble, and has much to do with their love of self and their own inclinations, . . . God desires to lead them farther. He seeks to bring them out of that ignoble kind of love to a higher degree of love for Him, to free them from the ignoble exercises of sense and meditation (whereby, as we have said, they go seeking God so unworthily and in so many ways that are unbefitting), and to lead them to a kind of spiritual exercise wherein they can commune with Him more abundantly and are freed more completely from imperfections . . ." (*Night* I,8,3).

Whatever the reason might be, it involves a transition from the experience of one kind of pleasure to the experience of another kind of pleasure which is more subtle, at least at first. As long as the beginner has not yet learned how to perceive this new level of pleasure, he will have a feeling of emptiness, corresponding to the first dark night (factor two in the prayer experiences of the Questionnaire on Spirituality). John of the Cross instructs the beginner to wait attentively on God (*Night* II,10,4). Little by little a new kind of inner concentration will be experienced, which is peaceful but not yet really enjoyable. This period corresponds to factors seven and fifteen in the Questionnaire on Spirituality. Rather than being absorbed in pleasure, the beginner is merely observant, trying to discover the first feelings of pleasure. This inner advertence is effortless and passive (*Night* I,9,6).

The practice of concentration in the stages of contemplation which follow this period involves a recurrence at ever deepening levels in the libido of this alternation between pleasure and lack of pleasure, or at times, even of pain. The principle of reward and punishment applies here. The contemplative has to pay for the happy experiences by suffering the unhappy periods (*Flame* I,19). When the experience of pleasure dominates the mind and emotions are absorbed in a kind of inner recreation and rest. This brings insights and enlightenment. When the contemplative has grown accustomed to this stage for some time, he begins to think he is at the end of the development. The data confirm this observation of John of the Cross. Of the seven subjects who thought they were more advanced than the others, six were in this middle stage. In actual fact, they had only experienced about half the pleasurable and less than half of the unpleasurable experiences possible, in the Questionnaire on Spirituality.

The goal of unitive prayer is the complete involvement of the self in the pleasurable experiences. In this middle stage, the self can still be a bystander, observing the pleasurable experiences in prayer without becoming entirely involved. The results are what John of the Cross calls spiritual gluttony and spiritual pride. The contemplative at this stage wants to possess God, the source of this pleasure, without being possessed by God in turn. The more the contemplative is able to observe in prayer, the less he is concentrated.

In order to progress beyond this stage, the contemplative has to go through an ever-deepening process of absorption in pleasure. The oscillation between pleasure-displeasure accomplishes this process. The greater the pleasure, the greater the corresponding displeasure, since the pain of withdrawal is felt all the more acutely. This is evident in the empirical data, where the build-up in pleasurable experiences (factors 1,8,4,5) corresponds to a build-up in unpleasurable experiences (factors 2,10,14). Toward the end of this process, the alternations become more and more rapid (factors 13,11). Along with this increase in intensity of experience, the distance from what is happening decreases. The result is full concentration and no observation. When this happens, the mystical experience becomes inexpressable, since in order to express the experience the self would have had to be a bystander. The degree of ineffability corresponds to the degree of absorption.

When the contemplative no longer has unpleasurable experiences, at least under normal circumstances (illness might be an exception), the self has become completely absorbed in the object of union, God. This in fact means that the fluctuations of the libidinal interest and energy, which characterized the earlier stages, have ceased. This can mean one of two things; either the pleasurable state of contemplation has achieved an independent status and remains undisturbed by the natural ups and downs of the libido, or the libido itself has become stabilized at the 'happy' pole. The empirical data do show that the stable subjects who are in the most advanced group have high scores on happy emotionality and low scores on unhappy emotionality. The question arises, however, whether this emotionally happy level preceded the development in contemplation and even helped to cause it, or whether the high level of happy emotionality is a result of it.

This development in libidinal concentration in contemplation constitutes the special atmosphere which makes prayer becomes a closed circuit of concentration, in Fortmann's words. The problem arises as to what the relationship might be between this highly charged libidinal circuit in prayer and the rest of the subject's libidinal interests? John of the Cross tells that the growth in contemplation is accompanied by a special kind of inner conflict, or war, which corresponds to factor 10. Up until almost the final stage in prayer this inner conflict increases. Thus, contrary to Fortmann, inner harmony and integration are not pre-requisites to prayerful concentration. On the contrary, the deeper the concentration in prayer, the greater the inner disharmony in the libido. In Fortmann's terminology, what is involved here is a conflict between the motives or values which attracted the subject to prayer in the first place, and other motives or values which the subject has not yet integrated into that first complex of motives. That this conflict can occur at all signifies that some basic inner disharmony or split exists in man's libido. This is the special concern of John of the Cross, to be presented in the following section.

A. The 'old man'

The optimism of pseudo-Dionysius is inadequate for explaining why so few men, with such great difficulty, return to the divine eros. If all of man's force of love is ultimately directed at union with the divine force of love, then why is not every man, from the very first moment of his life, united in mystical union with God? Or, why can not every man develop in a growth process toward this union with the divine eros? If all of creation is striving toward a return to God's love, then why is not all of mankind on the way to mystical union, or perhaps there already?

It is significant that immediately after expounding on the divine eros, pseudo-Dionysius then goes on to deal with the question why the demon has not come to union with the divine eros. In his subsequent reflection on evil, pseudo-Dionysius can find no positive reason why man should be hindered from union with the love of God. He states that the soul is free. Neither matter, nor the body, nor nature can hinder it. The question remains unanswered as to why so few men actually attain to mystical union.

It is the deeper insight of John of the Cross into the division in man's loves which answers the question. As has already been mentioned, he has a highly precise vocabulary for designating man's force of love for God, versus man's force of love for creatures. It is this division in man's desires which hinders mystical union. The antimony between these two sets of desires is caused by the fact, according to John of the Cross, that man actually seeks the same object (God) in both sets. Man perceives something of God in creation and mistakes this trace of the divine for God himself. In this case, one could call desires for creatures erroneous perception, since the trace of God in them is perceived imperfectly — incompletely, one-sidedly and rigidly. There would be no opposition between love of God and love of creation if man were content to accept creation for what it is. The reason for this transference of expectations for pleasurable satisfaction from God to substitutes for God is not in the first place a perverted will in man, but ignorance. Man does not know the ultimate object of his desire. He is in ignorance and darkness. Pseudo-Dionysius did not reflect on the double meaning of 'darkness'. It can mean the divine darkness in which the glory of God is hidden from man, but it can also mean the darkness of sin and ignorance in which man lives. In John of the Cross, this second meaning of darkness is taken into account. 'Darknesses' mean the affections for creatures which compete with the love of God (*Ascent* I,4, 1-3). In man's fallen state, he is ignorant of the good things of God (*Flame* III,70). He has not yet been introduced to the pleasure which can come from God, but he is confronted with pleasure from other sources. The evil of sin 'falls into' this ignorance (*Cant.* 26,14).

John of the Cross' view of man assumes, therefore, that man is aware of a desire for some satisfaction which is complete. Not knowing what the actual object of that desire is, he sets about trying to find something which will satisfy it. In his ignorance he mistakes the appropriate object of that desire for creatures. The moment of sin sets in when man expects from some creature the satisfaction which only God can give.

Attention was called in the first part of this chapter to the view that the desire for God is an erotic desire, containing both sensual and spiritual aspects. John of the Cross observes that the erroneous desire for God also seeks erotic satisfaction, although transferring this longing onto creatures. When the heart feels this desire in regard to natural goods, it experiences sensual delight and luxury (*Ascent* III,22,3). For instance, the transferral of this desire onto food (gluttony) produces luxury (*Ascent* III,25,5). So, too, does the desire to feel or touch pleasurable things (*Ascent* III,25,6). Transferring this desire onto another person, even in 'spiritual friendships', can produce spiritual luxury (*Night* I,4, 6-7).

John of the Cross seems to have a rule of thumb for determining when the desire for creatures competes with the desire for God. As one grows toward God, such attachments may or may not help one progress. If they do help, they should be strengthened and purified (*Night* I,4,7). However, if such attachments seem to prevent this growth toward God this is because one is expecting from that attachment a satisfaction which only God can give. Such an attachment would have become a closed system, and would end in projection, to use Fortmann's terms. One would be projecting the desire for God onto an object which is not adequate for satisfying that desire. This will be discussed more extensively later.

The problem involved here is the paradox which John of the Cross notes, namely that the heart becomes captive of that which it possesses with its desire. The theme which he develops from this is that the heart is driven toward possessing something. Its desire is like a cavern which has a profound capacity for experiencing the vehement thirst for God. But the heart is usually unaware or ignorant of this hunger for God because it has its attention fixed on desires for creatures (*Flame* I,18). When these caverns are filled with affections for creatures the heart does not notice its great emptiness and thirst for God (*Flame* I,18). Although these caverns are capable of containing a desire for God himself, the smallest and most insignificant thing can capture the heart's attention and make man unaware of this hunger for God (*Flame* III, 18-22). However, when the heart does become aware of this thirst for God within it, it can become completely absorbed, undone or melted in its desire for possession of God (*Flame* a I,7). Since this desire to possess is inherent in man's heart, the crucial point is not to eliminate the drive to possess, but to enlighten the heart about the real object of its desire:

"In everything we should let ourselves be guided by the law of Christman and of his Church . . . and in this way to remedy our ignorances." (*Ascent* II,22,7)

"Any soul that really loves can not remain satisfied nor be contented until it actually possesses God." (*Cant.* 6,4)

". . . perfect spiritual life is the possession of God in the union of love." (*Flame* I,32)

"The heart can not be in peace and calm without possession . . ." (*Cant.* 9,6)

The 'old man' is therefore the man who is not yet aware of the real object of his desire. He is busy trying out various objects, to see if they can satisfy his desire. Either he does this by alternating from one object of desire to the next, or by extending his desire as much as possible in one direction, onto one object.

B. Erroneous desire

What interests John of the Cross are 'the secret places of the desires' (*Ascent* I,1,4). The key concept in his line of interest is possession. A study in erotic desire is at the same time a study in possession. When man erroneously transfers his desire for God onto temporal, moral or even spiritual goods, he expects a satisfaction from them which is unreasonable. What interests John of the Cross is the way this unreasonable drive toward possession of some created object affects the object of that desire as well as the way it affects the one doing the desiring. Thus before John of the Cross devotes much attention to finding ways to enlighten man about the real object of his desire, he first pays a lot of attention to describing almost clinically the kinds of effects which erroneous perception can produce.

John of the Cross pays the most attention to two main kinds of possessions, material and spiritual goods. He places the most emphasis upon the possession of spiritual goods, perhaps since in his life as a friar he would presumably have more contact with this sort of possession than with material possession. Nevertheless his views on avarice show some insight into the matter. The only things which he actually calls idols are money and the religious practices of men. In regard to money he draws attention to the phenomenon that the desire to have money can expand into the desire to possess as much money as possible. The paradox is that man becomes the captive of that which he possesses. Ironically man is willing to make sacrifices for money which he would consider unreasonable to make for God. When his money diminishes, man is even ready to sacrifice his life (*Ascent* III,3,10). John of the Cross interprets this as a sacrifice to an idol. The irony of erroneous perception therefore is that when the will is attached to things other than God, but expecting a satisfaction which only God can give, the will possesses nothing, but rather is possessed by the things themselves (*Ascent* III,20,3).

John of the Cross criticizes even more sharply the desire to possess spiritual goods and moral goods as if they were God. He refers for instance to men who delight in the high morality of their motives, to the point that they think they possess morality. He states that it would be better for such men to be deprived of these motives (*Ascent* III,35,5). He even goes so far as to state that man should take no delight in moral action except inasmuch as it is inspired by the love of God (*Ascent* III,27,4). The reason he is so strict on the subject of moral good is because he concedes that morality, perhaps more than all other kinds of good, does produce a ligitimate delight in possessing it. Man can not possess anything better in this life. (*Ascent* III,27,2). Precisely because moral good is in itself so good, the more man will tend to substitute moral good for God himself.

Regarding religious matters, John of the Cross goes into great detail, revealing the countless ways man has of possessing spiritual goods in such a manner as to stifle the desire for God himself. No modern writer has given such a sharp and perceptive criticism of this naive religiosity, based upon the satisfaction of immature needs, and he has. He refers to the religious practices which people maintain, ostensibly in God's honor, but in fact for man's own pleasure, to satisfy man's desire to possess God on man's own terms:

"The sons of Israel made a feast to their idol, thinking that they made a feast to God." (*Ascent* III,28,2)

To begin with, man makes himself content with his own grasp or understanding of religious matters. He obtains these ideas about God, not so much from the Scriptures, as from his own reasonings, from intuitions, from all kinds of 'visions', from imaginings, from feelings, etc. These various kinds of concepts about God are dealt with in book two of the *Ascent*, where he goes into the various kinds of spiritual communications which people say they have. His conclusion is that the soul will consistently exhibit the tendency in regard to all these spiritual 'goods' to possess them as a kind of personal claim on God. This is precisely contrary to God's intention in such matters for he gives man the chance to understand him via these means in order to spur man on to seek him for himself. John of the Cross rejects man's attempts to grasp God with his reasonings and feelings because such means are inadequate.

In the *Ascent* John of the Cross criticizes mainly religious practices of the masses, such as pilgrimages, ceremonies and processions in which statues of the saints are highly adorned, elaborate prayer rituals in which every tiny detail has to be precisely just so, special regard for the way an oratory is decorated, etc. In the *Night*, he goes into the more refined forms of spiritual possessiveness. Only here does he deal with the root cause of man's tendency to transfer the desire for God onto other objects. By possessing goods other than God, especially spiritual goods, a secret pride grows in man whereby he becomes satisfied with himself (*Night* I,2,1). Here, once again, the accent is on the secrecy, the hiddenness of this pride. Man is unaware that this pride exists within him. This is especially evident regarding spiritual goods. Book one of the *Night* is a psychological study in the effects of the hidden workings of pride in man's spiritual life. Man's whole behavior becomes infected with this pride. He prefers to instruct others than to be taught, he delights in making a show of his adeptness in spiritual matters, he does not hesitate to reprove and correct others, whenever he is criticized he says that he has not been understood, he flees from solid criticism as from death itself, he resolves much, setting up the highest goals for himself, he prefers dealing with God in public rather than in private, he likes for others to see his spirituality and devotion, he can not confess his sins and shortcomings honestly, but has to excuse himself, he dislikes praising others and loves to be praised himself, he is full of envy and disquiet, he seeks out confessors who do not know him to confess true sins, and so forth. In the matter of spiritual friendships, he feels a 'luxury of spirit' which makes him perform his actions with a certain bravado and vain gratification, out of regard for the persons present. He also criticizes such friendships when the sensual aspect of it comes to predominate and attention is taken away from God.

A clear-sighted study in spiritual greed is found in chapter three of book one of the *Night*. John of the Cross makes fun of beginners who run from first one kind of devotion to another, from one spiritual book or writer to another, burdening themselves with all kinds of trinkets and crosses, and spiritual advice and counsel. He attributes this kind of behavior to the spirit of possession. He observes that a man who is seeking God for himself grows weary of all this multiplicity and curiosity, and begins to seek God in truth. In more advanced stages in the spiritual life, spiritual greed assumes more serious proportions. The more the soul has savored of God's love, and the more the desire for God has been awakened to some extent, the greater the tendency of the heart will be to make itself content with these spiritual graces, rather than aiming at God himself. For this reason John of the Cross repeatedly warns against attachment to reasonings about God or to any mystical phenomena or to any spiritual good whatsoever, because of the spirit of possession which inevitably will accompany such things. From attachment to reasonings about God, a presumption grows which is a branch of pride (*Ascent* II,21,11). Without ones even noticing it or feeling it this self-satisfaction will grow to the point that one will not even notice it even when one is in it up to ones ears (*Ascent* III,9,1). Pride becomes a habit (*Night* I,12,9). Instead of being zealous for God's glory they are zealous for their own pride and presumption (*Flame* III,59). It is unfortunate that John of the Cross paid so little attention to this, the root cause of erroneous perception in desire, and so much attention to the erroneous desire itself. He even calls desire itself a sin, rather than the spirit of pride which is at its root.

It should be pointed out that John of the Cross does not say that man should give up material, moral or spiritual goods. Rather he says that the will should renounce them. Hereby he shifts the accent from the renunciation of possessions as such, to the renunciation of the will's possessiveness in regard to them (*Ascent* I,5,2). Purification of the spirit is therefore the purification, of the memory's ability to hoard up and possess the reminiscences of these goods, since the will possesses these goods, not by their actual ownership, but by storing them up in the memory (*Ascent* II,6,2).

What makes the asceticism of John of the Cross seem too extreme is his viewpoint that every desire of the will must inevitably grow out of proportion and displace the desire for God. For this reason, he denounces even the smallest liking or preference for certain foods, clothes, etc. Perhaps in a cloister these were so important because all the grander kinds of possessions were prohibited by the Rule.

As chapter one brings to light, John of the Cross makes no distinction between sinful desires and lawful or ethically irrelevant desires. For him all man's desires are in some way tainted by this hidden displacement of the desire for God. He is aiming at purifying man *from* desire, not at purifying man *in* his desires. This is a cloister spirituality, as he himself admits, in the prologue, no. 9, of the *Ascent*. Yet, although his viewpoint is exaggerated, it contains many points which reveal his keen observation of human behavior. In book three of the *Ascent* he gives an almost clinical description of the effects of diseased desire. The mind becomes blunted with regard to God, a kind of spiritual blindness sets in, and the judgment can no longer honestly assess the worth of the desired object (*Ascent* III,19,3). This is because the heart has divinized the object of its desires. It no longer loves the created good for itself, but as a substitute for God. When the heart has gone so far as to expect divine satisfaction from a creature, the inevitable occurs — the desired thing can not possibly satisfy the desire for God. Instead of realizing this, the heart becomes dilated and craves increasingly more of the desired object. The will becomes 'fat' and 'swollen' through the acquisition of more and more of the desired object (*Ascent* III,19,5). Paradoxically or perhaps ironically, the more man craves something, the less he really appreciates or enjoys it. In fact, the heart comes to attach very little importance to the actual object of its desire, nor does it trouble itself about it, nor does it esteem it very highly.

The effect of this expansion of desire into a 'creature' is that the heart becomes wholly absorbed in it, forgetting all else. It becomes carried away and in this obsession with the desired object it eventually comes to neglect other matters which deserve its attention. The result is a failure to perform ones duty in life; or a mere outer or perfunctory performance of duty, due to compulsion or habit, and not from love of duty. This can entail moral lapse, malice or injustice. Finally the obsessions which desire can lead to, cause relapse into 'mortal sin' through covetousness (*Ascent* III,19,7). The irony of this is that by forsaking God, the heart's desire for some infinite satisfaction is not thereby eliminated. The desire for God remains, although disguised. But since this desire is insatiable, the heart makes such unreasonable demands on some created good that no object whatsoever except God could possibly fulfill them. The desire will never be satisfied and therefore its thirst and greed will only increase:

"For it is of these that God Himself speaks through Jeremias saying, 'They have forsaken Me, Who am the fountain of living water, and they have digged to themselves broken cisterns that can hold no water.' " (*Ascent* III,19,7)

The final stage in this diseased form of desire is idolatry, which is complete identification with the object desired (*Ascent* III,19,10). The final result is that the desired object drags the heart down to the level of the object. In all these effects of displaced desire, John of the Cross traces the progressive loss of spiritual freedom. The freedom of desire which man exercises in regard to anything less than God inevitably leads to spiritual slavery to the object of desire.

What is missing here is a reflection in John of the Cross upon the deeper motives behind this displacement of desire. He reflects only briefly on man's limited nature, the condition of this life (*Night* II,17,6; *Canticle* 11,3; 19,1; 33,5; *Flame* 1,6; 1,36; 4,8). He implies that man, precisely because he is limited, seeks something infinite and unlimited. The problem is that such an object is by definition beyond the condition of this life. Due to man's ignorance of the infinite dimension of his desire, he sets his goals too low, preferring the illusion of limitless satisfaction. This is the darkness of man's ignorance, from which man's fallen state originates. Man is so limited that he is not even capable of knowing what he is capable of, namely of desiring the infinite. In spiritual development, John of the Cross warns constantly against setting ones aims too low and being therefore too quickly satisfied with graces or favors in prayer. Repeatedly he has to emphasize that man's goal is complete spiritual freedom, which is the result or by-product of mystical union with God. This complete spiritual freedom is also the final aim of redemption (*Ascent* I,4,6; III,5,3). It is therefore false modesty when the Christian does not aim at this highest form of union, but rather makes himself content with lower forms of prayer. Each Christian is destined to fully possess God, i.e. the only kind of possession which does not drag the heart down to the level of the object desired. Rather, God, by taking possession of the heart of man, raises it up to a level which transcends it.

C. Critical reflections on the diagnosis of John of the Cross

Some of the insights voiced in John of the Cross' views on spiritual freedom are echoed by modern theologians. J. B. Metz, in his critical review of modern attempts to equate redemption with socio-political emancipation[51], emphasizes that freedom should not be reduced to these areas in life, but should be expanded to include freedom from guilt and suffering, from the finiteness of death and mortality. Before going on to reflect further upon how conformity with the desired object − Christ − frees the heart from its limited condition and captivity to erroneous desire, it is necssary to reflect on the experiential basis of John of the Cross' view of the 'old man'. No attempt has been made as yet to test its validity. Up until now what has been presented has been just his opinion.

As already mentioned, in chapter two, the empirical data show that his extreme standpoint on rejecting all desires except the desire for God has nothing to do with achieving mystical advancement. Rather, these strict views correlate only with conformity to a cloister ideal. Therefore, the items on the Questionnaire on Spirituality concerning these views on asceticism proved to be irrelevant: 1) the idea that purification means avoiding all forms of idolatry, in the sense of excessive desire for something instead of God, and 2) the idea that purification means doing away with excessive self-love. It should be noted that all these ideas about purification stress man's action, an action which is always negative − getting rid of some undesirable quality.

Going back to Fortmann, his analysis of distraction shows certain similarities to John of the Cross' description of the 'old man'. Fortmann[52] classifies three main kinds of distraction:
1. a vague, superficial distraction which arises when there is no distinct goal or orientation, and the libidinal level of desire is low: dreaminess.
2. A real split in the person, caused when there is a disagreement between

what one wants to think about and that which one thinks about as a matter of course because ones desire is usually orientated toward it.
3. a split which occurs when unwanted thoughts intrude, perhaps because the repressive mechanisms are temporarily relaxed, while the attention is directed toward something else.

The first kind of distraction is not taken into consideration by John of the Cross, except in a few scattered remarks about 'weak' souls. He seems to assume that most people are driven by a strong desire for something. Fortmann states that this strong will toward some goal can only arise when the person has a determination to establish an identity or a self[53]. This corresponds in many ways to the term 'ego-strength', already discussed in chapter two. The data show that the emotional level in subjects with a weak ego-strength is low, both in regard to happy as well as unhappy emotionality. One could speculate that this first type of distraction arises when the libidinal level is not sufficiently aroused, which results in a kind of drowsiness.

The second kind of distraction applies more directly to what John of the Cross is dealing with. A person who as a matter of course is oriented toward some drive like success, wealth, achieving recognition, etc. will discover that these desires intrude during prayer. 'Erroneous desire' would seem to cause this second kind of distraction. The direction of this distraction could also be turned around, however. A person who as a matter of course is oriented toward contemplation and contemplative values, might experience distraction when he is required by circumstances to concentrate on other goals. In this second kind of distraction there is no active repression of the non-dominant desire. Here there is merely a certain priority or hierarchy of desires.

In the third kind of distraction there is a real repression of a set of desires. In this case the desire for God would be driven underground or even denied. Or, vice-versa, the desire for God could be construed to demand a complete repression of other sexual or erotic desires. During prayer, these repressed sexual feelings, or other kinds of libidinal frustrations such as hostility, would cause distraction.

Which kind of distraction corresponds to the inner war or conflict which increases along with the depth of concentration in contemplation? In stable subjects, the second kind of distraction is probably occuring. In neurotic subjects, the third kind of distraction might occur. More will be said about this in the discussion of the dark night.

Fortmann insists that real distraction comes from this inner lack of integration, and not from disturbances in the surroundings. His remedy is to find whatever it is that is causing the conflict, see its relative value in the light of 'divine values', and accept it in an inner act of surrender. He says that the obsessive power of the source of conflict is only increased when one adopts a negative attitude toward it and tries to get rid of it.

The paradox between the first kind of distraction and the other kinds of distraction becomes evident here. To be able to be aroused enough to concentrate at all, ones emotional level or libidinal energy has to be aroused. But when the libidinal attraction to some object is too great, it becomes obsessive and impedes concentration. When this emotional level can not be reduced or put in the right perspective, prayer becomes difficult. Perhaps this explains why the libidinal circuit of concentration in contemplation can come into conflict with other libidinal desires. The closer the two kinds of libidinal attraction, the greater the potential conflict might be. Since the closest parallel to erotic attraction in contemplation is erotic attraction in human relationships, mainly man-woman relationships, one would expect the greatest degree of disharmony here, but also potentially the greatest integration could occur here.

What is missing in John of the Cross' study in eroticism is a way to integrate eroticism in human contacts with divine eroticism. The closest he comes to seeing an integration is in his last work: "All creatures from above and from below have their life and force and duration in God" (*Flame* 4,5). He envisages God's force of love as present in all levels of creation. Yet this view does not include any reflection upon the way the levels of creation could help each other come to God. He can only admit the possibility that in the state of perfect mystical union, it is possible to love creation in and through God (*Flame* 4,5). But he never states the reverse, namely that creatures could help the soul love God in and through the erotic force present in creatures. It is precisely this view of creation which destinguishes John of the Cross from pseudo-Dionysius, who saw creation as containing a hierarchy of 'erotès' who share in the erotic force which streams forth from God and which returns back to God: (*Div. Names*, ch. 4, sec. 12).

". . . die höheren Wesen durch ihre Fürsorge den niedrigeren angehören, die gleichgeordneten durch ihr Zusammenhalten (einander), die niedrigsten aber durch göttliche Rückwendung zu den ersten (den höheren angehören)."[54]

The source of this erotic love in creation comes from God and strives to return to God (cf. Plotinus, *Enneads*, III,5,4). These 'erotès' do not compete with the love of God; rather they cooperate with the divine eros to help each other rise up to the primal eros. The higher creatures (angels) take care of the lower ones; the creatures on an equal level help each other by holding on to each other (cooperating); the lower creatures by returning to God through the higher beings.This is the reason why it is so hard to adapt the insights of John of the Cross to modern readers, especially non-celibates. He has no vision of the integration of the various kinds of eroticism on the path to God. In his view the rivalry is absolute, admitting no ethically lawful or even irrelevant desires which do not compete with the love of and for God.

Perhaps this is not so much the fault of John of the Cross, as the entire spiritual tendency of the Christian tradition. A similar view can be found in Origen's commentary on the "Song of Songs":

"When the passion of love is directed to diverse skills, whether manual crafts or occupations needful only for this present life — the art of wrestling, for example, or of running — or even when it is expended on the study of geometry or music or arithmetic or similar branches of learning, neither in that case does it seem to me to be used laudably. The only laudable love is that which is directed to God or to the virtues of the soul."[55]

Origen regards these things, which Plato called the 'preliminary studies', to be of little value. Plato might have agreed that anyone who is content to remain at the lower grades of love was acting wrongly. But this does not mean that the preliminary stages are without value, as long as they are a means to an end and not an end in themselves. The same thing applies most especially to human love relationships, which could be the preliminary studies 'par excellence' to divine love. The following interviews are intended to show how the integration between eroticism in human relationships can occur with eroticism in prayer. Five of the most advanced subjects were interviewed on the subject of friendships with a member of the opposite sex, four nuns and one friar. It should be mentioned that the phenomenon of friendships with members of the opposite sex occurred among all levels of prayer development, that is, in all five groups. But since the topic at hand is the way this kind of erotic relationship can be integrated with the experience of advanced contemplation or unitive prayer, the experiences of these most advanced subjects throw the most light on the subject.

Regarding the actual nature of these friendships, it should also be noted that the individuals involved only saw each other on the average of about once a month. Due to the cloister situation, the actual physical manifestation of love was usually rather restricted, although not always. Intimate contact, therefore, can not be assumed at least on the physical level. Contact was mainly a matter of communication by telephone or letters. All the subjects interviewed, however, did describe how these relationships had awakened erotic feelings. Since some subjects were more articulate than others, the text of only one nun and one friar will be presented here because they seemed the best able to express the relationship:

MM: "Does such a friendship arise because your prayer life has developed so deeply, or does the friendship account for this prayer development?
Subject: "I think it is reciprocal. Before I met him I had already experienced that a new

dimension was entering my prayer life and that I was being placed into God, as it were. I lost my feeling of self thereby. This gave me a terrible feeling of fear and dread. At that time I also experienced an openness toward God and a desire to experience more, but I was afraid to let myself undergo this being swept up in God's love. When I first met this man we talked about this and he helped me get over the fear of this unknown dimension. He showed me that I had to learn to open myself up for God's love. And I really think that in friendships one learns to do this, too. But it works the other way around as well. After experiencing that openness in God and being set outside oneself, you retain something of that openness in regard to others. You must retain that, otherwise that openness is not authentic. In the beginning of such a friendship I wanted to tell everything I experienced in prayer, but he has taught me not to want to always express things in words. If you always use words to express prayer experiences you destroy something in your relationship to God. You get stuck at the level of reasoning. Now I know that in a friendship you can be silent because you think, he knows that already or he experiences that, too."

MM: "Would you say that this friendship has involved a struggle against the tendency to try to possess the other? Or against being possessed by the other?"

Subject: "In the beginning there were tensions because we had to try to orient everything toward God, since it really did take some possession of you. I have been working for years not to let it take entire possession of me. In the beginning my attention was directed to such things as when will I see him again, what will I say when I see him, how nice that someone else thinks I am attractive and worthwhile, etc. You seek yourself so quickly in such relationships. As the years passed it seems as if my desire has been purified of this egoism. Now it is not a hindrance to my prayer life but an expansion or extension of myself. It used to occupy my thoughts during prayer, but now if I think about him I just try to pray together with him through to God. If this deeper dimension did not develop, the friendship would have become dull. I must say, I have grown enormously through this by becoming more mature and independent. The tension between the two kinds of love must be there in order for it to grow to a deeper level and before you can integrate it in the love of God. If you really love someone else you want him to develop in his love for God, too. You don't try to restrain him from reaching his deepest possible development. You learn to love a little bit the way God loves."

MM: "Thus you do not love him possessively now. What would you think if he were to go and get married? Priests do get married nowadays, you know."

Subject: "Oh, that would be terrible! Just awful!"

Comment: The subject's final remark seems to indicate that the detachment and lack of possessiveness which she claims to have attained are not as fully realized as she thinks. Further questionning about her attitude toward a possible rival, another woman, revealed that she would feel a clash of interests. Both women would be competing for his exclusive love. The subject did state that if such a situation were to develop, she would completely break the bond she had with him. This could be interpreted in two ways: either she would do that from altruism, to free him, or she would do that to force his hand and pressure him to make a decision. An interview with another subject, a friar, also brought to light the central importance of possession and being possessed in such 'spiritual' friendships. In the case of the friar, it concerns several friendships which he had at the same time, only one of which was serious.

MM: "Does the tension between wanting to possess the other or being possessed by the other play a role in your relationship with her?"

Subject: "I think that this is precisely the point where the tensions occur. Love has to be refined, purified at this point. That can occur simply by the disappointments and the distance and the fact that each has his/her own activities . . . That all acts to purify love. I think that you are invited in and through love not so much to allow the other to be free as to help free each other. You send each other out away from the security which you have between you. That security is necessary, too, and good in itself. You can support each other in it. And I think that is the way God's love is, too. First he invites us to the security he gives us and then he sends us out from it to do our work. But I think that you lose this liberating effect which it can have when you try to build your house on it, so to speak. That would make the relationship exclusive, so that no one else could enter. Everyone else would be a visitor or an alien there. Then I would have the feeling as if I were building a house for always and forever, to go and sit in it and have my feelings protected from all outside influences, from especially those who are lonely and on the outside. Maybe we should strive to let many people into that house or perhaps to be at home everywhere."

MM: "Does the fact that someone else wants to possess you also play a role?"

Subject: "That does play a role. I experience it as a struggle. On one hand there is a very serious aspect to it, something that belongs to love itself, the desire to reserve someone for yourself. That desire goes without saying. But I want to add that I wish to avoid the over-hasty conclusion that you should be purified from that desire. You have to learn to grow in and through it toward maturity."

Comment: In both interviews, the problem with exclusivity and possession is centered around the possible rival, another man or woman. Neither subject considered the possibility that God might be a 'jealous lover', whose love might be opposed to that of the friend. Instead, both subjects considered the way God loves to be the ideal. God can love many people at the same time, and man should try to learn from God how to do that. Another subject made a remark which opens the way to integrate the eroticism of man-woman relationships with divine eroticism:

Subject: "That friendship stands in the great space of God's love. There is the actual encounter. However, there is also loneliness there. The deepest experience of God occurs in solitude. In God I let the incompleteness of the human relationship be fulfilled. I do not know how. But in God I know that the friendship is always renewed and grows in depth."

In this remark the sister adds something which neither pseudo-Dionysius nor John of the Cross considered. Human relationships not only can help one grow toward God's love, but the reverse can also occur — the erotic relationship with God can help the human relationship grow and deepen. Since what is involved here, nevertheless, is a cloistered nun, one suspects that she means the frustrations which the cloister imposes on any such relationship (the lack of physical contact, for instance) are resolved or integrated in prayer. Before anything can be said which is truly relevant to the modern laity, therefore, further research should be done with subjects formed in the western contemplative tradition but who are now leading the life of a layman or laywoman.

194

These interviews pose some questions to John of the Cross' view of the 'old man', but also support some of his positions. His view that man must reject all possessiveness except the desire to possess and be possessed by God is called into question. Rather these subjects accept the fact that possessiveness is part and parcel of human desires or loves, although they maintain that it must be refined and purified. The interviews show that this involves a struggle, even for these highly advanced contemplatives. Some kind of purification of the drive to possess is indeed necessary, in order to avoid stifling the love and the object of that love itself. The solution which these subjects seem to imply is that their struggle is aided by trying to follow the example which God sets. In God's relationship with man he is both possessive, yet makes man free. As one sister said, she tried to learn to love the way God loves. This identification with the model, God's way of loving, perhaps indicates a more positive way to relate to 'creatures' than that which John of the Cross envisaged. The 'preliminary studies', that is, the love of material, intellectual, moral and spiritual goods and especially the love of another person, educate man's ability to love. These preliminary loves do not necessarily impede the love of God, rather they help man prepare for it by opening up his libidinal interest in things and people. Only when man is not given an example or a model to follow which shows him how to integrate these loves with the source of love, God's eros, will he lose perspective.

D. *The role of techniques*

It is beyond the scope of this study to go deeply into the similarities and dissimilarities between oriental meditation techniques and western ascetical and contemplative techniques. A few words in passing, however, based upon the concrete experiences of three subjects, indicate that the problem is more complex than it might seem. As already mentioned in the introduction to this chapter there is a tension in prayer between finding ones self and surrendering it. The data indicate that neurotics have difficulty in letting go of their self. The fact that two of the most neurotic subjects in the EEG study used techniques spontaneously during prayer raises some questions. What was the motive behind this use of techniques? Was it meant to aid relaxation? Then why didn't they become much more relaxed than they did? Was it a tactic to maintain self-control and to resist the dynamism of the erotic attraction to God, a dynamism which presumably would threaten their feeling of self-sufficiency? The story of the wise cat in the introduction to chapter three illustrates the ambiguity of any technique. The temptation of a technique is that it gives one a feeling of self-reliance or self-control, precisely in the practice of a technique which ostensibly aims at loosening ones tense grip on oneself. This suggests tnat the self-surrender necessary to concentration in contemplation, based upon an inner harmony or integration, was not present in these subjects.

Another subject who will be quoted on pp. 206-208, the case history in hysteria, also used a technique. At the time of her cure from hysteria she had also begun to practice Zazen, the sitting meditation in Zen. She did not mention this in the story of her case history, since the practice of Zen began at about the end of the cure. At the time of her cure, she had discovered by introspection during prayer that her main problem was her tendency to lose herself in her many activities. She lost her self-control too easily. In the Zen meditation she continued her cure by training herself to concentrate upon her body as the seat of her personal identity. This taught her to come back to herself, to regain self-control. When she felt the symptoms of hysteria beginning, she would restrict her usual exuberance by meditation in this way, which amounted to an exercise in self-containment. In this case, increasing her feeling of identity or 'self' actually helped her to achieve inner harmony and integration. The conclusion seems to be that oriental meditation techniques can be used with highly differing motives, and with a wide range of results, both positive and negative, depending on the psychological structure of the subject.

Many similarities can be observed between the way prayer is practiced in western cloisters and the way Zen is practiced in oriental cloisters. As the description of the Zen hall in the EEG study in chapter two shows, the special atmosphere there resembles a chapel. Incense is burning, a bell rings to signal the beginning of the meditation session, each member of the community has his special seat, the meditation is done by assuming a special posture, a special dress is worn, an image of the object of identification (Buddha) is placed in front of those meditating in the hall, etc. In the chapels of the Carmelite nuns, the same atmosphere dominates. Each prayer session is signalled by the ringing of a bell, candles and/or incense are burning, each sister has her assigned seat, they wear a special dress or habit, they assume a special kneeling position, an image of the object of identification (a crucifix, an image of Christ, etc.) is placed in front of the sisters in the chapel. All these various things are designed to awaken certain associations with meditation or prayer, and as such they, too, are 'techniques'. The reason for these aids to concentration in the place of prayer is given by Fortmann:

"The transition from the profane to the holy must thus be made conscious and accentuated. It helps concentration in prayer when one does not just step from the daily work into prayer. The two spheres are too far apart and it is too difficult to build up concentration in prayer without orienting oneself fully and resolutely toward it."[56]

What is the psychological mechanism at work in these techniques? Fortmann suggests that three factors are at work here:

1. The force of habit, or the 'perseverence tendency'.
This means that the desired mood or thoughts will arise more easily when one has oriented oneself in that direction in the past. The repetition of a certain technique or meditative or prayerful posture in a certain surrounding, in a certain way, will awaken this mood.

2. The reproduction tendency through association.
When two associations were brought together at some earlier time, then later on, the presence of one of these associations will awaken the memory of the other. When some prayer experience took place before a certain picture or in a certain place at a certain time, etc. then returning to that object or place will reawaken that prayer experience by association. This only applies, however, when one is already in the mood.

3. Orientation toward a certain kind of imagination.
It is not so much a matter of which things one meditates upon as whether one is directed toward God while meditating or praying. One begins by placing oneself in God's presence, with a renewal of faith and by realizing what one is about to do. This is the particular function of the image of the object of identification in front of the person praying. By looking at an image of Christ, or perhaps of Mary or some saint, one becomes oriented toward a goal.
Fortmann concludes that these 'techniques' are necessary, even for laymen:

"Thus prayer should become a particular complex of its own, built upon associations and its own tension so that the profane occupations can no longer be disturbing. This does not mean that the profane complexes should be made inaccessible for the sphere of prayer. Asceticism refers here to 'virtual prayer' or walking in the presence of God."[57]

After considering the difficulties involved in prayer, however, Fortmann seems to realize that these techniques are insufficient to create the moral preparation for prayer. The whole problem becomes a matter of self-surrender. He then formulates a different, or ethical, set of conditions for prayer:
1. surrender and acceptance of the here and now of reality,
2. distance from the milieu and concentration upon higher values,
3. opening up oneself, having interest in God and ones fellow man.
These new conditions require a self-forgetfulness or self-emptying. He then goes on to describe how this opening up of the libido is achieved: through the establishment of relationships of trust, love and hope, i.e. the theological virtues. This will be developed in the following section.

Fortmann had indicated that concentration in prayer was the result of two steps, already mentioned in the introduction to this chapter:
1. achieving inner harmony or integration, and
2. going on from there to find the adequate or appropriate approach to the object of concentration by identifying with it.

But as the preceding section has shown, it is very difficult to find the way to achieve inner harmony or integration without already having found the way to identify with the model or object of contemplation. The self-surrender required before inner harmony can be achieved in fact is made possible by the second step. The author suggests that the steps toward concentration in prayer should be reversed. The way to inner harmony is found when one first of all identifies with the object of concentration, namely Christ. In more traditional terminology, this is called the imitation of Christ. As the interviews at the end of the preceding section have shown, the way the subjects came to integrate their various kinds of loves was by imitating the way God loves. The practice of techniques, either eastern or western (including affective asceticism, which could also be classified as a technique), does not necessarily help in this self-surrender. Fortmann voices the suspicion that the western emphasis on what he calles the 'dangerous self'[58] will contaminate the way a westerner practices any technique toward inner harmony. The technique becomes something which one has to master, it becomes an achievement, whereby the self-orientation of the westerner is only strengthened. Even in the techniques designed to create associations in the place where prayer is practiced are ego-oriented: they make one concentrate upon ones past experiences, ones habits, ones associations, etc. Only the third function of these techniques, the orientation toward the object or goal via an image, attracts the would-be contemplative out of himself. John of the Cross goes more deeply into this third function of techniques, which in fact transcends or surpasses the technique. He does this by showing the way the contemplative identifies with Christ, both actively and passively. The role of the theological virtues is central here.

A. Identification with the desired object: the imitation of Christ

1. The active imitation of Christ.

The process by which the human heart gradually becomes free from its tendency to mistake the desire for God as a desire for 'creatures' begins with baptism but does not end there. Baptism, which cleanses the soul from sin and initiates it into the life of Christ is just the beginning in a lifelong growth toward God. The absence of sin is not enough for salvation — the soul must also have a positive development in love for God:

"In order to arrive at such a high degree of perfection to which the soul aims, it is not enough for it to be clean and purified from all imperfections, but rather it must also have great force and a very sublime love." (*Cant.* 20,1)

What attracts the attention here, again, is the association of force and love; what John of the Cross is referring to here is the force of love, eros. He indicates both an active and a passive way by which the heart can grow in this likeness of Christ, that is, to grow until it attains the force of love which Christ possesses. The active way in the imitation of Christ is the conscious attempt to follow Christ's example in ones actions:

"Carry a daily appetite to imitate Christ and to regard all things as Christ would have regarded them" (*Ascent* I,13,3).

"Learn to suffer imitating the Son of God in his life and mortifications, which is the road toward reaching all spiritual good." (*Ascent* II,29,9)

"Imitate Christ, who is sublimely holy, and you will never err." (*Counsels*, 2,63)

The greater part of the *Ascent* is devoted to showing how the heart learns to imitate the poverty of spirit which Christ had. In this active imitation the accent lies upon the subjective attitude rather than the actual deed. The ideal is the exinanition of Christ, that is, the emptying of oneself in nakedness of spirit. This theme of the poverty of spirit is a variation of John of the Cross' main theme, possession and dispossession (*Ascent* I,13,4; II,7,2-12; *Counsels*, prologue, 2; 3,4). He especially warns against hoarding up spiritual favors and graces in prayer, which impede the way of the cross (*Cant.* 3,5).

2. *The passive imitation of Christ.*

As if becoming disillusioned with man's ability to imitate Christ actively, John of the Cross develops a correction to his optimism in the *Ascent*, in his elaboration of the theme of exinanition or kenosis in the *Night*. He observes that man's fallen state has left his will so weak that man can do very little himself to grow to the strength of love which God calls him to:

"However greatly the soul itself labours, it cannot actively purify itself so as to be in the least degree prepared for the Divine union of perfection of love, if God takes not its hand and purges it not in that dark fire, in the way and manner that we have to describe." (*Night* I,3,3)

This extension of the theme of the imitation of Christ develops into a view of Christ as the interior teacher who gives man an education in love:

"If you, in your love, oh good Jesus, do not soften the soul, it will always persevere in its natural hardness." (*Counsels* 1,28)

"The delectable science which she says here that He taught her is mystical theology, the secret science of God, which spiritual men call contemplation — this is most delectable, since it is science through love, the which love is its master and that which makes it to be wholly delectable. And inasmuch as God communicates to the soul this science and knowledge in the love wherewith He communicates Himself to her, it is delectable to her understanding, since it is a science which pertains thereto; and likewise it is delectable to her will, since it consists in love, which pertains to the will." (*Cant.* 27,5)

"Besides teaching the soul there how to love : . . he makes it love with the force he loves it with." (*Cant.* 38,4)

In man's weak or impure state, the force of this love resembles fire which purifies man and causes him pain and suffering. Fire, a symbol which John of the Cross uses about 54 times in this respect[59], symbolizes the divine love, which purges man's appetites of all 'strange fire', i.e. the erroneous desire for God which is mistakenly transferred to creatures, or 'idols' (Lev. 10,1) (*Ascent* I,5,7). He sometimes attributes this fire to Christ and other times to the Holy Spirit. In his last work, the *Flame*, he works out this distinction: the fire's source is Christ, but when the flame reaches out to man, to 'burn' or purify his heart, the Holy Spirit is at work. The 'passive imitation of Christ' is the endurance of this education in love by fire. The active agent is the Holy Spirit:

"This flame, which is the Holy Spirit, is wounding the soul and destroying and consuming in it the imperfections of its evil habits; and this is the operation of the Holy Spirit, wherein He prepares it for Divine union and the transformation of love in God." (*Flame* 1,19)

"He who is not born anew in the Holy Spirit can not see this kingdom of God, which is the state of perfection." (*Ascent* II,5,5)

The theme of possession is central to this passive imitation of Christ. Just as Christ emptied himself (kenosis), so the Christian must empty himself of all other desires which possess him, and give himself entirely over to the desire for God, in being totally possessed by the Holy Spirit (*Flame* 1,1). The likeness of Christ is perfect when man can say that he no longer lives, but rather Christ lives in him (*Cant.* 12,7; 26,3; *Flame* 2,34). The goal or reward is the total possession of God, since just as the Christian is surrendering himself to God, at the same time God is surrendering Himself to the Christian:

"And thus between God and the soul a reciprocal love is being formed in conformity of union and matrimonial surrender, in which the goods of both, which are the divine essence, are possessed by each one freely due to the voluntary surrender of the one to the other; both possess them together." (*Flame* 3,79)

The passive imitation of Christ is a passive way of the cross. It consists in

200

enduring or suffering the oppressiveness of God's love. In learning to experience a much greater force of love, or of eros, than man is usually able to experience, suffering must necessarily accompany this growth. The paradox is here: in order to be able to experience an increasingly greater degree of pleasure, man has to experience an increasingly greater suffering. The heart experiences this education in love as a hostile, invading force, which nauseates it (*Night* II, 5,6; 11,7; 11,11; 16,9; *Flame* 2,26). It goes through the pains of hell. Indeed, this dark night is a premature introduction into purgatory's fire (*Night* II,6,2). Suffering is induced, not only almost physically from the force of God's love, but also because life itself inflicts trials during this period. Like Job, the Christian will lose his friends, material goods, reputation, family, etc. (*Night* II,6,3). The soul is strengthened and accompanied in this by the force of God's love which is darkly present (*Night* II,11,7; 16,9). The soul should not become frightened at the horrors of this dark night, since it is the only path to spiritual freedom (*Night* II,22,1-2).

At this point the soul's inner state is one of great disharmony:

"This is a painful disturbance, involving many misgivings, imaginings and strivings which the soul has within itself, wherein, with the apprehension and realization of the miseries in which it sees itself, it fancies that it is lost and that its blessings have gone for ever." (*Night* II,9,7)

The reason this statement is so important is because, in the Questionnaire on Spirituality, this description of spiritual torment correlated highly with neuroticism. Neurotic subjects who were in no way advanced mystics had nevertheless experienced this inner lack of integration. On the other hand, very advanced mystics, who were unusually stable, had also gone through such experiences during the dark night. The implication is that the 'dark night' of passive purification is a depressed state which occurs in the mystic as a transitional period in a growth process, but which is chronic in the neurotic. The few neurotic subjects who had actually progressed in prayer to the point of the dark night of passive purgation, experienced it to a much more intense degree than stable subjects. Unstable subjects with a weak 'ego-strength', in fact, tended to fall back to a more superficial prayer form when the unhappy experiences became too great. John of the Cross attributes the source of this suffering to too much self-knowledge, arising when man becomes aware of the limits of his ability to love. Fortmann's description of 'weak' or neurotic types, given in the introduction to this chapter, is relevant here — i.e. they suffer from a kind of libidinal impotence or lack of expansiveness. As a consequence they are unable to support the force of God's love. The libidinal level is too low. The low scores of such subjects on happy emotionality, and in some cases, on any kind of emotionality, happy or unhappy, confirms this.

John of the Cross states that many people go through a period in life when they begin to experience dissatisfaction with created goods, in a kind of inner emptiness (*Night* I,8,4). In fact, he states that the great majority of 'recollected persons' enter this phase. Thus, he sees a certain degree of depression as a normal phase in human development. The second phase of this depression, the dark night of passive purification, eventually follows this first phase, although not always immediately. Only very few people, not even the half, will actually experience the dark night of passive purification in all its intensity, at least in this life. Nevertheless, each man must go through this period, if not in this life, then in the next, in purgatory (*Night* II,7,12). In fact, John of the Cross states that the reason he undertook to explain what the dark night is, is because so many people experience it, without being able to discover its meaning (*Night* II,22). He sees it as a normal development in the affective growth of man, and not as some peculiar stage in mysticism alone.

He gives this period of depression meaning by placing it within the framework of affective redemption. The dark night is the night of faith, in which the soul learns to rely on God's force of love and not on its own forces. The invading force of God's eros makes the heart realize its own misery and sin all the more clearly (*Night* II,5,5). The soul becomes undone in inner torment, both natural and spiritual (*Night* II,6,5). However, precisely by becoming aware of its immersion in its own miseries (*Night* II,7,3), the soul is freed from every kind of 'evil spirit' (*Night* II,9,3). This introduces the motif of the 'cure' which the dark night brings – precisely by being made aware of its illness, the soul can be cured. The darkness of faith will eventually give way to the light of faith, and affective healing. In this period of passive purgation, the 'old man' dies off and the 'new man' the likeness to Christ, is born (*Night* I,4,2).

3. *The active side of the passive imitation: faith.*
Pseudo-Dionysius developed the theme of the divine darkness of contemplation (skotos). Gregory the Great reflected on 'unknowing faith' and the darkness of man's fallen state. It was John of the Cross who connected these concepts and arrived at the idea of the darkness of faith. He proposes the darkness of faith as a remedy to the darkness of man's fallen state and limited condition. In the increasing depression of the dark night, one does not survive by fighting the shadows, but by lighting a candle. This candle is faith:

"For, in telling us to look to the faith whereof the prophets spake, as to a candle that shines in a dark place, he is bidding us remain in the darkness, with our eyes closed to all these other lights; and telling us that in this darkness, faith alone, which likewise is dark, will be the light to which we shall cling." (*Ascent* II,16,15)

John of the Cross states again and again that the only suitable means to arrive at union with God is through faith (*Ascent* II,30,5; 2,9; 8,1; 26,11; *Flame* 3,48). He states that the reason why faith can lead man out of the darkness of his limited condition is because it orients man toward the goal or the object of his desire, which is God, in such a way that man can transcend his own limited vision of what that goal is like:

"For, even as God is infinite, so faith sets Him before us as infinite; and, as He is Three and One, it sets him before us as infinite; and, as God is darkness to our understanding, even so does faith likewise blind and dazzle our understanding. And thus, by this means alone, God manifests Himself to the soul in Divine light, which passes all understanding. And therefore, the greater is the faith of the soul, the more closely it is united with God." (*Ascent* II,9,1)

Furthermore, faith surpasses the things which one can feel or experience libidinally in prayer, experiences which only give the illusion of understanding something about God's love (*Ascent* II,11,7). By relying on dark faith, man overcomes the limitations of his ability to love. He expands his libidinal capacities only when he sets no limits to love — but man can only do this by surpassing his emotional and intellectual limits through faith, which opens up new perspectives. The more man relies on blind faith, the more he will grow in love or eros:

". . . the abyss of faith in which the understanding has to remain in darkness and has to proceed in darkness by love, in faith, and not by much reasoning." (*Ascent* II,29,5)

"The more the soul is pure and careful in faith, the more it will have of infused charity from God." (*Ascent* II,20,6)

". . . by means of which faith, God infuses into them charity and increases it within them, together with the act thereof, which is to love more . . ." (*Cant.* 26,8)

"It is after the manner of faith in which we love God without understanding Him." (*Cant.*, prologue, 2)

"Faith is the proximate and proportionate means for the understanding in order for the soul to arrive at the divine union of love." (*Ascent* II,2,9)

What John of the Cross is referring to here is an existentially situated faith, or, in his own words, 'living faith' (fe viva). This concept of faith has recently been explored by G. Muschalek, who elaborates upon the idea that faith is a way of knowing only insofar as the believer's own existence has been renewed[60]. The 'old man' has to be replaced by the renewed man, the man of faith or the likeness of Christ. This is the central difference between the meaning of 'faith' in John of the Cross and the kind of intellectual faith evident in the pseudo-*Soliloquia*, as mentioned in chapter three, where faith means adherence to the articles of the Creed. Muschalek makes the perceptive statement that the darkness of faith arises from the non-possession of God. Correspondingly, the light of faith will dawn as the 'new man' comes closer and closer to possessing God. Here again, the theme of possession enters the picture. The darkness of the via negativa is the darkness of the non-possession of God.

Along with the theme of the darkness of faith comes the theme of the hiddenness or secrecy of faith. Faith is a secret ladder (*Night* II,15,11), along which the other two theological virtues (love and hope) reach man. These three theological virtues disguise the self (*Night* II,21,3). This disguise protects the self from 'sensuality' and from the 'demons' (*Night* II,22,1). This secret ladder is the ladder toward divine union, and before the self can climb it, it must be denuded and hidden in this disguise (*Night* II,24,3-4). Once the self is stripped of its pride or self-love, it is able to enter a deep recollection and inner peace, finding itself removed far from the 'enemy'. As a result, the darkness of erroneous desire is removed and the desire for God is awakened (*Night* II,25, 3-4). To explain how this happens, he quotes the biblical text (Mt. 6,3), "The right hand should not know what the left hand is doing." What is the function or the meaning of all this secrecy and hiddenness? It is necessary for the soul to be hidden from the 'enemy', for some reason. The poem which John of the Cross composed, in which the mystical path is indicated which the soul has to take, describes this secrecy:

1. "Upon a dark night
   With desires inflamed in love,
   – Oh happy chance!
   I went out without being noticed,
   My house being now at rest;

2. In darkness and secure
   By the secret ladder, disguised,
   – Oh happy chance!
   In darkness and secure,
   My house being now at rest."
   (Introduction to *Ascent* and *Night*)

At this point it seems possible to speculate on the nature of the 'enemy', sensuality and the 'demon' (*Night* II,22,1), in the process of affective redemption. If the theory of Glueck and Stroebel, discussed in the EEG study[61] in chapter two, is correct, then meditation relaxes the usual mechanisms whereby the self represses disturbing or unwanted libidinal material. One wonders if John of the Cross' 'enemy' might not be Glueck and Stroebel's repressed sexual frustrations, hositilities, murderous tendencies, etc. The problem involved in contemplation is that it raises the level of and interest in libidinal desires. It is an education in love. But at the same time that the loving aspects of the libido are activated, the other aspects of the libido can also be aroused. How can the freeing of the libido be accomplished so that its effects are salvific or healing and not pernicious? John of the Cross, too, observed that when one of the passions is aroused, the other passions follow it (*Ascent* III,26,6). He classifies two sets of passions: happy ones (joy, hope) and unhappy ones (fear, pain). In his early work, the *Ascent*, he teaches that all these passions are to be eliminated. The ideal is impassibility. Later on, in his last work, the *Flame*, he comes to a different view. The ideal is to be consumed in passions (*Flame* 2,30), but in such a way that they are all ordered or integrated in accordance with the dominant goal, love of God (*Cant.* 28,4). The contemplative experiences the passions, but refers them always to the object of identification, God. The 'house' of passions has to be put to rest before the soul can see God (*Night* I,14,1). In many ways, the first view of John of the Cross resembles the idea of Fortmann, that the person has to achieve inner harmony or integration before he can concentrate in prayer. John of the Cross' insistence upon a strict affective asceticism is a logical consequence of this view: "Being now free from the bother of the natural passions, . . . one enjoys in security and quiet the participation in God" (*Cant.* 24,5). The later formulation, however, suggests a different kind of ethical or moral preparation. The healing of the libido is accomplished when the self is dressed or disguised in the theological virtues. What is the function, then, of these virtues?

The empirical data in chapter two show that the theological virtues are one of the main factors in mystical development. The statements of John of the Cross which were used in the Questionnaire on Spirituality to describe the action of the theological virtues were:

"Trust in God, who will not fail to give what is needful for the way, until He brings one into the clear and pure light of love." (*Night* I,10,3)

"Purity of heart is nothing less than the love which comes from God's favor." (*Night* II,12,1)

"The spirit is purified and enlightened only through love." (*Night* II,12,1)

"When love is perfect then occurs the transformation of the soul through love to God." (*Ascent* I,2,4)

These statements instruct the Christian to do only one thing, to trust God. They do not state that one must love only God. In fact, the statement, "Direct the will to God with love." (*Ascent* II,29,7), which was also used in the Questionnaire on Spirituality, did not correlate with mystical advancement. This suggests that the working order or sequence in the theological virtues is this: man begins by trusting God, which in turn makes it possible for God to communicate more of His love to him. Hope increases as faith increases. The virtue of faith (and hope) is active; the virtue of love is receptive, and in fact is not a matter of will power. The theological virtues work to integrate man into a relationship with God of inter-dependency. The empirical data show that the theological virtues correlate negatively with the variables 'independence', 'neuroticism' and 'unhappy emotionality'. This could mean that independent subjects, who tend to be unhappy and neurotic, are not able to establish this inter-dependent relationship as well as dependent, stable and happy subjects. The theological virtues act to help the subject establish a 'tie that binds' with the object of identification, Christ. They counteract self-sufficiency, or self-love.

To illustrate the way the theological virtues work in healing the libido, a case history is presented here, taken from a report written by the subject 08 (see page 267). Her current psychological results show her to be rather emotional, in the happy sense, extremely extravert, stable, with no tendency toward psycho-somatic neuroticism. She has a relatively high 'ego-strength' and an unusually low score on hysteria (conversion neurosis). Her score on test reliability is slightly better than average. A striking aspect of her psychological profile is her extremely high need for group support and her extreme sensitivity to what is socially desirable. Her scores on the Questionnaire on Spirituality show her to be one of the most advanced mystics in group one. Although her current psychological profile is quite good, her case history, however, reveals a struggle with hysteria (conversion neurosis), which she finally won without any professional help.

Previous to her entry in the Carmelite Order, she had always been inclined to long for death whenever any conflict upset her. She was a particularly exuberant type. In her work as a social worker, however, she often ran into more formal or reserved people who did not understand her. She began to let this upset her, and the desire for death returned. She pictured death as a way to a life without pain and suffering, a kind of nirvana. She became aware, when she was about twenty-five, that this was merely an escape. She then decided not to flee suffering any longer. Instead, she deliberately sought it, by entering the cloister. Shortly after her junior profession, which meant that a dispensation would have been necessary if she were to leave, she began to have suicidal thoughts. She put them out of her mind when she realized that her suicide would signify a reproach against her fellow sisters.

After that, she began to have periods of paralysis. At first complete paralysis, then later on attacks of partial paralysis. In these attacks her body resembled that of a corpse: stiff, motionless, unable to eat, to see, or to react to the surroundings. In the partial attacks she felt very weak and could only lie in bed. She described the course of her illness and cure this way:

"Suddenly I was confronted with a death for which I was not prepared and which I had not counted on. I no longer longed for death but rather death had its hold on me. I could not resist it and I could not move. I could not cry out. I was powerless in every respect. I waited until death had done its work. That lasted about an hour; then life returned. My reaction was to realize that this was the consequence of my over-enthusiastic effort in the group . . . an effort which was not free from self-seeking. The next morning, I stood up, joyful and full of courage. I told no one about it. I realized I would have to become less active. This hard lesson in paralysis would overcome me often. An active nature does not become passive very easily. I felt guilty about being so concentrated upon myself.

Once this purification (the subject's word for paralysis) ocurred in the dining room, where I could not hide it. The Mother Superior came over to look at me and she was shocked. She immediately called the doctor because she thought I was dying and I could not tell her that it would go away soon. The doctor came, had me breathe into a paper sack, and understood nothing about what I had experienced. The next morning I stood up as usual and could go back to work.

The attack began usually with a terrible headache. The strangest thing was that I did not feel really sick. The doctor gave me different medicines every three weeks, but they did no good. The attack began as follows: I would not feel very well. I felt somewhat uncertain, uncomfortable, nauseous, with a tendency to retch, no appetite. My first impression was always that I was catching the flu. I noticed an oppressive feeling in my stomach. I became clammy, cold and hot. My whole body became over-sensitized, painful. My strength simply went away. Finally everything became hazy and I had to go to bed.

The doctor could never find anything wrong with me. Only once did he ask if I had any inner conflicts. I answered vaguely that I did. I tried to talk with my spiritual director about this but he did not want to discuss it. All I got was a little laugh out of him and I had to make do with that.

I began to look for the blame for these attacks in myself rather than in things or events outside of me. The problem was to discover what precisely was involved. It had something to do with purifying my inner attitude in faith, hope and love. During the attacks as I lay in bed this reflection began to dawn on me. I began to feel myself intensely in the grasp of the Lord. This being grasped was different every time. Sometimes I simply felt myself to be abnormal and thought that they would bring me to a sanatorium. In that light I was in a totally different world. I discovered the reason for this partial paralysis, this powerlessness. It always involved reducing my involvement, my desire to achieve something and get recognition. There really were conflicts, thus, but I only noticed them in the light of God's pure love, when it shone over me. The Almighty stood, as it were, with two large clear eyes above me and in that clear light my whole life lay open and nude. During this purification I experienced myself as being very abnormal. This did not make me anxious. On the contrary, it seemed quite understandable to me. I saw that I needed to be healed but that this would take time. All together, it took several weeks. Every time I had to overcome the desire to achieve and do something for the group in order to mean something to the group. I had to learn that my contribution to the group did not consist in doing anything but in being. I simply had to respond to God's love for man, and in the experience of that love, quite concretely, to let God be seen by others. As soon as I could say 'yes' to this insight, I was always healed from the attack. Now when I feel a headache coming on, I sit down and try to relax by moderating my activity. For about two years now, I haven't had these attacks any more.

To accept that the Lord was at work in and through these events required a lot of faith and courage. I could never have imagined that body and soul are so intensely linked with each other. Whenever anyone seriously dares to dig deeply in his bodily ailments and searches for their cause within himself rather than outside himself, then in many cases he will get well in this way for good. By resorting to medicines or adaptation techniques, a person can merely evade himself. The confrontation with yourself requires a lot of courage but it is worth it. I can understand now why monks went into solitude for a while. Something like that would have done me a lot of good, too. Man is so great that he can discover his own lack of redemption in his own body, that he can do penance in his body for his sins, and that he can accept the grace of redemption, too, in his body by opening himself up to it. In this way, too, his body becomes a participant in the grace of resurrection. The pain is not a punishment from God but a consequence of the lack of redemption in man and in creation. Hereby man can discover via his bodily disturbances, whether physical or psychical, at which point he is still not redeemed." (trans.: M.M.)

The affective redemption involved in this case history did not consist of affective asceticism. The subject's basic orientation toward the group is still extremely great, as her scores show. However, the anxiety which this used to cause has decreased. She no longer feels threatened when she does not receive the love and recognition from the group which she needs. Her healing came when she experienced being loved by God, which brought her the insight that she did not need to achieve or do anything to merit love. The only thing which she did do, as she says, was to persist in faith. The theological reflection on this healing effect that comes from experiencing the free gift of God's love centers around the concept of unmerited grace, as H. L. Zindinger states:

"Die 'Motivlosigkeit' der Liebe Gottes ist somit so zu verstehen, dass diese Liebe keinerlei äusseres Motiv hat, weder ein positives in den greifbaren Eigenschaften des geliebten Gegenstandes – des Menschen – noch ein negatives (so dass man auch sagen kann, Gott liebt den Menschen, obwohl er wertlos ist), sondern *sich selbst motiviert* – und ob sich der Eros in diesem Punkte wirklich so sehr von der Agape unterscheidet, wird noch zo klären sein.
"Was die Theologie über das Wesen der Liebe auszusagen hat, bleibt . . . was sie über die Wirkung der (göttlichen) Liebe zu sagen weiss: sie vernichtet die Gesetzlichkeit und zerstört den Libertinismus, positiv formuliert: sie ermöglicht die Freiheit und die Erkenntnis – beides deshalb, weil sie die Angst nimmt. *Liebe ist der Gegensatz zur Angst* – die Angst zerstört die Liebe, die Liebe zerstört die Angst. Hier ist die Parallel der biblischen Aussage zum tiefenpsychologische Befund wieder deutlich."[62]

In the case history just quoted, the experience of God's love was the impulse which allowed the subject to reduce her anxiety in social contacts. It made her aware of her deeper needs and aspirations, while at the same time 'hiding' herself from herself, so that she could bear the truth. The loss of self which this experience of God's love caused, helped her to see herself objectively. The reason she could accept the naked truth about her abnormal condition and even realize the psychological meaning of the paralysis (something which a hysteric almost never realizes), was because she was 'clothed' in the reassuring security of God's love, something which she experienced, too, in a bodily way.

This hiddenness characterizes a great deal of the actual experience of mystical union. The sufferings of the dark night are interspersed with periods of relief and blessings. The pleasurable prayer experiences return and it is as if God took the soul out of the purifying oven to show it what he had been doing. Then God returns it to the crucible of love, and the darkness and hiddenness of the process of educating in love continues (*Night* II,7,4-7).

It is this education in unmerited love which helps the contemplative gain inner harmony. The active agent in this is the erotic force of the love of the

Holy Spirit. This education is a hidden ladder, since the heart is not fully aware of this desire within it. It is in darkness and this growth in love is hidden to it (*Night* II,20,6). With each climb to a higher step, however, i.e. with each increase in the degree of love, much more is revealed to it by love. Finally, toward the end of the dark night, the light of faith begins to dawn. The darkness of faith is replaced by the light of faith, and the contemplative comes to resemble the object of identification, Christ. One becomes like that which one contemplates.

Before going on to discuss the possibilities which deep prayer can open up, it is necessary to review briefly the problems involved in concentrated or deep prayer. As the section on the kinds and degrees of concentration in prayer has already mentioned, the increase in concentration corresponds to an ever-deepening experience of pleasure. In a kind of self-perpetuating cycle, the experience of pleasure is followed by an experience of displeasure, which is followed by an experience of pleasure. Each time, the degree of pleasure increases, and correspondingly the absence of that pleasure in the negative cycle becomes ever greater, too. What is the basic psychological mechanism at work here? The principle of purification is this alternation, according to Lindinger:

"Auf den Höhepunkten der Liebe, im Orgasmus wie in der Ekstase ... ist der Egoismus mit dem Altruismus tatsächlich identisch ... Denn der Akt der Liebe ... *ist* Selbstpreisgabe. Der Mensch aber wil sich nicht hergeben, dazu hängt er zu sehr an sich selbst. Er will sich selber für sich selber haben. Das höchste Glück aber findet er nur, wo er sich selber hergibt. Auf den Höhepunkten der Liebe spürt er das und *kann* es auch – und *findet* darin das höchste Glück. Sobald er aber von diesen Höhepunkten wieder heruntersteigt und reflektiert, revoltiert er dagegen, wenn auch meist unbewusst ... Der Mensch leidet darunter, dass er nicht fassen kann, warum er diese Last der Selbstpreisgabe auf sich nehmen muss, um das höchste Glück, das er für sich sucht, zu finden."[63]

If one wants to call this pendulum course, between the experience of God and the lack of that experience, the way of the cross, one has a grasp of the basic intention of John of the Cross' view on the passive imitation of Christ.

B. The 'new man': the likeness of Christ

The old adage that you become like that which you contemplate applies just as much to Christian contemplation as to oriental meditation. The Zen Buddhist monk quoted in chapter two, in the EEG study, tells how the ideal of Zen meditation is to become like Buddha, sitting under a tree and reflecting on all the suffering he had gone through, without being emotionally involved. The ideal of the Christian contemplative is to be crucified with Christ on a tree. What is the emotional involvement once this ideal has been attained?

The likeness with Christ will be discussed in this section along two main lines: 1) the likeness to the Word, the Divine Wisdom (the Sophia) which dwells in the Son of God, and 2) the likeness to Christ risen, in the actual bodily effects of this identification.

1. *Identification with the Divine Wisdom.*

John of the Cross associates the Divine Wisdom with counsel, clarity, guidance, knowing, the sun, and especially the light of faith. Through faith man receives enlightenment concerning God, the mysteries of the Incarnation, concerning God's action in events and persons (*Cant.* 7,2; *Ascent* III,12,1; II,27,2; 2,4). Faith teaches man (*Cant.* 7,5; *Ascent* II,29,7). This is the light of faith, which is divine in its origin (*Ascent* I,8,6; II,5,6; 9,1; 9,3; 14,10; 14,13; 15,3; 27,5). His teaching about enlightenment or illumination with the Divine Wisdom can be summed up by saying that God, the source of this divine light, communicates his truth to man in the union of love through faith. The element of love is essential here. The seven grades or degrees of wisdom correspond to the seven degrees of love (*Flame* I,12-13). 'To know' in divine illumination means to experience God's wisdom in a love relationship.

Since so many of the subjects in the empirical study had indeed experienced mystical union to some degree, it is possible to see if these two aspects of mystical union (love and knowledge) appear in the empirical results. The illumination of the intellect through faith is described in factor four, which the neutral judges called 'thinking contemplation', and which John of the Cross would have called 'intellectual visions'. The items in this factor were:

"These successive words always come when the spirit is recollected and absorbed very attentively in some meditation; and, in its reflections upon that same matter whereupon it is thinking, it proceeds from one stage to another, forming words and arguments ... with great facility and distinctness ... so that it seems not to be doing this itself, but rather it seems that another person is supplying the reasoning within its mind or answering its questions or teaching it." (*Ascent* II,29,1)

"For it will come to pass that, when a person is inattentive to a matter and it is far from his mind, there will come to him a vivid understanding of what he is hearing or reading. This is with respect to that which God is in His works, and herein are included the other articles of our Catholic faith." (*Ascent* II,26,16; 27,1)

"This kind of vision, or, to speak more properly, of knowledge of naked truths, is very different from ... seeing bodily things with the understanding; it consists rather in comprehending and seeing with the understanding the truths of God, whether of things that are, that have been or that will be ..." (*Ascent* II,26,2)

"God often represents many things to the soul and teaches it much wisdom." (*Ascent* II,16,3)

As already discussed in chapter two, the more experiences the subjects have had in mystical and contemplative prayer (factors 1 and 8), the more experiences they also have in this factor four, thinking contemplation. This illumination of the intellect accompanies mystical union. On the other hand, factor two, which described man's inability to understand or experience God, declined in importance in proportion to the advancement in prayer. What seems to supplant this 'unknowing' of factor two, the 'via negativa', is illumination as described in factor four. This enlightenment corresponds to the growth in assimilation or identification with the Divine Wisdom.

To emphasize the specific character of this enlightenment, it is necessary here to return briefly to the thought of Fortmann. In his article, "Het heldere licht"[64] (translated: the clear light), written shortly before his death, Fortmann tries to synthesize the Christian teaching about the Eternal light with the Buddhistic teaching about the Great Light. Overlooking the fact that similar symbols in different religions may be based upon widely differing views of man, Fortmann all too easily equates these two kinds of light. He supports these theological acrobatics by appealing to the authority of pseudo-Dionysius. Fortmann states that at the time pseudo-Dionysius wrote ($\pm$ 6th century), the mentalities of east and west had not yet grown so far apart. Therefore pseudo-Dionysius' description of the divinity as a cascade of light (in *Celestial Hierarchy*, not in the mystical works discussed in chapter three), who communicates his light to all creatures, corresponds somewhat to the Buddhistic teaching about enlightenment or 'satori'. A further inspection of the thought of pseudo-Dionysius is absent in Fortmann, who borrows from D. Rutledge[65].

What Fortmann leaves out of the discussion are the mystical works of pseudo-Dionysius, namely *The Mystical Theology* and *Divine Names*, ch. 4, already discussed in chapter three. He seems unaware that pseudo-Dionysius envisaged God not only as the source of light, but also as the source of all love, all eros. The 'return' to God is not only the return of the little light to the Great Light, but is also the return of the little eros ('erotès') to the Great or Primal eros. Perhaps Fortmann could overlook this so fundamental aspect of the Christian teaching on light because, as has already been mentioned, Fortmann considered love for God to be a clear light which can not be experienced sensually[66]. It is a purely spiritual love which receives no support from sense perception[67]. He speaks indeed of a clear light, but not of a warm light. The libidinal context of this enlightenment is disregarded.

Not so, John of the Cross. For him, illumination is the glow which comes from the warmth of mystical union. The symbol of warmth refers to the thirst of love (*Night* I,11,1). Although he often refers to warmth, he combines it with the symbol of light in only a few passages (*Night* II,12,7; *Flame*

3,76; 3,80). This yearning desire for God is associated in the *Flame* with a whole family of 'hot' symbols: glow, fire, spark, flaming sword of love, flaming arrow of love, cauterization, sores and wounds of love's burning, etc. The living love from God reaches out to man with its flame, which at first purifies man and then ignites his heart. The light of wisdom is obtained through the suffering which the fire of love causes when it purifies man (*Night* II,5,1; 10,3; 12,2; *Cant.* 34,12). Enlightenment, therefore, is obtained precisely through the way of suffering, and not by avoiding suffering through mystical detachment. God's light and love purify man the way fire purifies precious metals.

The direction in these symbols is from God to man. This implies that the 'desiderium Dei' is not so much man's desire for God, but God's desire for man. This is why John of the Cross can say, "If the soul is looking for God, then its Lover is looking for it much more" (*Flame* 3,28). This echoes the idea in pseudo-Dionysius that eros is divine in its origin. In describing the final stage, when the creature has returned back to the divine eros and light, John of the Cross uses the symbol of a log that has completely caught on fire, giving forth both light and warmth. The symbol of fire, not of light, is the final or ultimate symbol of mystical union in the Christian tradition, because it recognizes the libidinal aspect of divine union.

The erotic or sexual connotations in the theme of the spiritual marriage enter the picture here again. The reason nuptial imagery is appropriate for describing enlightenment is given by J. W. Dixon:

"To know and to desire are parts of the same act. We know with the same flesh that desires and the attempt to know outside desire falsifies the knowing, which would be no more than a private fate were it not that we also falsify the known. We desire with the same flesh that knows, and the attempt to desire without knowing impoverishes the desire, which would be no more than a private failure were it not that we thereby impoverish the desired.

The rhythms and tonalities of our knowing are shaped by our desiring. If the knowing is itself unsexed (as some undoubtedly is), its direction, its purpose, its use is shaped by the tone of the dominant sexuality, as the virginal purity of mathematics becomes the major tool of the engineer's conquering."[68]

"The imagery that is emerging here may have rhetorical use as a heuristic device, but more is involved than picturesque or emotive speech. Erotics is the art and science of sexuality, the knowing of sexuality as, in its completion, a relation between a man and a woman. To speak of 'the erotics of knowing' is to take the sexual relation between a man and a woman as a paradigm of knowing anything as, in the moral enterprise, knowing is a paradigm of the sexual relation. To use such a paradigm — or metaphor — requires exploring its full range for insight into the act studied; the whole range of sexuality becomes in some way interpretative of some aspect of knowing . . . The model of the true marriage becomes the model for true knowing . . ."[69]

For this reason, the symbolism of the spiritual marriage can be especially revealing when it is used to describe what the Christian will experience when he or she comes to the full likeness or identification with the Divine

Wisdom. This parallel will be dealt with here under two headings: increasing communication and increasing beauty, in the transition from the 'spiritual betrothal' to the final stage, the 'spiritual marriage'. Finally, the actual role of the body in divine union will be briefly considered.

a. Increasing communication.

In his last work, *The Living Flame of Love*, John of the Cross reviews briefly the stages of growth by which the 'old man' is replaced with the 'new man', formed in the image of Christ in justice and holiness (*Flame* 2,33). These stages of growth can be summarized roughly as the stage of the spiritual betrothal and the spiritual marriage. As in the more modern view of betrothals, the two lovers involved have already experienced union, to some degree, long before marriage. The idea that mystical union only occurs in the final stage of spiritual development, the spiritual marriage, is a religious parallel to the cultural pattern of earlier times, when intercourse occurred only in marriage (ideally) and not before. In mystical union, as John of the Cross describes it, the spiritual betrothal also contains mystical union, although this is only a union of love and grace. In the final stage, the spiritual marriage, there is furthermore communication between God and man (*Flame* 3,24). Just as intercourse can have increasingly more meaning as the degree of communication and intimacy deepens, so, too, mystical union can increase in meaning or depth. In the spiritual betrothal, the Holy Spirit anoints the believer with the unctions of love, preparing him or her for mystical union in the way a bride (groom) is prepared for the wedding. God's love acted in the first stage to purify the 'old man'. It was oppressive and painful. In the final stage, the fire of God's love is no longer oppressive. Rather, it is so soft that it is like waters of life which satisfy the thirst of the spirit (*Flame* 3,8).

The increase in communication in the spiritual marriage comes about because man has come to understand the language of God (*Flame* 3,37). This increased communication transforms the believer into the 'new man', who is spiritually free:

". . . in this present communication and transformation of love which the soul now enjoys in this life . . . she feels the new spring of liberty, enlargement and joy of spirit . . ." (*Cant.* 39,8)

"Contemplation is information and divine love together." (*Flame* 3,32)

"The soul, like one that has gone forth from this dungeon and imprisonment, and is brought into the recreation of spaciousness and liberty, feels and experiences great sweetness of peace and loving friendship with God together with a ready abundance of spiritual communication." (*Night* II,7,4)

The light of enlightenment, this divine communication, is the light of possession. In the spiritual marriage, the contemplative possesses God and

213

all the attributes of God, his glory, freedom and wisdom (*Flame* 1,21).

b. Increasing beauty.

The final result is that God transforms the believer, making him as beautiful as fire itself (*Night* II,10,1). He becomes transformed into the beauty of the Divine Wisdom, the Word of God (*Cant.* 36,7). Iconography represents the Sophia, the Divine Wisdom, not as a light, but as a woman with red hands and a red face. This goes back to an older tradition which represented every angel or messenger from God with flaming hands and face[70]. This signifies that in bringing the message to man from heaven, the angel caught on fire. Although it is most unlikely that John of the Cross ever saw an icon of the Sophia, his grasp of the essentials of her identity is close to that of the icon.

John of the Cross works out the theme of beauty by associating it with the Divine Wisdom. He states that there are two degrees or kinds of beauty. There is the lesser beauty, the beauty of creatures, which is caused by their possessing a minor degree of wisdom. This he calls 'evening wisdom'. The greater beauty, that of the Divine Wisdom, is the 'morning wisdom' (*Cant.* 36,6). The minor beauty is the result of God's having passed by (i.e. having created the world):

"Scattering a thousand graces, He passed through these groves in haste, and looking upon them as he went, left them, by his glance alone, clothed with beauty." (*Cant.*, stanza 5)

The rivalry between creation and God, so typical of John of the Cross, is resolved in this theme of beauty. The contemplative soul expresses, in the *Canticle*, the desire to see as much as possible of the minor beauty, i.e. the beauty of creation, as well as the major beauty, i.e. God. The two kinds of beauty form a unity (*Cant.* 36,7). He is able to arrive at this synthesis because the concept of the Divine Wisdom is very closely linked with the act of creation (*Cant.* 5,1). In fact, the only mention John of the Cross makes of a harmony between God and creation is in reference to the Divine Wisdom and its beauty (*Cant.* 15,27).

Because man is created by God, he is already clothed with the beauty and dignity of the minor wisdom. But man also has the possibility of becoming clad with the major wisdom or beauty by becoming like the Divine Wisdom:

"Transform me in the beauty of Divine Wisdom, which is the Word, the Son of God." (*Cant.* 36,7)

The 'new man' in Christ is at the same time man at his most beautiful. It is interesting to note that John of the Cross has in mind both masculine and feminine beauty, corresponding to both a bride's mysticism as well as a bridegroom's mysticism. He almost never uses the Spanish word 'belleza' to describe this beauty, since it is a word which usually refers to feminine beauty. Rather, he uses the word 'hermosura', which can refer just as much to the handsomeness of a man as the beauty of a woman. Whether the Divine Wisdom itself is masculine or feminine is ambiguous. The Spanish word for wisdom, 'sabiduría', is feminine, so whenever John of the Cross refers to the Divine Wisdom, he uses the pronoun 'she'. However, as the quote above shows, the Divine Wisdom is identified with the Word, the Son of God, which would make it masculine.

The description of the believer's preparation for the transformation into the beauty of the Sophia in the spiritual marriage, however, corresponds to the preparation of the bride. This is because John of the Cross is thinking, not so much about the individual believer, as the whole people of God, the nation of Israel or the Church, both of which are referred to as 'she'. In the betrothal, which begins with baptism, God starts adorning the believer, who is destined to share the beauty of the celestial king (or queen). Using the text of Ezechiel, which describes the beauty treatment which God gave Israel, John of the Cross sketches briefly in symbols this preparation for union:

"And I washed thee with water (baptism), and I washed away the blood from thee, and I anounted thee with oil, and clothed thee with colours and shod thee with hyacinth, and girded thee with fine linen and clothed thee with fine garments. And I decked thee with ornaments, put bracelets on thy hands and a chain on thy neck. And upon thy mouth I put a jewel, and in thy ears earrings and a crown of beauty upon thy head. And thou were decked with gold and silver, and clothed in fine linen and broidered silks and many colours; bread very choice and honey and oil didst thou eat, and thou becamest of mighty beauty . . ." (*Cant.* 23,6)

The meaning of these symbols is given in the following stanza. The believer is made beautiful in the perfection of love. The adornments and gifts are the virtues which the believer possesses in strength and perfect spiritual peace. The ecclesiastical or communal character of this transformation in beauty is underlined again in the following text:

"Let us so act that, by means of this exercise of love aforementioned, we may attain to seeing ourselves in Thy beauty in life eternal: that is, that I may be so transformed in Thy beauty, since I shall have Thy own beauty; so that, when one of us looks at the other, each may see in the other his beauty, the beauty of both being Thy beauty alone, and I being absorbed in Thy beauty; and thus I shall see Thee in Thy beauty and Thou wilt see me in Thy beauty . . . This is the adoption of the sons of God . . . And thus . . . (the Church) will share in the very beauty of the Spouse in the day of her triumph, which will be when she sees God face to face." (*Cant.* 36,5)

In both the texts quoted above, John of the Cross brings the theme of beauty into an ecclesiological context. He refers in the first text, not to an individual queen such as Esther, but to the people of Israel. In the second text, although beginning with an individual's experience, he enlargens this to include all the church, the mystical body of Christ. However, just as the individual experience is a parallel to the communal experience in baptism, so, too, the individual's experience at the 'day of triumph' will be parallel to that of the whole church body. The role of the body of the individual believer is just as much a part of the transformation into beauty as the role of the mystical body of Christ, the church. This theme of the bodily likeness receives a further extension in John of the Cross' treatment of resurrection.

2. *The bodily likeness.*

In this concluding section the usual reference point, the empirical data, will be left behind. What is being considered here is something which is beyond the scope of empiricism, but which is not necessarily beyond the rules of logic. The logical implications of the likeness to Christ are drawn.

John of the Cross himself maintained an empirical approach to the matter of the bodily manifestations of mysticism, to the distress of his contemporaries who failed to appreciate his scepticism. Stories abound about his 'hard' attitude. A famous stigmatic was to be found in the neighborhood of a convent where he was staying. He had no desire to go and see her, but finally he gave in to the insistent urging of his friends. However, he took along a wet sponge. When he finally did meet her, he merely proceeded to wipe off the so-called 'stigmata'. Her fraud became all too evident. On another occasion, a woman went into what seemed to be ecstasy. Since this happened in a crowded church during a service, a sensation was caused. John of the Cross happened to be celebrating Mass there. He saw the disturbance and instructed a friar to throw water in her face. She allegedly could neither see nor hear anything in her ecstatic trance. When the friar made the motion to throw the water, the glass broke off at the stem and a piece flew in her face. She dodged it, and was not hit. Everyone saw this and drew the obvious conclusion. She was laughed out of the church. Thus, John of the Cross subjected such phenomena to empirical 'research' where possible. He did not reject such bodily manifestations if the empirical test proved that the phenomenon was authentic. But more often than not, the fraud was revealed.

Thus, when John of the Cross does speak about the actual bodily effects of divine union, he is speaking with the same kind of educated naivete or empirical openness which Fortmann advocated. He knows that fraud is possible but does not exclude the possibility that authentic bodily phenomena can occur. His rule of thumb is, the bodily manifestation must correspond to the spiritual state:

"God, generally speaking, gives no mercy to the body without first and primarily performing it in the soul. When the seraph wounded St. Francis, wounding the soul with love in the five wounds (of Christ), their effect went out, too, to the body, impressing them also in the body." (*Flame* 2.13)

216

In the mystical theology of John of the Cross, the transformation into the 'new man' also includes a certain bodily transformation. The beginner's body is not experienced in the libidinal force of God's love and therefore it can not bear much of the divine 'touch':

"That touch is not continuous nor intense because it would disconnect the soul from the body." (*Cant.* 7,4)

Later on the experience is better assimilated, symbolized by wine in this quote:

"The drink is diffused and poured out through all the members and veins of the body." (*Cant.* 26,5)

Finally the experience of union is completely integrated in the body:

"Now its soul and body and all its powers and all its abilities are employed in the things which belong to the service of the Bridegroom." (*Cant.* 28,2)

"All the ability of my soul and body . . . all is moved by love and in love." (*Cant.* 28,8)

"And in this good which comes to the soul the unction of the Holy Spirit sometimes overflows into the body, and this is enjoyed by all the substance of sense and all the members of the body and the very marrow and bones, not as feebly as is usually the case, but with a feeling of great delight and glory, which is felt even in the remotest joints of the feet and hands. And the body feels such glory in the glory of the soul that it magnifies God after its own manner, perceiving that He is in its very bones, even as David said, 'All my bones shall say, "God, who is like unto Thee?" ' And since all that can be said concerning this matter is less than the truth, it suffices to say of the bodily experience, as of the spiritual, that it savours of eternal life." (*Flame* II,22)

"Thou art become marvellously glad with all the harmony of thy soul and even of thy body, which has become a Paradise watered by springs Divine." (*Flame* III,7)

To modern theologians such concrete references to the body's participation in the experience of God and even of eternal life seem naive. Vergote states:

"The resurrection of the body is by tradition the object of our hope. But do we dare to say that the resurrected body is the real body, namely that which experiences pleasure and happiness? When many no longer dare to speak about the resurrection, is that then perhaps because they are only thinking about the miraculous event of the resurrection, which has become suspect? They fail to recognize in the resurrected body the paradigmatic expression of libidinal bodiliness."[71]

What John of the Cross is attempting to explain in symbolic and poetical language, as well as in concrete observations of bodily sensations, is that the body, too, grows in the likeness of Christ. Thereby it follows the imitation of Christ to its logical conclusion, namely the resurrection of a body which can experience the pleasure of the 'wedding feast', the introduction into eternal life. Perhaps the main difference between the earthly body and the body of the life to come is that the resurrected body will be

217

able to bear a much more intense contact with God, because its capacity for pleasure will have been expanded. According to John of the Cross, the real cause of dying, when the 'new man' dies, is not some natural cause, such as illness or old age. These may appear to be the causes to 'outsiders', but the real cause is an impulse of God's love which so overwhelms the body's ability to support pleasure, that the body dies:

"Their spirits are wrested away by nothing less than some loving impulse and encounter far loftier and of greater power and strength than any in the past, for it has succeeded in breaking the web and bearing away a jewel, which is the spirit." (*Flame* I,30)

Returning finally to Fortmann, the problem which he ran into in trying to bring the Christian experience of death into harmony with the Buddhistic view of death is that the biological reality of the body had to recede into the background. Fortmann writes in the article already referred to, "The clear light", that it is possible to obtain a certain distance or detachment from the body by thinking, 'Not I live, but Christ lives in me.' What he did not stop to consider was that the body in the Christian experience, precisely in and through pain can come to resemble Christ's body. The trouble which Fortmann has is essentially that which distinguishes the Christian view of life from the Buddhist view: in Buddhism there is no reflection on the positive acceptance of suffering and there is no possibility of a resurrection. Fortmann's problem was also an existential one. While dying of cancer himself, the issue of finding detachment from pain was not so much a theological as a psycho-somatic issue. A more detached Fortmann is found in an earlier article, written several years before his death[72]:

"We have no other means to capture the mysterious reality of the after life than that of the biblical and liturgical images. They are the most adequate approach to a dimension of reality which in principle lies outside our ability to understand, of which 'no ear had heard nor has ever entered anyones mind'. Of course one can object with Marx that that dimension does indeed come from man, that all belief in a resurrection and a happier existence after death is the wish dream of an immature humanity, an escape for the oppressed heart of man from the misery of this world, an illusion which serves merely to help man survive *here.* That is the last and most powerful attack which can be made on the Christian belief, because it is so reasonable: we are discontent with this life and therefore we *create* incessant illusions. However, this is no proof. The fact that we have a need for the consolation which lies in the resurrection does not prove that it is merely fantasy. It proves that only when one starts with the point of view that every religious expectation has to end up as a deception. Disbelief is an a priori, just as much as belief is.

However, he who feels able to believe should be careful not to ruin his belief with a dry rationalism which wants to know exactly what happens in an area where only images can take one further. He must let the images be and bear them in him with respect. He should *dare* to let himself be consoled by the images. True, he must not reject criticism. On the contrary, he should support it as far as possible. But where it is not possible, because the area itself is inaccessible to criticism, there he must keep modestly silent.

It is not beneath our human condition to find comfort in these images. It would be so only if God's mercy had been proven to be illusory and the loneliness of dying — without God — was a scientifically proven fact."

The route covered in this study of Christian mysticism has been indicated in the foreword. It is directed toward a re-evaluation of the body in western spirituality and toward a comparison of the role of the body·in Christian mysticism with the role of the body in oriental meditation techniques. The very negative treatment of the body so characteristic of western spirituality is shown in the strict ascetical teaching of John of the Cross in chapter one. Chapter two has put this negative view to the test and has discovered that asceticism has nothing to do with mystical advancement. Hereby a serious attack has been made on the foundations of the traditional western monastic or cloistered spirituality. Put more· positively, an opening has been made for a new body-oriented spirituality which is more suited to the life of the modern layman.

The difference in the role of the body between western and oriental spirituality is explored very concretely in the EEG study in chapter two. The Maharishi, the leader of the Transcendental Meditation movement, states that the nervous system is the main bodily function involved in meditation. By strengthening the nervous system the meditator gains inner peace and rest. This study suggests that this is the valuable finding of the TM movement, a finding which should be incorporated into the practice of Christian prayer, too. However, as the reports of the subjects show, in Christian mysticism not just the nervous system but the entire body is involved in the experience of divine union. That is, the whole range of bodily sensuality or eroticism is involved. The author has suggested that this libidinal experience of the divine could enrich the experience of TM.

Chapter three then goes on to show how the 'via negativa' in no way implies a rejection of the body. The historical study presented here tries to clear the air of prejudices about the supposedly purely spiritual nature of Christian mysticism. The role of eroticism is examined in its original context in pseudo-Dionysius. Finally, chapter four explores precisely that area of human, bodily experience, i.e. the libido, which oriental meditation techniques bypass. This orientation toward erotic love supplies the main motive or dynamism behind Christian mysticism. The author shows that this search for pleasure in ones own body is less egotistical than might appear. Indeed, it is the search for affective redemption. The identification with the object of love and union, Christ, provides the libidinal attraction in prayer. The actual implications of bodily eroticism in prayer are dealt with: sexual feelings in prayer, the specific differences in approach to prayer in men and women, the repercussion upon the rest of the libido and the way this affects repressed desires and inner conflicts. Finally, the logical conclusion is drawn that if the experience of the divine in Christian mysticism is so body-oriented, then the goal of the Christian mystical union must also be body-oriented. Both the means to union and the union itself must involve the body. For this reason the Christian teaching of the resurrection of the body is the logical conclusion to the affective redemption, the liberation of eroticism, which Christian mysticism aims at. The possibilities which this conformity to the risen Christ open up are further explored, possibilities which lie outside the scope of oriental meditation, but which are central to Christian mysticism. Through this reflection upon the role of the body in prayer, one can conclude that eroticism in the prayer of union is not sublimation or projection of sexual desire, but actual participation in the divine eroticism of God's love.

Notes

Notes to the Preface:

[1] For example, see the stereotypes of 'introvert' and 'extravert' mysticism in:
Butler, C., *Western Mysticism*, London, 1927.
Master, R. & Houston, J., *The Varieties of Psychedelic Experience*, N.Y., 1966.
Reypens, L., s.v. "Ame: structure d'aprés les mystiques," *Dictionnaire de Spiritualité, Ascétique et Mystique*, vol. I, Paris, 1937, 433-469.
Stace, W. T., *Mysticism and Philosophy*, London, 1960.
Underhill, E., *Mysticism*, N.Y., 1955.
[2] Vergote, A., *Psychologie religieuse*, Brussels, 1966[3], pp. 157-158.
[3] Schoonenberg, P., "Ervaringen en voorstellingen van Gods transcendentie," *Politiek of mystiek?*, (Schillebeeckx, E., ed.), Brugges, 1973, pp. 51-68.
[4] e.g. Cox, H., *The Seduction of the Spirit*, N.Y., 1973, section I, ch. 3, "The House of Reason."
[5] For a concise review of attitudes of psychiatrists and psychologists regarding the 'psychopathology' of mysticism see:
Campbell, A., *Seven States of Consciousness*, London, 1973, pp. 112-122.
[6] Dietrich, H., "Über Hysterie in Mystik und Mystik in Hysterie," *Confinia Psychiatrica*, 6, (1963), pp. 232-241.
Leuba, J. H., *The Psychology of Religious Mysticism*, London & Boston, 1925[1], 1972[2].
Moller, H., "Affective Mysticism in Western Civilization," *Psychoanalytic Review*, 52, (1965), pp. 115-130.
Prince, R. & Savage, C., "Mystical states and the concept of regression," *Psychedelic Review*, 8, (1966), pp. 59-75.
Spoerri, T., "Beitrage zur Ekstase," *Bibl. Psychiatrica et Neurologica*, no. 132, (Karger, E., ed.), Basel & N.Y., 1968[2].
[7] Eysenck, H. J., *Readings in Extraversion/Introversion*, vol. I, London, 1970, p. 265. (Since Eysenck's definition of 'extraversion' will be used throughout this study his term 'extraversion' will be used instead of the more usual term 'extroversion'. For his definition of extraversion, see p. 70 ff, ch. 2 in this Study.)
[8] Hood, R., "Psychological strength and the report of intense religious experience," *Journal for the Scientific Study of Religion*, 13 (1974), pp. 65-71. For a wider, more positive view of regression see:
Allison, J., "Adaptive regression and intense religious experiences," *Journal of Nervous and Mental Disease*, 145 (1967), pp. 452-463.
[9] Roldán, A., *Introducción a la ascética diferencial*, Madrid, 1962.
[10] Contrary to Stace, see above, footnote 1.

Notes to Chapter One.

[1] Bataillon, M., *Erasmo y España*, Mexico & Buenos Aires, 1950[2], vol. 2, pp. 369-370.

² Cf. Eulogio de la Virgen del Carmen, O.C.D., "Illumination" and "Illuminisme et illuminés", *Dictionnaire de Spiritualité*, vol. 7, 1346 & 1367.

³ Both *The Spiritual Canticle* and *The Living Flame of Love* occur in two versions, called A and B. Version B has been used throughout this study except in the 'Questionnaire on Spirituality' in chapter two and where specifically stated with the indication (A).

⁴ For further information on the life and works of John of the Cross see e.g.:
Baruzi, J., *Saint Jean de la Croix et le problème de l'expérience mystique*, Paris, 1924, 1931².
Bruno de J. M., O.C.D., *St. Jean de la Croix*, Brugges, 1961.
Crisógono de Jesús Sacramentado, O.C.D., *San Juan de la Cruz, su obra científica y su obra literaria*, 2 vols., Madrid, 1929. (English translation: *The Life of St. John of the Cross*, N.Y., 1958.)
Cristiani, L. (Mgr.), *St. John of the Cross*, N.Y., 1962.
Efrén de la Madre de Dios, O.C.D., *San Juan de la Cruz y el misterio de la stma. Trinidad en la vida espiritual*, Zaragoza, 1947.
Matias del Niño Jesús, O.C.D. (ed.), *Vida y obras completas de San Juan de la Cruz* (the biography of Crisógono, revised and annotated), BAC, vol. 15, Madrid, 1972⁶.
Peers, A., *Handbook to the Life and Times of St. Teresa and St. Jean of the Cross*, London, 1954.
Peers, A., *The Complete Works of St. John of the Cross*, 3 vols., Westminster, Maryland, 1964.
Ruíz, F., O.C.D., *Introducción a San Juan de la Cruz: el escritor, los escritos, el sistema*, BAC, vol. 279, Madrid, 1968.

⁵ Ruíz, F., *Op. Cit.*, p. 153.

⁶ All translations of John of the Cross' writings are taken from A. Peers, *The Complete Works of St. John of the Cross*, 3 vols., N.Y., 1964.

⁷ Mager, A., *Mystik als seelische Wirklichkeit*, Graz, 1945, p. 209.

⁸ Ruíz, F., *Op. Cit.*, pp. 451-452.

⁹ Peters, J., O.C.D., *Geloof en mystiek*, Louvain, 1957.

¹⁰ Bendiek, J., *Art. Cit.*, p. 100.

¹¹ Gregory the Great, *Morales sur Job (Sources Chrétiennes 32), p. 91, introduction.*

¹² Cordero, F., "La teología espiritual de Santa Teresa de Jesús, reacción contra el dualismo neoplatónico", *Revista Española de Teología*, vol. 30 (1970), 1 & 2, p. 3-38.

¹³ *Ibid.*, p. 7.

¹⁴ Verbeke, G., *L'evolution de la doctrine du pneuma du stoicisme a s. Augustin*, Paris, 1943, p. 43.

¹⁶ Cf. the revised version of Crisógono's biography in: Matias del Niño Jesús, *Vida y obras completas de San Juan de la Cruz*, Madrid, 1972, p. 62-63.

¹⁷ *Ibid.*, p. 79.

¹⁸ *Ibid.*, p. 227, n. 113.

¹⁹ *Ibid.*, p. 269.

²⁰ Morel, G., *Op. Cit.*, p. 64.

²¹ Lucien Marie de St. Joseph, "S. Jean de la Croix," *Dict. de Spiritualité*, vol. 8, col. 408-447.

²² *Ibid.*, col. 443.

²³ Matias, *Op. Cit.*, prologue.

²⁴ Cf. footnote 15.

²⁵ Trueman, E. W., *Op. Cit.*, p. 324.

²⁶ For a sample of the passages in John of the Cross to which the Spanish Inquisition objected see: "Reply of RPM Fray B. Ponce de León, Prima Professor of Theology in the University of Salamanca, to the Notes and Objections Which Were Made Concerning Certain Propositions Taken From the Book of our Father Fray John of the Cross" (July 11, 1622), in: Peers, A., *The Complete Works of St. John of the Cross*, vol. III, Appendices, pp. 355-404. Especially propositions II, IX, XXIV and above all XL are important since they involve the

duality of human/divine, sense/spirit, to which the Inquisition had objections.
[27] Commented upon in: Eulogio de S. Juan de la Cruz, *La transformación total del alma en Dios según S. Juan de la Cruz*, Madrid, 1963.
[28] Lucien Marie de St. Joseph, *L'expérience de Dieu: Actualité du message de Saint Jean de la Croix*, Paris, 1968, especially pp. 277-280.
[29] Cf. footnote 12.
[30] Gabriel of St. M. Magdalene, *Spiritual Commentary on the Constitutions of the Discalced Carmelite Nuns* (Geestelijk commentaar op de Constituties van de Ongeschoeide Carmelitessen) (translated from French by the sisters in Hulst, Zeeland, Holland, 1942.)
[31] *Ibid.*, p. 60 (trans.: MM)

Notes to Chapter Two:

[1] Gregory of Nyssa, *In Scripturae verba 'Faciamus hominem ad imaginem nostram'*, Migne PG 44, 257, B-C.
[2] The selection of psychological tests was made with the help of Dr. G. van Vliet and various other psychologists at the University of Nijmegen. The statistical analyses were made with the assistance of Dr. A. van der Ven, P. van Teeuwen, H. van der Hoeven and others in the department of mathematical psychology at the Univ. of Nijmegen.
[3] Greeley, A. M., *Ecstasy: A way of knowing*, New Jersey, 1974.
[4] The Dutch translation used was by J. C. Peters and J. A. Jacobs, *Joannes van het Kruis, Mystieke Werken*, Gent, 1975.
[5] Kampen, D. van, "De 'Personality Questionnaire' van Eysenck & Eysenck: een factor-analytisch onderzoek," *Nederlands Tijdschrift voor de Psychologie*, 31/1 (1976), pp. 23-34.
[6] Hood, R. W., "Psychological strength and the report of intense religious experience," *Journal for the Scientific Study of Religion*, 13 (1974), pp. 65-71.
[7] Nuttin, J. & Beuten, B., *Handleiding bij de persoonlijkheidsinventaris MMPI*, Louvain Univ. Press, Louvain, 1969, pp. 37-38.
[8] Hood, R. W., "The Construction and Preliminary Validation of a Measure of Reported Mystical Experience," *Journal for the Scientific Study of Religion*, 14 (1975), pp. 29-41.
[9] Acknowledgments should be extended to the department of EEG in the Institute of Neurology at the Catholic University of Nijmegen for putting their equipment and services so generously at the disposal of this study; especially for the guidance of the neurologist, Dr. S.L.H. Notermans and for the services of the EEG operant, J. van der Wee, the programmer, Ir. H. de Weert and the technician, J. Kap.
[10] Fortmann, H., *Aandachtig Bidden*, Nijmegen, 1945 (dissertation).
[11] Jung, C. G., *Psychologischen Typen*, Zürich, 1946, pp. 624-641.
[12] Cf. Gray, J., "Strength of the Nervous System, Introversion-Extraversion, Conditionability and Arousal," in: *Readings in Extraversion-Introversion*, (H. J. Eysenck, ed.), London, 1970², vol. I, pp. 49-77.
[13] Eysenck, H. J., *The Biological Basis of Personality*, Springfield, Ill., 1967.
[14] Orlebeke, J. F., *Aktivering, extraversie en sterkte van het zenuwstelsel*, Assen, 1972, p. 59.
[15] Eysenck, H. J., *Readings in Extraversion-Introversion*, vol. III, pp. 60-61, 71-81, 97-99, 499-512.
[16] Orlebeke, *Op. Cit.*, pp. 54-78.
[17] *Ibid.*, p. 128.
[18] Savage, R., "Electro-cerebral activity, extraversion and neuroticism," *British Journal of Psychiatry*, 110 (1964), p. 98.
[19] Eysenck, H. J., *The Biological Basis of Personality*, p. 68.
[20] Gale, A., "The Psychophysiology of Individual Differences: Studies of Extraversion and the

223

EEG," in: *New Approaches in Psychological Measurement* (P. Kline, ed.), London, 1973, pp. 211-256.

[21] *Ibid.*, p. 234.

[22] *Ibid.*, p. 233.

[23] See p. 267 appendix.

[24] See p. 54 chapter two.

[25] Brown, B., "Emotional Influences," *The Alpha Syllabus: A Handbook of Human EEG Activity* (Brown, B & Klug, J., eds.), Springfield, Ill., 1974, pp. 204-219.

[26] Woolfolk, R. L., "Psychophysiological Correlates of Meditation," *Archives of General Psychiatry,* 32 (1975), pp. 1326-1333.

[27] Das, N.N. & Gastaut, H., "Variations de l'activité du coeur et des muscles squelettiques au cours de la méditation et de l'extase yogique," *Electroencephalographie Clin. Neurophysiol.,* Supplement 6 (1955), pp. 211-219.

[28] Wenger, M. A. & Bagchi, B.K., "Studies of autonomic functions in practitioners of Yoga in India," *Behavioral Sciences,* 6 (1961), pp. 312-323.

[29] Bagchi, B. K. & Wenger, M.A., "Electrophysiological correlates of some Yogi exercises," *Electr. Clin. Neurophysiol.,* Suppl. 7 (1957), pp. 132-149.

[30] Anand, B. K., Chhina, G. S., Singh, B., "Some aspects of electroencephalographic studies in Yogis," *Electr. Clin. Neurophysiol.,* 13 (1961), pp. 452-456.

[31] Hirai, T., "Electroencephalographic Study on the Zen Meditation," *Seishin Shinkegaku Zasshi* (Psychiatria et Neurologia Japonica) (Tokyo), 62/1 (1060), 76-105. Abstract in: Hirai, T., *Zentralblatt für die gesamte Neurologie und Psychiatrie,* 158 (1960), p. 144.

[32] *Ibid.* (translated for the author by Noboyuki Kajiwara)

[33] Kasamatsu, A. & Hirai, T., "An electroencephalographic study on the Zen meditation (Zazen)," *Psychologia,* 12 (1969), pp. 205-225.

[34] Zen Master Hakuun Yasutani Roschi, translated by Fumio Hashimoto, in: "Fukan-Zazen-gi", *Wunderbare Katze und andere Zen-texte* (K. Dürckheim, ed.), Weilheim Oberbayern, 1964, p. 83.

[35] Pagano, R. P., Rose, R. M., Stivers, R. M., Warrenburg, S., "Sleep during transcendental meditation," *Science,* 191 (1976), pp. 308-310.

[36] Benson, H., Beary, J. F., Carol, M. P., "The relaxation response," *Psychiatry,* 37 (1974), pp. 37-38.

[37] Wallace, R. K., Benson, H., Wilson, A. F., "A wakeful hypometabolic physiological state," *Am. Journal of Physiol.,* 221 (1971), pp. 795-799.

[38] Banquet, J. P., "Spectral analysis of the EEG in meditation," *Electr. Clin. Neurophysiol.,* 35 (1973), pp. 143-151.

[39] Schwartz, G. E., "Pros and cons of meditation: Current findings on physiology and anxiety, self-control, drug abuse and creativity," lecture at the 81st annual convention of the American Psychological Association, Montreal, 1973.
Orme-Johnson, D. W., "Autonomic Stability and Transcendental Meditation," *Psychosom. Medicine,* 35 (1973), pp. 341-349.

[40] Emerson, V. F., "Can belief systems influence neurophysiology: Some implications of research on meditation," *Newsletter Review* (Montreal), 5 (no. 1 & 2), 1972, pp. 20-31.

[41] Doxey, N. C. S., "The high alpha state – a distinct state of consciousness?", paper presented at the South African Psychological Association Congress, Witwatersrand University, Johannesburg, July, 1972.

[42] *Ibid.,* p. 6.

[43] Johnson, L. C., "A psychophysiology for all states," *Psychophysiology,* 6/5 (1970), pp. 501-516.

[44] Doxey, N. C. S., *Art. Cit.,* p. 8.

[45] Glueck, B. C. & Stroebel, C. F., "'Biofeedback and Meditation in the Treatment of Psychi-

atric Illnesses," *Comprehensive Psychiatry*, 16, no. 4 (1975), pp. 303-321.

[46] Sperry, R. W., "Brain bisection and consciousness," *Brain and Conscious Experience* (Eccles, J., ed.), Berlin, Heidelberg, N.Y., 1966, pp. 298-313.

[47] Jung, C. G., *Op. Cit.*, p. 47.

[48] Many thanks to the psycho-physiologist, A. Gale, for his advice in the writing up of this experiment.

[49] For further information regarding details of the procedure and the reasons for adopting certain methods of measurement, consult the parties mentioned note 9, ch. 2. The author was not present at all planning sessions and can not bear complete responsibility for the actual design and execution of the experiment.
Gratitude must be extended at this point to the "Stichting Nijmeegse Universiteits Fonds" (SNUF) for generously subsidizing the costs of the subjects' travel to the Institute of Neurology at Nijmegen and for helping with the costs of the psychological testing.

[50] The term 'combination' designates a combination of drowsy, tense and irritated EEG patterns. The drowsy patterns differed from a normal drowsy EEG pattern since no gradual transition occurs from alpha to theta activity and because no increase in beta or vertex activity occurs. Rather the theta arises abruptly. The subjects report being alert rather than drowsy even though they sometimes have a high proportion of waxing and waning or sleep spindles. Their behavior, as observed during both the routine EEG and the prayer sessions, exhibited irritation at environmental stimuli and restlessness. This EEG pattern was therefore accompanied from time to time with many artifacts. Due to all these considerations, the term 'combination' was ranked as the most tense stadium on the scale.

[51] Gevins, A. S., Yeager, C. L., Diamond, S. L., Spire, J., Seitlin, G. M., Gevins, A. H., "Automated Analysis of the Electrical Activity of the Human Brain (EEG): A Progress Report," *Proceedings of the Instit. of Electrical and Electronics Engineers*, 63/10 (1975), pp. 1382-1399.

[52] Fortmann, H., *Op. Cit.*, p. 44.

[53] *Ibid.*, 23-24.

Notes to Chapter Three:

[1] Dürckheim, K. (Graf), *Wunderbare Katze und andere Zen-Texte*, Weilheim Oberbayern, 1964, col. p. 61-72.

[2] Lucien-Marie de St. Joseph, "S. Jean de la Croix," *Dict. de Spiritualité*, vol. 8, p. 432.

[3] Lucien-Marie, *L'expérience de Dieu: Actualité du message de Saint Jean de la Croix*, Paris, 1968, p. 277.

[4] Many thanks are extended to A. J. M. Davids for his help with this chapter.

[5] Ivánka, E. von, *Von den Namen zum Unnennbaren*, Einsiedeln, no date.
Tritsch, W., *Dionysius Areopagita: mystische Theologie und andere Schriften*, München, 1956.
Gandillac, M. de, *Oeuvres Complètes du Pseudo-Denys L'Aréopagite*, Paris, 1943.

[6] Ivánka, E., *Op. Cit.*, p. 10.

[7] *Ibid.*, p. 24.

[8] *Ibid.*, p. 16.

[9] Bernhart, J., *Die philosophische Mystik des Mittelalters*, München, 1922.

[10] Waldmann, M., "Thomas von Aquin und die 'Mystische Theologie' des Pseudo-Dionysius' ", *Geist und Leben*, 22 (1949), pp. 121-145.

[11] Roques, R., "Denys l'Aréopagite," *Dict. de Spiritualité*, vol. 3, pp. 283-284.

[12] Vanneste, J., "La théologie mystique du pseudo-Denys l'Aréopagite", *Studia Patristica*, vol. 5, (1962), pp. 401-415.

(The reason why no mention is made in this study of the three ways (via purgativa, illuminativa, unitiva) in pseudo-Dionysius is because they play no role in his mystical works. Cfr. Vanneste, J., "La doctrine des trois voies dan la *Théologie Mystique* du Pseudo-Denys l'Aréopagite," *Studia Patristica*, vol. 8, part 2 (1966), pp. 462-467.)

[13] Ivanka, *Op. Cit.*, p. 27.

[14] Stiglmayr, J., "Aszese und Mystik des sog. Dionysius Areopagita", *Scholastik*, vol. 2 (1927), pp. 161-207.

[15] *Ibid.*, p. 205.

[16] Ivanka, E. von, *Plato Christianus*, Einsiedeln, 1964, pp. 284-285.

[17] Völker, W., *Kontemplation und Ekstase bei Pseudo-Dionysius Areopagita*, Wiesbaden, 1958, p. 173: although Völker calls the 'nous' the contemplative organ in pseudo-Dionysius, he can find only about two texts in his mystical works which state this (*Div. Names*, ch. 1,1 (588B), and *Myst. Th.* I,3 (1001A).

[18] Stiglmayr, *Ibid.*

[19] Gross, J., *Entstehungsgeschichte des Erbsündendogmas*, München, vols. 1-4, 1960-1972.

[20] *Ibid.*, vol. 2, p. 211.

[21] Stiglmayr, *Op. Cit.*, p. 176.

[22] Bouyer, L., "Le pseudo-Denys et la mystique des pères," *Histoire de la Spiritualité Chrétienne*, vol. 1, Paris, 1966, pp. 473-503.
Völker, who asserts that apatheia in pseudo-Dionysius is a central theme, can only find 3 texts which use this term: EN II,3,8 (404C); CH 7,1 (205D); Ep. 10 (1117B), in: *Op. Cit.*, p. 39-40.

[23] Gross, *Op. Cit.*, vol. 2, pp. 204-205.

[24] Cf. Kern, W., "Übel", *Lex. f. Th. u. Kirche*, vol. 10, 1960², p. 431.

[25] E.g. Greshake, G., *Gnade als Konkrete Freiheit: Pelagius und Augustinus*, Mainz, 1972.
Stoeckle, B., "Erbsündige Begierlichkeit," *Münchener Theologische Zeitschrift*, 14 (4) (1963), pp. 225-242.
Heijke, J., "God in het diepst van de gedachte," *Bijdragen*, 16 (1955), pp. 357-377.

[26] Crisógono, *San Juan de la Cruz* . . ., Madrid, 1929, p. 34 (trans. MM).

[27] Efrén de la Madre de Dios, *San Juan de la Cruz*, Zaragoza, 1947, p. 205. (trans.: MM)

[28] *Ibid.*, p. 180, footnote 64. (Trans.: MM.)

[29] Matias (ed.), *Vida y obras*, BAC, Madrid, 1972, pp. 56-57 (Crisógono's biography, revised and annotated).

[30] Gross, J., *Op. Cit.*, vol. 2, pp. 241-243.

[31] Bruno de Jesús María, *Saint Jean de la Croix*, Paris, 1929, p. 13.

[32] Steggink, O., "L'enracinement de Saint Jean de la Croix dans le tronc de l'ordre car-mélitain," *Actualité de Jean de la Croix* (Lucien-Marie & J. M. Petit, eds.), Brugges, 1970, pp. 51-78.

[33] Translation by Werling, N. G., "The Book of St. John, 44", chs. 3-6, *The Sword*, 4 (1940), pp. 153-154.

[34] Quiroga, Jesús-María, *Historia de la vida y virtudes del ven. P. Fr. Juan de la Cruz*, Brussels, 1628, bk. 1, ch. 4, p. 35 (quoted by Eulogio de la Virgen del Carmen in "Saint Jean de la Croix", s.v. "Denys l'Aréopagite en Occident," *Dict. de Spiritualité*, vol. 3, col. 400. (trans.: MM.)

[35] Matias, *Op. Cit.*, p. 61, footnote 99.

[36] Crisógono, *Op. Cit.*, p. 35. (trans.: MM.)

[37] *Ibid.*, p. 59 (trans.: MM.)

[38] Gregorius Magnus, *Moralia in Job*, Migne, PL 75, 746A; 75, 713C, 509; 76, 782.

[39] Gillet, R., "Mystique Grégorienne," *Dict. de Spiritualité*, vol. 6, pp. 899-902.

[40] For the influence of Augustine upon the dualism in Gregory the Great, cfr.: Grégoire le Grand, *Morales sur Job*, Sources Chrétiennes, 32, introduction.

Butler, C., *Western Mysticism: The Teaching of St. Augustine, Gregory and Bernard on Contemplation and Contemplative Life*, London, 1927².

[41] Aubin, P., S.J., "Intériorité et extériorité dans les Moralia in Job de Saint Grégoire le Grand", *Rech. Sc. Rel.*, 62 (1974), pp. 117-166.

[42] Baruzi, J., *Saint Jean de la Croix et le problème de l'expérience mystique*, Paris, 1931², p. 305; footnotes on pp. 306-307 list all his uses of 'oscuras', 'tinieblas', 'tiniebla', 'noche'.

[43] Cf. "Augustine: Apocryphes", *Dict. de Spiritualité*, vol. 1 (2), 1134, no. 16.

[44] Bruno, *Op. Cit.*, p. 134, footnote 1, p. 160, footnote 2.

[45] Peers, A., *Op. Cit.*, vol. 3, p. 341.

[46] Cfr. *Clavis Patrum Latinorum*, (E. Dekkers, ed.), Steenbrugge, 1951¹.

[47] Bataillon, M., *Erasmo en España*, México & Buenos Aires, 1950², vol. 1, pp. 55-56.

[48] Adolfo de la Madre de Dios, "Inquisition", s.v. "Espagne", *Dict. de Spiritualité*, vol. 4 (2), 1165.

[49] Cfr. Corella, Sierra A., *La censura de libros y papeles en España y los índices y catálogos españoles de los prohibidos y expurgados*, Madrid, 1947. (This book could unfortunately not be obtained by the author.)

No mention of the *Soliloquios* is found in F. H. Reusch, *Der Index der verbotenen Bücher*, vol. 2.1, Aalen, 1967, but G. Quiroga's Index is only dealt with in a general way. Cfr. F. Reusch, *Indices Librorum Prohibitorum des Sechzehnten Jahrhunderts*, Tübingen, 1886, for the complete Index of Quiroga.

There is also no reference to the *Soliloquios* in the *Index Librorum Expurgatorum*, Madrid, 1584 by Gaspar Quiroga; only the commentaries by Erasmus and Vives on Augustine are mentioned.

[50] Bataillon, *Op. Cit.*, vol. 1, p. 344, n.3.

[51] It was not possible for the author to obtain a copy of Baconthorpe's works. The only extensive treatment of them available was in: Matias, *Op. Cit.*, p. 59-60, footnotes 80-93.

[52] Orcibal, J., *Saint Jean de la Croix et les mystiques rhéno-flamands*, Brugge, 1966, p. 25.

[53] Durantel, J., *Saint Thomas et le Pseudo-Denis*, Paris, 1919.

Waldmann, M., "Thomas von Aquin und die 'Mystische Theologie' des Pseudo-Dionysius", *Geist und Leben*, vol. 22, (1949), p. 121-145.

[54] Winklhofer, T. A., "Joh. vom Kreuz und die Surius Übersetzung der Werke Taulers," *Theologie in Geschichte und Gegenwart* (M. Schmaus, ed.), München, 1957, pp. 317-348.

[55] Proceso Apostólico de Jaén, fº 156.

[56] Jerónimo de San José, *Historia del ven. P. Fr. Juan de la Cruz*, Madrid, 1912, ch. 3, 64, c.18 (1614¹), (trans. MM). Quoted by P. Silverio, *Dictámenes de espíritu*, vol. 4, p. 351, as mentioned by Eulogio, "St. Jean de la Croix", *Dict. de Spiritualité*, vol. 3 (sub verb. "Influence de pseudo-Denys en Occident"), p. 401.

[57] *Ibid.*, pp. 401-407.

[58] Ivanka, *Plato Christianus*, pp. 284-285.

[59] Ivanka, E. von, "Die unmittelbare Gotteserkenntnis als Grundlage des natürlichen Erkennens und als Ziel des übernatürlichen Strebens bei Augustin," *Scholastik*, 13 (1938), p. 533.

[60] *De Trinitate*, bk. 15, ch. 24 (trans. S. McKenna, *Saint Augustine, The Trinity*, Washington, D.C., 1963.)

[61] Trueman, E. W., *El crisol del amor*, Barcelona, 1967, ch. 12.

[62] Ivanka, *Op. Cit.*, p. 536.

[63] Matias, *Op. Cit.*, p. 56, footnote 56 (trans. MM.)

[64] *Ibid.*, p. 57 (trans. MM.)

[65] *Ibid.*, p. 59 (trans. MM.)

[66] *Ibid.*, p. 60, cf. footnote 89.

[67] Jerónimo, *Op. Cit.*, bk. I, ch. 4,2; quoted in Efrén, *Op. Cit.*, p. 202 (trans. MM.)

[68] Ruíz, F., "Cimas de contemplación," *Eph. Carm.*, 13 (1962), p. 293 (trans. MM.)

[69] Viller, M. & Rahner, K., "Die areopagitischen Schriften," *Aszese und Mystik in Väterzeit*, Freiburg, 1939, p. 238-239.

[70] Ivanka, *Plato Christianus*, p. 286.

[71] Quiroga, Jesús María, *Historia de la vida y virtudes del ven. P. Fr. Juan de la Cruz*, p. 37 (trans. MM). (Many thanks to the theological library of the University of Louvain for putting this valuable book at the author's disposal.)

Notes to Chapter Four:

[1] Winklhofer, T. A., *Die Gnadenlehre in der Mystik des Hl. Johannes vom Kreuz*, Freiburg, 1936, p. 7.

[2] Fortmann, H. M. M., *Als ziende de Onzienlijke*, Hilversum/Antwerp, 1964-1968.

[3] Despite his rather extensive review of Fortmann's works, the logical connection between the various stages in Fortmann's intellectual development has been neglected by P. A. van Gennep, *Het kwetsbare midden: Persoon en werk van Han Fortmann*, Bilthoven, 1973.

[4] Fortmann, H., *Als ziende de Onzienlijke*, vol. 2, p. 255.

[5] Fortmann, H., *Aandachtig bidden*, Nijmegen/Utrecht, 1945, p. 98.

[6] *Ibid.*, p. 51.

[7] *Ibid.*, p. 147 (trans.: M.M.)

[8] *Ibid.*, p. 111.

[9] *Ibid.*, p. 136.

[10] *Ibid.*, p. 143.

[11] Schillebeeckx, E., "Het geloof functionerend in het menselijk zelfverstaan," *Het Woord in de geschiedenis*, Bilthoven, 1969, p. 52 (trans.: MM.)

[12] Vergote, A., *Het huis is nooit af*, Antwerp/Utrecht, 1974, p. 240 (transl.: MM.)

[13] *Ibid.*, p. 245. (trans.: MM.)

[14] *Ibid. (transl.: MM.)*

[15] Cf. Leuba, J. H., *The Psychology of Religious Mysticism*, London/Boston, 1972[2], (1925[1]), for an example of this reductionist view.

[16] Ledergerber, K., *Die Auferstehung des Eros: Die Bedeutung von Liebe und Sexualität für das künftige Christentum*, Münich, 1971, p. 103.

[17] *Ibid.*, p. 50.

[18] Jung, C., *Psychologischen typen*, Zürich, 1946 (1926[1]), p. 278.

[19] A poignant expression of this situation appeared recently in a French cartoon, which depicts a group of nine men standing in a baren parking lot in a new complex of office buildings, where no vegetation or any form of nature is present. Amid this sterile desert of concrete and glass, one man, presumably a manager, says: "L'important sera de créer un climat érotique." (*Marie Claire*, Nov., 1976)

[20] Brown, N.O., *Life Against Death*, London, 1970[5], p. 50.
For an example of the view that eroticism in western mysticism is per se narcissistic, see: Moller, H., "Affective Mysticism in Western Civilization," *Psychoanalytic Review*, 52 (1965), pp. 115-130. (re: Teresa of Avila)

[21] Fortmann, H., *Aandachtig bidden*, p. 187.

[22] Ledergerber, *Op. Cit.*, p. 71.

[23] Ussel, J. van, *Intimiteit*, Deventer, 1975.

[24] *Ibid.*, p. 26-27 (trans.: MM.)

[25] Oechslin, R. L., "Eckhart", *Dict. de Spiritualité*, vol. 4 (1), col. 101-102.

[26] Arntzen, M. J., *Mystieke rechtvaardigingsleer*, Kampen, 1956, p. 121.

[27] *Martin Luthers Werke: Kritische Gesamtausgabe*, Weimar, 1883, 9,99.36-100.3.

[28] Ozment, S., *Homo Spiritualis*, Leiden, 1969.

[29] *Ibid.*, p. 3.
[30] Schubart, W., *Religion und Eros*, München, 1941, pp. 1-2; quoted by N. Frenkle, *Der Traum, die Neurose, das religiöse Erlebnis*, Zürich, 1974, pp. 42-43.
[31] Greeley, A., *Ecstasy: A Way of Knowing*, New Jersey, 1974.
[32] Peters, J., *Geloof en mystiek*, Louvain, 1957, p. 56 (trans.: M.M.).
[33] Vergote, A., *Interprétation de langage religieux*, ch. 2,1 ("Désir de l'infini ou désir indéfini?"), Paris, 1974, pp. 135-155.
[34] Luis de San José, *Concordancias de las obras y escritos del doctor de la iglesia San Juan de la Cruz*, Burgos, 1948.
[35] Cf. *Merriam-Webster Pocket Dictionary*, N.Y., 1968[29], p. 167: "erotic: relating to or dealing with sexual love."
[36] Cf. Footnote 23.
[37] *Proceso Apostólico de Jaén*, f⁰ 156.
[38] Cf. Pseudo-Dionysius, *Divine Names*, ch. 4,14 (Migne PG 3, 712 C), and ch. 4, 17 (713 D).
[39] References to God's force of love: *Night*, prol. 2; II,5,6; 10,7; 11,4; 11,7; 13,9; 6,9; *Canticle* 13,1-2; 25,10; 30,11; 31,1; 38,3; 38,4; *Flame* 2,2; 2,3; 2,5; 2,18;
References to man's force of love, directed to God: *Ascent* III,28,6-7; 29,2; 44,2; *Night* II,4,2; 9,7; 11,2; 11,4-5; 13,8; 16,14; 19,2; 19,3; 19,4; *Canticle* 3,10; 17,1; 29,3; 30,1; 40,1; 40,5; *Flame* 1,12; 1,13; 1,17; 1,33; 1,34; 2,10; 2,13; 2,14; 2,26; 2,34.
References to man's force of love for creatures: *Ascent* III,26,4; 26,7; 27,5; *Night* I,11,1-2; 13,11; II,3,1; 13,11; 16,4; *Canticle* 15,30; *Flame* 3,47; 4,5.
[40] For a recent attempt to reappraise the theological depth of the symbolism of the "Song of Songs" in its communal meaning, see: Tillmans, W. G., "De oude Paradijssymboliek, een verkenning," *Bijdragen*, 36 (1975), pp. 350-390. Cfr.: A. Goosen, *Achtergronden van Priscillianus' christelijke ascese*, Nijmegen, 1976, p. 246, n. 188, re: several writers in the Patristic period who develop the more individual and ascetical approach to bride's mysticism.
[41] Beirnaert, L., "La signification du symbolisme conjugal dans la vie mystique," *Expérience Chrétienne et Psychologie*, Paris, 1964, pp. 417-431.
[42] Ginneken, P. van, *Psychologische krachtlijnen in het monastieke leven*, 1976.
[43] Hulsbosch, A., "Christus, de scheppende wijsheid van God," *Tijdschrift voor Theologie*, 11 (1971), pp. 66-77.
[44] García-Lorca, F., *De Fray Luis a San Juan*, Madrid, 1971.
[45] Peers, A., *The Complete Works of St. John of the Cross*, vol. 2, p. 23, n. 2.
[46] Cf. *Canticle* 13,2; *Night*, prologue, 2.
[47] Fortmann, H., *Als ziende de Onzienlijke*, vol. 3-a, pp. 248-249. (trans.: M.M.)
[48] Plato, *Republic*, 490, A, 7ff.
[49] Rist, J. M., *Eros and Psyche*, Toronto, 1964, p. 203.
[50] Fortmann, H., *Aandachtig bidden*, p. 115.
[51] Metz, J. B., "Erlösung und Emanzipation," *Erlösung und Emanzipation*, (Quaestiones Disputatae, 61), Basel, 1973, pp. 120-140.
[52] Fortmann, H., *Op. Cit.*, p. 82.
[53] *Ibid.*, p. 116.
[54] Pseudo-Dionysius, *Divine Names*, ch. 4,12 (Migne PG 3,710) translation by Ivanka, E. von, *Dionysios Areopagita: Von den Namen zum Unnennbaren*, Einsiedeln, (no date).
[55] Rist, *Op. Cit.*, p. 209 (Origen. Migne PG 13, 71 B-C).
[56] Fortmann, H., *Op. Cit.*, p. 130. (trans.: M.M.)
[57] *Ibid.*, p. 131. (trans.: M.M.)
[58] Fortmann, H., *Oosterse renaissance*, Bilthoven, 1970, pp. 56-63.
[59] References to fire: *Ascent* I,2,2; 8,3; 21,6; 31,6; III,31,2; *Night* I,3,3; II,6,5; 9,3; 10,1; 10,7; 11,1; 11,7; 12,1; 12,2; 12,5; 12,7; 20,6; *Canticle* 1,17; 1,20; 3,8; 10,5; 13,1; 13,12; 26,4; 26,19; 31,2; 39,14; *Flame*, prologue, 3; 4; 1,3; 1,4; 1,5; 1,11; 1,16; 1,19; 1,22; 1,23; 1,25; 1,27; 1,33;

2,2; 2,3; 2,5; 2,7; 2,8; 2,9; 2,10; 2,11; 2,25; 2,26; 2,29; 3,8 (3x); 3,9 (3x).

[60] Muschalek, G., *Glaubensgewissheit in Freiheit* (Quaest. Disp. 40) 1968, pp. 67-74.
[61] See footnote 45 p. 224, chapter two.
[62] Lindinger, H., "Gott ist Liebe: Ein Beiträge zum tiefenpsychologischen und theologischen Verständnis von Eros und Agape," *Evangelische Theologie*, 33 (1973), p. 169 (a criticism of Nygren, *Eros und Agape*, 1952).
[63] *Ibid.*, p. 176.
[64] Fortmann, H., *Oosterse renaissance*, p. 64-67.
[65] Rutledge, D., *In search of a yogi*, Bombay, 1964, p. 44.
[66] Fortmann, H., *Aandachtig bidden*, p. 136.
[67] *Ibid.*, p. 143.
[68] Dixon, J. W., "The Erotics of Knowing," *Anglican Theological Review*, 56 (1974), p. 3.
[69] *Ibid.*, p. 6-7.
[70] Frutaz, A. P., "Sophia," *Lexikon für Theologie und Kirche*, vol. 9, p. 886, 1964[2].
[71]. Vergote, A., *Het huis is nooit af*, p. 242. (trans.: M.M.)
[72] Fortmann, H., "Latijnse uitvaart," *Hoogtijd*, Utrecht, 1966, pp. 107-108. (trans.: M.M.)

Appendix

SCALE OF INNER WELL-BEING

(questionnaire designed by Dr. H. J. M. Hermans
and Drs. J. C. M. Tak-Van de Ven)
(Translated and published with permission of the authors)

Instructions:
Below you will find several statements which can be completed in various ways by choosing among the words or sentences which are presented. If a word or sentence is applicable to you make an 'X' to the left of it. Make only one 'X' for each statement. Do not skip over any statement and proceed as quickly as possible.

1. I feel
   .... unhappy seldom
   .... unhappy rather often
   .... unhappy quite often

2. I think that I
   .... have much too little self-confidence
   .... have too little self-confidence
   .... have sufficient self-confidence

3. In my free time I participate in
   .... many activities
   .... rather few activities
   .... very few activities

4. I have the feeling of being powerless
   .... never
   .... seldom
   .... often
   .... always

5. In general I feel that there is
   .... a great distance between myself and others
   .... a somewhat great distance between myself and others
   .... little distance between myself and others

6. I have the feeling of not being myself
.... very often
.... rather often
.... seldom

7. When I am alone I feel
.... often lonely
.... seldom lonely

8. I have feelings of guilt
.... seldom
.... rather often
.... quite often

9. I laugh with joy
.... seldom
.... sometimes
.... often

10. I have a feeling of freedom
.... to a great degree
.... to some degree
.... to only a small degree

11. I feel
.... often anxious
.... seldom anxious

12. I like children
.... very much
.... rather well
.... not very much

13. I am jealous
.... often
.... seldom
.... never

14. I feel
.... not very healthy
.... rather healthy
.... very healthy

15. I feel worthless
.... often
.... sometimes
.... seldom
.... never

16. I am
.... very quickly discouraged

.... somewhat quickly discouraged
.... not discouraged very quickly

17. I have a feeling of inner emptiness
   .... always
   .... often
   .... once in a while
   .... never

18. I feel bored
   .... never
   .... once in a while
   .... often

19. My interest in what happens around me is
   .... very great
   .... not so great

20. .... I often dislike myself.
   .... I seldom dislike myself.
   .... I never dislike myself.

21. Feelings of inferiority bother me
   .... a very great deal
   .... rather much
   .... very little

22. The confidence I have in others is
   .... very little
   .... a little
   .... a great deal

23. .... I have much trouble with periods of depression.
   .... I seldom have any trouble with periods of depression.

24. In general I worry
   .... a very great deal
   .... somewhat
   .... very little

25. I rely on my feelings
   .... usually
   .... not often
   .... usually not

26. I have the feeling that
   .... I have no aim in life
   .... I have very little aim in life
   .... I have an aim in life

27. I enjoy myself

.... very often
.... rather often
.... not much
.... very little

28. In general I have
.... a great deal of energy
.... not much energy
.... little energy

29. I feel depressed
.... very often
.... rather often
.... seldom

30. In contact with others I feel
.... very sure of myself
.... not so sure of myself
.... not at all sure of myself

31. Contact with the people I know gives me
.... very much satisfaction
.... much satisfaction
.... not so much satisfaction
.... little satisfaction

32. My hobbies please me
.... very much
.... much
.... not very much

33. When I notice that someone does not like me
.... I feel very dejected
.... I feel rather dejected
.... I do not feel dejected very readily

34. I have the feeling that life is full of promise
.... often
.... sometimes
.... seldom
.... never

35. Introspection is something which I do
.... often
.... not often

For further discussion of this test and its application plus a discussion of the variable 'happy emotionality' see the entire issue of:
Gedrag, tijdschrift voor psychologie, 1, no. 1 (1973). Although this is a Dutch review, most of the articles are in English.

Also: H. J. M. Hermans, *Value Orientations and Their Development: Theory and Methods of Self-Confrontation*, Swets & Zeitlinger, Amsterdam, 1976.

Also: H. J. M. Hermans, *Value Orientations and Their Development: Theory and Methods of Self-Confrontation*, Swets & Zeitlinger, Amsterdam, 1976.

TEXT OF THE QUESTIONNAIRE ON SPIRITUALITY

Instructions:

You find hereby the questionnaire about the spirituality of John of the Cross. Please place your number, not your name, at the top of this page. It is important that everyone return this questionnaire before the end of the month.

1. This questionnaire is intended to test certain ideas of John of the Cross against the reality of your own experiences. In order to answer these questions it is not necessary for you to have read his works. It is, however, necessary for you to read the instructions well at the beginning of each section. In the following section (I) you will be asked which of the statements from John of the Cross expresses your *present* way of praying. 'Present' means within the last month. To the right of each question you will find a series of numbers, from '0' to '5': 0 1 2 3 4 5 .

If the statement from John of the Cross expresses your experiences in prayer completely then circle the five: 0 1 2 3 4 ⑤. If the statement expresses your prayer experience fairly well, but not entirely, circle the four: 0 1 2 3 ④ 5 . If the statement only expresses your experience for about 50%, then circle the three: 0 1 2 ③ 4 5 . If the item expresses your experience to a very limited degree, circle the two. Circle the one if the item only describes your prayer experience very incidentally. If the statement does not express your prayer experience at all, then circle the zero.

2. You are requested to answer the questions from your own experience, not from your knowledge of certain theories about prayer. All answers are good, if they reflect your personal experience. Thus do not be concerned about whether your answers are in accordance with any doctrine. You may even answer inconsequently or contradict yourself if this reflects your own experience.

3. Be careful not to skip over or to forget any question. Always make a decision and mark something, even when you find it difficult. This is very important for the experiment.

4. At the end of section one (I) return to the first question and place an (X)

to the right of all the questions which express or describe any experience in prayer which you have *ever* had in the past, up to and including the present.

The Questionnaire on Spirituality

Section One: Prayer Experiences.

1. "(God) is wont to bestow on (the soul) certain enkindling touches of love, which like a fiery arrow strike and pierce the soul and leave it wholly cauterized."
2. "(the soul is) ... left dry and empty and in darkness."
3. "These considerations and forms and manners of meditation are necessary ... in order to gradually feed and enkindle the soul with love by means of sense."
4. "... so sweet and so delectable are the wounds of love ..."
5. "The language of God, since it is very intimate and spiritual ... transcends every sense and at once makes all harmony and capacity of the outward and inward senses to cease and be dumb."
6. "Naught comes to the soul at this time than bitterness."
7. "It is necessary for the soul to be given material for meditation, and to make interior acts of its own account, and so to take advantage of the spiritual heat and fire which come from sense."
8. "... as when one suddenly awakens, the will is enkindled in loving, desiring, praising, giving thanks, doing reverence, esteeming and praying to God with savour of love."
9. "The spirit feels itself here to be deeply and passionately in love, for ... inasmuch as this love is infused, it is passive rather than active ... what the soul does here is to give its consent."
10. "In the darkness of my understanding and the constraint of my will, ... remaining in the dark in pure faith ..."
11. "This is an ... activity wrought by means of images, forms and figures that are fashioned and imagined."
12. "... The Holy Spirit brings to pass the glorious vibrations of His flame ..."
13. "Without knowing how it comes to pass, and without any efforts of its own, the soul enters farther into its own interior depths ..."
14. "So many and so grievous are the afflictions of this night, ... that all that can be said thereof is certainly less than the truth."
15. "When ... one is able to see that the soul is not occupied in that repose and knowledge, one will need to make use of meditation ... One uses sometimes the one and sometimes the other, at different times."
16. "The soul is conscious of the sweetness of love ..."
17. "Sometimes, when the soul has done nothing to produce it, it feels this sweet inebriation of its spirit and the enkindling of this Divine wine within its inmost substance."
18. "... these wounds of love ... leave the soul wounded and grieving ..."
19. "(the soul is) without being able to think of any particular thing or having the desire to do so."
21. "... the sorrow and the grief which (the soul) suffers ordinarily in God's absence (fill it entirely)."
22. "... the spiced wine ... love's sweetness and spiritual delight, and its effect are both accustomed to last long ..."
23. "The soul understands without effort ... and receives only that which is given to it."
24. "With the yearnings ... of a lioness going to seek her cubs when they have been taken away from her and she finds them not, does this wounded soul go forth to seek its God."

236

25. "The interior words . . . which at certain times come to the spirit by supernatural means without the intervention of any of the senses . . . seem to the spirit as if a third person communicates them formally."

26. "In this spiritual sleep which the soul has . . . it possesses and enjoys all the calm and rest and quiet . . ."

27. ". . . love alone . . . is that which now moves and guides (the soul), and makes it to soar upward to its God along the road of solitude, without its knowing how or in what manner."

28. "The yearnings for God become so great in the soul that the very bones seem to be dried up by this thirst and the natural powers to be fading away, and their warmth and strength to be perishing through the intensity of the thirst of love."

29. "(the soul) finds so many and such abundant spiritual communications and apprehensions, both in sense and in spirit, wherein they oftentimes see imaginary and spiritual visions . . . these things come together with other delectable feelings."

30. "Now God no longer afflicts me; no longer oppresses me; no longer wearies me as he used to do . . ."

31. "This touch does not last long nor is it powerful. Rather it discontinues after a short time."

32. "The soul . . . is conscious of this complete undoing of itself in its very substance, together with the direst poverty, wherein it is, as it were, nearing its end."

33. "God often represents many things to the soul, and teaches it much wisdom."

34. "These rays were communicated with such loftiness and such power that the soul was made to issue forth from herself in rapture and ecstasy."

35. "This 'jumping of the sparks' is sometimes a most subtle touch of the soul by the Beloved, which sometimes occurs when one is the least attentive to it."

36. "The soul notices that 'I know not what' is missing or must still happen. This impedes it from completely enjoying the periods of refreshment."

37. "These things are set before the soul supernaturally. These may be presented to the exterior senses, as are locutions and words audible to the ear; or, to the eyes, visions of saints, and of beauteous radiance; or perfumes to the sense of smell; or tastes and sweetnesses to the palate; or other delights to the touch . . ."

38. "(the soul) sees and tastes abundance and inestimable riches . . .

39. "The soul feels itself far from being favoured."

40. "Thou dost touch the soul the more, penetrating deeply within it . . ."

41. "Despite the fact that it could appear as if one were doing nothing and wasting time, one has enough to do by practicing patience and persevering in doing nothing."

42. "The soul feels itself full of all good and free of all evil."

43. "If sometimes the soul prays it does so with such lack of strength and of sweetness that it thinks that God neither hears it nor pays heed to it."

44. "The soul may not now try to find sweetness and fervour . . . The soul must walk with loving advertence to God, without making specific acts, but conducting itself passively."

45. "When it comes to pass that the soul is conscious of being led into silence, and hearkens, it must forget even the practice of that loving advertence of which I have spoken."

46. "This is a painful disturbance, involving many misgivings, imaginings and strivings which the soul has within itself . . . This causes vehement spiritual groans and cries; when it has the necessary strength and power it dissolves into tears, although this relief comes but seldom."

47. ". . . there are wont to occur to the memory and fancy, at certain times, many and various forms and imaginations, and to the sensual part of the soul many and various motions and desires . . ."

48. ". . . the soul . . . experiences and has fruition of an inestimable feast of love."

49. ". . . God has set a cloud before (the soul) through which its prayer cannot pass."

50. ". . . after each of these periods of relief the soul suffers once again, more intensely and

keenly than before."

51. "These successive words always come when the spirit is recollected and absorbed very attentively in some meditation; and, in its reflections upon that same matter whereon it is thinking, it proceeds from one stage to another, forming words and arguments . . . with great facility and distinctness . . . so that it seems not to be doing this itself, but rather it seems that another person is supplying the reasoning within its mind or answering its questions or teaching it."

52. ". . . this touch of God brings great satisfaction and comfort to the substance of the soul."

53. "Although at times through its benignity (the flame) gives the soul a certain amount of comfort . . . yet, both before and after this happens, it compensates and recompenses it with further trials."

54. ". . . this fire afflicts it (the soul) not, but rather enlarges it; it wearies it not, but delights it . . ."

55. "(the soul) is unable to raise its affection or its mind to God, neither can it pray to Him."

57. "For it will come to pass that, when a person is inattentive to a matter and it is far from his mind, there will come to him a vivid understanding of what he is hearing or reading . . . This is in respect to that which God is in his works, and herein are included the other articles of our Catholic faith."

58. "(the soul) tastes a marvellous sweetness and spiritual delight, finds true rest and Divine light and has lofty experience of the knowledge of God."

59. "The will becomes conscious of its natural hardness and aridity with respect to God."

60. ". . . (this flame) joyfully and happily exercises the arts and playings of love."

61. ". . . all the senses and faculties are empty, idle and at rest from their own operations . . . What the soul does at this time is to wait lovingly upon God, which is to love in continuation of unitive love."

62. "Because the soul sees that it is so full of misery, it can not believe that God loves it or has any reason to, or ever will have."

63. "This kind of vision, or, to speak more properly, of knowledge of naked truths is very different from that of which we have just spoken in the 24th chapter. For it is not like seeing bodily things with the understanding; it consists rather in comprehending and seeing with the understanding the truths of God, whether of things that are, that have been or that will be . . ."

64. "The soul finds all the rest and relaxation it desires."

65. "The soul has to suffer the existence of two contraries within it, warring against the habits and properties of the soul."

66. ". . . so deeply and profoundly does (God) wound (the soul) that it causes it to melt in love."

67. "The soul is like to the empty vessel waiting to be filled; like to the hungry man that desires food . . ."

68. "(The soul feels itself) . . . from the very inmost part of its substance to be flowing veritable rivers of glory, abounding in delights . . ."

Section Two: The following words describe some general activities which can take place during prayer. the instructions are the same as in section one. Do not leave any items blank.

1. napping
2. thinking about or musing over not more than two texts
3. changing often ones position (sitting differently, shifting weight, etc.)
4. suddenly bringing some wishes or intentions to mind
5. nodding
6. letting all sorts of thoughts come to mind
7. paying attention to every sound
8. receiving something, experiencing something, without being able to express it

9. becoming dull
10. making an effort to still the thoughts
11. being irritated by bodily discomforting situations (the temperature, drafts, the weather, uncomfortable clothing, lack of fresh air, itch, hunger, coughing, etc.)
12. being made restful during or as a result of prayer
13. waking up suddenly
14. paying attention to the time
15. making an effort to awaken or call up certain feelings in regard to God
16. being reminded of earlier experiences of God's presence
17. yawning
18. 'talking' with God about insights, events, etc.
19. As a preparation for prayer, making use of one or more of these activities: breathing techniques, turning music on, going walking or bicycling, always repeating the same word or words, reciting familiar texts or words out loud, or any other repetitive and simple action.
20. being overcome by certain emotions in regard to God
21. just barely moving the hands or the feet, almost without noticing it
22. trying to recall God's presence as a preparation for prayer
23. having difficulty in sitting still
24. becoming aware of the surroundings all of a sudden after being 'out of it' for a bit
25. quite consciously praying for certain wishes or intentions
26. having difficulty in setting plans, problems, conflicts, hurt feelings out of ones mind
27. having difficulty in holding ones head up (not due to illness or age)
28. being irritated by light, the smallest sound, movements in the surroundings
29. having trouble sitting up straight (not due to illness or age)
30. continually hoping that some disturbance will cease (such as noise from traffic, a telephone, bells, whispers, music, coughing, etc.)
31. becoming more relaxed while sitting, and slumping down a little
32. after prayer (especially when it does not succeed) plunging into some physical activity such as just walking around, running, bicycling, housework, eating, gardening, or some other movement which does not demand much concentration in order to 'blow off steam'.

Section Three: The asceticism of Saint John of the Cross. To what extent do the following sentences from the works of John of the Cross express your own ideas at the moment? If a sentence appeals to you completely, then circle the five. The instructions are the same as in section one. Give only your own opinion. Do not leave any item blank. Consider all the questions critically. Before answering look over all the statements first.

1. "This is what spiritual persons call the Purgative Way. In this operation the soul endures great suffering and experiences grievous afflictions in its spirit, which . . . make it to faint and grieve at its own self-knowledge." (*Living Flame of Love* A I, 19)
2. "When the soul tastes of the spirit, it conceives a distaste for all that pertains to the flesh." (*Flame* A III, 32)
3. ". . . evangelical perfection . . . consists in the detachment and emptiness of sense and spirit." (*Flame* A III, 47)
4. "Faith voids and darkens the understanding as to all its natural intelligence . . . Hope voids and withdraws the memory from that which it is capable of possessing . . . Charity . . . voids and annihilates the affections and desires of the will for whatever is not God." (*Dark Night of the Soul*, bk. II, ch. 21, no. 11)
5. "Endeavor to detach the soul from all coveting and solicitude of any kind for higher things, (in prayer)." (*Flame* A III, 34)
6. "It is not necessary that the will should be so completely purged with respect to the passions, since these very passions help it to feel impassioned love." *Dark Night*, II, 13,3.

239

8. "The more the soul rejoices in any other thing than God, the less completely will it center its rejoicing in God." (*Ascent* III, ch. 16, 2)
9. "The Christian must rejoice, not in the performing of good works and the following of good customs, but in doing them for the love of God alone." (*Ascent* III, ch.27, 4)
10. "(the soul) has gradually to deprive itself of desire for all the worldly things . . ." (*Ascent* I, 2, 1)
11. "It is necessary for the soul . . . to pass through this dark night of mortification of the desires and denial of pleasures in all things." (*Ascent* I, 4, 1)
12. "The soul . . . cannot actively purify itself so as to be in the least degree prepared for the Divine union of perfection of love." (*Night* I, 3, 3)
13. "In order to come to union with the wisdom of God, the soul has to proceed rather by unknowing than by knowing." (*Ascent* I, 4, 5)
14. "The whole business of attaining to union with God consists in purging the will from its affections and desires." (*Ascent* III, 16, 3)
15. "Cleanness of heart is nothing less than the love and grace of God." (*Dark Night* II, 12, 1)
16. ". . . purity of soul . . . means that there clings to the soul no creature affection." (*Ascent* III, 3, 4)
17. "One single affection remaining in the spirit . . . suffices to hinder it from feeling or experiencing . . . the delicacy and intimate sweetness of the spirit of love." (*Dark Night* II, 9, 1)
18. "(The spirit) is cleansed and illumined with love only." (*Dark Night* II, 12, 1)
19. "Trust in God . . . who will not fail to give what is needful for the road, until He bring one into the clear and pure light of love." (*Dark Night*, I, 10, 3)
20. "For when . . . love is perfect . . . the transformation of the soul is wrought through its love." (*Ascent* I, 2, 4)

Section IV: Your own spirituality. The instructions are the same as in the preceding section. Always give your own personal opinion.

1. The process of purification consists mainly of acting justly and doing ones duty.
2. The process of purification consists mainly in renouncing all pleasure apart from God.
3. The process of purification consists mainly of detachment from all desires for creatures.
4. The process of purification consists mainly of renouncing all exaggerated love of self.
5. Tho process of purification consists mainly of letting go of all idols, 'strange Gods'.
6. The process of purification consists mainly of the purifying work of God's love.
7. I have had much support from the descriptions of prayer of John of the Cross because they express many of my own experiences.
8. I have never had much profit from the descriptions of prayer of John of the Cross because I do not agree with his ideas about how prayer should develop.
9. I have never had much profit from the descriptions of prayer of John of the Cross because I prefer a more sober spirituality.
10. Although the descriptions of prayer of John of the Cross do appeal to me, I have never been able to find my own prayer experiences in them.
11. The theme of the 'spiritual marriage' which occurs so often in the works of John of the Cross appeals to me personally.
12. Although the counsel of John of the Cross about the process of purification does appeal to me, I have never really been able to put it into practice.
13. I have never had much profit in the sort of asceticism which John of the Cross advocates because I do not agree with his ideas about how that process should be seen.
14. I have actually been able to put the advice about asceticism of John of the Cross into practice; and I do so, day in and day out.
15. In general I prefer the advice of John of the Cross about asceticism to his teaching about prayer or his descriptions of prayer.

240

16. John of the Cross is too strict for my taste.
17. My own prayer experiences are much more sober than those of John of the Cross.
18. My favorite spiritual writer is much more human than John of the Cross.
19. My favorite spiritual writer is John of the Cross.
20. I read very often in the works of John of the Cross.
21. I used to read a lot in the works of John of the Cross, but not recently.

Section (V): The idea of God. (Omitted because of the undifferentiated answers of the subjects.)

Section VI: Personal assessment.
Below you see two lines, 'A' and 'B'. Place on line 'A' a cross at the place which corresponds with your own assessment of your prayer advancement. For example, if you think that you are as advanced in prayer as possible, then place a cross to the extreme right of the line, as indicated here: _____ X
If you think that you are advanced, but not as far as possible, then place the cross a bit to the center, as indicated here: _____ X _____
If you think you are about in the middle, then place the cross in the middle.
If you consider yourself not particularly advanced, place the cross a little to the left.
If you think you are not at all advanced, place the cross at the extreme left.

LINE'A': _____

On line 'B': Place a cross where you think the prayer life of the others in your community, on the average, lies. The instructions are the same as for line 'A'.
LINE 'B': _____

(Constructed with the help of Drs. R. Meertens, social psychologist, and Drs. A. Sinnige-Breed, clinical psychologist.)
(The translations of the quotations from John of the Cross are taken from A. Peers, *The Complete Works of St. John of the Cross*, Westminster, Maryland, The Newman Press, 1964. To make it easier to read the passages, some quotations have been shortened or slightly changed to make the context of the sentence clearer.)

TABLE 1. *Cluster Analysis of section one: Prayer experiences.* (for the content of each item, see the copy of the test, pp. 236-238)

Cluster A: happy prayer experiences. *Cluster B:* unhappy prayer experiences.

Test Item	Corr.	Re-test Item	Corr.	Test Item	Corr.	Re-test Item	Corr.
19	0.842	68	0.811	6	0.758	2	0.798
9	0.788	52	0.811	50	0.684	59	0.758
60	0.764	4	0.801	46	0.642	47	0.728
22	0.761	12	0.766	14	0.638	39	0.716
66	0.756	19	0.763	53	0.621	21	0.675
52	0.742	26	0.762	32	0.602	50	0.674
55	0.726	35	0.756	43	0.568	3	0.664
58	0.724	8	0.751	21	0.559	10	0.663
54	0.721	22	0.748	65	0.542	14	0.660
42	0.715	17	0.748	7	0.531	32	0.636
4	0.715	1	0.746	2	0.515	62	0.622
40	0.713	16	0.731	62	0.493	43	0.608
38	0.713	58	0.719	47	0.479	46	0.591
12	0.710	9	0.717	67	0.476	53	0.570
68	0.704	40	0.716	11	0.470	49	0.536
27	0.698	66	0.706	15	0.468	65	0.523
8	0.666	13	0.702	10	0.457	41	0.505
61	0.647	54	0.697	3	0.437	6	0.501
26	0.644	27	0.662	49	0.436	11	0.490
48	0.640	38	0.661	59	0.430	7	0.443
13	0.638	48	0.661	39	0.401		
17	0.636	61	0.656	28	0.390		
1	0.632	18	0.652				
35	0.600	5	0.623	Rel:	0.8124	Rel:	0.8871
18	0.597	60	0.621				
16	0.584	33	0.609				
5	0.570	55	0.604				
63	0.533	28	0.580				
64	0.524	24	0.558				
30	0.517	42	0.540				
57	0.514	36	0.539				
23	0.512	23	0.538				
36	0.476	57	0.537				
33	0.474						

Rel: 0.9537 Rel.: 0.9587
(Rel: = correlate of internal consistency, or reliability.)

TABLE 2. *Correlations with distractions in prayer. Cluster C.*

Test: cluster analysis

Item	Corr.	
7	0.60	tense, distracted
9	0.56	drowsy
17	0.56	yawning
32	0.56	restless
29	0.53	restless
6	0.53	distracted
15	0.52	attempted concentration
14	0.52	restless

Rel.: .8467

Re-test: cluster analysis

Item	Corr.	
29	0.81	restless
32	0.71	restless
9	0.71	drowsy
17	0.71	yawning
26	0.68	distraction
14	0.65	restless
1	0.64	drowsy
7	0.61	tense, distracted
13	0.61	sleepy

Rel.: .9032

TABLE 3. *Cluster Analysis of section three: ascetical views. Cluster D.*

Test Item	Corr.		Conformity: Corr.	Re-test: Item	Corr.		Conformity Corr.:
12	0.766	mild	0.47	9	0.810	strict	0.48
16	0.750	strict	0.52	2	0.789	strict	0.45
14	0.736	strict	0.39	10	0.768	strict	0.57
17	0.729	strict	0.40	16	0.752	strict	0.52
6	0.727	mild	0.37	4	0.731	strict	0.42
13	0.716	mild	0.25	5	0.724	mild	0.47
5	0.711	mild	0.47	1	0.715	mild?	0.44
19	0.703	mild	0.33	8	0.689	strict	0.51
4	0.698	strict	0.42	3	0.681	strict	0.31
20	0.680	mild	0.24	14	0.674	strict	0.39
10	0.674	strict	0.57	17	0.667	strict	0.40
8	0.670	strict	0.51	12	0.667	mild	0.47
3	0.668	strict	0.31	20	0.612	mild	0.24
2	0.655	strict	0.45	13	0.599	mild	0.25
18	0.629	mild	0.00	11	0.589	strict	0.51
9	0.601	strict	0.48				
15	0.566	mild	0.39				
11	0.563	strict	0.51				
1	0.528	mild?	0.44				
7	0.499	mild	0.30				

Rel.: 0.9285

Rel.: 0.9241

TABLE 4. *Cluster analysis of section four: attitudes toward John of the Cross. Cluster E.*

Test Item	Corr.	Conformity		Re-test Item	Corr.
14	0.669	0.38		7	−0.718
3	0.661	0.50		2	−0.640
7	0.633	0.22		14	−0.598
11	0.628	0.15		20	−0.581
2	0.613	0.41		19	−0.574
19	0.590	0.30		3	−0.561
6	0.507	0.35		11	−0.493
20	0.582	0.36		4	−0.309
4	0.486	0.15			
5	0.414	−0.14			
				9	0.703
8	−0.650	−0.38		8	0.697
13	−0.625	−0.20		13	0.658
9	−0.604	−0.22		10	0.617
16	−0.566	−0.22		18	0.617
10	−0.524	−0.28		16	0.596
18	−0.430	−0.13		17	0.408
21	−0.309	−0.35			

Rel.: 0.8526   Rel.: 0.8544

TABLE 5. *Correlation matrix between sumscores of clusters*

Test:

	A	B	C	D	E
A	1.0				
B	0.12	1.0			
C	-0.14	0.47	1.0		
D	0.48	-0.12	-0.19	1.0	
E	0.44	-0.09	-0.15	0.78	1.0

Re-test:

	A	B	C	D	E
A	1.0				
B	0.03	1.0			
C	-0.23	0.50	1.0		
D	0.45	0.16	-0.09	1.0	
E	0.67	-0.01	-0.35	0.67	1.0

244

TABLE 6. *Factor reliabilities, test/re-test.*

Present Experiences	Rel.	Past Experiences Rel.
Pleasurable mystical experience (factor 1, positive emotionality)	0.8852	0.8985
Active rational meditation (factor 6, emotionally neutral)	0.8088	0.4534
Emotional contemplation (Factor 8, emotionally positive)	0.7884	0.8683
Intellectual visions (factor 4, emotionally neutral)	0.7849	0.7579
Non-emotional contemplation (factor 7)	0.7647	- - -
Mixed pleasurable/unpleasurable mystical experiences (factor 11)	0.7383	0.6961
Distracted, troubled prayer (factor 10, emotionally neutral)	0.7054	0.2146
Unhappy mystical experiences (factor 13)	0.7033	0.7033
Very unhappy mystical experience (factor 14)	0.6945	0.6822
Passive contemplation (factor 15, emotionally neutral)	0.6836	- - -
The inability to pray (factor 2, emotionally neutral)	0.6706	0.6552
Active visual meditation (factor 3, emotionally neutral)	0.5177	0.1764

Reliability correlates above about 0.6750 are considered reliable.
Unreliable factors, present prayer experiences: 2,3
Unreliable factors, past prayer experiences: 2,3,6,10

TABLE 7. *The Factors in Prayer Experience* (only items with the highest loadings are included, i.e. above 0.6000) (all translations taken from A. Peers, *The Complete Works of St. John of the Cross*)

Factor 1: "Emotionally pleasurable mystical experience".

Item:		*Loading*
19.	"... the soul, in this continual feast ..., enjoys all delight and tastes all sweetness." (*Spiritual Canticle*, A, XXX, 8)	0.9214
60.	"... (this flame) joyfully and happily exercises the arts and playings of love." (*Living Flame of Love*, A, I, 8)	0.8906
66.	"... so deeply and profoundly does (God) wound (the soul) that it causes it to melt in love." (*Flame*, A, I, 7)	0.8868
68.	"(The soul feels itself) ... from the very inmost part of its substance to be flowing veritable rivers of glory, abounding in delights ..." (*Flame*, A,I,1)	0.8744
55.	"... the soul is as if enraptured, immersed in love and wholly one with God." (*Canticle*, B, XXVI,14)	0.8334
54.	"... this fire afflicts it not (the soul) but rather enlarges it; it wearies it not, but delights it ..." (*Flame*, A, II,3)	0.8313
38.	"(the soul) sees and tastes abundance and inestimable riches ..." (*Canticle*, A, XIII,4)	0.8065
40.	"Thou dost touch the soul the more, penetrating deeply within it ..." (*Flame*, A, II,18)	0.8294
52.	"... this touch of God brings great satisfaction and comfort to the substance of the soul ..." (*Canticle*, A, XIII,14)	0.8219
22.	"... the spiced wine ... love's sweetness in the soul ... and its effect are both accustomed to last long ..." (*Canticle*, A, XVI, 7)	0.8218
58.	"(the soul) tastes a marvellous sweetness and spiritual delight, finds true rest and Divine light and has lofty experience of the knowledge of God." (*Canticle*, A, XIII,4)	0.8118
9.	"The spirit feels itself here to be deeply and passionately in love, for ... inasmuch as this love is infused, it is passive rather than active ... what the soul does here is to give its consent." (*Dark Night*, II, XI,2)	0.8074
27.	"... love alone ... is that which now moves and guides (the soul), and makes it to soar upward to its God along the road of solitude, without its knowing how or in what manner." (*Dark Night*, II, XXV,4)	0.8007
8.	"... as when one suddenly awakens, the will is enkindled in loving, desiring, praising, giving thanks, doing reverence, esteeming and praying to God with savour of love." (*Canticle*, B, XXV, 5)	0.7930
12.	"... The Holy Spirit brings to pass the glorious vibrations of His flame ..." (*Flame*, B, I,17)	0.7864
4.	"... so sweet and so delectable are the wounds of love ..." (*Canticle*, A, IX,2)	0.7549
1.	"(God) is wont to bestow on (the soul) certain enkindling touches of love, which like a fiery arrow strike and pierce the soul and leave it cauterized." (*Cant.*, I, 9)	0.7336
17.	"Sometimes, when the soul has done nothing to produce it, it feels this sweet inebriation of its spirit and the enkindling of this Divine wine within its inmost substance." (*Canticle*, A, XVI, 7)	0.7146
48.	"... the soul ... experiences and has fruition of an inestimable feast of love." (*Canticle*, A, XIII,4)	0.7037
42.	"The soul feels itself full of all good and free of all evil." (*Cant.*, 14,4)	0.6968

61. "... all the senses and faculties are empty, idle and at rest from their own operations ... What the soul does at this time is to wait lovingly upon God, which is to love in continuation of unitive love." (*Cant.* 16,11) 0.6938

13. "Without knowing how it comes to pass, and without any efforts of its own, the soul enters farther into its own interior depths ..." (*Dark Night* II, ch. 23,4) 0.6732

63. "This kind of visions, or, to speak more properly, of knowledge of naked truths is very different from that of which we have just spoken in the 24th chapter. For it is not like seeing bodily things with the understanding; it consists rather in comprehending and seeing with the understanding the truths of God, whether of things that are, that have been or that will be ..." (*Ascent* II, ch. 26,2) 0.6716

35. "This 'jumping of the sparks' is sometimes a most subtle touch of the soul by the Beloved, which sometimes occurs when she is least attending to it." (*Cant.* 25,5) 0.6347

16. "One tastes the taste of love in oneself." (*Ascent* II, ch. 14,2) 0.6345

18. "These wounds of love leave the soul behind in a crying pain of love." (*Cant.* I,18) 0.6053

Factor 2: The inability to pray.

Item		Loading
49.	"... God has set a cloud before (the soul) through which its prayer cannot pass." (*Dark Night*, II, ch. 8,1)	0.8706
56.	"(the soul) is unable to raise its affection or its mind to God, neither can it pray to Him." (*Dark Night, II, ch. 8, 1*)	0.8346
43.	"If sometimes it prays it does so with such lack of strength and of sweetness that it thinks that God neither hears it nor pays heed to it." (*Dark Night*, II, ch. 8, 1)	0.8034
59.	"The will becomes conscious of its natural hardness and aridity with respect to God." (*Flame*, B,I,23)	0.6743
39.	"The soul feels itself far from being favoured." (*Dark Night*, II, ch. 5,7)	0.6284

Factor 3: "Active, visual prayer".

Item		
11.	"This is an ... activity wrought by means of images, forms and figures that are fashioned and imagined ..."	0.8357

Factor 4: "Intellectual visions."

Item		
51.	"These successive words always come when the spirit is recollected and absorbed very attentively in some meditation; and, in its reflections upon that same matter whereon it is thinking, it proceeds from one stage to another, forming words and arguments ... with great facility and distinctness ... so that it seems not to be doing this itself, but rather it seems that another person is supplying the reasoning within its mind or answering its questions or teaching it." (*Ascent*, II, ch. 29, 1)	0.7916
57.	"For it will come to pass that, when a person is inattentive to a matter and it is far from his mind, there will come to him a vivid understanding of what he is hearing or reading." "This is with respect to that which God is in His	

works, and herein are included the other articles of our Catholic faith."
(*Ascent*, II, ch. 26,16; ch. 27,1)   0.7282

63.   "This kind of vision, or, to speak more properly, of knowledge of naked truths is very different from that of which we have just spoken in the 24th chapter. For it is not like seeing bodily things with the understanding; it consists rather in comprehending and seeing with the understanding the truths of God, whether of things that are, that have been or that will be . . ."
(*Ascent*, II, ch. 26, 2)   0.7082

33.   "God often represents many things to the soul, and teaches it much wisdom."
(*Ascent*, ch. 16, 3)   0.7051

Factor 5: "Sensational mystical phenomena".

34.   "These rays were communicated with such loftiness and such power that the soul was made to issue forth from herself in rapture and ecstasy." (*Canticle*, A, 12,1)   0.8627

29.   "(the soul) finds so many and such abundant spiritual communications and apprehensions, both in sense and in spirit, wherein they oftentimes see imaginary and spiritual visions . . . these things come together with other delectable feelings. (*Dark Night*, II, ch. 2, 3)   0.8570

37.   "These . . . are set before the soul supernaturally. These may be presented to the exterior senses, as are locutions and words audible to the ear; or to the eyes, visions of saints, and of beauteous radiances; or perfumes to the sense of smell; or tastes and sweetnesses to the palate; or other delights to the touch . . ." (*Ascent* II, ch. 17,9)   0.7828

Factor 6: "Active, rational prayer."

15.   "When . . . one is able to see that the soul is not occupied in that repose and knowledge, one will need to make use of meditation . . . One uses sometimes the one and sometimes the other, at different times." (*Ascent* ch, 15,1)   0.8123

7.   "It is necessary for the soul to be given material for meditation, and to make interior acts of its own account, and so to take advantage of the spiritual heat and fire which come from sense." (*Flame* A III,30)   0.7396

3.   "These considerations and forms and manners of meditation are necessary . . . in order to gradually feed and enkindle the soul with love by means of sense." (*Ascent* II, ch. 12,5)   0.6687

Factor 7: "Emotionally neutral contemplation"

45.   "When it comes to pass that the soul is conscious of being led into silence, and hearkens, it must forget even the practice of that loving advertence of which I have spoken." (*Flame* III,35)   0.8610

23.   "The soul understands without effort . . . and receives only that which is given to it." (*Ascent* II, ch. 15,2)   0.6623

Factor 8: "Emotional contemplation"

26.   "In this spiritual sleep which the soul has . . . it possesses and enjoys all the calm and rest and quiet . . ." (*Cant.* A 13,22)   0.8588

17.   "Sometimes, when the soul has done nothing to produce it, it feels this sweet inebriation of its spirit and the enkindling of this Divine wine within its

248

inmost substance." (*Cant.* A 16,7)   0.7146

61.   "... all the senses and faculties are empty, idle and at rest from their own
       operations ... What the soul does at this time is to wait lovingly upon God,
       which is to love in continuation of unitive love." (*Cant.* 16,11)   0.8313

16.   "The soul is conscious of the sweetness of love ..." (*Ascent* II, ch. 14,12)   0.8062

23.   "The soul understands without effort ... and receives only that which is
       given to it." (*Ascent* II, ch. 15,2)   0.6635

13.   "Without knowing how it comes to pass, and without any efforts of its own,
       the soul enters farther into its own interior depths ..." (*Night* II, 23,4)   0.6371

19.   "The soul, in this continual feast ... enjoys all delight and tastes all sweet-
       ness." (*Cant.* A 30,8)   0.6048

5.   "The language of God, since it is very intimate and spiritual ... transcends
       every sense and at once makes all harmony and capacity of the outward and
       inward senses to cease and be dumb." (*Night* II, 17,3)

Factor 10: "Distracted, troubled prayer"

65.   "The soul has to suffer the existence of two contraries within it, warring
       against the habits and properties of the soul." (*Flame* I,22)   0.8182

47.   "... there are wont to occur to the memory and fancy, at certain times,
       many and various forms and imaginations, and to the sensual part of the
       soul many and various motions and desires ..." (*Canticle* A 25,2)   0.7905

7   "It is necessary for the soul to be given material for meditation, and to make
       interior acts of its own account, and so to take advantage of the spiritual heat
       and fire which come from sense." (*Flame* A, III,30)   0.6328

Factor 11: Mixed pleasurable/unpleasurable mystical experience.

50.   "... after each of these periods of relief the soul suffers once again, more
       intensely and keenly than before." (*Night* II, ch. 10,7)   0.8269

53.   "Although at times through its benignity (the flame) gives the soul a certain
       amount of comfort ... yet, both before and after this happens, it compen-
       sates and recompenses it with further trials." (*Flame* I,19)   0.7037

24.   "With the yearnings ... of a lioness going to seek her cubs when they have
       been taken away from her and she finds them not, does this wounded soul
       go forth to seek its God." (*Dark Night* II, ch. 13,8)   0.6244

32.   "The soul ... is conscious of this complete undoing of itself in its very
       substance, together with the direst poverty, wherein it is, as it were, nearing
       its end." (*Dark Night* II, ch. 6,6)   0.6181

46.   "This is a painful disturbance, involving many misgivings, imaginings and
       strivings which the soul has within itself ... This causes vehement spiritual
       groans and cries; when it has the necessary strength and power it dissolves
       into tears, although this relief comes but seldom." (*Dark Night* II, ch. 9,7)   0.6004

Factor 13: Unpleasurable mystical experience.

21.   "... the sorrow and the grief which (the soul) suffers ordinarily in God's
       absence ... (fill it entirely)." (*Cant.* A I,8)   0.8414

6.   "Naught comes to the soul at this time but bitterness." (*Dark Night* II, ch.
       10,8)   0.7176

24.   "With the yearnings ... of a lioness going to seek her cubs when they have

249

	been taken away from her and she finds them not, does this wounded soul go forth to seek its God." (*Dark Night* II, ch. 13,8)	0.6244
2.	"(the soul is) . . . left dry and empty and in darkness." (*Dark Night* II, 6,4)	0.6966
14.	"So many and so grievous are the afflictions of this night, . . . that all that can be said thereof is certainly less than the truth." (*Dark Night* II, ch. 7,2)	0.6701
28.	"The yearnings for God become so great in the soul that the very bones seem to be dried up by this thirst and the natural powers to be fading away, and their warmth and strength to be perishing through the intensity of the thirst of love." (*Dark Night* I, ch. 10,1)	0.6549
46.	"This is a painful disturbance, involving many misgivings, imaginings and strivings which the soul has within itself . . . This causes vehement spiritual groans and cries; when it has the necessary strength and power it dissolves into tears, although this relief comes but seldom." (*Dark Night* II, ch. 9,7)	0.6004

Factor 14: Very unpleasurable mystical experience.

14.	"So many and so grievous are the afflictions of this night, . . . that all that can be said thereof is certainly less than the truth." (*Dark Night* II, ch. 7,2)	0.8828
32.	"The soul . . . is conscious of this complete undoing of itself in its very substance, together with the direst poverty, wherein it is, as it were, nearing its end." (*Dark Night* II, ch. 6,6)	0.7588
10.	"In the darkness of my understanding and the constraint of my will, . . . remaining in the dark in pure faith . . ." (*Dark Night* II, ch. 4,1)	0.7008
46.	"This is a painful disturbance, involving many misgivings, imaginings and strivings which the soul has within itself . . . This causes vehement spiritual groans and cries; when it has the necessary strength and power it dissolves into tears, although this relief comes but seldom." (*Dark Night*, II, ch. 9,7)	0.6638
2.	"(the soul is) . . . left dry and empty and in darkness." (*Dark Night* II, ch. 6,4)	0.6427
67.	"The soul is like to the empty vessel waiting to be filled; like to the hungry man that desires food . . ." (*Cant.* A, IX,5)	0.6170

Factor 15: Passive, restful contemplation.

13.	"Without knowing how it comes to pass, and without any efforts of its own, the soul enters farther into its own interior depths . . ." (*Night*, II, ch. 23,4)	0.7410
25.	"The interior words . . . which at certain times come to the spirit by supernatural means without the intervention of any of the senses . . . (seem) to the spirit like a third person who communicates them formally." (*Ascent* II, 30,1)	0.7015
20.	"(the soul is) without being able to think of any particular thing or having the desire to do so." (*Dark Night* I, ch. 9,6)	0.6641

TABLE 8. *Factor analysis (oblique factor structure) of section one: Test.*

Factor one		Factor two		Factor three		Factor four		Factor five	
19	0.9214	49	0.8706	11	0.8257	51	0.7916	34	0.8627
60	0.8906	56	0.8346	3	0.4171	57	0.7282	29	0.8570
66	0.8868	43	0.8034	47	0.3977	63	0.7082	37	0.7828
68	0.8744	59	0.6743	48	-0.4495	33	0.7051		
55	0.8334	39	0.6284	61	-0.4132	27	0.5809		
54	0.8313	2	0.6149	55	-0.3375	58	0.5802		
38	0.8065	6	0.5735			59	-0.4775		
40	0.8294	14	0.5634						
52	0.8219	10	0.5376						
22	0.8218	41	0.5342						
9	0.8074	48	-0.4494						
58	0.8118								
27	0.8007								

Factor one		Factor six		Factor seven		Factor eight		Factor nine	
8	0.7930								
12	0.7864	15	0.8123	45	0.8610	26	0.8588	62	0.7394
4	0.7549	7	0.7396	23	0.6623	17	0.8394		
1	0.7336	3	0.6687	40	0.5763	61	0.8313		
17	0.7146	5	-0.5747	30	0.5515	16	0.8052		
48	0.7037	23	-0.4395	7	-0.4813	23	0.6635		
42	0.6968	63	-0.3855			13	0.6371		
61	0.6938					19	0.6048		
13	0.6732					5	0.6018		
63	0.6716					27	0.6006		
35	0.6347					55	0.5899		
16	0.6345								

Factor one		Factor ten		Factor eleven		Factor twelve		Factor thirteen	
18	0.6053								
5	0.5944								
26	0.5943	65	0.8182	50	0.8269	31	0.6952	21	0.8414
23	0.5886	47	0.7905	53	0.7037	33	0.5940	6	0.7176
64	0.5774	7	0.6328	24	0.6244	27	0.5492	24	0.6967
33	0.5262	59	0.5643	32	0.6181	48	0.5077	2	0.6966
30	0.5205	32	0.4869	46	0.6004			14	0.6701
59	-0.4505	23	-0.5360	18	0.5992			28	0.6549
		5	-0.4470	65	0.5740			46	0.6440
				1	0.5676			50	0.5753
				28	0.5595			43	0.5614
				14	0.5544			18	0.5298

Factor fourteen		Factor fifteen	
14	0.8828	13	0.7410
32	0.7588	25	0.7015
10	0.7008	20	0.6641
39	0.6785	5	0.5553
46	0.6638	27	0.5331
2	0.6427	44	0.5042
67	0.6170	30	0.4974
43	0.5968		
21	0.5930		
49	0.5681		
65	0.5635		
50	0.5463		

251

(cut-off line is generally 0.5000)

TABLE 9. *Correlations among factors:*

Group One: 'Positive Passive Experience'

	1	8	4	7	15	12
1	1.0					
8	.66	1.0				
4	.52	.39	1.0			
7	.49	.48	.46	1.0		
15	.47	.35	.46	.47	1.0	
12	.43	.18	.71	.37	.32	1.0
(5)	.40	.29	.33	.32	-.01	.34

Group Two: 'Negative Passive Experience'

	2	14	13	11
2	1.0			
14	.61	1.0		
13	.56	.78	1.0	
11	.43	.67	.72	1.0
(10)	.25	.42	.29	.31

Correlations between group one and group two:

	2	14	13	11	(10)
1	-.25	-.09	.01	.32	-.25
8	-.38	-.35	-.17	.06	-.51
4	-.11	-.21	-.23	.25	-.20
7	-.02	-.08	-.11	.21	-.45
15	.20	.19	.00	.17	-.12
12	-.03	-.09	-.14	.18	-.09
(5)	.01	.09	.12	.36	-.99

Correlations between passive prayer
(factors 7,8) & active prayer (6,10,3)

	6	10	3
7	-.42	-.45	-.03
8	-.43	-.51	-.34

Corr. factor 6 & factor 10 = 0.4764
Corr. factor 6 & factor 3 = 0.1499

252

TABLE 10. *First Test (proportional sumscores on factors, i.e. % of the maximum number of points possible, rounded off): Prayer experiences, present and past.*

		Factors: present experiences												past experiences								
		8	6	10	3	1	4	15	7	2	11	13	14	8	6	10	4	1	11	2	13	14
Subjects: Group I	28	100	13	20	00	99	95	100	95	00	00	00	14	100	100	100	75	100	100	100	100	100
	08	100	07	33	00	100	95	100	100	16	64	26	43	100	100	100	100	100	100	100	100	100
	40	96	40	07	00	86	30	60	75	04	28	11	20	100	00	33	50	100	60	80	86	71
	01	92	13	27	00	89	40	64	85	36	72	57	60	100	100	100	100	100	100	100	100	100
	31	88	07	13	80	80	80	92	90	00	08	09	23	100	33	100	75	100	95	100	100	100
	10	86	13	00	00	78	45	84	100	08	20	26	17	100	33	67	75	95	60	40	71	71
	12	86	27	13	00	83	100	68	90	00	08	06	00	100	100	33	100	95	40	100	57	71
	22	84	47	67	20	59	40	96	45	76	56	69	69	100	100	33	50	53	60	60	43	71
	30	84	73	47	40	79	65	48	90	00	48	46	20	100	100	100	100	89	100	100	100	100
	51	84	53	20	00	77	85	72	90	00	12	09	23	100	67	00	100	79	20	00	29	57
Group II	44	76	80	73	60	77	20	84	65	76	68	69	74	100	100	67	50	100	60	100	71	57
	47	72	67	73	00	47	25	52	65	04	04	06	17	70	33	100	25	47	00	20	00	29
	25	72	33	73	00	60	60	72	70	52	56	43	60	90	00	33	75	100	80	40	43	57
	03	70	33	73	20	54	60	76	55	56	52	54	49	70	67	100	50	53	60	100	57	43
	20	70	80	67	60	64	60	48	75	24	44	29	29	70	100	67	50	74	80	60	57	57
	18	66	27	27	00	63	30	56	80	00	16	03	06	70	67	33	75	74	60	00	14	57
	38	64	73	80	40	54	80	44	60	44	12	14	29	60	100	100	75	53	20	60	14	29
	23	62	60	40	40	56	45	40	45	28	36	14	37	60	100	100	25	42	40	100	29	57
	33	62	53	27	00	46	05	20	55	00	00	06	14	70	100	100	25	53	00	20	00	43
	13	60	33	67	20	39	60	72	70	04	48	54	46	60	67	100	50	42	60	40	57	100
	34	60	53	67	00	21	45	40	40	00	32	14	40	80	67	100	50	42	40	60	43	29
	48	60	67	73	00	43	25	64	50	84	100	86	94	100	100	100	75	84	100	100	86	57

253

Group III

	8	6	10	3	1	4	15	7	2	11	13	14	8~	6	10	4	1	11	2	13	14
09	56	00	00	00	24	00	88	75	20	00	00	29	60	67	33	00	53	00	80	43	29
x26	56	40	53	00	37	75	48	75	44	16	40	34	70	33	67	75	53	20	80	43	57
19	50	47	73	00	49	25	36	45	16	56	51	54	60	33	67	50	47	80	40	43	57
x15	50	80	33	00	64	25	36	30	20	24	40	34	80	67	33	25	68	40	60	43	71
x11	48	40	40	20	52	60	60	55	20	08	23	37	50	100	67	100	47	00	00	14	43
x24	48	73	13	00	11	05	40	60	24	12	23	34	50	100	33	00	11	00	20	43	43
x32	46	20	00	00	08	15	00	25	00	00	00	09	50	100	33	25	16	00	100	43	57
x14	44	80	33	00	56	25	28	30	08	12	29	23	50	67	00	00	53	40	60	29	57
02	42	73	67	80	22	30	20	30	68	16	26	26	40	100	67	00	21	00	80	29	43
06	42	33	20	00	36	45	40	20	16	16	09	51	30	33	33	00	37	20	20	14	43
39	42	00	00	00	11	35	56	50	56	00	11	31	100	67	67	50	100	80	100	71	86
54	40	87	67	40	23	20	44	15	12	04	11	31	30	100	67	00	21	00	20	14	29
52	40	20	40	20	41	05	36	45	64	48	43	49	–	–	–	–	–	–	–	–	–

'x' placed at extreme left, by the subject's number, indicates those subjects who thought their prayer life was more advanced than that of the others.

Group IV

	8	6	10	3	1	4	15	7	2	11	13	14	8	6	10	4	1	11	2	13	14
21	36	73	80	00	62	90	28	55	08	52	11	20	60	100	67	100	63	60	100	86	86
53	34	67	07	00	16	50	28	70	32	16	20	17	17	–	–	–	–	–	–	–	–
29	32	33	60	00	06	00	40	55	28	08	09	23	40	67	100	00	42	20	40	57	43
x37	30	47	13	00	17	25	20	40	12	24	17	49	60	100	33	50	32	60	80	57	86
46	30	87	67	60	28	40	60	60	56	40	29	51	60	100	67	50	42	80	100	43	43
45	26	73	73	00	25	00	40	15	28	60	57	60	70	100	100	00	63	80	60	86	86
55	24	80	53	60	31	25	16	20	60	36	40	51	10	100	67	00	32	40	80	43	57
16	22	53	07	40	35	05	44	65	56	52	89	74	100	100	33	75	95	100	80	86	100
35	20	13	00	00	26	05	04	20	04	04	03	00	100	100	100	50	79	100	100	71	100

Group V	8	6	10	3	1	4	15	7	2	11	13	14	8	6	10	4	1	11	2	13	14
36	16	60	73	20	17	25	04	40	56	52	37	63	10	100	67	25	16	60	80	29	57
43	12	87	53	60	19	45	12	30	52	48	57	80	70	100	67	00	79	60	60	57	86
07	12	20	53	60	00	55	20	45	76	00	06	26	10	67	67	25	05	20	80	14	14
04	12	67	67	80	08	10	08	00	64	16	20	26	20	67	67	00	32	40	60	43	43
49	10	47	20	00	01	00	04	00	40	04	06	23	10	100	100	25	21	20	100	43	57
05	10	13	13	20	02	25	12	05	00	04	03	06	00	00	33	00	11	00	40	14	00
50	10	60	33	40	18	25	36	05	48	08	17	26	10	67	33	00	11	00	80	14	29
27	08	60	67	00	00	00	04	15	88	28	40	74	50	100	100	00	32	20	80	43	71
17	06	13	73	00	04	00	24	10	48	32	57	74	40	67	67	00	37	20	60	57	71
42	04	67	100	00	05	15	24	25	100	32	46	80	10	67	100	00	05	20	100	43	71

TABLE 11. *Averages of the proportional (%) sumscores of each group on each factor, past and present, rounded off.*

	8	6	10	3	1	4	15	7	2	11	13	14	8	6	10	4	1	11	2	13	14
I	90	27	27	14	83	70	76	85	16	36	26	29	100	67	67	75	89	80	80	86	86
II	62	53	60	20	53	45	56	60	32	40	31	40	80	67	100	50	63	60	60	43	57
III	46	47	33	12	34	30	40	45	28	16	23	34	50	67	33	25	47	20	60	43	57
IV	28	60	40	20	27	25	32	40	36	32	31	37	60	100	67	50	58	60	80	71	86
V	10	27	53	28	07	20	16	20	56	24	29	49	20	67	67	00	26	20	80	43	43

Subjects who have experienced ecstasy: 28, 08, 01, 30, 25, 20, 52, 35
(Subject 41 was dropped from both the first test and the re-test because she did not follow the instructions.)

255

TABLE 12: *Re-test (proportional sumscores in percentages, rounded off).*
Prayer experiences, present and past.

		Factors: present experiences												past experiences								
		8	6	10	3	1	4	15	7	2	11	13	14	8	6	10	4	1	11	2	13	14
Group I	28	86	13	07	00	94	100	88	100	00	04	03	14	100	100	100	100	100	100	100	100	100
	08	84	13	07	00	83	80	68	90	00	44	31	31	100	100	100	100	95	100	100	100	100
	40	94	53	20	00	89	20	68	90	04	28	31	17	100	67	100	75	100	100	100	100	100
	01	90	27	33	20	87	65	60	85	44	76	77	74	100	100	100	100	100	100	100	100	100
	31	82	13	07	00	89	90	84	80	04	24	11	23	100	100	100	100	100	100	100	100	100
	10	94	13	07	00	86	55	96	95	08	20	14	14	100	33	67	100	100	40	40	43	71
	12	90	40	07	40	81	65	48	70	00	16	09	11	100	67	67	75	100	60	100	71	57
	22	12	53	60	20	21	20	20	25	60	36	20	54	70	100	100	75	21	100	100	71	86
	30	72	73	67	00	67	45	68	80	72	68	71	63	100	100	100	100	100	100	100	100	100
	51	92	53	27	00	96	85	84	90	00	20	14	17	100	67	100	100	100	100	60	86	100
Group II	44	88	80	67	80	82	40	92	55	72	80	66	77	100	100	100	75	100	80	100	71	86
	47	56	53	73	00	47	30	52	65	16	12	09	23	80	100	67	25	53	60	60	29	43
	25	86	60	73	20	82	65	76	80	36	48	49	54	100	100	100.	100	100	60	40	43	43
	03	62	53	53	60	49	60	52	40	68	32	34	46	60	100	100	25	47	40	80	29	43
	20	78	67	40	20	35	15	28	35	00	00	03	03	90	100	67	50	89	80	100	86	100
	18	54	60	13	20	62	30	36	50	00	04	00	06	60	67	00	00	89	60	00	00	29
	38	36	67	73	40	34	45	36	45	80	64	74	77	50	100	100	75	53	100	100	100	100
	23	36	67	33	40	38	45	28	15	60	44	43	54	30	100	67	50	42	40	100	43	71
	33	52	53	20	20	49	30	28	40	00	12	09	09	80	100	33	25	63	20	00	29	,43
	13	48	27	27	00	38	40	48	40	12	60	51	46	80	67	100	75	37	80	20	57	57
	34	74	67	33	00	59	55	48	50	00	20	40	26	90	100	67	75	74	20	40	71	43
	48	46	73	67	00	32	05	68	60	32	56	54	63	100	100	100	75	100	100	80	86	100

256

	8	6	10	3	1	4	15	7	2	11	13	14	8	6	10	4	1	11	2	13	14
09	48	27	20	00	35	10	56	55	28	24	37	54	40	67	33	00	42	20	100	43	71
26	34	33	40	40	13	50	28	55	20	08	20	37	80	100	100	100	74	60	100	43	71
19	44	60	67	40	41	50	40	25	16	64	63	63	60	100	100	75	47	80	40	71	86
15	76	60	67	00	71	40	64	80	16	32	40	29	90	100	67	75	95	60	40	43	43
11	38	73	60	00	44	40	28	40	28	24	20	31	60	100	100	50	68	60	60	29	57
24	46	73	40	20	13	05	44	55	72	20	26	60	50	100	67	00	16	00	100	29	71
32	46	00	00	00	25	00	12	15	00	00	00	00	70	67	33	00	37	00	60	29	43
14	32	100	60	00	37	15	32	45	00	24	29	29	30	100	100	25	58	60	40	86	71
02	—	— did not follow instructions						—	—	—			—	—	—	—	—	—	—	—	—
06	36	20	13	40	25	35	16	40	28	08	00	20	50	33	33	25	42	00	20	00	29
39	26	00	00	00	06	00	28	40	92	08	17	40	90	00	67	75	84	100	100	100	100
54	18	73	47	20	14	10	16	30	24	00	00	17	30	100	67	00	32	00	00	00	29
52	36	27	27	40	35	35	32	20	40	20	31	31	90	100	67	25	79	40	80	86	57

	8	6	10	3	1	4	15	7	2	11	13	14	8	6	10	4	1	11	2	13	14
21	30	73	73	20	40	60	36	70	48	72	46	66	80	100	100	75	63	100	100	86	100
53	28	87	40	00	13	50	20	30	08	04	03	03	70	100	33	75	53	20	80	29	57
29	36	60	47	00	08	00	36	45	16	12	14	26	50	67	67	00	11	20	80	29	57
37	22	40	33	40	07	15	32	.25	56	12	26	34	60	100	100	25	21	40	100	57	71
46	52	80	67	40	37	40	72	60	48	32	46	49	70	100	100	75	68	60	100	57	71
45	08	87	100	40	07	10	20	15	60	56	69	86	90	100	100	50	74	100	100	100	100
55	50	73	60	40	51	45	48	45	72	40	43	46	40	100	100	25	53	40	100	43	57
16	20	80	60	60	34	35	28	55	52	60	60	54	100	100	100	75	79	100	80	100	100
35	40	33	13	00	35	15	28	45	00	00	03	03	90	100	67	50	89	80	100	86	100

	8	6	10	3	1	4	15	7	2	11	13	14	8	6	10	4	1	11	2	13	14
36	18	20	00	00	12	00	12	20	28	00	23	20	10	100	33	00	05	00	80	14	14
43	58	73	67	40	43	40	60	55	44	64	66	54	80	100	100	75	79	80	100	71	71
07	24	40	47	60	03	20	28	35	48	00	06	14	10	33	67	00	11	20	60	00	29
04	16	80	80	60	11	10	20	30	08	28	29	43	20	100	100	00	05	40	00	00	14
49	12	13	07	00	03	15	12	05	48	00	00	29	70	100	100	25	42	40	100	43	71
05	08	13	07	00	04	20	08	35	04	00	00	00	10	00	00	00	05	40	20	00	29
50	36	53	33	60	09	35	32	20	64	04	17	29	20	100	33	25	05	00	100	14	57
27	00	73	67	00	00	00	04	05	80	28	40	74	40	100	100	00	37	60	100	57	86
17	10	20	60	00	02	05	24	15	40	28	51	63	30	33	67	00	05	40	00	00	14
42	26	93	60	00	01	00	44	40	88	20	51	71	50	100	33	00	11	40	100	57	71

(Group V)

TABLE 13. *Averages of the proportional (%) sumscores of each group on each factor, past and present, rounded off.*

	8	6	10	3	1	4	15	7	2	11	13	14	8	6	10	4	1	11	2	13	14
I	80	33	27	08	80	65	68	80	20	32	29	31	100	67	100	100	89	100	100	86	86
II	56	60	47	24	61	40	48	50	32	36	34	43	80	100	67	50	68	60	60	57	57
III	40	47	40	16	29	25	32	40	28	20	23	34	60	67	67	12	58	40	60	43	57
IV	32	67	53	26	25	30	36	45	40	36	34	40	70	100	100	50	58	60	100	71	86
V	20	47	40	20	08	15	24	25	44	16	29	40	30	67	67	12	21	40	60	29	43

Subjects who have experienced ecstasy: 28, 08, 01, 30, 25, 07, 35

TABLE 14. *Correlations between psychological variables and individual items describing prayer experiences.*

I. *Neuroticism.*

Corr. Item
0.44 47. "There are wont to occur to the memory and fancy, at certain times, many and various forms and imaginations, and to the sensual part of the soul many and various motions and desires." (factor 10)
0.38 65. "The soul has to suffer the existence of two contraries within it, warring against the habits and properties of the soul." (factor 10)
0.32 59. "The will becomes conscious of its natural hardness and aridity with respect to God." (factor 2)

258

0.32	32.	"The soul . . . is conscious of this complete undoing of itself in its very substance, together with the direst poverty, wherein it is, as it were, nearing its end." (factors 11,14)
0.32	46.	"This is a painful disturbance, involving many misgivings, imaginings, and strivings which the soul has within itself . . . This causes vehement spiritual groans and cries; when it has the necessary strength and power it dissolves into tears, although this relief comes but seldom." (factors 11,13,14)
0.32	50.	". . . after each of these periods of relief the soul suffers once again, more intensely and keenly than before." (factor 11)
-.42	64.	"The soul finds all the rest and relaxation it desires." (factor 1)
-.42	42.	"The soul feels itself full of all good and free of all evil." (factor 1)
-.33	23.	"The soul understands without effort and receives only that which is given." (factors 7,8)

II. *Psycho-somatic neuroticism.*

0.39	32.	"The soul . . . is conscious of this complete undoing of itself in its very substance, together with the direst poverty, wherein it is, as it were, nearing its end." (factors 11,14)
0.35	2.	"The soul is left dry and empty and in darkness." (factors 2,14)
0.31	59.	"The will becomes conscious of its natural hardness and aridity with respect to God." (factor 2)

III. *Extraversion.*

Factor 8: "Contemplation".
Corr. *Item.*

0.37	26.	"In this spiritual sleep which the soul has it possesses and enjoys all the calm and rest and quiet . . ."
0.33	17.	"Sometimes, when the soul has done nothing to produce it, it feels this sweet inebriation of its spirit and the enkindling of this Divine wine within its inmost substance."
0.34	16.	"The soul is conscious of the sweetness of love . . ."
0.32	23.	"The soul understands without effort and receives only that which is given to it."
0.23	13.	"Without knowing how it comes to pass, and without any efforts of its own, the soul enters farther into its own interior depths . . ."

Factor 7: "Passive prayer"

0.31	45.	"Whenever the soul experiences itself being placed in that silence and in that listening, then it must forget the practice of loving attention which I spoke about . . ."
0.32	23.	See above.
0.38	30.	"Now God no longer oppresses me, no longer constrains me . . . as he used to."
-0.38	7.	"It is necessary for the soul to be given material for meditation, and to make interior acts of its own account, . . ."

Factor 1: Pleasurable mystical experience

0.37	57.	"For it will come to pass that, when a person is inattentive to a matter and it is far from his mind, there will come to him a vivid understanding of what he is hearing or reading . . ." (also in factor 4).
0.34	68.	"The soul feels itself, from the very inmost part of its substance, to be flowing veritable rivers of glory, abounding in delights."
0.32	64.	"The soul finds all the rest and relaxation it desires."

0.32   58.   "The soul tastes a marvellous sweetness and spiritual delight, finds true rest and Divine light and has lofty experience of the knowledge of God."

0.28   60.   "This flame joyfully and happily exercises the arts and playings of love."

IV.   *Test Unreliability.* (very few items correlated significantly.)

0.27   55.   "The soul is as if enraptured, immersed in love and wholly one with God."

-0.31   47.   "There are wont to occur to the memory and fancy, at certain times, many and various forms and imaginations, and to the sensual part of the soul many and various motions and desires."

V.   *Social desirability.*

Factor 1: "Pleasurable mystical experience".

0.44   16.   "The soul is conscious of the sweetness of love." (also in factor 8).

0.40   55.   "The soul is as if enraptured, immersed in love and wholly one with God."

0.38   68.   "The soul feels in itself, from the very inmost part of its substance, to be flowing veritable rivers of glory, abounding in delights."

0.38   42.   "The soul feels itself to be full of all that is good and free of all evil."

0.37   38.   "The soul sees and tastes abundance and inestimable riches."

0.35   48.   "The soul experiences and has fruition of an inestimable feast of love."

0.35   60.   "This flame joyfully and happily exercises the arts and playings of love."

0.35   64.   "The soul finds all the rest and relaxation it desires."

0.34   17.   "Sometimes, when the soul has done nothing to produce it, it feels this sweet inebriation of its spirit and the enkindling of this Divine wine within its inmost substance."

0.33   54.   "This fire afflicts it not but rather enlarges it; it wearies it not, but delights it."

0.32   58.   "The soul tastes a marvellous sweetness and spiritual delight, finds true rest and Divine light and has lofty experience of the knowledge of God."

0.31   4.   ". . . so sweet and so delectable are the wounds of love . . ."

0.31   9.   "The spirit feels itself here to be deeply and passionately in love, for inasmuch as this love is infused, it is passive rather than active. What the soul does here is to give its consent."

0.31   30.   "Now God no longer oppresses me, no longer constrains me, . . . as he used to."

Factor 10: "Distracted prayer".

-0.32   65.   See under 'Neuroticism'.

-0.45   47.

-0.31   59.

Factor 2: "The first dark night- the inability to pray."

-0.34   43.   "If sometimes the soul prays it does so with such lack of strength and of sweetness that it thinks that God neither hears it nor pays heed to it."

-0.32   39.   "The soul feels itself far from being favoured."

VI.   *Ego strength* (Barron Ego Strength Scale): all significant correlations were negative.

-0.35   32.   "The soul is conscious of this complete undoing of itself in its very substance, together with the direst poverty, wherein it is, as it were, nearing its end." (factor 11)

-0.33   59.   "The will becomes conscious of its natural hardness and aridity with respect to God." (factor 2)

-0.27 3. "These considerations and forms and manners of meditation are necessary in order to gradually feed and enkindle the soul with love by means of sense."

-0.26 14. "So many and so grevious are the afflictions of this night, that all that can be said thereof is certainly less than the truth." (factor 14)

VII. *Hysteria* (MMPI Hysteria Scale): all significant correlations were positive.

(It is noteworthy that so few correlations were found, and that only 'intellectual' visions are correlated, not the 'sensational' visions, or ecstasy.)

0.30 51. "These successive words always come when the spirit is recollected and absorbed very attentively in some meditation; and, in its reflections upon that same matter whereon it is thinking, it proceeds from one stage to another, forming words and arguments with great facility and distinctness, so that it seems not to be doing this itself, but rather it seems that another person is supplying the reasoning within its mind or answering its questions or teaching it."

0.28 63. "This kind of vision, or, to speak more properly, of knowledge of naked truths is very different from that of which we have just spoken in the 24th chapter. For it is not like seeing bodily things with the understanding; it consists rather in comprehending and seeing with the understanding the truths of God, whether of things that are, that have been or that will be . . ."

0.28 31. "This 'scattering of sparks' is a most subtle touch of the soul by the Beloved which sometimes takes place when one is the least attentive to it."

VIII. *Age.* (very few correlations were found.)

0.33 48. "The soul experiences and has fruition of an inestimable feast of love."
0.31   9. "The spirit feels itself here to be deeply and passionately in love, . . ."
0.30 42. "The soul sees and tastes abundance and inestimable riches."
0.30 42. "The soul feels full of all that is good and free of all evil."

IX. *Happy emotionality.* (almost all the correlations were with factors 1 and 8)

Corr.	Item
0.50	64
0.48	48
0.47	16
0.45	68
0.44	42
0.44	17
0.42	60
0.41	30
0.40	26
0.39	54
0.39	19
0.37	55
0.37	58
0.36	35
0.36	38
0.35	66
0.31	4

-.37   47 (factor 10)
-.35   59 (factor 2)
-.33   50 (factor 11)
-.28   65 (factor 10)

X.   *Unhappy emotionality*

-.43   64 (factor 1)
-.40   48 (factor 1)
-.34   23 (factor 1)
-.34   27 (factor 1)
-.32   42 (factor 1)
0.43   65 (factor 10)
0.42   47 (factor 10)
0.41   59 (factors 2, 13, 14)
0.39   21
0.36   46
0.34   50
0.33   6
0.30   14

CULTURAL VARIABLES
Scale of Inter-Personal Values, etc.

I.   *Need for group support:*

0.28   (59)   "The will becomes conscious of its natural hardness and aridity with respect to God."

0.22   62.   "Because the soul sees that it is so full of misery it can not believe that God loves it or has any reason to do so or ever will have."

-0.36   23.   "The soul understands without effort and receives only that which is given."

II.   *Need for recognition:*

0.41   65.   "The soul has to suffer the existence of two contraries within it, warring against the habits and properties of the soul." (factor 10)

III.   *Leadership:*

0.31   (34)   "These rays communicated with such loftiness and such power that the soul was made to issue forth from herself in rapture and ecstasy." (factor 5)

0.31   (46)   "This is a painful disturbance, involving many misgivings, imaginings and strivings which the soul has within itself . . ." (factor 11)

IV.   *Female:* (since only 9 male subjects were involved here, and 45 females, the correlations are somewhat distorted).

0.39   23.   "The soul understands without effort and receives only that which is given."

0.37   13.   "Without knowing how it comes to pass, and without any efforts of its own, the soul enters farther into its own interior depths . . ."

0.34   44.   "The soul may not now try to find savour and fire. The soul does nothing other than to direct its loving attention to God."

262

-0.35   47.   "There are wont to occur to the memory and fancy, at certain times, many and various forms and imaginations, and to the sensual part of the soul many and various motions and desires."

-0.34   11.   "This is an activity wrought by means of images, forms and figures that are fashioned and imagined." (factor 3: active, visual prayer)

V.   Conformity:

Corr.   Item   (all items in factor 1)

0.46   9.   "The spirit feels itself here to be deeply and passionately in love, for . . . inasmuch as this love is infused, it is passive rather than active . . . what the soul does here is to give its consent."

0.37   18.   "These wounds of love leave the soul behind in a crying pain of love."

0.36   1.   "God is wont to bestow on the soul certain enkindling touches of love, which like a fiery arrow strike and pierce the soul and leave it cauterized."

0.35   4.   ". . . so sweet and so delectable are the wounds of love."

0.33   66.   "So deeply and profoundly does God wound the soul that it causes it to melt in love."

0.33   8.   "As when one suddenly awakens, the will is enkindled in loving, desiring, praising, giving thanks, doing reverence, esteeming and praying to God with savour of love."

0.32   12.   "The Holy Spirit brings to pass the glorious vibrations of His flame."

0.32   40.   "Thou dost touch the soul the more, penetrating deeply within it."

0.31   19.   "The soul, in this continual feast, enjoys all delight and tastes all sweetness."

-.28   56.   "The soul is unable to raise its affection or its mind to God, neither can it pray to Him."

VI.   Altruism: (items in factors 1 and 8)

0.40   13.   "Without knowing how it comes to pass, and without any efforts of its own, the soul enters farther into its own interior depths."

0.39   9.   "The spirit feels itself here to be deeply and passionately in love, for inasmuch as this love is infused, it is passive rather than active. What the soul does here is to give its consent."

0.33   17.   "Sometimes, when the soul has done nothing to produce it, it feels this sweet inebriation of its spirit and the enkindling of this divine wine within its inmost substance."

0.31   27.   "Love alone is that which now moves and guides the soul, and makes it to soar upward to its God along the road of solitude, without its knowing how or in what manner."

0.30   40.   "Thous dost touch the soul the more, penetrating deeply within it."

VII.   Experimental Group   (almost the same items are involved in the correlations as with 'conformity', except that here the correlation is negative)

Corr.   Item

-0.39   8.   see under 'conformity' (factor 1)

-0.37   1.   see under 'conformity'

-0.37   66.   see under 'conformity'

-0.36   40.   see under 'conformity'

-0.36   4.   see under 'conformity'

-0.30   12.   see under 'conformity'

-0.40	14.	"So many and so grevious are the afflictions of this night, that all that can be said thereof is certainly less than the truth." (factor 14)
-0.40	18.	see under 'conformity' (factors 1 and 11)
-0.39	24.	"With the yearnings of a lioness going to seek her cubs when they have been taken away from her and she finds them not, does this wounded soul go forth to seek its God." (factor 11)
-0.38	50.	"After each of these periods of relief the soul suffers once again, more intensely and keenly than before." (factor 11)
-0.37	1.	see under 'conformity' (factors 1 and 11)
-0.31	53.	"Although at times through its benignity the flame gives the soul a certain amount of comfort . . . yet, both before and after this happens, it compensates and recompenses it with further trials." (factor 11)

VIII. *Related cultural items* (almost all the correlations were with factors 1 and 8)

Independence		*Higher Education*	
Corr.	Item	Corr.	Item
-0.55	9	-0.52	9
-0.51	38	-0.52	40
-0.50	18	-0.49	4
-0.50	1	-0.46	23
-0.49	55	-0.45	38
-0.48	4	-0.45	8
-0.48	66	-0.45	60
-0.45	8	-0.44	66
-0.42	13	-0.43	58
-0.41	19	-0.42	52
-0.39	12	-0.39	12
-0.38	17	-0.39	22
-0.37	40	-0.38	68
-0.35	54	-0.38	19
-0.34	60	-0.37	13
-0.34	68	-0.36	27
-0.32	27	-0.32	1
-0.31	23	-0.32	54
-0.31	48	-0.32	55
-0.30	58	-0.30	18

TABLE 15.
Psychological Variables.

	N	NS	E	T	SD	+	−	ES	Age	H
Neuroticism (N)	1.00									
Psycho-Somatic Neuroticism (NS)	0.42	1.00								
Extraversion (E)	-.40	-.30	1.00							
Test Unreliability (T)	-.33	.00	-.04	1.00						
Social Desirability (SD)	-.59	-.48	.49	.64	1.00					
Happy Feelings (+)	-.74	-.46	.57	.21	.57	1.00				
Unhappy Feelings (−)	.84	.25	-.46	-.30	-.46	-.70	1.00			
Barron Ego-Strength Scale (ES)	-.59	-.58	.25	-.00	.29	.50	-.46	1.00		
Age	-.38	-.12	.07	.40	.34	.15	-.33	.00	1.00	
Hysteria Scale (H)	-.01	.25	-.04	-.23	-.26	-.00	-.08	-.24	.01	1.00

Cultural Variables:

	S	C	R	I	A	L	F	Ex	Ed
Group Support (S)	1.00								
Conformism (C)	-.49	1.00							
Recognition (R)	.26	-.14	1.00						
Independence (I)	.31	-.57	-.32	1.00					
Altruism (A)	-.52	.44	-.40	-.50	1.00				
Leadership (L)	-.33	-.37	-.12	-.00	.00	1.00			
Female (F)	-.22	.26	-.24	-.10	.28	-.03	1.00		
Experiment. Group (Ex)	.18	-.48	-.09	.37	-.10	.12	-.43	1.00	
Higher Education (Ed)	.24	-.31	.11	.31	-.34	.11	-.53	.43	1.00
(Psych. Variables)									
Age	-.11	.21	-.17	-.10	.18	-.19	—	.05	-.53
Neuroticism	.20	.17	.28	.07	-.30	-.03	—	-.09	.11
Extraversion	-.16	-.11	-.15	.01	.26	.20	—	.11	-.01
Unhappy Feelings	.26	-.29	.46	-.10	-.27	.18	—	-.04	-.04
Test Unreliability	-.18	.25	-.03	-.40	.28	-.07	—	-.22	-.12
Social Desirability	-.10	.03	-.02	-.40	.33	.07	—	.06	-.14

There was no significant correlation with the other psychological variables.
(cut-off line is generally 0.20)

Survey:
The 'favorable' psychological variables can be grouped together on the basis of their positive inter-correlations: extraversion, happy feelings, social desirability, Ego-strength, altruism, low score on neuroticism. The 'unfavorable' variables are: neuroticism, psycho-somatic neuroticism, introversion, low Ego-strength, hysteria, unhappy feelings, need for group support and recognition. *Cultural variables generally do not correlate with the psychological variables.*

265

CANONICAL CORRELATION ANALYSIS:
PSYCHOLOGICAL VARIABLES AND PRAYER FACTORS

TABLE 16. *Unfavorable psychological variables and sumscores on factor 8 (emotional contemplation) and factor 1 (pleasurable mystical experiences)*

	Canonical Variate Predictors	Canonical Variate Criteria
1. Factor 8, present experiences	0.94	0.39
2. Factor 1, present experiences	0.77	0.32
3. Factor 8, past experiences	0.91	0.38
4. Factor 1, past experiences	0.81	0.33
5. Neuroticism	-0.23	-0.55
6. Psycho-somatic neuroticism	-0.11	-0.26
7. Introversion (signs on 'extra-version' reflected)	-0.37	-0.90
8. Unhappy emotions	-0.27	-0.64

Predictors: 1-5   Canonical correlation: 0.41
Criteria: 5-8   Probability level: 0.68

TABLE 17. *Favorable psychological variables and sumscores on factor 8 and factor 1.*

	Canonical Variate Predictors	Canonical Var. Criteria
1. Stability (signs on 'neuroticism' reflected)	-0.26	-0.54
2. Extraversion	-0.27	-0.44
3. Happy emotions	-0.46	-0.96
4. Factor 8, present experiences	-0.90	-0.43
5. Factor 1, present experiences	-0.93	-0.44
6. Factor 8, past experiences	-0.79	-0.38
7. Factor 1, past experiences	-0.68	-0.33

Predictors: 4-7   Canonical Correlation: 0.48
Criteria: 1-3   Probability level: 0.15

266

TABLE 18. *Unfavorable psychological variables and sumscores on factor 6 (active meditation), factor 10 (distraction, troubled prayer), and factor 3 (visual meditation) (present only)*

		Canonical Variate Predictors	Canonical Var. Criteria
1.	Factor 6	-0.46	-0.26
2.	Factor 10	-0.83	-0.47
3.	Factor 3	-0.71	-0.40
4.	Neuroticism	-0.43	-0.77
5.	Psycho-somatic neuroticism	-0.32	-0.57
6.	Introversion	-0.43	-0.77
7.	Unhappy emotions	-0.45	-0.80

Predictors: 1-3   Canonical correlation: 0.56
Criteria: 4-7   Probability level: 0.033

Technical note: In a canonical correlation analysis the number of variables should not exceed ¼ the number of subjects. In these canonical correlation analyses presented in Tables 16-18, the number of subjects could not be more than 50, because four subjects had not correctly filled in the questions about past prayer experiences. Therefore they had to be dropped. On the other hand, they could be incorporated again into the canonical correlation analyses in Tables 25-26 because only present prayer experiences are involved. For this reason then the number of variables in Tables 25-26 could be increased to 13, that is, because the total number of subjects involved was raised to 54.

TABLE 19. *Subjects and Their Psychological Scores (subjects ranked according to Table 10, p. 300)* (For the explanation of the abbreviations, see p. 269.)

	N	NS	E	T	SD	IW+	IW-	Sp.	Cn.	Rg.	In.	Al.	Ld.	ES	Hys.(?)	A	B	Age	Ex.	Ed.
28	2	6	4	3	5	88	0	VH	M	M	VL	VH	M	40	72(x)	1	2	52	2	6
08	5	1	9	4	9	69	22	H	H	M	VL	M	M	44	37	4	4	48	2	2
40	2	2	10	9	9	88	5	M	VH	M	VL	H	M	42	39(3)	?	?	71	1	4
01	2	1	8	1	7	69	11	L	M	L	VL	VH	H	44	53	3	3	50	3	6
31	3	10	3	3	3	69	5	H	H	M	VL	VH	M	42	60	4	4	60	2	2
10	1	5	10	1	4	92	0	L	H	L	L	VH	M	49	60	4	4	37	2	2
12	1	9	8	6	9	69	11	M	VH	L	VL	VH	M	41	61	3	3	64	2	3
22	8	5	1	2	4	38	61	H	H	M	VL	H	L	36	54	1	3	61	2	2
30	8	8	1	4	3	31	67	M	H	VH	VL	M	M	35	53	3	3	55	1	2
51	1	1	4	8	10	81	17	M	L	M	VL	VH	L	43	41(5)	1	5	58	3	3

(Group I)

	N	NS	E	T	SD	IW+	IW-	Sp.	Cn.	Rg.	In.	Al.	Ld.	ES	Hys.(?)	A	B	Age	Ex.	Ed.
Group II 44	7	9	1	5	3	62	44	M	VH	H	VL	H	L	37	49	1	3	30	1	4
47	9	2	1	1	2	25	27	M	VH	H	VL	M	L	40	44	2	2	55	3	7
25	2	6	4	1	3	69	11	M	H	M	L	H	M	44	54	3	3	33	2	2
s03	3	4	4	2	2	75	27	M	L	H	L	H	M	49	59	3	3	28	4	7
20	4	6	3	5	2	44	44	H	M	M	L	H	L	40	53	3	3	63	2	2
18	1	2	7	2	5	88	11	M	VH	M	L	VL	L	44	54	4	4	68	2	6
38	2	2	3	7	5	81	22	M	H	VL	VL	H	M	46	54	1	4	33	2	2
23	1	6	3	6	7	56	11	M	H	L	L	H	M	45	61	2	2	63	2	3
s33	1	1	8	3	9	92	0	M	H	M	VL	VH	L	44	54	3	3	47	5	6
13	2	5	8	6	9	62	17	M	H	H	L	VH	L	41	56	3	3	29	2	6
34	10	9	5	3	2	50	38	M	M	L	M	VH	M	34	60	1	3	34	2	6
48	4	9	7	5	3	62	27	L	H	VL	VL	VH	H	37	70(x)	4	4	55	1	?
Group III 09	4	6	2	5	4	31	22	M	H	L	L	VH	L	38	65(4)	3	3	61	2	1
s26	3	5	8	1	3	69	27	H	L	L	M	H	M	44	51	4	3	48	4	7
19	8	8	10	1	5	62	83	M	H	H	VL	VH	L	44	60	3	4	38	2	2
s15	1	2	9	8	10	88	11	M	H	L	VL	VH	M	46	47	5	3	65	2	6
s11	3	3	3	2	6	62	11	H	M	M	M	H	L	51	57	5	4	53	5	7
24	1	2	9	4	5	75	5	VL	VH	H	VL	VH	M	44	46	5	3	44	2	6
32	1	2	3	6	4	81	5	M	VH	L	M	M	M	46	47	4	3	67	2	6
s14	1	2	5	7	9	75	11	M	VH	VH	VL	H	L	41	53(4)	4	3	73	2	4
s02	9	5	6	1	2	69	44	VH	L	H	M	M	M	41	61	4	4	37	3	7
s06	1	5	1	1	5	50	11	H	H	L	L	H	VL	47	53	3	3	65	3	6
39	4	9	7	2	4	50	38	VH	VL	M	M	M	M	31	63	1	3	54	5	6
s54	1	2	1	4	7	75	0	VL	M	L	L	VH	VH	46	58	1	2	54	3	6
52	7	9	4	6	4	37	38	VL	H	H	L	H	M	36	49	2	2	48	3	3
Group IV 21	5	7	3	1	1	49	17	M	H	M	L	H	L	36	??	1	?	49	3	2
s53	3	2	10	1	8	75	17	M	L	M	L	H	H	41	54	?	?	67	3	3
29	3	4	7	7	9	50	50	M	VL	H	M	M	H	47	47	1	1	37	4	7
37	3	9	4	9	8	37	11	M	H	L	L	VH	M	36	68	5	1	77	5	6
46	9	9	1	6	1	25	50	L	VH	L	L	VH	M	34	51	1	4	35	1	6
45	9	3	1	7	7	44	89	VH	M	VH	VL	M	L	36	39	2	3	24	1	6
55	9	8	1	2	3	31	61	H	L	H	M	H	VL	31	46(4)	3	?	62	3	3
16	5	2	4	1	4	50	22	M	VH	L	VL	VH	M	50	47	1	2	62	2	2
35	4	2	6	2	5	81	17	M	VL	L	H	VH	M	47	51	3	3	49	2	6
Group V s36	10	5	3	4	3	31	83	M	M	H	VL	VH	M	37	63	1	1	45	3	7
43	7	8	5	2	1	57	17	M	VH	L	VL	VH	M	32	61(3)	3	3	27	1	6
07	6	3	5	1	2	62	38	H	M	H	L	M	M	45	72	2	3	32	4	7
04	7	9	3	9	7	38	50	H	m	m	l	vh	l	41	56	1	1	29	4	7
49	5	8	6	1	3	50	17	H	M	M	M	M	M	41	51	2	2	62	5	6
05	10	9	1	1	1	14	72	M	M	L	M	M	M	47	55	1	1	31	4	7
s50	6	7	1	6	5	69	11	M	M	M	L	H	L	49	61	3	3	44	3	7
s27	1	4	4	4	4	49	11	M	VH	M	L	VH	VL	48	41	2	3	47	2	4
17	7	9	1	2	1	31	78	H	M	H	L	M	L	32	65	1	3	48	2	7
s42	2	9	1	6	2	62	0	VH	M	M	VH	M	L	43	54	1	3	49	1	6

s = (placed at the extreme left of the subject's number) Superior, spiritual director, or ex-Superior, or substituting Superior in the Superior's absence (due to illness).

(x) This subject has a severe medical condition with symptoms similar to hysteria (vomiting, nausea, loss of appetite, etc.)

268

Key to Abbreviations:

N   = Neuroticism (Scale: 1-10; 5 = average score of the Dutch population)
NS   = Psycho-somatic neuroticism
E   = Extraversion
T   = Test unreliability
SD   = Social desirability
IW+ = Inner Well-being Test, happy emotions (Scale: percentages of the points possible)
IW− = Inner Well-being Test, unhappy emotions (Scale: percentages of the points possible)

Scale of Inner-personal Values:

Sp. = Need for group support   VL = very low, compared with the general population
Cn. = Conformity   L   = low
Rg. = Need for recognition   M   = medium
In. = Independence   H   = high
Al. = Altruism   VH = very high
Ld. = Leadership qualities

ES = Barron Ego-Strength Scale (The adjusted scale contains only 60 items; the norm is 40 ±)
Hys. (?) = MMPI Hysteria Scale: Scale is in percentages (50 = average)
         (Since both the Barron Ego-Strength Scale and the Hysteria Scale contain a few questions which are not applicable to subjects in cloisters, as many as two unanswered questions were allowed. By subjects who left more than 2 questions blank, the number of unanswered questions is mentioned between parentheses (?).
A   = The subject's assessment about his/her own stage of development in prayer.
B   = The subject's assessment of the average level of advancement in prayer of the group. (Scale: 1-5. Five = the furthest stage of advancement.)
Ex. = Degree of experimenting allowed in the group. (Scale: 1 = very strict; 2 = moderate, 3 = a flexible group, 4 = an experimental group, 5 = individual living alone.
Ed. = Level of education (7 = university level)

269

Subjects ranked as in Table 10, p. 253.

	N	NS	E	T		N	NS	E	T
28	1	5	7	7	53	5	2	10	3
08	2	1	10	1	29	4	4	8	1
40	2	2	6	9	37	2	10	5	8
01	2	1	7	1	46	9	2	1	5
31	1	7	5	5	45	10	6	2	3
10	1	5	10	1	55	9	9	1	3
12	1	8	6	8	16	1	2	6	1
22	6	7	2	6	35	3	2	3	4
30	8	9	1	2	36				
51	1	4	3	8	43	4	8	3	4
44	7	8	2	6	07				
47	6	5	1	1	04				
25	2	6	2	1	49	4	6	7	1
03	8	4	3	1	05	7	5	1	2
20	1	6	4	1	50	2	8	1	6
18	1	2	7	1	27	1	4	6	7
38	4	3	6	1	17	7	10	1	1
23	1	5	1	5	42	1	7	1	4
33	1	3	10	2					
13	2	4	8	7					
34	9	9	4	1	Subjects 21, 36, 07, 04				
48	5	9	8	3	did not send their re-tests back.				
09	1	8	4	9					
26	3	3	9	1					
19	8	7	10	1					
15	1	1	9	5					
11	1	4	4	3					
24	1	3	5	3					
32	1	2	2	2					
14	1	1	6	8					
02	9	5	10	1					
06	1	2	2	1					
39	2	6	6	2					
54	2	2	2	8					
52	9	4	3	3					

TABLE 20. *Factor Analysis of Section Two.*

Distractions in Prayer

Factor 1: "*Tense, distracted state.*"

Loading	Item	
0.872	30.	continually hoping that some disturbance will stop (e.g. traffic noise, a telephone ringing, whispering, music, coughing, etc.)
0.798	28.	being irritated by light or the smallest noise or movements
0.748	11.	being irritated by uncomfortable circumstances such as the temperature, drafts, the weather, itching, uncomfortable clothing, etc.

Factor 2: "*Drowsiness.*"

0.797	9.	becoming dull and drowsy
0.777	1.	dozing off
0.716	5.	nodding
0.702	6.	bringing all sorts of thoughts to mind

Factor 3: "*Attempted relaxation and concentration.*"

0.758	22.	trying to remember God's presence as a preparation for prayer
0.722	15.	making an effort to awaken certain feelings in regard to God
0.708	10.	making an effort to still the thoughts
0.603	6.	bringing all sorts of thoughts to mind

Factor 4: "*Relaxed, remembering*".

0.621	16.	being reminded of previous experiences of God's presence
-0.697	21.	putting the hands or the feet in a a lighty different position
-0.640	19.	as a preparation for prayer, doing one or more of these activities: yoga exercises, turning music on, walking or bicycling, constantly repeating the same word or words, reading a familiar text out loud, or any other repetitive and mechanical, simple movement or action.
-0.54	22.	trying to remember God's presence as a preparation for prayer

Factor 5: "*Restlessness.*"

0.827	14.	checking the time
0.691	3.	changing position often
0.684	32.	after prayer, especially when it did not suceed, taking up some physical activity such as just walking around, bicycling, household chores, eating, gardening, or any other movement which does not require much concentration.
0.668	23.	having difficulty in sitting still
0.629	29.	having trouble sitting straight (not due to age or illness)
0.567	19.	as a preparation for prayer, doing one or more of these activities: see above.

271

Factor 1: "Tense, distracted state"

Item, section two:	Items, section one:
30. irritation	67. very unpleasurable prayer experience (factor 14)
28. irritation	43. inability to pray (factor 2)
	49. inability to pray
	59. inability to pray
11. irritation	7. active rational meditation (factor 6)
	11. active visual meditation (factor 3)
	43. inability to pray (factor 2)
	57. intellectual vision (factor 4)

Factor 2: "Drowsiness"

9. becoming drowsy	2. inability to pray (factor 2)
	3. active visual meditation (factor 3)
	6. inability to pray (factor 2)
	7. active rational meditation (factor 6)
	11. active visual meditation (factor 3)
	21. unpleasurable experience (factor 13)
	47. distracted, troubled prayer (factor 10)
1. dozing off	47. distracted, troubled prayer (factor 10)
5. nodding	– – – –
6. distraction: bringing all sorts of things to mind.	6. unpleasurable experience (factor 13)
	11. active visual meditation (factor 3)
	21. unpleasurable experience (factor 13)
	47. distracted, troubled prayer (factor 10)
	59. inability to pray (factor 2)
	65. distracted, troubled prayer (factor 10)

Factor 3: "Attempted relaxation and concentration"

22. remembering God's presence	2. unpleasurable experience (factor 13)
	3. active visual meditation (factor 3)
	6. unpleasurable experience (factor 13)
	7. active rational meditation (factor 6)
	10. very unpleasurable experience (factor 14)
	15. active rational meditation (factor 6)
	43. inability to pray (factor 2)
	44. passive, restful contemplation (factor 15)
15. trying to awaken emotions for God	3. active visual meditation (factor 3)
	6. unpleasurable experience (factor 13)

	7. active rational meditation (factor 6)
	15. active rational meditation (factor 6)
	47. distracted, troubled prayer (factor 10)
	49. inability to pray (factor 2)
	59. inability to pray (factor 2)
	65. distracted, troubled prayer (factor 10)

10. stilling the mind	2. unpleasurable experience (factor 13)
	7. active rational meditation (factor 6)
	6. unpleasurable experience (factor 13)
	10. very unpleasurable experience (factor 14)
	32. very unpleasurable experience (factor 14)
	43. inability to pray (factor 2)
	47. distracted, troubled prayer (factor 10)
	49. inability to pray (factor 2)
	65. distracted, troubled prayer (factor 10)

Factor 4: "Relaxed, remembering"

16. remembering past prayer experiences (positive loading)	24. unpleasurable experience (factor 13) 42. pleasurable experience (factor 1) 58. pleasurable experience (factor 1) 56. inability to pray (factor 2)
21. changing position of hands and feet (negative loading)	7. active rational meditation (factor 6) 11. active visual meditation (factor 3) 15. active rational meditation (factor 6)
19. techniques (negative loading)	– – –
22. remembering God's presence (negative loading)	2. unpleasurable experience (factor 13) 3. active visual meditation (factor 3) 6. unpleasurable experience (factor 13) 7. active rational meditation (factor 6) 10. very unpleasurable experience (factor 14) 15. active rational meditation (factor 6) 43. inability to pray (factor 2) 44. passive, restful contemplation (factor 15)

Factor 5: "Restlessness"

14. checking the time	3. active visual meditation (factor 3) 41. inability to pray (factor 2) 59. inability to pray (factor 2)
3. changing position	– – –
32. moving around	2. inability to pray factor 2) 47. distracted, troubled prayer (factor 10) 59. inability to pray (factor 2) 65. distracted, troubled prayer (factor 10)

23. moving around	2. inability to pray (factor 2)
	41. inability to pray (factor 2)
	56. inability to pray (factor 2)
29. slumping	3. active visual meditation (factor 3)
	15. active rational meditation (factor 6)
19. techniques	– – –

TABLE 22. *Section Three: Ascetical views.*
Correlations with Ascetical Views:

'Loving' items:	Cl. A	A.	N.	–	Ind.	Exp.	Educ.	Age
6. "Direct the will to God with love."	–	0.38	-0.38	-0.28	-0.51	-0.47	-0.28	–
15. "Purity of heart is nothing less than the love which comes from God's favor."	0.39	0.38	-0.38	-0.53	-0.21	-0.35	-0.42	0.47
18. "The spirit is purified and enlightened only through love."	–	–	–	–	–	-0.35	-0.23	–
19. "One must trust God; He will not withhold that which is necessary for the way, until he has brought the soul to the clear and pure light of love."	0.37	0.34	-0.35	-0.36	-0.33	-0.48	-0.40	0.32
20. "When love is perfect then occurs the transformation of the soul through love to God."	0.37	0.32	–	–	-0.41	-0.22	–	–
5. "One must detach oneself from all pleasurable feelings in prayer and from specific intellectual acts."	0.41							
13. "One must pray by 'unknowing' rather than by knowing."	0.40							
17. "A single attachment is enough to prevent ones enjoying the pleasure of love in prayer."	0.39							

Cl. A = cluster A (mystical prayer)
A   = Altruism
N   = Neuroticism
–   = Unhappy emotions
Ind.   = Independence
Exp.   = Experimental group
Educ. = Higher education
(For the content of the other items in section three, see pp. 239-240, appendix)

Undifferentiated correlations with prayer 'items' (conformistic items) & cultural variables:

Items: Sec. 3	1	4	8	9	12	18	19	40	66	Con-for-mity	Inde-pend.	Exper. group.
01 mild?	0.32	0.29	0.39	0.41	0.28	0.28	0.25	0.31	0.36	0.44	-0.32	-0.46
02 strict	0.37	0.42	0.46	0.50	0.27	0.46	0.44	0.38	0.50	0.45	-0.48	-0.39
03 strict	0.28	0.35	0.40	0.43	0.37	0.41	0.30	0.41	0.45	0.31	-0.27	-0.52
04 strict	0.34	0.41	0.31	0.38	0.31	0.37	0.33	0.41	0.52	0.42	-0.29	-0.53
05 mild	0.39	0.35	0.44	0.50	0.34	0.44	0.37	0.35	0.41	0.47	-0.24	-0.52
06 love	0.16	0.15	0.32	0.34	0.20	0.11	0.19	0.17	0.22	0.37	-0.51	-0.47
07 mild	0.37	0.31	0.33	0.33	0.17	0.34	0.33	0.24	0.28	0.30	-0.44	-0.18
08 strict	0.40	0.39	0.27	0.34	0.14	0.56	0.21	0.21	0.34	0.51	-0.35	-0.55
09 strict	0.33	0.39	0.40	0.44	0.37	0.31	0.32	0.25	0.53	0.48	-0.37	-0.58
10 strict	0.35	0.41	0.24	0.28	0.16	0.50	0.21	0.25	0.35	0.57	-0.31	-0.51
11 strict	0.30	0.30	0.23	0.20	0.16	0.52	0.13	0.24	0.30	0.51	-0.26	-0.69
12 mild	0.37	0.32	0.37	0.40	0.28	0.42	0.30	0.31	0.38	0.47	-0.33	-0.47
13 mild	0.33	0.35	0.39	0.40	0.32	0.35	0.35	0.34	0.42	0.25	-0.25	-0.49
14 strict	0.18	0.28	0.31	0.23	0.22	0.39	0.23	0.26	0.29	0.39	-0.24	-0.49
15 love	0.33	0.33	0.27	0.50	0.33	0.28	0.37	0.46	0.33	0.39	-0.21	-0.35
16 strict	0.37	0.36	0.36	0.42	0.30	0.39	0.29	0.37	0.36	0.52	-0.30	-0.50
17 love	0.35	0.26	0.28	0.31	0.09	0.37	0.28	0.25	0.34	0.40	-0.29	-0.51
18 love	0.23	0.19	0.23	0.26	0.10	0.18	0.30	0.21	0.26	–	-0.18	-0.35
19 love	0.34	0.32	0.35	0.40	0.29	0.27	0.31	0.31	0.29	0.33	-0.33	-0.48
20 love	0.17	0.19	0.20	0.18	0.22	0.24	0.37	0.27	0.26	0.24	-0.41	-0.22

TABLE 23. *Canonical Correlation Analysis: Ascetical views (mild) and contemplative and mystical prayer (past and present).*

Variables	CVp	CVc
1. Present contemplative prayer (factor 8) (sumscores)	0.83	0.56
2. Present mystical prayer (factor 1)	0.78	0.53
3. Past contemplative prayer	0.95	0.64
4. Past mystical prayer	0.76	0.52
5. Ascetical item '5'	0.55	0.82
6. Ascetical item '7'	0.31	0.46
7. Ascetical item '13'	0.51	0.76
8. Ascetical item '15'	0.25	0.37
9. Ascetical item '18'	0.39	0.58
10. Ascetical item '19'	0.58	0.85
11. Ascetical item '20'	0.26	0.38
12. Ascetical item '6' (section four)	0.53	0.78

Predictors: 1-4 Canonical correlation: 0.68
Criteria: 5-12 Probability level: 0.20
CVp = canonical variate of the predictors
CVc = canonical variates of the criteria

TABLE 24. *Ascetical views (strict) and contemplative and mystical prayer (past and present):*

Variables	CVp	CVc
1. Present contemplative prayer	0.65	0.14
2. Present mystical prayer	0.65	0.14
3. Past contemplative prayer	0.10	0.02
4. Past mystical prayer	0.31	0.07
5. Ascetical item '2'	0.06	0.27
6. Item '4'	0.08	0.36
7. Item '8'	-.07	-.31
8. Item '10'	-.02	-.10
9. Item '11'	-.00	-.02
10. Item '14'	-.07	-.33
11. Item '16'	0.08	0.36
12. Item '17'	0.08	0.35

Predictors: 1-4
Criteria: 5-12

Canonical Correlation: 0.22
Probability level: 0.99

TABLE 25. *The co-determinants to concentration in prayer.*

Variables	CVp	CVc
1. Present emotional contemplative experiences (sumscores, factor 8)	0.93	0.69
2. Present pleasurable mystical experiences (sumscores, factor 1)	0.99	0.74
3. Extraversion	0.23	0.31
4. Happy emotionality	0.41	0.47
5. Social desirability	0.35	0.55
6. Conformity	0.33	0.44
7. Independence	-0.53	-0.72
8. Higher education	-0.48	-0.65
9. Administrative position	-0.30	-0.40
10. 'Via negativa' (item 5, sec. 3)	0.42	0.57
11. 'Via negativa' (item 13, sec. 3)	0.40	0.54
12. Theological virtues (item 19, sec. 3)	0.38	0.51
13. Theological virtues (item 6, sec. 4)	0.38	0.51

Predictors: 1-2
Criteria: 3-13

Canonical correlation: 0.74
Probability level: 0.0043

276

TABLE 26. *The co-determinants to concentration in prayer.*

Variables	CVp	CVc
1. Present emotional contemplative experiences (sumscores, factor 8)	0.95	0l74
2. Present pleasurable mystical experiences (sumscores, factor 1)	0.98	0.76
3. Extraversion	0.24	0.31
4. Happy emotionality	0.35	0.46
5. Social desirability	0.41	0.53
6. Conformity	0.32	0.42
7. Independence	-0.53	-0.69
8. Higher education	-0.48	-0.62
9. Administrative position	-0.30	-0.39
10. 'Via negativa' (item 5, sec. 3)	0.43	0.55
11. 'Via negativa' (item 13, sec. 3)	0.41	0.53
12. Theological virtues (item 19, sec. 3)	0.38	0.50
13. The elimination of self-love (item 4, sec. 4)	-0.19	-0.24

Predictors: 1-2   Canonical correlation: 0.77
Criteria: 3-13   Probability level: 0.0011

STATISTICAL ANALYSIS
OF THE POWER DENSITY SPECTRAL ANALYSIS:
A MULTIVARIATE ANALYSIS OF VARIANCE

In the original design the following analysis of variance factors were distinguished:
1. prayer with two levels, a non-concentrated condition and a concentrated state.
2. localization with six levels, i.e. positions T4-T6, T6-P4, P4-Pz, Pz-P3, P3-T5, T5-T3. Positions F8-T4 and T3-F7 were disregarded because of possible artifacts.
3. polarity with two levels, monopolarity and bipolarity.
4. psychological type with two levels, introversion and extraversion (neuroticism was not included because the analysis would have become too complicated).

Each subject was measured under each level combination of the first three factors. The fourth factor divided the subject into two groups: introverts and extraverts. Eight dependent variables were measured. The first four were the average frequency of delta, theta, alpha and beta rhythm respectively. The second four were the absolute power of these rhythms in the same order. Other possible variables, such as peak power, peak frequency

277

and relative power were not included because they were so highly inter-dependent.

Since the main point of interest was the factors 'prayer' and 'type' and their interaction, it was decided to perform an analysis of variance with these factors only. Furthermore a detailed examination of the mean values of the different level combinations taken over the subjects led to the conclusion that the differences of the means for 'localization' and 'polarity' could be disregarded. That is, there was no appreciable difference between data from the bipolar and the monopolar recordings nor from the various positions. The analysis of variance with 'prayer' and 'type' was performed on the mean scores of the subjects taken over the level combinations of localization and polarity. So, for each person a mean value was computed over 12 observations. The mean scores are given in the following Table I on the next page.

For each separate type of rhythm an analysis of variance was done separately. In fact what is involved here is called a repeated measurements design. It was not possible to use normal analysis of variance procedures since the observations under the different conditions are not independent.

Therefore, the multivariate approach to the analysis of variance of repeated measurements was used[1]. The results are shown in Table II, page 279. In no case was a significant effect found on a 0.05 level of significance. If one uses a 0.10 level of significance, which is highly unusual in scientific research, one finds a significant difference between the two types and between the prayer conditions for total power in the alpha band. A significant type effect was also found for total power in the delta band[2].

[1] Bock, R. D., *Multivariate Statistical Methods in Behavioral Research*, N.Y., 1975, ch. 7.
[2] Acknowledgments must be extended to A. van der Ven and H. van der Hoeven, who did this statistical analysis and who helped in preparing this report.

TABLE I. *Mean Scores.*

	delta (A.F.)	theta (A.F.)	alpha (A.F.)	beta (A.F.)	delta (T.P.)	theta (T.P.)	alpha (T.P.)	beta (T.P.)
1021.000 N	1.442	5.442	10.108	18.600	3.867	0.900	2.700	1.325
2021.000	1.492	5.475	10.258	18.733	3.783	0.925	3.692	1.400
1031.000 N	1.667	5.367	10.433	18.258	4.225	1.192	5.042	1.958
2031.000	1.650	5.450	10.300	18.250	4.450	1.475	4.892	2.400
1041.000 N	1.342	5.375	9.933	18.958	8.242	1.208	17.525	3.217
2041.000	1.533	5.325	9.967	18.683	5.300	1.200	17.333	2.167
1051.000	1.792	5.408	9.742	18.300	13.075	3.250	24.042	5.933
2051.000	1.767	5.483	9.808	18.275	11.550	2.717	23.267	5.342
1101.000	1.742	5.592	9.942	17.525	8.075	3.483	33.800	8.150
2101.000	1.783	5.600	9.883	17.500	7.417	3.050	26.050	7.567
1121.000	1.650	5.417	10.292	17.250	5.650	1.308	5.583	5.575
2121.000	1.575	5.392	10.558	17.733	5.683	1.167	4.517	5.917
1012.000	1.783	5.767	9.208	17.600	19.692	14.642	109.200	20.517
2012.000	1.717	5.758	9.292	17.792	17.892	12.058	108.683	22.350
1062.000	1.408	5.625	9.325	18.925	7.192	1.217	10.850	1.508
2062.000	1.483	5.708	9.267	18.883	7.325	1.633	12.017	1.458
1072.000	2.000	5.433	9.700	17.525	13.683	6.050	54.450	7.742
2072.000	1.917	5.617	9.475	17.517	17.242	6.683	52.425	7.017
1082.000	1.667	5.850	8.800	17.667	9.058	5.817	99.833	8.608
2082.000	1.692	5.842	8.733	17.617	7.692	4.858	97.483	7.050
1092.000	1.642	5.617	9.692	17.700	10.617	3.417	47.325	5.975
2092.000	1.658	5.567	9.875	18.150	8.758	2.508	32.542	4.850
1112.000	1.308	5.417	10.308	16.683	18.717	2.158	18.317	7.083
2112.000	1.392	5.383	10.792	16.958	10.392	1.683	14.008	7.625
1132.000 N	1.600	5.325	10.508	18.625	5.083	1.142	6.742	3.392
2132.000	1.600	5.342	10.542	18.742	4.983	1.158	7.825	3.408

(A.F.) = average frequency
(T.P.) = total power
First column: 1 = non-concentrated state in prayer, 2 = concentrated prayer
Second and third column: number of the subject
Fourth column: 1 = introvert, 2 = extravert
N = Neurotic (score of 7 to 10 on 'N' scale)

TABLE II. *Multivariate Analysis of Variance.*

	Step Down F		Univariate F
	Interaction Type vs Prayer	Main effect Type	Main effect Prayer
delta (A.F.)	.6207	.8910	.4592
theta (A.F.)	.8853	.1059	.2492
alpha (A.F.)	.4088	.1744	.2988
beta (A.F.)	.7169	.4423	.1524
delta (T.P.)	.9697	*.0814*	.1688
theta (T.P.)	.7644	.1487	.1465
alpha (T.P.)	.6977	*.0802*	*.0907*
beta (T.P.)	.6337	.2398	.4834

(values for the different EEG variables in relation to the different effects.)

279

TABLE III. *Correlation Matrix*

Key:

1. Level of arousal (routine EEG)
2. Synchronization of alpha waves (routine EEG)
3. Alpha spreading (routine EEG)
4. Theta spreading (routine EEG)
5. Neuroticism (N scale, ABV)
6. Extraversion (E scale, ABV)
7. Happy emotionality (+ scale, Positief Welbevinden)
8. Unhappy emotionality (− scale, Positief Welbevinden)
9. Emotional contemplation
10. Mystical experience
11. Active rational prayer
12. Distracted prayer
13. Non-emotional contemplation
14. Alpha abundance (routine EEG)
15. Theta abundance (routine EEG)
16. Level of arousal (prayer EEG)
17. Synchronization of alpha waves (prayer EEG)
18. Alpha spreading (prayer EEG)
19. Theta spreading (prayer EEG)
20. Alpha abundance (prayer EEG)
21. Theta abundance (prayer EEG)
22. Independence (Scale of Inter-Personal Values)

	1	2	3	4	5	6	7	8	9	10
1	1.0000									
2	-0.6085	1.0000								
3	0.1398	0.1820	1.0000							
4	-0.4444	0.3648	0.6536	1.0000						
5	0.5443	-0.5963	0.0107	-0.2717	1.0000					
6	-0.4070	0.7033	0.3213	0.2934	-0.3227	1.0000				
7	-0.6154	0.7265	0.0485	0.3208	-0.8512	0.4831	1.0000			
8	0.6111	-0.7223	-0.0435	-0.3124	0.8510	-0.4800	-0.9999	1.0000		
9	-0.2848	0.5030	0.2608	0.2848	-0.3856	0.4668	0.4399	-0.4381	1.0000	
10	-0.2497	0.3730	0.2805	0.2975	-0.2887	0.3572	0.3490	-0.3477	0.9691	1.0000
11	0.3601	-0.0900	-0.2959	-0.3370	0.0598	-0.3669	-0.0300	0.0278	-0.2455	-0.3626
12	0.3226	-0.1718	-0.3919	-0.1403	0.3027	-0.2937	-0.2868	0.2861	-0.3103	-0.3397
13	-0.4423	0.5271	0.1018	0.2315	-0.5398	0.5181	0.5631	-0.5624	0.8875	0.8534
14	-0.1055	0.1556	0.6722	0.4650	-0.2719	0.1518	0.1711	-0.1691	0.0289	0.1066
15	-0.3100	0.1242	0.3257	0.7645	-0.0800	0.0764	0.2222	-0.2146	0.0530	0.0653
16	0.4744	-0.6707	-0.0466	-0.2530	0.9036	-0.3368	-0.8403	0.8390	-0.5916	-0.4836
17	-0.4462	0.7355	0.2901	0.4172	-0.7668	0.4158	0.7885	-0.7855	0.7639	0.6968
18	-0.2864	0.2833	0.3129	0.4591	-0.0708	0.1856	0.1970	-0.1949	0.0434	0.1363
19	0.0506	-0.1975	0.2303	0.2027	0.1042	0.0286	0.0560	-0.0605	-0.0236	0.0679
20	-0.0594	0.3304	0.6637	0.4436	-0.5018	0.3339	0.3251	-0.3243	0.3752	0.3658
21	-0.0784	-0.0113	0.3568	0.2966	-0.0374	0.1349	0.1670	-0.1700	0.1319	0.2419
22	0.4048	-0.4536	-0.4606	-0.5856	0.3200	-0.4384	-0.2111	0.2046	-0.6746	-0.6241

	11	12	13	14	15	16	17	18	19	20

11	1.0000								
12	0.4815	1.0000							
13	-0.4335	-0.2988	1.0000						
14	-0.5975	-0.4945	0.1280	1.0000					
15	-0.1442	0.0201	-0.0087	0.0492	1.0000				
16	0.0568	0.3066	-0.6858	-0.2040	-0.1431	1.0000			
17	-0.1529	-0.3703	0.7472	0.3065	0.2079	-0.9221	1.0000		
18	-0.2078	0.0424	0.0459	0.4014	0.0400	0.1146	0.0999	1.0000	
19	-0.3773	0.1021	0.1535	0.3475	0.0589	0.1686	-0.1470	0.2831	1.0000
20	-0.3838	-0.3616	0.4345	0.8125	-0.1132	-0.4375	0.5178	0.3445	0.3203	1.0000
21	-0.4661	-0.0557	0.2726	0.5922	-0.0913	0.0435	0.0759	0.5847	0.8607	0.5650
22	0.2176	0.3669	-0.5341	-0.1390	-0.2161	0.3260	-0.4900	-0.2453	0.2222	-0.4270

	21	22
21	1.0000	
22	0.0574	1.0000

TABLE IV. *Introversion/Extraversion and Prayer Periods (combined means)*

average frequency of alpha	Introverts	Extraverts	
poor concentration	10.07Hz	9.65 Hz	(S.D. = 0.5826)
good concentration	10.13 Hz	9.71 Hz	

total power of alpha	Introverts	Extraverts	
poor concentration	14.78 MMV2	49.53 MMV2	(S.D. = 36.5284)
good concentration	13.29 MMV2	46.43 MMV2	

TABLE V. *Locality vs. Introvert (I) and Extravert (E) (combined means)*

Locality:	theta band: total power	alpha band: total power	
T4-T6	I: 2.3 MMV2	I: 20.6 MMV2	(S.D. theta = 3.6328
	E: 5.8 MMV2	E: 72.2 MMV2	S.D. alpha = 36.5284)
T6-P4	I: 1.7 MMV2	I: 15 MMV2	
	E: 3.8 MMV2	E: 37 MMV2	
P4-Pz	I: 1.2 MMV2	I: 11 MMV2	
	E: 3.9 MMV2	E: 46 MMV2	
Pz-P3	I: 2 MMV2	I: 15.4 MMV2	
	E;: 5.7 MMV2	E: 53 MMV2	
P3-T5	I: 2 MMV2	I: 11 MMV2	
	E: 4.6 MMV2	E: 35 MMV2	
T5-T3	I: 1.6 MMV2	I: 10.6 MMV2	
	E: 4.2 MMV2	E: 44.5 MMV2	

TABLE VI. *Difference scores, visual assessment of the EEG.*

Factor 8 (emotional contemplation), Factor 1 (mystical experience).

Subjects with high sumscores:	level of arousal baseline	prayer	synchronization baseline	prayer	alpha spreading baseline	prayer	alpha abundance baseline	pray
01	3	2 = +1	4	4 = 0	3	2 = −1	4	4 =
03	2	3 = −1	3	3 = 0	1	1 = 0	3	3 =
08	3	3 = 0	3	3 = 0	2	2 = 0	3	3 =
09	2	2 = 0	3	3 = 0	1	1 = 0	3	3 =
10	2	2 = 0	4	4 = 0	2	3 = −1	4	4 =
14	4	4 = 0	2	2 = 0	1	1 = 0	2	2 =
Subjects with low sumscores:								
02	4	4 = 0	3	2 = +1	1	1 = 0	2	1 =
04	5	5 = 0	1	1 = 0	2	2 = 0	3	3 =
05	5	5 = 0	1	1 = 0	2	1 = +1	4	3 =
06	2	2 = 0	2	3 = −1	1	1 = 0	3	2 =
07	1	5 = −4	3	1 = +2	1	3 = −2	3	2 =
11	2	2 = 0	4	3 = +1	2	1 = +1	3	3 =
12	4	3 = +1	3	3 = 0	1	1 = 0	3	3 =
13	4	3 = +1	3	2 = +1	1	2 = −1	3	3 =

TABLE VII. *Factor 6 (active, rational meditation).*

Subjects with high sumscores	level of arousal baseline	prayer	synchronization baseline	prayer	alpha spreading baseline	prayer	alpha abundance baseline	pray
02	4	4 = 0	3	2 = +1	1	1 = 0	2	1 =
04	5	5 = 0	1	1 = 0	2	2 = 0	3	3 =
11	2	2 = 0	4	3 = +1	2	1 = +1	3	3 =
12	4	3 = +1	3	3 = 0	1	1 = 0	3	3 =
14	4	4 = 0	2	2 = 0	1	1 = 0	2	2 =
Subjects with low sumscores								
01	3	2 = +1	4	4 = 0	3	2 = +1	4	4 =
03	2	3 = −1	3	3 = 0	1	1 = 0	3	3 =
05	5	5 = 0	1	1 = 0	2	1 = +1	4	3 =
06	2	2 = 0	2	3 = −1	1	1 = 0	3	2 =
07	1	5 = −4	3	1 = +2	1	3 = −2	3	2 =
08	3	3 = 0	3	3 = 0	2	2 = 0	3	3 =
09	2	2 = 0	3	3 = 0	1	1 = 0	2	3 =
10	2	2 = 0	4	4 = 0	2	3 = −1	4	4 =
13	4	3 = +1	3	2 = +1	1	2 = −1	3	3 =

or 10 (distracted, troubled prayer)

jects with sumscores	level of arousal		synchronization		alpha spreading		alpha abundance	
	baseline	prayer	baseline	prayer	baseline	prayer	baseline	prayer
NE	4	4 = 0	3	2 = +1	1	1 = 0	2	1 = +1
NI (retest)	2	3 = −1	3	3 = 0	1	1 = 0	3	3 = +1
NI	5	5 = 0	1	1 = 0	2	2 = 0	3	3 = 0
SI	4	3 = +1	3	3 = 0	1	1 = 0	3	3 = 0
SE	4	3 = +1	3	2 = +1	1	2 = −1	3	3 = 0
–	1	5 = −4	3	1 = +2	1	3 = −2	3	2 = +1
NI	4	4 = 0	2	2 = 0	1	1 = 0	2	2 = 0
jects with sumscores:								
SE	3	2 = +1	4	4 = 0	3	2 = +1	4	4 = 0
NI	5	5 = 0	1	1 = 0	2	1 = +1	4	3 = +1
SI	2	2 = 0	2	3 = −1	1	1 = 0	3	2 = +1
E	3	3 = 0	3	3 = 0	2	2 = 0	3	3 = 0
SE	2	2 = 0	3	3 = 0	1	1 = 0	3	3 = 0
SE	2	2 = 0	4	4 = 0	2	3 = −1	4	4 = 0
SE	2	2 = 0	4	3 = +1	2	1 = +1	3	3 = 0

= Neurotic   (ABV scores between 7-10 on neuroticism scale)
Introvert   (ABV scores between 1- 3 on extraversion scale)
= Extravert   (ABV scores between 7-10 on extraversion scale)
Stable   (ABV scores between 1-3 on neuroticism scale)
hnical note: A rank correlation could not be carried out because the number of subjects was below minimum, 20.

283

Bibliography

SOURCES:

1. *St. John of the Cross:*

Bruno de Jesús María, O.C.D., *Saint Jean de la Croix*, Paris, Librairie Plon, 1929. (also in: *Les Études Carmélitaines*, Brugges, Desclee de Brouwer, 1961).

Crisógono de Jesús Sacramentado, O.C.D., *San Juan de la Cruz, su obra científica y su obra literaria*, 2 vols., Madrid, Editorial Avila, 1929.

Efrén de la Madre de Dios, O.C.D., *San Juan de la Cruz y el misterio de la stma. Trinidad en la vida espiritual*, Zaragoza, Editorial 'El Noticiero', 1947.

Jerónimo de San José, O.C.D., *Historia del Ven. P. Fr. Juan de la Cruz*, Madrid, Diego Díaz de la Carrera, 1614 (reprinted in 1912).

Matías del Nino Jesús & Lucinio Ruano, O.C.D. (eds.), *Vida y obras de San Juan de la Cruz* (revised and annotated biography of Crisógono), (Biblioteca de Autores Cristianos, 15), Madrid, La Editorial Católica, 1972[6].

Peers, A. E., *The Complete Works of St. John of the Cross*, 3 vols. (text and historical material from the critical edition of P. Silverio de Santa Teresa), Westminster, Maryland, The Newman Press, 1964.

Quiroga, José de Jesús María, O.C.D., *Historia de la vida y virtudes del Ven. P. Fr. Juan de la Cruz*, Brussels, J. Meerbeeck, 1628.

Silverio de Santa Teresa, C.D. (ed.), *Obras de S. Juan de la Cruz, Doctor de la Iglesia: Procesos de Beatificación y Canonización*, vol. 5 (Biblioteca Mística Carmelitana, 14), Burgos, El Monte Carmelo, 1931.

2. *Miscellaneous:*

Augustine, A., *The Trinity* (S. McKenna, trans.), Washington, D.C., Catholic University of America Press, 1963.

Grégoire le Grand, *Morales sur Job* (Sources Chrétiennes, 32), R. Gillet & A. Gaudemaria, ed. & trans.), Paris, Editions du Cerf, 1950.

Petrus Lombardus, *Senteniarum Libri IV*, Paris, 1553 (also in: Migne, J.P. (ed.), *Patrologia Latina*, vol. 192, 521-962, Paris, 1857-66).

(Pseudo) Augustine, *Meditationes, Soliloquia et Manuale*, Antwerp, Steelsius, 1557.

(Pseudo) Dionysius Areopagita, *Patrologia Graeca* (J. P. Migne, ed.), vol. 3, 119-1064, Paris, 1857-66.

Translations:

Gandillac, M. de, *Oeuvres Complètes de Pseudo-Denys L'Aréopagite*. Paris, Aubier, 1943.

Ivanka, E. von, *Dionysius Areopagita: Von den Namen zum Unnennbaren*, Einsiedeln, Johannes Verlag, no year.

Tritsch, W., *Dionysios Areopagita: Mystische Theologie und andere Schriften*, Munich, Barth Verlag, 1956.

Quiroga, G., *Index Librorum Expurgatorum*, Madrid, A. Gomez Regium, 1584.

Regel en Constitutiën der Ongeschoeide Nonnen van de Orde der Allerh. Maagd Maria van den Berg-Carmel, Rome, 1928. (Commentary: Fr. Gabriel of the St. M. Magdalene, Dutch trans., Hulst, Zeeland, 1942).

Thomas Aquinas, *Scriptum Super Sententiis*, Paris, P. Lethielleux, 1929.

Werling, G., "The Book of St. John, 44", (translation of *Liber Institutionum Primorum Monachorum*), *The Sword*, 4 (1940), 20-24, 152-160.

THEOLOGICAL-HISTORICAL LITERATURE:

Adolfo de la Madre de Dios, "Inquisition", s.v. "Espagne", *Dictionnaire de Spiritualité*, vol. 4 (2), Paris, Beauchesne, 1961, col. 1165.

Arntzen, M. J., *Mystieke rechtvaardigingsleer*, Kampen, Kok, 1956 (Dutch).

Aubin, P., "Intériorité et extériorité dans les 'Moralia in Job' de Saint Grégoire le Grand, *Recherches de Science Religieuse*, 62 (1974), 117-166.

Auer, A., "Ansätze einer Laienspiritualität", s.v. "Frömmigkeit", *Lexikon für Theologie und Kirche*, vol. 4, Freiburg, Herder, 1960², 404-405.

Baruzi, J., *Saint Jean de la Croix et le problème de l'expérience mystique*, Paris, Librairie Féliz Alcan, 1931².

Bataillon, M., *Erasmo en España*, México & Buenos Aires, Fondo de Cultura Económica, 1950².

Bavel, T. J. van, *Augustinus*, Baarn, Het Wereldvenster, 1970.

Bendiek, J., "Got und Welt nach Joh. vom Kreuz," *Philosophisches Jahrbuch*, (1972), 88-105.

Bernhart, J., *Die philosophische Mystik des Mittelalters*, Munich, Reinhardt, 1922.

Blanchard, P., "Expérience trinitaire et expérience mystique d'après Saint Jean de la Croix", *L'Année Théologique*, 1948, 293-310.

—, "L'espace intérieur chez saint Augustin d'après de Livre X des 'Confessions' ", *Augustinus Magister* (Études Augustiniennes), Paris, 1954, 535-542.

—, "La doctrine et la méthode de libération spirituelle chez saint Jean de la Croix," *Carmel*, 1969, 24-41, 97-118.

Bouyer, L., "Le pseudo-Denys et la mystique des pères," *Histoire de la Spiritualité Chrétienne*, I, Paris, Aubier, 1966, 473-503.

Brouwer, J., *De Psychologie der Spaansche Mystiek*, Amsterdam, H.J. Paris, 1931.

Butler, C., *Western Mysticism: The Teaching of SS. Augustine, Gregory and Bernard on Contemplation and Contemplative Life* (2), London, 1927.

Cavallera, F., "Augustine: Apocryphes", *Dict. de Spirit.*, vol. 1(2), col. 1134.

Cordero, F. G., "La teología espiritual de santa Teresa de Jesús, reacción contra el dualismo neoplatónico," *Revista Española de Teología*, 30 (1970), no. 1 & 2, pp. 3-38.

Corella, Sierra A., *La censura de libros y papeles en España y los índices y catálogos españoles de los prohibidos y expurgados*, Madrid, 1947.

Cox, H., *The Seduction of the Spirit*, N.Y., Simon & Schuster, 1973.

Cristiani, L., *St. John of the Cross*, N.Y., 1962.

Dekkers, E. (ed.), *Clavis Patrum Latinorum*, Steenbrugge, 1951¹.

Dixon, J. W., "The Erotics of Knowing", *Anglican Theological Review*, 56 (1974), 3-16.

—, "Paradigms of Sexuality," *Anglican Theological Review*, 56 (1974), 151-170.

Durantel, J., *Saint Thomas et le Pseudo-Denis*, Paris, Librairie F. Alcan, 1919.

Dürckheim, K. Graf, *Wunderbare Katze und andere Zen-Texte*, Weilheim Oberbayern, Otto Wilhelm Barth Verlag, 1964.

Eulogio de la Virgen del Carmen, O.C.D., "Saint Jean de la Croix," s.v. "Denys l'Aréopagite en Occident," *Dict. de Spirit.*, vol 3, 400.

—, *San Juan de la Cruz y sus escritos*, Madrid, Ediciones Cristianidad, 1969.

—, & Ruiz, F., "San Juan de la Cruz" (commentary and bibliography), *Ephemerides Carmelitana*, 19 (1968), 45-88.

—, "Illumination", *Dict. de Spirit.*, vol. 7, col. 1346.

—, "Illuminisme et illuminés", *Dict. de Spirit.*,vol. 7, col. 1367.

Eulogio de San Juan de la Cruz, *La transformación total del alma en Dios seqún S. Juan de la Cruz*, Madrid, Editorial de Espiritualidad, 1963.

García-Rodriguez, C. M. F., "El fondo del alma," *Revista Española de Teología*, 8 (1948), 458 ff.)

Garrigou-Lagrange, R., "St. Thomas et Saint Jean de Croix," *Vie Spirituelle*, (Oct., 1939), p. 27.

Goosen, A., *Achtergronden van Priscillianus' christelijke ascese*, Nijmegen, 1976.

Gillet, R., "Mystique Grégorienne," *Dict. de Spirit.*, vol. 6, cols. 899-902.

Grabmann, M., "Zur Psychologie der Mystik," *Der Katholische Gedanke*, Munich Theatiner Verlag, 1922.

Greshake, G., *Gnade als Konkrete Freiheit: Pelagius und Augustinus*, Mainz, Grünewald, 1972.

—, "Der Wandel der Erlösungsvorstellungen in der Theologiegeschichte," *Erlösung und Emmancipation*, (Quaestiones Disputatae, 61), Basel, Herder, 1973, pp. 69-101.

Gross, J., "Ur- und Erbsünde in der Theosophie des Pseudo-Dionysius," *Zeitschrift für Religions u. Geistesgeschichte*, vol. 4, (1952), pp. 32-42.

—, *Entstehungsgeschichte des Erbsündesdogmas*, Munich, Reinhardt, 1960-1972.

Hauserr, I., "Les Orientaux connaissent-ils les 'nuits' de saint Jean de la Croix?", *Orientalia Christiana Periodica*, 12 (1946), pp. 5-46.

Hendrikx, E., *Augustins Verhältnis zur Mystik (Ein patristische Untersuchung)*, Würzburg, Rita Verlag, 1936.

Heijke, J., "God in het diepste van de gedachte," *Bijdragen*, 16 (1955), 357-76.

Ivanka, E. von, "Von Platonismus zur Theorie der Mystick," *Scholastik*, 11, (1936), 163 ff.

—, "Die unmittelbare Gotteserkenntnis als Grundlage des natürlichen Erkennens und als Ziel des übernatürlichen Strebens bei Augustin," *Scholastik*, 13 (1938), 521-543.

—, "Apex Mentis: Wanderung und Wandlung eines stoischen Terminus," *Zeitschrift für katholische Theologie*, 72 (1950), 129-176.

—, *Plato Christianus*, Einsiedeln, Johannes Verlag, 1964.

Kern, W. "Übel," *Lexikon für Theologie und Kirche*, vol. X, 1960², 431.

Koch, J., "Augustinischen und dionysischen Neuplatonismus," *Kant. Studiën*, 48 (1956), 117-133.

Leblond, G., *Fils de lumière: L'inhabitation personnelle et spéciale du Saint-Esprit en notre âme selon saint Thomas d'Aquin et saint Jean de la Croix*, Sain Léger-Vauban, Yonne, 1961.

Ledergerber, K., *Die Auferstehung des Eros: Die Bedeutung von Liebe und Sexualität für das künftige Christentum*, Munich, Pfeiffer, 1971.

Lucien-Marie de Saint Joseph, *L'Expérience de Dieu*, Paris, Edition du Cerf, 1968.

—, "S. Jean de la Croix," *Dict. de Spirit.*, vol. 8, cols. 408-447.

Luis de San José, O.C.D., *Concordancias de las obras y escritos del doctor de la iglesia San Juan de la Cruz*, Burgos, Tipografía de 'El Monte Carmelo', 1948.

Mager, A., *Mystik als Seelische Wirklichkeit*, Graz, Verlag Pustet, 1945.

—, *Mystik als Lehre und Leben*, Innsbruck, 1934.

Marcelo del Niño Jesús, O.C.D., *El tomismo de San Juan de la Cruz*, Burgos, Tipografía de 'El Monte Carmelo', 1930.

Maritain, J., *Les degrees du savoir*, Brugge, Paris, Desclee de Brouwer, 1932.

—, "S. Jean de la Croix: practicien de la contemplacion," *Études Carmélitaines*, 16 (1931), 62-109.

Mesters, G., "Johannes vom Kreuz: Leben, Werke, Persönlichkeit und Lehre," *Lexikon Für Theologie und Kirche*, vol. 5, 1051-1052 (bibliography).

Metz, J. B., "Freiheit," *Handbuch Theologischer Grundbegriffe*, (I), (H. Frisch, ed.), Munich, Kösel Verlag, 1963, 403-414.

—, "Erlösung und Emanzipation," *Erlösung und Emanzipation* (Quaestiones Disputatae, 61),

Basel, Herder, 1973.

—, & Fiorenza, F. P., "Der Mensch als Einheit von Leib und Seele," *Mysterium Salutis*, 2, Einsiedeln, Benziger, 1965, 584-636.

Mosis, R., *Der Mensch und die Dinge nach Johannes vom Kreuz*, Würzburg, Echter Verlag, 1964.

Morel, G., *Le sens de l'existence selon Saint Jean de la Croix*, Paris, Aubier (Éditions Montaigne), 1960.

Murray, T., "The 'man' of St. Augustine and St. Thomas," Proceedings of the *American Catholic Philosophical Association*, 24 (1959), 90-96.

Muschalek, G., *Glaubensgewissheit in Freiheit*, (Quaestiones Disputatae, 40), Freiburg, Herder, 1968.

Oechslin, R. L., "Eckhart," *Dict. de Spirit.*, vol. 4 (1), 101-102.

Orcibal, J., *Saint Jean de la Croix et les mystiques rhéno-flamands*, Brugges, Desclée de Brouwer, 1966.

Orozco, E., *Poesia y mística*, Madrid, Ediciones Guadarrama, 1959.

Ottonello, P. P., *Bibliografia de s. Giovanni della Croce*, Rome, Edizioni del Teresianum, 1967.

Ozment, S., *Homo Spiritualis (Studies in Medieval and Reformation Thought*, vol. 6), Leiden, Bril, 1969.

Peers, A., *Handbook to the Life and Times of St. Teresa and St. John of the Cross*, London, Burns & Oates, 1954.

Pepin, F., *Noces de Dieu; le symbolisme nuptial du 'Cantico espiritual' de saint Jean de la Croix à la lumière du 'Canticum Canticorum'*, Paris, Desclée de Brouwer, Bellarmin-Montreal, Tournai, 1972.

Peters, J., *Geloof en mystiek: een theologische bezinning op de geestelijke leer van Sint Jan van het Kruis*, Louvain, E. Nauwelaerts, 1957.

—, "La doctrina protestante moderna y la doctrina sobre la fe en san Juan de la Cruz," *Revista de Espiritualidad*, 16 (1957), 429-448.

—, & Jacobs, J. A., *Johannes van het Kruis: Mystieke Werken*, Gent, Carmelitana, 1975².

Puech, H. C., "La ténèbre mystique chez le Pseudo-Denys," *Études Carmélitaines*, 23 (2), (1938), 33-53.

Ratzinger, J., "Vorfragen zu einer Theologie der Erlösung," *Erlösung und Emanzipation* (Quaestiones Disputatae, 61), Freiburg, Herder, 1973, 141-155.

Reusch, F. H., *Die Indices librorum prohibitorum des sechzehnten Jahrhunderts gesammelt u. herausgegeben*, Tübingen, Bibliothek des Litterarischen Vereins in Stuttgart, 12, 1886.

—, *Der Index der verbotenen Bücher*, 3 vols. Aalen, Scientia Verlag, 1967.

Reypens, L., "Âme: Structure d'après les mystiques," *Dict. de Spirit.*, vol. 1, Paris, 1937, 433-469.

Rist, J. M., *Eros und Psyche (Studies in Plato, Plotinus and Origen)*, Toronto, Univ. of Toronto Press, 1964.

Rondet, H., "L'anthropologie religieuse de saint Augustin, *"Recherches de Science Religieuse*, 29 (1939), 163-196.

Roques, R., "Le primat du transcendant dans la purification de l'intelligence selon le Pseudo-Denys," *Revue d'Ascese et de Mystique*, 23 (1947), 142-169.

—, "Denys l'Areopagite," *Dict. de Spirit.*, vol. 3, Paris, 1957, 246-286.

—, *L'Universe dionysien*, Paris, Aubier, 1954.

Ruiz, F., "Cimas de contemplación: exégesis de *Llama de amor viva,"* Ephemerides Carm., 13 (1962), 257-298.

—, *Introducción a San Juan de la Cruz: El escritor, los escritos, el sistema*, (Biblioteca de Autores Cristianos), Madrid, La Editorial Católica, 1968.

—, "Vida teologal durante la purificación interior, en los escritos de san Juan de la Cruz," *Revista de Espiritualidad*, 18 (1959), 341-379.

Sanson, H., *L'esprit humain selon saint Jean de la Croix*, Paris, Faculty of Letters of Algeria, 1953.

Schillebeeckx, E., "Het geloof functionerend in het menselijk zelfverstaan," *Het woord in de geschiedenis* (Burke, T. P., ed.), Bilthoven, Nelissen, 1969.

—, "Beschouwingen rond de 'exercitia spiritualia', *Tijdschrift voor Geestelijk Leven*, 4 (1), (1948), 202-211.

—, "Stilte gevuld met parabels," *Politiek of mystiek?* (special number of *Tijdschrift voor Theologie*, Brugges, Desclée de Brouwer, 1973, 69-81.

Schoonenberg, P., "Ervaringen en voorstellingen van Gods transcendentie," *Politiek of mystiek?*, Brugges, Desclée de Brouwer, 1973, 51-68.

Schöpf, A., "Die Verinnerlichung des Wahrheits Problems bei Augustinus," *Revue des Études Augustiniennes*, 13 (1967), 85-95.

Stace, W. T., *Mysticism and Philosophy*, N.Y. & Philadelphia, MacMillan, 1961.

Steggink, O., "L'enracinement de Saint Jean de la Croix dans le tronc de l'ordre carmélitain," *Actualité de Jean de la Croix* (Lucien-Marie & Petit, J. M., eds.), Brugges, Desclée de Brouwer, 1970, 51-78.

Stiglmayr, J., "Aszese und Mystik des sog. Dionysius Areopagita," *Scholastik*, 2 (1927), 161-207.

Stoeckle, B., *Die Lehre von der erbsündlichen Konkupiszenz in ihrer Bedeutung für das christliche Leibethos*, Ettel, 1954 (reprinted in: "Erbsündige Begierlichkeit," *Münchener Theol. Zeit.*, 14 (1963), 225-242.)

Theodorou, A., "Die Lehre von der Vergöttung des Menschen bei den griecheschen Kirchenvätern," *Kerygma und Dogma*, 7 (1961), 283-310.

Tillmans, W. G., O.C.D., "De oude paradijssymboliek, een verkenning," *Bijdragen*, 36 (1975), 350-390.

Troelstra, S., *Geen enkel beeld, mystieke weg, deprojektie en individuatie bij San Juan de la Cruz*, Assen, van Gorcum, 1977.

Truemen-Dicken, E. W., *El crisol de amor*, Barcelona, Herder, 1967.

Turbessi, G., *Vita contemplativa: Dottrina tomistica e sua relazione alle fonti*, Rome, 1944.

Underhill, E., *Mysticism*, N.Y., Meridian Books, 1955.

Ussel, J. van, *Intimiteit*, Deventer, Slaterus, 1975².

Vanneste, J., "La doctrine des trois voies dans la Théologie Mystique du Pseudo-Denys l'Aréopagite," *Studia Patristica*, vol. 8 (2), (1968), 462-467.

—, "La théologie mystique du pseudo-Denys l'Aréopagite," *Studia Patristica*, vol. 5 (1962), 401-415.

Verbeke, G., *L'evolucion de la doctrine du pneuma du stoicisme à s. Augustin*, Paris, Desclée de Brouwer, 1945.

Vergote, A., *Interpretation de langage religieux*, Paris, Editions de Seuil, 1974.

—, "De Geest, kracht tot heil en geestelijke gezondheid," *Leven uit de geest*, (Theologische peilingen aangeboden aan E. Schillebeeckx), Hilversum, Gooi & Sticht, 1974, 180-195.

—, *Het huis is nooit af*, Antwerp, Utrecht, De Nederlandsche Boekhandel, 1974.

Viller, M. & Rahner, K., *Aszese und Mystik in der Väterzeit*, Freiburg, Herder, 1939.

Völker, W., *Kontemplation und Ekstase bei Pseudo-Dionysius Areopagita*, Wiesbaden, F. Steiner Verlag, 1958.

Waldmann, M., "Thomas von Aquin und die 'Mystische Theologie' des Pseudodionysius," *Geist und Leben*, 22 (1949), 121-145.

Weger, K., *Theologie der Erbsünde*, (Quaestiones Disputatae, 44), Freiburg, Herder, 1970.

Weier, W., "Die instrospective Bewustseinswahrnemung beim hl. Augustine und bei Descartes," *Franziskanische Studien* (Münster), 50 (1968), 239-250.

Winklhofer, T. A., "Joh. vom Kreuz und die Surius Übersetzung der Werke Taulers," *Theologie in Geschichte und Gegenwart*, (Schmaus, M., ed.), Munich, K. Zink, 1957,

317-348.

—, *Die Gnadenlehre in der Mystik des hl. Johannes vom Kreuz*, Freiburg, Herder, 1936.

Woroniecki, H., "Les éléments dionysiens dans le thomisme," *Collectanea Theologica*, 17 (1936), 25-40.

PSYCHO-PHYSIOLOGICAL LITERATURE
AND PSYCHOLOGICAL LITERATURE:

Afferman, R., "Sünde und Erlösung in tiefenpsychologischer Sicht," *Erlösung und Emanzipation*, (Quaestiones Disputatae, 61), Freiburg, Herder, 1973, 15-29.

Alexander, F., "Buddhistic training as an artificial catatonia," *Psychoanalysis*, 19 (1931), 129 ff.

Anand, B., Chhina, G., & Singh, B., "Some aspects of electroencephalographic studies in yogis," *Electroencephalography & Clinical Neurophysiology* (E.Cl.N), 13 (1961), 452-456.

Bagchi, B. & Wenger, M., "Electrophysiological correlates of some yogi exercises," *E.Cl.N.*, Supplement no. 7 (1957), 132-149.

—, "Simultaneous EEG and other recordings during some yogic practices," *E.Cl.N.*, 10 (1958), 193 (abstract).

Banquet, J. P., "EEG and Meditation: Spectral analysis of EEG during transcendental meditation," *E.Cl.N.*, 33 (1972), 454 (abstract).

Benson, H., "The relaxation response," *Psychiatry*, 37 (Feb. 1974), 37-42.

Boudreau, L., "Transendental meditation and yoga as reciprocal inhibitors," *Journal of Behavioral Therapy & Experimental Psychiatry*, 3 (1972), 97-98.

Brosse, T., "Études instrumentales des techniques du Yoga. Expérimentation psychosomatique," *Ecole francaise d'extrême orient*, vol. 52, Paris, 1963.

Brown, B. B. & Klug, J. W., *The Alpha Syllabus: A Handbook of Human EEG Alpha Activity*, Springfield, Ill., C. C. Thomas, 1974.

Brown, F. M., William, S. S. & Blodgett, J. T., "EEG kappa rhythmus during transcendental, meditation and possible perceptual threshold changes following," Kentucky Academy of Science, Nov. 19, 1971 (paper).

Brown, N. O., *Life Against Death: The Psychoanalytical Meaning of History*, London, Chaucer Press, 1970[5].

Campbell, A., *Seven States of Consciousness: A vision of possibilities suggested by the teaching of Maharishi Mahesh Yogi*, London, V. Gollancz, 1973[2].

Das, N. N. & Gastaut, H., "Variations de l'activité du coeur et des muscles squelettiques au cours de la méditation et de l'extase yogique," *E.Cl.N.*, Supplement 6 (1955), 211-219.

Davy, M., "Limitations of psychoanalysis in the approach to mysticism," *Psyche* (Paris), 4 (1949), 105-116.

Day, D. N., *Meditation: A Multistage Learning Model* (dissertation for School of Business Administration, Univ. of Calif., Berkeley, May, 1971[2] (available from P.O. Box 108, Tomales, Calif., 9492, U.S.A.).

Dietrich, H., "Über Hysterie in Mystik und Mystik in Hysterie," *Conf. Psychiat.*, 6 (1963), 232-241.

Doxey, N. C. S., "The high alpha state: a distinct state of consciousness?", paper presented at the South African Psychological Association Congress, Witwatersrand University, Johannesburg, July, 1972.

Eccles, J., (ed.), *Brain and Conscious Experience*, (Study week, 1964, of the Pontificia Academia Scientiarum), Berlin, Heidelberg, N.Y., Springer Verlag, 1966.

Emerson, V. F., "Can belief systems influence neurophysiology: Some implications of research on meditation," *Newsletter Review* (Montreal), vol. 5, no. 1 & 2 (1972), 20-31.

Eysenck, H. J., *The Biological Basis of Personality*, Springfield, Ill., C. C. Thomas, 1967.

—, *Readings in Extraversion/Introversion*, London, Staple Press, 1970[2].

Fingarette, H., "The ego and mystic selflessness," *Psychoanalytic Review*, 45 (1958), 5-40.

Fortmann, H. M. M., *Aandachtig Bidden* (dissertation), Nijmegen, Dekker & v. d. Veght, 1945.

—, *Hoogtijd*, Utrecht, Ambo, 1966.

—, *Als ziende de Onzienlijke*, Hilversum/Antwerp, P. Brand, 1964-1968, 4 vols.

—, *Oosterse renaissance*, Bilthoven, Ambo, 1970[3].

—, *Heel de mens*, Bilthoven, Ambo, 1972.

Frenkle, N. J., *Der Traum, die Neurose, das religiöse Erlebnis*, Zürich, Einsiedeln, Köln, Benziger, 1974.

Gale, A., "The Psychophysiology of Individual Differences: Studies of Extraversion and the EEG," *New Approaches in Psychological Measurement* (kline, P., ed.), London, Wiley & Sons, 1973, 211-256.

Gennep, P. A. van, *Het kwetsbare midden (Persoon en werk van Han Fortmann)*, Bilthoven, Ambo, 1973.

Gevins, A. S., Yeager, C. L., Diamond, S. L., Spire, J., Zeitlin, G. M., Gevins, A. H., "Automated Analysis of the Electrical Activity of the Human Brain (EEG): A Progress Report," *Proceedings of the Instit. of Electrical and Electronics Engineers*, 63/10 (1975), 1382-1399.

Ginneken, P. van, *Psychologische krachtlijnen in het monastieke leven*, 1976 (unpublished thesis for Fac. of Psych. of Religion, Univ. of Louvain).

Glueck, B. C. & Stroebel, C. F., "Biofeedback and Meditation in the Treatment of Psychiatric Illnesses," *Comprehensive Psychiatry*, vol. 16, no. 4 (Aug., 1975), 303-321.

Graham, J., "Auditory Discrimination in Meditators," Univ. of Sussex, Psych. Dept., Brighton, England. Unpublished manuscript (June, 1971).

Greeley, A., *Ecstasy: A way of knowing*, New Jersey, Prentice Hall, 1974.

Hirai, T., "EEG changes during the concentrated relaxation," *Seishin Shinkegaku Zasshi* (Psychiatria et Neurologia Japonica) (Tokyo), 62/1 (1960), 76-105.

—, (abstract in:) *Zentralblatt für die gesamte Neurologie und Psychiatrie*, 158 (1960), 144.

Hood, R. W., "Religious orientation in religious experience," *Journal for the Scientific Study of Religion*, 9 (1970), 285-291.

—, "A comparison of the Allport and Feagin scoring procedures for intrinsec/extrinsec religious orientation," *Journal for the Scientific Study of Religion*, 10 (1971), 370-374.

—, "Psychological strength and the report of intense religious experience," *Journal for the Scientific Study of Religion*, 13 (1974), 65-71.

—, "The construction and preliminary validation of a measure of reported mystical experience," *Journal for the Scientific Study of Religion*, 14 (1975), 29-41.

James, W., *The Varieties of Religious Experience*, N.Y., Modern Library, 1902.

Johnson, L. C., "A psychophysiology for all states," *Psychophysiology*, 6/5 (1970), 501-516.

Jung, C. G., *Psychologischen Typen*, Zürich, Rascher Verlag, 1946 (1926[1]).

Kampen, D. van, "De 'Personality Questionnaire' van Eysenck & Eysenck: een factoranalytisch onderzoek," *Nederlands Tijdschrift voor de Psychologie*, 31/1 (1976), 23-34.

Kanellakos, D. P. & Ferguson, P. C., *The psychobiology of Transcendental Meditation, an annotated bibliography* (available at MIU, 1015 Gayley Ave., Los Angeles, Calif., 90024, U.S.A.), 1973.

Kasamatsu, A. & Hirai, T., "An electroencephalographic study on the Zen meditation (Zazen)," *Psychologia*, 12 (1969), 205-225.

Laubry, C. & Brosse, T., Data gathered in India on a yogi with simultaneous registration of the pulse, respiration, and electrocardiogram, *Presse Medicale*, 44 (1936), 1601-1604.

Leuba, J. H., *The Psychology of Religious Mysticism*, London & Boston, Routledge & Kagan, 1972 (2), (1925[1]).

Lindinger, H., "Gott ist Liebe: Ein Beitrag zum tiefenpsychologischen und theologischen

Verständnis von Eros und Agape," *Evangelische Theologie*, 33 (1973), 164-181.

Maréchal, J., *Études sur la Psychologie des Mystiques*, Paris, Brugges, Desclée de Brouwer, 1938².

Maslow, A., *Toward a Psychology of Being*, Princeton, 1962.

Masters, R. & Houston, J., *The Varieties of Psychedelic Experience*, N.Y., Dell. Pub. Co., 1966.

Meissner, W. W., *Foundations for a Psychology of Grace*, New Jersey, Paulist Press, 1966.

Moller, H., "Affective mysticism in western civilization," *Psychoanalytic Review*, 52 (1965), 115-130.

Müller-Pozzi, H., *Psychologie des Glaubens*, Munich, Kaiser Verlag, 1975.

Nuttin, J. & Beuten, B., *Handleiding bij de persoonlijkheidsinventaris MMPI* (Studia Psychologia), Louvain, Univ. of Louvain Press, 1969.

Okuma, T., Kogu, E., Ikeda, K. & Sugiyama, H., "The EEG of Yoga and Zen practitioners," *E.Cl.N.*, 9 (1957), 51.

Orlebeke, J. F., *Aktivering, extraversie en sterkte van het zenuwstelsel*, Assen, van Gorcum, 1972.

Orme-Johnson, D. W., "Autonomic stability and transcendental meditation," *Psychosomatic Medicine*, 35 (1973), 341-349.

Pagano, R. R. et al., "Sleep during transcendental meditation," *Science*, 191 (1976), 308-309.

Prince, R. & Savage, C., "Mystical states and the concept of regression," *Psychedelic Review*, 8 (1966), 59-75.

Roldán, A., *Introducción a la ascetica diferencial*, Madrid, Editorial Razón y Fe, 1962.

Salman, D. H., "New approaches to the classification of mystical states," *Newletter Review*, vol. 5, no. 1 & 2 (1972), 1-2.

Sargant, W., "The physiology of faith," *British Journal of Psychiatry*, 115 (1969), 505-508.

Savage, R., "Electro-cerebral activity, extraversion and neuroticism," *British Journal of Psychiatry*, 110 (1964), 98.

Schwartz, G. E., "Pros and cons of meditation: Current findings on physiology and anxiety, self-control, drug abuse and creativity," paper read before the 81st annual convention of the American Psychological Association, Montreal, 1973.

Simonov, P. V., "Basic (alpha) EEG rhythm as electrographic manifestation of preventive inhibition of brain structuures," *Progress in Brain Research*, 22 (1968), 138-147.

Spoerri, T. (ed.), *Beiträge zur Exstase* (Bib. Psychiatrica et Neurologica, no. 134), Basel, Karger, 1968.

Staal, F., "Het wetenschappelijk onderzoek van de mystiek," *de Gids*, no. 1 & 2, 3-34; 108-132.

Tart, C. T. (ed.), *Altered States of Consciousness*, N.Y., Wiley & Sons, 1969.

Vergote, A., *Psychologie religieuse*, Brussels, C. Dessart, 1966³.

Wallace, R. K., "The physiological effects of transcendental meditation," *Science 167 (1970), 1751-1754.*

—, *"The physiology of meditation,"* *Scientific American*, 226/2 (1972), 84-90.

—, "A wakeful hypometabolic physiological state," *Am. Journal of Physiology*, 221 (1971), 795-799.

Wenger, M. & Bagchi, B. K., "Studies of autonomic functions in practitioners of Yoga in India," *Behavioral Science*, 6 (1961), 312-323.

Woolfolk, R. L., "Psychophysiological Correlates of Meditation," *Archives of General Psychiatry*, 32 (1975), 1326-1333.

Indices

294

Leadership, 30, 58, 61, 63, 66-67, 262, 265, 267-269.
Libido, 50, 51, 52, 54, 55, 59, 61, 62, 63, 64, 68. 69, 70, 72, 73, 78, 88, 89, 105, 106, 107, 108, 109, 150, 151, 161, 162, 163, 165, 166-178, 179, 181, 189, 191, 197, 201, 203, 204, 205, 211, 212, 219.
Limbic circuit, 70, 88, 90, 91, 101, 102.
MMPI, 30, 31, 68.
MPI, 29.
Neuroticism, 29, 46, 50, 51, 53, 54, 64, 68, 70, 71, 72, 73, 74, 92, 99, 100, 102, 103, 157, 195, 201, 205, 206, 258-259, 265, 266, 267-269, 270, 274, 277, 279, 280, 283.
Pilot study, 94.
Pilot test, 26.
Power density spectral analysis, 103-105, 277-281.
Psychological inventories, 24, 29-31, 65, 88, 231-234, 267-269, 270.
Psychological types, xiii, 23, 24, 50, 65, 66, 201, 277-279.
Psychological variables, 25, 45, 46, 47, 48, 50, 54, 56, 59, 63, 64, 65, 69, 99, 105, 114, 153, 258-262, 265, 266, 267-269, 270.
Psycho-physiology, 51, 64, 69-109, 149-151.
Psycho-somatic neuroticism, 46, 74, 206, 259, 265-266, 267-269, 270.
Regression, xiii, 221.
Reliabilities, 32-34, 38-39, 242-244, 245.
Religious variables, 63, 64, 65, 69 (see also 'Asceticism', 'Contemplation', 'Testing', Pleasurable mystical experiences', 'Unpleasurable mystical experiences', 'Altruism', 'Religious superiors', etc. in index of theological subjects).
Re-testing, 26, 29, 33, 45, 242-244, 245, 256-258, 270.
Social desirability, 29, 46, 47, 48, 68, 260, 265, 267-269, 276-277.
Spreading of alpha waves, theta waves, 98, 102-104, 180, 282-283.
Stability, 52, 65, 69, 70, 71, 72, 75, 92, 101, 190, 201, 266, 283.
Strong nervous system, 51, 68, 70-75, 91, 101, 103, 107, 109, 219.
Tension, 33, 50, 53, 54, 64, 67, 98, 101, 105, 106, 193, 194, 195, 197, 225, 243.
Test reliability, 33, 45, 47-50.
Theta waves, 76, 81, 85, 96, 98, 103, 277, 279, 280, 281.

t-Test of dependent samples, 98, 104-105.
Unhappy emotionality, 30, 33-34, 37, 38, 39, 40, 42, 44, 46, 53, 54, 56, 64, 68, 70, 71, 72, 74, 102, 103, 157, 190, 201, 205, 262, 265, 266, 267-269, 274.
Visual assessment (EEG), 94-105, 282-283.
Weak psychological type, 39, 50, 51, 52, 64, 69, 71, 72, 103, 109, 178-179, 190, 201.

2. INDEX OF PERSONS AND AUTHORS

296

Christian Mysticism:
Transcending Techniques

SUMMARY

This study deals with a two-fold problem. In the first place, a need exists today among the laity to relate oriental meditation techniques, which are so popular now, to western contemplative traditions. Secondly, the laity and especially the youth find much of the mystical teaching of a western writer like St. John of the Cross (1542-1591) inapplicable to the modern situation. Chapter one shows how difficult it is to extricate his mystical teaching from a framework of dualisms: spirit/body. Creator/creation, love for God/love for creatures. Rather than attempt a hermeneutical approach through a 'literature study', the author goes directly to the experiences of members of the contemplative order, the Discalced Carmelites, which John of the Cross and Teresa of Avila founded. An empirical study was conducted among 54 members of this order to determine if the mystical teaching of John of the Cross is correct and if it can be dissociated from his ascetical teaching. The subjects were given five psychological tests, a questionnaire on spiritual experience and ascetical attitudes. Also, EEG (electroencephalographic) recordings were made.

The results showed conclusively that strict ascetical attitudes and practices are not related to contemplative/mystical experience. Rather the degree of prayer development is related to a complex of co-determinants: a high degree of happy emotionality, a low degree of anxiety, extraversion, social and religious dependency, normal ego strength, and stability. The theological attitudes involved are the emphasis upon the theological virtues and the practice of the 'via negativa'. The psychological traits suggest that what Eysenck calls a 'strong nervous system' is a necessary prerequisite to mystical/contemplative development. Therefore a psychophysiological (EEG) study was conducted to see if the EEG data of the most advanced contemplatives might correspond to what he predicts one will find by a stable extravert, i.e. a strong nervous system. The results showed that the most advanced contemplatives produced EEG data very similar to those of Zen and Yoga meditators. However, whereas the oriental meditation techniques seem to enhance or cultivate a strong nervous system, the Christian contemplative tradition seems merely to build upon the pre-existing strong nervous system of the subject, without enhancing it. The suggestion is made that Christian contemplatives might profit from practicing oriental techniques in combination with prayer to attain concentration.

The structure of Christian contemplation seems to be a complex of three movements:

1. a phase of inner recollection or concentration in which both outer and inner distractions are inhibited. Strong nervous systems are better able to achieve this than weak nervous systems.

2. a phase of libidinal or erotic concentration in a dialectic of happy/unhappy mystical experiences, which increases in intensity and momentum of alternation. Whereas the first phase could be fostered through techniques which aid concentration, the second phase presupposes a high libidinal or emotional level in the subject. This too, is part of the profile of the strong nervous system, as the data show. This erotic attraction is made possible by an object of desire and identification. In Christian contemplation this is the symbol of Christ.

3. a phase of ecstatic encounter with the object of union. The three phases do not cancel out as the next phase arrives. Rather each phase seems to continue to be present as the under-lying framework within which the next phase can emerge.

This study could be considered as the extension of the problem which the late Professor H. Fortmann had dealt with in his dissertation, *Aandachtig bidden* (1945) (concentrated prayer), and in his later studies on oriental spirituality. This current study tests his insights and intuitions with modern, empirical means. It furthermore tries to arrive at a reflection on the relationship between western and oriental contemplative traditions, a reflection which Fortmann did not come to, perhaps due to his premature death. Since Fortmann's dissertation did not deal with mystical prayer, this study tries to supplement his work by concentrating mainly on the prayer of mystical union. The libidinal basis for this form of prayer, a matter which entirely escaped Fortmann, is especially explored, in chapter four. A theological reflection on the context within which this libidinal dialectic occurs, namely the 'via negativa', is offered in chapter three. Hereby an attempt is made to give the modern laity a key to understanding the mystical teaching of traditional western spiritual writers, so that their mystical insights can be made accessible.

300